Signing
FOR
DUMMIES®
2ND EDITION

Withdrawn

by Adan R. Penilla II, PhD, and Angela Lee Taylor

WILEY

John Wiley & Sons, Inc.

Signing For Dummies®, 2nd Edition

Published by
John Wiley & Sons, Inc.
111 River St.
Hoboken, NJ 07030-5774
www.wiley.com

For general information on our other products and services, please contact our Customer Care Department within the U.S. at 877-762-2974, outside the U.S. at 317-572-3993, or fax 317-572-4002.

For technical support, please visit www.wiley.com/techsupport.

Wiley publishes in a variety of print and electronic formats and by print-on-demand. Some material included with standard print versions of this book may not be included in e-books or in print-on-demand. If this book refers to media such as a CD or DVD that is not included in the version you purchased, you may download this material at http://booksupport.wiley.com. For more information about Wiley products, visit www.wiley.com.

Library of Congress Control Number: 2012936424

ISBN 978-1-118-11758-3 (pbk); ISBN 978-1-118-26260-3 (ebk); ISBN 978-1-118-22452-6 (ebk); ISBN 978-1-118-23775-5 (ebk)

Manufactured in the United States of America

10 9 8 7 6 5 4 3 2 1

WILEY

About the Authors

Adan R. Penilla II, PhD, NAD IV, NIC, CI/CT, and SC: L, is currently employed as a Video Relay Service interpreter. He also works at Colorado State University as an American Sign Language instructor and at Pueblo Community College as an English instructor. He freelance interprets for the Colorado 10th Circuit Court and the Pueblo Police Department. He is also a mentor for the Colorado Registry of Interpeters for the Deaf for courtroom interpreting.

Dr. Penilla was an interpreter for the American Delegation at the World Federation of the Deaf (Vienna, 1995). He has authored "The Middle East in ASL," "Countries from around the World in ASL," "Cities from around the World in ASL," "Name Sign Properties in ASL," and "Quick Study Bar Charts in ASL" (1st and 2nd editions Quick Study BarCharts). He has also written several DVDs for Signs of Development.org and Sign Media, Inc.

Dr. Penilla also lectures at national, state, and RID-sanctioned conferences and workshops on various topics regarding ASL and English.

He recently had the honor of presenting at the 2011 National RID Conference in Atlanta.

To find out more about Dr. Penilla and his lectures, go to www.aslworld matters.com.

Angela Lee Taylor, born deaf, is a native of Dixon, Illinois. Taylor graduated from the Illinois School for the Deaf in 1985 and received her bachelor's degree from Gallaudet University in 1997. Taylor has taught ASL for Pikes Peak Community College, the Colorado School for the Deaf and the Blind, and the community. Taylor has annually coordinated for the statewide Deaf and Hard of Hearing Symposium. She is a tutor for the Shared Reading Project (SRP) and is also involved with the American Sign Language Teachers Association of Colorado (ASLTAC). Taylor resides in Pueblo, Colorado, with her husband, Lindsey, and their border collie/blue heeler mix, Chip.

Dedication

(From lead author, Adan)

To my parents, Adan and Aurora Penilla — Mom and Dad. Thanks for your generosity in love, patience, and giving. You have helped me more than you know.

Dad, whenever I have a challenge before me, I still hear you: "Buckle down."

Mom, a better friend was never born.

Author's Acknowledgments

(From lead author, Adan)

My four sisters plus one, you have been a blessing throughout the years. Thanks for the support and encouragement in all I do. As Mom used to say, you're making memories. We have remained friends as adults, and I am proud of each of you.

Leland Paul Reeck — ID, you have been a wonderful co-lecturer, research partner, colleague, and honest editor of my work. You're a good man and a greater friend. As iron sharpens iron . . . SP

Chrissy Guthrie, thanks for editing this book. Your help has made this book possible. I could not have written it without your patience.

Lastly, thank you to technical reviewer Jeff Choate, copy editor Todd Lothery, illustrator Lisa Reed, and the rest of the crew from John Wiley & Sons, Inc. I have learned much from you.

Publisher's Acknowledgments

We're proud of this book; please send us your comments at http://dummies.custhelp.com. For other comments, please contact our Customer Care Department within the U.S. at 877-762-2974, outside the U.S. at 317-572-3993, or fax 317-572-4002.

Some of the people who helped bring this book to market include the following:

Acquisitions, Editorial, and Vertical Websites

Senior Project Editor: Christina Guthrie

(Previous Edition: Jennifer Connolly, Kathleen Dobie)

Acquisitions Editor: Michael Lewis

Copy Editor: Todd Lothery

Assistant Editor: David Lutton

Editorial Program Coordinator: Joe Niesen

Technical Editors: Jeffrey Choate, Leland Paul Reeck, CI/CT

Vertical Websites: Jenny Swisher, Marilyn Hummel

Editorial Manager: Christine Meloy Beck

Editorial Assistants: Rachelle Amick, Alexa Koschier

Art Coordinator: Alicia B. South

Cover Photos: © PhotoSpin, Inc./Alamy

Cartoons: Rich Tennant (www.the5thwave.com)

Composition Services

Project Coordinator: Sheree Montgomery

Layout and Graphics: Carrie A. Cesavice, Cheryl Grubbs, Corrie Niehaus

Proofreaders: Lindsay Amones, Shannon Ramsey

Indexer: Estalita Slivoskey

Illustrator: Lisa Reed

CD Producer: Her Voice Unlimited, LLC

CD Talent: CD Talent provided by Indiana School for the Deaf

Diane Hazel Jones, MA; Deaf Education, CSC;L

Danny Lucero, BA in Deaf Studies from Gallaudet University

Janet Etkie Schwall, BA, CDI

Dave Tester, Teacher

Christine Wood, ASL Teacher

Donald Yates, Teacher Assistant

Publishing and Editorial for Consumer Dummies

    Kathleen Nebenhaus, Vice President and Executive Publisher

    Kristin Ferguson-Wagstaffe, Product Development Director

    Ensley Eikenburg, Associate Publisher, Travel

    Kelly Regan, Editorial Director, Travel

Publishing for Technology Dummies

    Andy Cummings, Vice President and Publisher

Composition Services

    Debbie Stailey, Director of Composition Services

Contents at a Glance

Introduction *1*

Part 1: Getting Started *7*
Chapter 1: Finding Out That You Already Know a Little Sign 9
Chapter 2: Warming Up with Signing Grammar Basics 21
Chapter 3: Starting to Sign Basic Expressions 47
Chapter 4: Getting Your Numbers and Times Straight 73
Chapter 5: Signing at Home 87

Part 11: American Sign Language in Action *107*
Chapter 6: Asking Questions and Making Small Talk 109
Chapter 7: Asking for Directions 137
Chapter 8: Dining and Going to the Market 159
Chapter 9: Shopping Made Easy 187
Chapter 10: The Signer About Town 215
Chapter 11: Takin' Care of Business 233
Chapter 12: Recreation and the Great Outdoors 247
Chapter 13: Here's to Your Health 277

Part 111: Looking into Deaf Life and Interpreting *297*
Chapter 14: The Deaf Community and Deaf Etiquette 299
Chapter 15: Interpreting: Are You Interested? 313
Chapter 16: Using Technology to Communicate 321

Part 1V: The Part of Tens *327*
Chapter 17: Ten Tips to Help You Sign like a Pro 329
Chapter 18: Ten Ways to Pick Up Sign Quickly 333
Chapter 19: Ten Popular Deaf Expressions 337

Part V: Appendixes *343*
Appendix A: Answer Key to Fun & Games 345
Appendix B: About the CD 347

Index *351*

Table of Contents

Introduction 1
About This Book 1
Conventions Used in This Book 2
Foolish Assumptions 3
How This Book Is Organized 3
    Part I: Getting Started 4
    Part II: American Sign Language in Action 4
    Part III: Looking into Deaf Life and Interpreting 4
    Part IV: The Part of Tens 4
    Part V: Appendixes 5
Icons Used in This Book 5
Where to Go from Here 6

Part 1: Getting Started 7

Chapter 1: Finding Out That You Already Know a Little Sign 9
Discovering Signs That Look like What They Mean 9
Building on the Basics of Sign — Gestures and Expression 11
    Spelling with your fingers 11
    Shaping up those hands 14
    Benefiting with body language 16
    Telling with your face 17

Chapter 2: Warming Up with Signing Grammar Basics 21
Explaining the Parts of Speech 21
    Distinguishing between noun/verb pairs 22
    Modifying with adjectives and adverbs 24
Talking Tenses 26
Structuring Sentences 28
    Subjecting yourself to nouns and verbs in simple sentences .. 28
    Placing subjects and objects 28
Exclaiming in Simple Sentences 35
Signing Conditional Sentences 40
Personification: The Secret of Agents 41
Providing Clarity with Facial Grammar 43

Chapter 3: Starting to Sign Basic Expressions **47**

Initiating a Conversation 47
    Attracting someone's attention 48
    Using greetings and closings 48
Getting Acquainted 53
    Sharing feelings and emotions 55
    Connecting your thoughts 58
    Talking about where you're from 59
Acting the Part: Constructed Dialogue and Constructed Action 68
    Constructed Dialogue 68
    Constructed Action 69

Chapter 4: Getting Your Numbers and Times Straight **73**

Counting on Numbers 73
    Getting from one to ten with cardinal numbers 74
    Ordering ordinal numbers 77
    Signing phone numbers and the like 78
Talking about Time 78
    Signing calendar dates 82

Chapter 5: Signing at Home **87**

Handling Signs about Your Home 87
    Touring all the rooms 91
    Furnishing your home 94
Hanging Out for the Holidays 100
Teaching the Tots 103
Keeping Track of Your Subjects in Space 105

Part II: American Sign Language in Action **107**

Chapter 6: Asking Questions and Making Small Talk **109**

Signing Key Questions: Six Ws, One H 109
Discussing Family, Friends, and More 114
    Family and friends 115
    Relating where you live and work 119
Using Possessives and Pronouns When Chatting 129
    Personal pronouns and possessives 130
    Demonstrative pronouns 132

Chapter 7: Asking for Directions **137**

Finding Your Way 137
Looking to Natural Landmarks 143
Searching the Streets 146
Transporting Yourself 149
Directing Your Sentences with Conjunctions 151

Chapter 8: Dining and Going to the Market **159**

    Eating Three Square Meals a Day 159

        Having breakfast 164

        Munching on lunch 166

        Enjoying dinner 170

    Dining Out 174

        Ethnic food around town 175

        Don't forget the drinks! 177

    Attention, Shoppers! 181

        Signing specialty stores 181

        Getting a good deal 183

Chapter 9: Shopping Made Easy **187**

    Clothes for All Seasons 187

        Fall fashion 191

        Spring style 194

        Summer suits 197

        Clothing by color 199

    All about Money 205

    Shopping Superlatives and Comparisons 210

Chapter 10: The Signer About Town **215**

    Making Plans 215

        Going to the movies 218

        Going to the theater 223

        Going to the museum 225

    Selecting Your Social Station 227

Chapter 11: Takin' Care of Business **233**

    Occupying Yourself with Occupations 233

    Sorting Office Supplies 238

    Getting to Work 242

Chapter 12: Recreation and the Great Outdoors **247**

    Exercising Your Right to Recreate 247

        Getting into the competitive spirit 247

        Setting out solo 254

    Playing Indoor Games 258

    Having Fun with Hobbies 260

    Seeing the Night Sky 262

    Getting the Weather Report 265

    Having Fun with Rhetorical Questions in ASL 270

Chapter 13: Here's to Your Health 277
Going to the Doctor..277
Signaling medical personnel.............................277
Figuring out how you feel 279
Expressing medical terms 281
Describing Ailments and Treatments 283
Pointing to Body Parts 286
Handling Emergencies 291

Part III: Looking into Deaf Life and Interpreting......... 297

Chapter 14: The Deaf Community and Deaf Etiquette 299
Digging into Sign's Past..299
Exploring the two schools of thought on Deaf communication....300
Examining when and how ASL began.........................301
Facing the Challenges of the Deaf Community 302
Putting the past behind us.................................302
You've come a long way, baby............................303
The Deaf as an Ethnic Group...................................305
Understanding Deaf culture...............................306
Knowing who falls into the Deaf cultural community.................306
Living as bilingual/bicultural people...................307
Being Sensitive to Being Deaf..................................308
Living together in a hearing world 308
Getting the Deaf perspective.............................309
Participating in the Deaf Community..........................309
Finding your place in the Deaf community................310
Communicating with new Deaf friends for the first time............311
Questions you shouldn't ask..............................312

Chapter 15: Interpreting: Are You Interested? 313
Knowing Where Interpreters Are Needed 313
Getting the Proper Training with Interpreting Classes............315
Certifying Your Success...315
Working for an Interpreting Agency............................317
Abiding by the Code of Professional Conduct.................318
Balancing Two Languages and Honing Your Skills............319

Chapter 16: Using Technology to Communicate 321
Can You See Me Now? Using Videophones....................321
Communicating with videophones.........................322
What to expect when using a video relay service 323
Keeping conversations private 324

Utilizing Other Communication Methods.................................324
    Texting 24/7...324
    Chatting visually 325

Part IV: The Part of Tens.................................. 327

Chapter 17: Ten Tips to Help You Sign like a Pro.................329

Watch Yourself and Others Sign...329
Discover Multiple Signs for Communicating One Thing.........................329
Practice Your Signing — with Others 330
Always Fingerspell a Name First...330
Adjust Your Eyes; Everyone's Signing Is Different 330
Use Facial Expressions like Vocal Inflections 330
Journal Your Progress...331
Get Some Signing Space..331
Don't Jump the Gun..331
Watch the Face, Not the Hands 332

Chapter 18: Ten Ways to Pick Up Sign Quickly 333

Volunteer at a Residential School for the Deaf............................333
Volunteer at Local Deaf Clubs...333
Attend Deaf Social Functions 334
Make Deaf Friends 334
Assist Deaf Ministries..334
Attend Conferences for Interpreters.......................................335
Work at Camps for the Deaf 335
Attend Silent Weekends..335
Go to Deaf Workshops and Deaf Conferences 336
Watch Sign Language Videos 336

Chapter 19: Ten Popular Deaf Expressions 337

Swallowed the Fish..337
Train Gone..338
Pea Brain...338
Shucks/Darn! 339
I Hope 339
Your Guess Is as Good as Mine...339
Cool!...340
Oh No! 341
That's Pretty Straight-Laced 341
Wow!..341

Part V: Appendixes *343*

Appendix A: Answer Key to Fun & Games. 345
Chapter 1 345
Chapter 2 345
Chapter 3 345
Chapter 4 345
Chapter 5 345
Chapter 6 345
Chapter 7 346
Chapter 8 346
Chapter 9 346
Chapter 10 346
Chapter 11 346
Chapter 12 346
Chapter 13 346

Appendix B: About the CD 347
System Requirements 347
Using the CD 348
What You'll Find on the CD 348
Troubleshooting 350
Customer Care 350

Index *351*

Introduction

· ·

Most of you have probably seen Deaf people use American Sign Language out in public — in restaurants, hospitals, airports, churches, and the like. To see people use this language to share ideas about every subject is remarkable and fascinating to watch. Now, you have a chance to enter the wonderful world of Deaf people. This book is an introduction for you to get your hands wet and a great refresher for those who need an easy and clear way to practice Sign.

About This Book

Signing For Dummies, 2nd Edition, is designed to give you a general understanding of the properties of Sign, as well as an understanding of Deaf culture. As you'll soon see, the language and the culture go hand in hand and can't be separated, and an understanding of both makes you a better signer. As you build your foundation in Sign, you'll see that it's a highly organized language with rules that govern it — rules that we explain in this book.

To clarify, *Signing For Dummies,* 2nd Edition, focuses solely on what's known as *American Sign Language* (ASL) because it's the most popular form of communication for the Deaf community in the United States.

This book is categorized according to subject. You can use each chapter as a building block for the next chapter or you can skip around wherever you please. Just find a subject that interests you and dig in, remembering that the most important thing is to have fun while you're figuring out this stuff.

After you understand a concept, we strongly recommend that you practice with others who are learning ASL or who are already proficient. Conversing with Deaf people is highly recommended as they are the experts. Doing so helps reinforce the knowledge you obtain from this book and allows others to help you hone your skills. If others understand you, you're probably on the right track. And if you don't understand something, don't despair. Talk to your Deaf friends or others who already know Sign.

Conventions Used in This Book

Here are some conventions we use to help you navigate this book:

- ✔ We capitalize the word *Sign* when we use it as another name for American Sign Language. We don't, however, capitalize it when we use it as a verb *(to sign)* or a noun (referring to a person — a *signer* — or to a specific sign).

- ✔ We always capitalize *Deaf* because it means culturally Deaf (whereas lowercase "deaf" simply means that someone has an audiological impairment and communicates in spoken English rather than ASL).

- ✔ Whenever we use Sign in lists, examples, and dialogues, we print it in ALL CAPS to show that it's the closest equivalent to its English counterpart.

- ✔ When we introduce a new sign, we **bold** it in the text so that you know you're about to learn a new sign.

- ✔ ASL doesn't use punctuation, so we add hyphens to show slight pauses in Sign translations.

- ✔ The text (Sign and its English translation) always comes before the illustration.

- ✔ To save space, manual numbers and words that are fingerspelled don't have illustrations. See Chapter 1 if you need help remembering how to sign a particular letter or number.

- ✔ A **Q** in a line of ASL indicates that you need to sign the manual question mark (flip to Chapter 6 for more on the manual question mark).

- ✔ Websites appear in `monofont`.

This book also includes a few elements that other *For Dummies* books do not. Here are the new elements that you'll find:

- ✔ **Signin' the Sign dialogues:** Seeing Sign in actual context helps you understand how to use Sign vocabulary. Many signs have more than one meaning, and in ASL there's more than one way to say something, so these dialogues can help you out with that.

- ✔ **Fun & Games activities:** These games at the end of the chapters help you practice Sign and are a good way to have fun while checking your progress. Some Fun & Games activities have pictures that help you develop your memory skills for Sign recognition.

Don't think of the translations of English sentences into ASL as word-for-word translations. In fact, many signs have no English equivalents. Throughout this book, you find English equivalents that are close in meaning to Sign but not exactly the same. Remember that ASL is a completely different language from English. Fortunately, many gestures that hearing people use are also used by Deaf people in ASL, so you already have a head start that you can build on.

Foolish Assumptions

We hate to assume anything about anyone, but when writing this book, we had to make a few foolish assumptions about you. Here they are (we hope we were right):

- You have little or no experience in this type of communication, but you have a genuine interest.

- You don't expect to become fluent in Sign after going through this book. You just want some basic vocabulary, and you want to see what particular signs look like by themselves and in simple sentences.

- You aren't interested in memorizing grammar rules; you just want to communicate. (In case you do happen to be interested in ASL grammar, Chapter 2 is dedicated to that topic, and other rules and concepts are sprinkled throughout the book.)

- You want to know a few signs to be able to communicate with Deaf friends, family members, and acquaintances.

- Because ASL satisfies a foreign language requirement in many colleges, you want to see whether ASL is for you.

- You met a pretty Deaf girl or a handsome Deaf guy, and knowing some Sign will really help out!

How This Book Is Organized

This book is divided by topic into parts and then further divided into chapters. Here we tell you what kind of information you can find in each part.

Part I: Getting Started

This part explains fingerspelling and the basic handshapes, facial expressions, and body language of Sign. We include some rules so that you can see how objects and action work together. You can make simple sentences with these basics. As a general tip, maximize your time in Part I. The rest of the book builds on this foundational content.

Part II: American Sign Language in Action

In this part, you find your time to shine; this is where the rules of Sign and action of Sign come together. Here you develop your ability to strike up conversations, ask for directions, and talk about dining and shopping. You also discover the signs for business terms, outdoor activities, and health-related words and expressions. This part essentially prepares you for a variety of types of discussions.

Part III: Looking into Deaf Life and Interpreting

In this part, you give your hands a rest and read how Deaf people function in the hearing world. This part captures the cultural component of ASL. You discover the history of Sign and some basics about Deaf etiquette. You also get a crash course in becoming an interpreter and find out how recent technology helps Deaf people communicate. This part gives you a more complete understanding of the Deaf world.

Part IV: The Part of Tens

Here you find some great ideas so that you can sign even better and faster. This part helps you get past any reluctance you may have and encourages you to feel more confident about signing in front of other people. You also gain an appreciation for the richness of ASL by seeing various idiomatic expressions that Deaf people use.

Part V: Appendixes

This book has two appendixes. Appendix A gives you all the answers to the Fun & Games questions. Appendix B provides detailed instructions for playing and using the CD that accompanies this book. The CD is designed to give you a fuller view of ASL and to make the most of your ability to learn.

Icons Used in This Book

To help you find certain types of information more easily, we include several icons in this book. You find them on the left-hand side of the page, sprinkled throughout:

This icon highlights tips and tricks that can make signing easier.

This icon points out interesting and important information that you don't want to forget.

To avoid making a blunder or offending a Deaf friend, pay attention to what these paragraphs have to say.

For those grammar buffs out there, this icon points out useful ASL grammar rules and concepts.

This icon draws your attention to pieces of information about the culture of the Deaf community.

This icon indicates Signin' the Sign dialogues and other elements that are featured on video clips on the CD, so that you can see Sign in action and practice with the signers.

Where to Go from Here

The beauty of this book is that you can begin anywhere you want. You may find it helpful to start with the first few chapters to get down the basics, but if that's not your thing, feel free to jump in wherever you want. Use the table of contents and the index to point you in the right direction. Find a subject that interests you, start signing, and have fun! Just remember, you're going to make mistakes, but don't let that discourage you. Instead, use those mistakes as opportunities to solidify and strengthen your foundation. Nothing worthwhile comes easily. Take your time, take notes, and let everyone take notice of your ability to sign!

Part I
Getting Started

The 5th Wave   By Rich Tennant

"You don't have to shout the words out once you know what they are, Derek. This is American Sign Language, not charades."

In this part . . .

These chapters lay the foundation for your understanding of American Sign Language. You'll likely find that you know more than you think. Sign language is enveloped with body language, facial expressions, numbers, and some spelling — all of which you use in English every day.

Chapter 1

Finding Out That You Already Know a Little Sign

In This Chapter

▶ Knowing some of ASL's iconic signs
▶ Communicating using gestures and facial expressions

Signing isn't difficult, although moving your hands, body, and face to convey meaning instead of just using your voice may seem odd at first. But with time, practice, and interaction, you'll see that hand movements can be meaningful. Your goal and reward is being able to meet and communicate with a whole new group of people — people who share your opinions, hobbies, and more. That's definitely worth the initial awkwardness!

This chapter illustrates the manual alphabet in American Sign Language and talks about hand and body movements. Here, we show you the basics of making handshapes and using facial expressions and body language to get your ideas across. And we start off by reassuring you that you already know some signs. Trust us — you do.

For example, Sign is interwoven in your gestures when you use your index finger to motion to someone to "come here," when you shake your head "yes" and "no," and when you give someone the "evil eye." When you put these in signing context, you convey volumes of information.

Discovering Signs That Look like What They Mean

Iconic or *natural* signs look like what they mean — the up and down motion of brushing your teeth that means **toothbrush**, for instance, or the right and left punches that mean **boxing**. Iconic signs always show action. Here are some examples:

BOXING: Looks like you're "putting up your dukes."

DRIVE: Pretend that you're steering a car.

EAT: Act like you're putting food in your mouth.

MILK: Have you ever seen a cow being milked? That's how you sign milk.

SWIMMING/POOL: Think of when you walk through the shallow end of the pool and extend your arms out in front of you to clear the water.

TOOTHBRUSH/BRUSH TEETH: If you've ever brushed your teeth with your finger, you made the sign for toothbrush and for brushing your teeth.

Like the sign for boxing, many sports signs are iconic. Check out Chapter 12 for more sports signs.

Being a winning receiver

If you have trouble reading someone's signs, check the context and then ask yourself, "What could this person mean?" Remember that it's okay to ask someone to repeat something, just like you do when you don't understand someone speaking to you. You can show a signer you're "listening" by nodding your head. If at any time someone is signing something to you and you begin not to understand, stop the person and let her know what you did understand and where you stopped understanding. This is perfectly acceptable. Don't wait for the person to finish a long, drawn-out thought and then say, "I don't understand."

Remember not to watch the signer's hands primarily. You want to watch the signer's hands through your peripheral vision. Keep your eyes on the whole picture, from the signer's abdomen on up to her head. The eyes, face, hands, and body movements tell the whole story.

Building on the Basics of Sign — Gestures and Expression

You already know that "speaking" ASL is mostly a matter of using your fingers, hands, and arms. What you may not understand yet is that facial expressions and body language are important and sometimes crucial for conveying and understanding signs and their meaning. If you're focused only on a signer's hands, you can easily miss the slightest rolling of the eyes, a raised eyebrow, or the signer "pointing" at something with his eyes. So expect to see hands on hips in frustration, eyes open wide in shock, and hands on mouths covering a hearty laugh. You know these gestures already and are off to a good start.

The following sections explain how you get nearly your whole body involved in ASL.

Spelling with your fingers

Signers use the manual alphabet (shown later in this section) all the time, especially beginners. Signers *fingerspell* — spell using the manual alphabet — certain words and, at first, people's names. So as a beginner, feel free to fingerspell any word you don't know the sign for. If you want to fingerspell two or more words in a row, such as a title or someone's first and last name, pause for just a second between each word.

In this book, any word that you fingerspell is shown in hyphenated letters. For example, *mall* is written as M-A-L-L. We usually don't take the space to show the hand signs for each letter; we leave it to you to find the appropriate letters here in this chapter.

Don't worry about being slow at fingerspelling. Remember, clarity is the goal, not speed. Silently mouth the letter sounds as you fingerspell the letters. Doing so helps you control your speed because you concentrate more on the letters. Don't pronounce each letter individually; pronounce the sounds as you fingerspell. If you're fingerspelling P-H-I-L-L-I-P, for example, mouthing "P-H" is incorrect. You want to mouth the "F" sound.

You may encounter Deaf people who fingerspell everything, even words that have a sign. This is called the *Rochester Method,* and some Deaf people are most comfortable communicating this way. Even the best interpreters can easily get lost trying to understand this method. The best way to follow what these signers are expressing is to watch their mouth movement and read their lips. You may not catch most of what's said, but if you do some lip-reading, remember the topic, and ask for clarification, you'll get by.

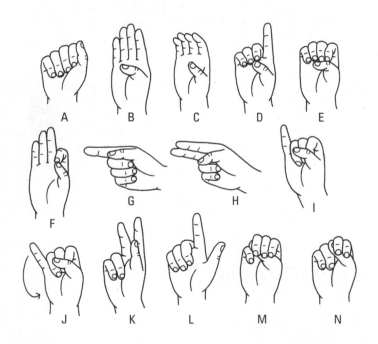

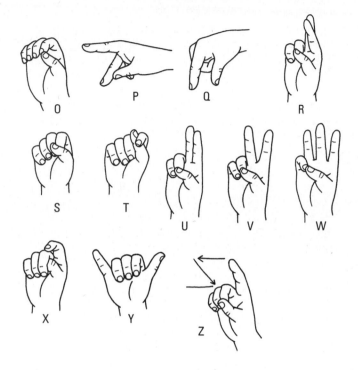

You sign, rather than fingerspell, some *initializations* — concepts such as **a.m.** and **p.m.,** which you sign as morning and evening, respectively. But you can fingerspell a word like **okay** as O-K, or you can just show the F handshape. Yes, it's a gesture, but it gets the point across. Remember, all languages use gestures, and ASL is no different.

A.M.

P.M.

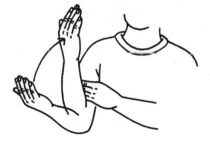

You may run across compound names that are abbreviated as two letters: Los Angeles (LA), San Francisco (SF), Burger King (BK), and Blue Ridge (BR). Remember to fingerspell the complete word before you abbreviate it, because L-A could mean Louisiana and B-R could mean Baton Rouge. The goal is to be clear; shortcuts and slang will come, so don't get ahead of yourself.

Shaping up those hands

Remembering a few simple points can help you make handshapes like a life-long signer. *Handshapes* are hand formations that you use to sign each letter of the alphabet; this is also called the *manual alphabet.* Your manual dexterity is like a voice that has the ability to sing, and it requires practice. Start with two-letter words and graduate to larger ones. As you start getting the feel for fingerspelling, you'll be using hand muscles that you didn't know you had, so you may notice a little soreness.

Handshapes are the individual letters of the manual alphabet, and fingerspelling is an action using the manual alphabet to create words.

In your excitement to sign, you face the possibility of overusing your hands. Like that singing voice, your hands need a little break as they get ready for the next step. To find out how to keep your hands limber, search for "hand exercises" on the Internet or talk to sign language interpreters.

In the rest of this section, we explain the basic conventions of handshapes.

For signing purposes, the hand you write with is called your *dominant hand* (some folks call it the *active hand*). The other hand is your *base hand* or *passive hand.* In this book, all the illustrations represent a right-handed signer — the right hand illustrates the dominant hand, and the left hand illustrates the passive hand. So, in a nutshell, if you see a sign with the right hand dominant and you're left-handed, use your left hand.

While your active hand does the work, your passive hand does one of the following:

- ✔ It mirrors the active hand.
- ✔ It displays one of seven basic handshapes, called *natural handshapes.*

The seven natural handshapes are the letters **A, B, C, S,** and **O** and the numbers **1** and **5.**

If you don't use your passive hand for these handshapes, you'll be breaking a rule in ASL. The Deaf person who is watching you sign may not know this particular rule, but she'll be thrown off. Therefore, follow this basic rule and stay ahead of the game.

You can use natural handshapes in a variety of ways. You may form the same handshape in one direction for a particular sign but in a different direction for another sign. For a sign such as **start,** you form the natural handshape (in this case, the number 5) in one direction. But for a sign such as **cook,** you form that same natural handshape in a different direction. Check out the following examples of active/passive handshapes that you use while signing:

START: Place your active index finger between your index and middle fingers of your passive hand, and then turn the active index finger outward — it looks like you're turning the ignition key in a car.

BUY: Hold out your passive hand, palm up in the 5 handshape. Use your active hand as you would to hand money to a salesclerk.

COOK: Hold your passive hand out, palm up. Lay your active hand across the top of it, palm down. Now flip your active hand over, then flip it back over, palm down.

When your passive hand mirrors the shape of your dominant hand, you move both hands either together or alternately. If moving them alternately, you move both hands in alternate directions at the same time. Here are some examples of alternating handshapes:

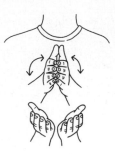

BOOK: Make this sign as if you're actually opening a book.

GIFT: Put both hands in front of you in the "X" handshape, but extend one a little farther away than the other from your body. At the same time, jerk your hands up a little bit, twice.

MAYBE

STORE: Keep your hands in the same shape and move them back and forth simultaneously.

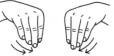

Benefiting with body language

Communicating a concept in Sign is often made clear by using body language. The meaning of **I don't know** comes through clearly when you raise your shoulders, tilt your head, and turn your palm up. Signing **I'm sick** is more easily understood when you accompany the sign with half-shut eyes, an open mouth, and a partially extended tongue. Another example is the word **no.** The speed at which you shake your head from side to side, with eyes open or shut, can say a lot about the degree of **no.** Quick, short body movements show an emphatic message; an exaggeratedly slow motion with an exaggerated facial expression conveys a similar message. In a word, the speed of the sign displays various tones. Check out the illustrations of these signs to see what we mean:

DON'T KNOW

SICK: Both hands move in a small circular motion.

NO: When you sign the word, close your eyes if you want to make it more emphatic.

Telling with your face

In Sign, you use your face to show emotion and add expression. Facial expressions tell you how the signer feels about the information he's signing. Your facial expression is just as important as your hand movements. Without the correct facial expression, the person watching you sign will either get the wrong message or need clarification to make sure that he understands your message correctly.

Don't be alarmed if you aren't understood, even if a Deaf person asks for clarification a couple of times for the same sentence. This means the person genuinely wants to understand what you mean, and it also affords you the opportunity to learn to express your thoughts by Deaf standards. This is an invaluable way of learning; don't shy away from this experience.

Sign expressions as if you actually "feel" that way. For example, you sign the word **sad** while you slump your shoulders down and make a sad facial expression. You sign **happy** just the opposite — keep your shoulders up and wear a smile. (Check out Chapter 3 for illustrations of these signs.)

Be sure that you maintain eye contact when you're signing, and, again, watch your conversational partner's face, not his hands. Your peripheral vision allows you to still see the hands, so don't worry about missing any signs.

Signin' the Sign

Belinda and Terry are getting ready for the holidays. Belinda wants to start shopping for Christmas presents.

Terry: Do you want a ride to the mall?
Sign: M-A-L-L — RIDE — WANT YOU Q

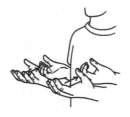

Belinda: Yes, I want to start buying Christmas gifts soon.
Sign: YES — SOON — CHRISTMAS GIFTS — START BUYING — WANT ME

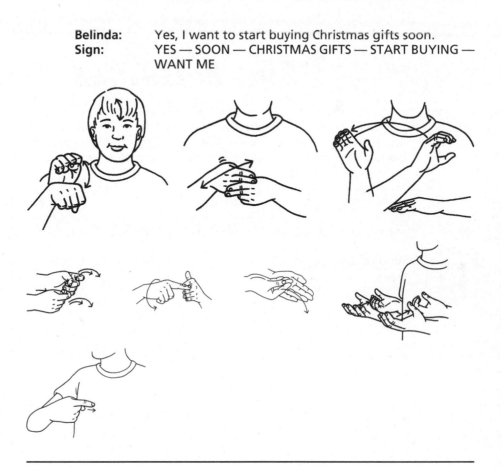

Fun & Games

Using the manual alphabet, practice fingerspelling your own name. Then finger-spell ten three-letter words of your choice. Refer to the manual alphabet, if needed, to double-check yourself.

Chapter 2

Warming Up with Signing Grammar Basics

....

In This Chapter

▶ Signing various parts of speech

▶ Indicating tenses in your signing

▶ Putting together some simple sentences

▶ Expressing exclamations

▶ Getting more complicated with conditional sentences

▶ Using personification and facial grammar

....

*I*n this chapter, we talk about the building blocks that you need to communicate in any language — nouns, verbs, adjectives, and adverbs — and we tell you how to put them together to form simple sentences. We also tell you how to get your body involved to express verb tenses.

Explaining the Parts of Speech

Both English and American Sign Language have subjects and verbs, as well as adjectives and adverbs that describe the subjects and verbs. Also, English and Sign both allow you to converse about the present, past, and future, so whatever English can do, Sign can do — visually. However, unlike English, ASL doesn't use prepositions as a separate part of speech. As a general rule, most prepositions in Sign, with a few exceptions, act as verbs.

The English language articles — *a, an,* and *the* — aren't used in Sign. Likewise, helping verbs, such as *am, is,* and *are,* aren't used in Sign, either. ASL is an active language, which means that helping verbs and being verbs aren't necessary.

Distinguishing between noun/verb pairs

Some nouns and verbs in Sign share the same handshapes. You distinguish the part of speech by signing the motion once if it's a verb and twice if it's a noun. Like any language, there are exceptions to the rule.

Though most nouns don't have a verb that looks the same, all but a few nouns need the double motion. Most of the noun illustrations in this book are represented by double arrows. We indicate which nouns don't follow the double-motion rule.

Table 2-1 shows a few noun and verb pairs.

Table 2-1	Nouns and Verbs with Shared Handshapes		
English Noun	*Sign*	*English Verb*	*Sign*
CHAIR		SIT	
PLANE		FLY	
CAR		DRIVE	

The following examples compare the noun/verb differences.

English: Please sit in this chair.
Sign: THIS CHAIR (point) — PLEASE — SIT

English: I like to fly small planes.
Sign: SMALL PLANES — FLY — LIKE ME

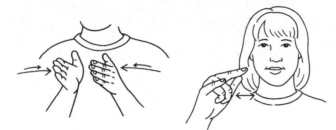

Modifying with adjectives and adverbs

In English, a modifier can come before or after the word it modifies, depending on the sentence. However, in Sign, you typically place the adjective or adverb — the modifier — after the word it modifies. But sometimes in Sign, you may find yourself expressing the modifier at the same time you sign the word it modifies, just by using your face.

Your facial expressions can describe things and actions in ASL. For instance, if something is small or big, you can show its size without actually signing **small** or **big.** You can describe a small piece of thread by pursing your lips, blowing out a little air, and closing your eyes halfway. If something is very thick, puff out your cheeks. You can convey that it's raining hard or that a car is moving fast by moving your eyebrows or shaping your mouth a certain way. (Turn to Chapter 1 for more on using expressions and body language.)

The following examples show adjectives and adverbs placed with nouns and verbs. We also provide tips on how to use facial expressions to really get your point across when describing things in Sign.

PRETTY GIRL: Raise your eyebrows, form your mouth into an "o" shape (like saying ooh), sign "pretty" and then "girl."

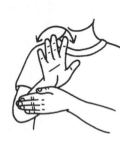

BAD MOVIE: Sign the word "movie" and then turn your mouth down in a frown and scrunch your eyebrows together while signing the word "bad."

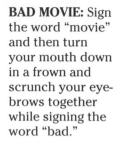

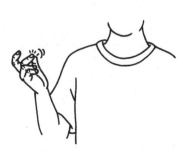

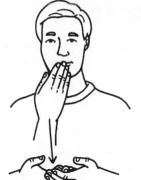

GOOD DOG: Sign the word "dog" first, then slightly smile and raise your eyebrows as you sign the word "good."

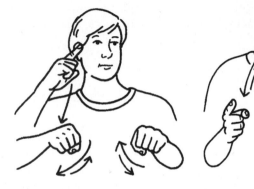

TALK LOUDLY or LOUDLY TALK

RUN VERY FAST: Sign the word "run" while scrunching your eyebrows together and clenching your jaw tight with your mouth slightly open.

Some adverbs used in English, such as the words *very* and *really*, are also used in ASL. Others must be incorporated into the verb by using facial expressions.

Talking Tenses

To communicate tenses in Sign, you need your hands *and* your body. Showing tense in ASL is partly a matter of where you sign in relation to your body.

Think of your body as being in the present tense, which is a fairly safe assumption, we hope.

To place everything you sign into past tense, you sign **finish** at chest level or higher, depending on the level of intensity, at either the beginning or end of the sentence (most signers do it at the beginning for clarity), while saying the word *fish,* a shortened version of *finish.* This sign signals that everything has already happened.

You can also use the **finish** sign when making an exclamation. (For more on this sign's uses, see the section "Exclaiming in Simple Sentences" later in this chapter.)

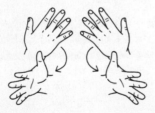

Signing in future tense works pretty much the same way as signing in past tense. You indicate future tense by signing and saying **will** at the end of a sentence. The farther you sign the word **will** from the front of your body, the farther into the future you go. Here's an example:

English: He will go later.
Sign: HE GO — WILL

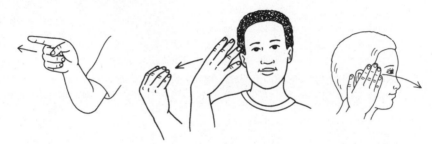

You can also sign **will** to show affirmation. For example:

English: Mike is walking over to my house.
Sign: MY HOUSE — M-I-K-E — WALKING — WILL

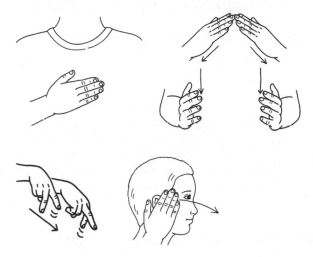

You can easily sign an event that's going to happen in the future. A simple rule to follow: Mention what's planned or intended and then sign **will.**

Here's a time-sensitive concept that doesn't quite fit into past, present, or future tense. To show that you're not yet finished with or you haven't even started a task, sign the unaccomplished deed and then sign **not yet** while shaking your head slightly from side to side, as if saying *no,* at the end of the sentence. You don't pronounce *not yet,* though; you simply sign it. The following sentence gives you an idea of how you can use this expression:

English: I haven't eaten.
Sign: ME EAT — NOT YET

Structuring Sentences

Putting a sentence together in English is pretty basic. You usually put it in subject-verb-direct object order, perhaps throwing in an indirect object between the verb and the direct object. In ASL, however, you can choose to assemble your sentence in different orders, depending on the dialogue.

You can sign simple sentences in a natural English order. However, most of the time, you can get your point across in a variety of ways.

Although Sign is an official language, it isn't a written one. Some people have attempted to make an artificial Sign system for writing purposes, but few people know it because its use is so limited. Because ASL isn't meant to be a written language, it has no punctuation. To write about Sign, as in this book, you must translate it as closely as possible into a written language such as English.

Subjecting yourself to nouns and verbs in simple sentences

Unlike English grammar rules, which dictate that the subject must go before the verb, Sign allows you to put the subject before or after the verb when dealing with simple sentences; it doesn't matter which word comes first. The same goes for exclamations; you can place them at the beginning or the end of a simple sentence (see the section "Exclaiming in Simple Sentences" later in this chapter). The following examples illustrate how simple sentences work.

English: He ran.
Sign: HE RAN
Sign: RAN HIM

English: She fell.
Sign: SHE FELL
Sign: FELL HER

Placing subjects and objects

To incorporate direct and indirect objects into your signing, first start with a basic subject-verb sentence. You can sign it in subject-verb or verb-subject order. Here are some examples:

English: He sells.
Sign: HE SELLS

English: I eat.
Sign: ME EAT

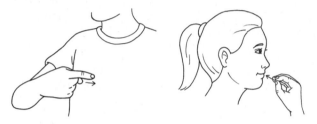

English: She drives.
Sign: SHE DRIVES

Although these short sentences get the point across, the world would be pretty boring if that's how people communicated all the time. So add a direct object to each of these sentences to make them a little more interesting.

In case you haven't had a grammar class in a few years, a *direct object* is a word that goes after the verb and answers the question *what?* or *whom?* However, in ASL, the direct object can go either before the subject or after the verb.

English: He sells food.
Sign: HE SELLS FOOD

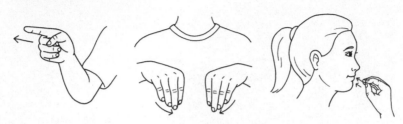

Sign: FOOD HE SELLS

English: I eat pizza.
Sign: ME EAT PIZZA

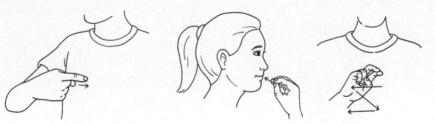

Sign: PIZZA ME EAT

English: She drives a car.
Sign: SHE DRIVES CAR

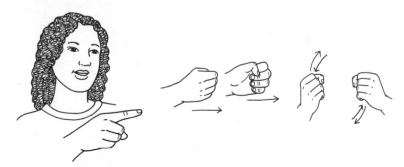

Sign: CAR SHE DRIVES

TIP

If you have a sentence that may be misunderstood if you change the word order, leave it in the natural English order. For example, if you want to say *Joe loves Sue,* you need to sign JOE LOVES SUE. Changing it around to SUE LOVES JOE doesn't convey the same meaning. (Having said that, we really hope that Sue does love Joe in return.)

Okay. So you're signing sentences with direct objects. Now, try to take your signing skills one step further by signing *indirect objects.* (Another quick grammar reminder: Indirect objects are words that come between the verb and direct object; they indicate who or what receives the direct object.) You place the indirect object right after the subject and then show the action. These sentences show you the correct order:

English: The girl throws the dog a bone.
Sign: DOG BONE — GIRL — THROW

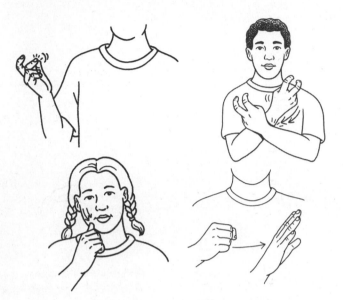

English: I gave the teacher an apple.
Sign: ME TEACHER — APPLE GAVE

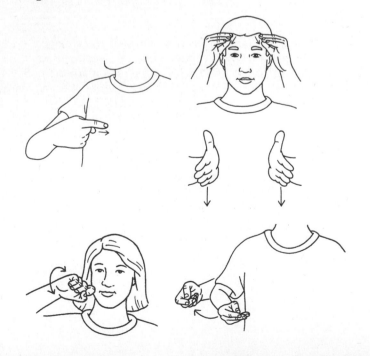

Signing sentences in an understandable order may be a bit tricky at first. If the person you're signing to is leaning forward, has an inquisitive look, or seems distracted, he or she probably doesn't understand you. You may want to try signing the thought in a different way.

Signin' the Sign

Linda and Buddy are at work. The restaurant will be opening in one hour, and they're taking a quick breather before it opens.

Linda: The chairs look nice.
Sign: CHAIRS — LOOK NICE

  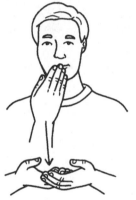

Buddy: That pizza smells good.
Sign: PIZZA — SMELLS GOOD

Linda: We're finished. I'm going to eat now.
Sign: WE FINISH — NOW — ME EAT

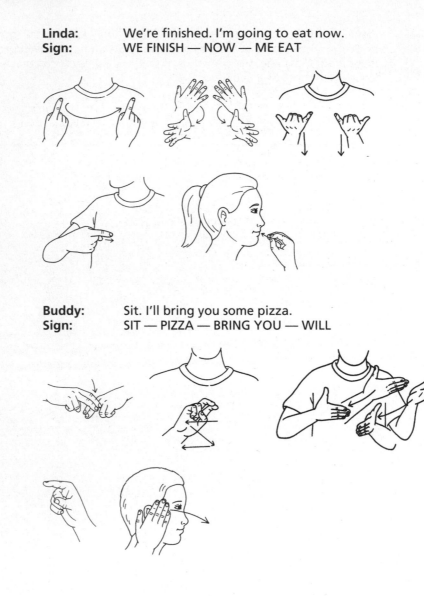

Buddy: Sit. I'll bring you some pizza.
Sign: SIT — PIZZA — BRING YOU — WILL

Linda:	Throw me an apple, too.
Sign:	APPLE — THROW ME — TOO

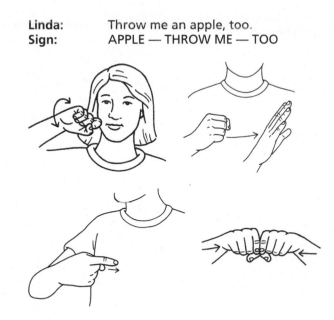

Exclaiming in Simple Sentences

Exclamations in all languages tell the listener how you feel about a subject. Sign is no different. Exclamation is used a lot in Sign; both signer and receiver use it. As in English, you can also use exclamation to show *how* strong you feel or don't feel about something. Other signers who are watching can sign what they feel about what you've signed, too. You can sign exclamations at the beginning or end of the sentence. Most, but not all, exclamations in Sign have English equivalents. Following is a list of some of the more popular Sign exclamations. Ask your Deaf friends to sign these expressions to get a clear picture because the face will tell a thousand words.

OH/I SEE

WHAT: This exclamation is fingerspelled simply as W-T; it's only used as a one-word exclamation (as "What?!").

COME ON

FINISH: Although finish is used at the beginning of a sentence to show past tense (see the section "Talking Tenses" earlier in this chapter), it's also used as humor in Sign to indicate "enough already" and as a reprimand meaning "stop that." You sign the word, using just one hand, and you pronounce the word "fish," which is a shortened version of the sign for "finish," as stated earlier. You can tell by the context of the conversation which way it's being used.

OH MY GOSH

WOW

OOH: (Also known as "flick"): Start with your hand in the "8" handshape, then change it to a "5" sign handshape using a quick flicking motion with your middle finger.

COOL

Signin' the Sign

Adan and Aurora will be celebrating their 50th wedding anniversary. Adan wants to stay home and celebrate, while Aurora wants to go out. See how their conversation unfolds.

Aurora: Wow! Our 50th anniversary!
Sign: ANNIVERSARY — 50 YEARS — US — WOW

Adan: Ooh, that's a long time!
Sign: (flick!) — LONG TIME — SO FAR

Aurora: Where do you want to celebrate?
Sign: CELEBRATION — WHERE GO — Q

Adan: The living room.
Sign: (point) — LIVING ROOM

Aurora: Oh, I see. Why?
Sign: OH I SEE WHY — Q

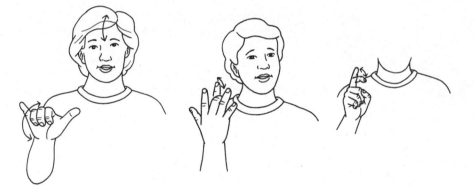

Adan: It's inexpensive.
Sign: CHEAP

Aurora:	You stop that!
Sign:	FINISH

Signing Conditional Sentences

A conditional sentence occurs when a circumstance is added to a sentence. A *circumstance* is a phrase that usually starts with a conditional word, such as "if" or "suppose."

Sign the conditional word while raising your eyebrows, but then follow with the rest of the conditional phrase and sentence with your eyebrows back down in their normal position.

Consider this example:

English: If you order beer, I'll order wine.
Sign: IF BEER ORDER YOU — WINE ORDER ME

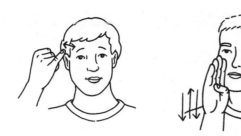

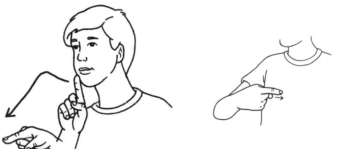

Personification: The Secret of Agents

In ASL, turning a verb into a person is called *personification.* You do it with
two simple motions: Sign the verb and then glide the heels of your hands
down the sides of your body with your fingers extended outward. The result
of this is an **agent.** Look at this list to see what we mean.

WRITE + AGENT = WRITER

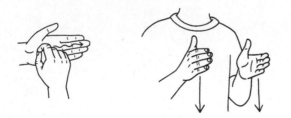

FLY + AGENT = PILOT

SUPERVISE + AGENT = SUPERVISOR

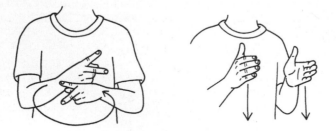

COOK + AGENT = CHEF

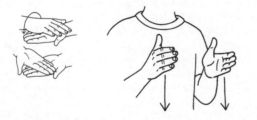

LAW + AGENT = LAWYER

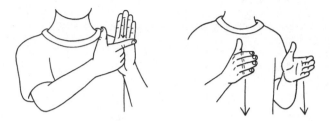

MANAGE + AGENT = MANAGER

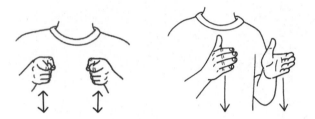

Providing Clarity with Facial Grammar

Facial grammar in ASL is information added to an ASL discourse that conveys the signer's degree of emotion, information that can be descriptive to a noun, or information that can be descriptive to the motion of the verb.

Imagine having a spoken conversation with no tonality. Things would get confusing very quickly. In ASL, facial and body expressions are equal to tonality in spoken English. They allow the addressee to understand the severity and emotion of the conversation. They offer extra information that words alone can't provide.

You've been using facial expressions all your life — thousands of expressions. So with Sign, all you need to do is add a subject and verb with that certain expression that only you can do, and you've arrived. Make sure you keep in mind that a little exaggeration of the facial expression is needed, for an obvious reason: ASL has no vocal tone. Exaggeration will come with ease; everybody is guilty of a little exaggeration now and then, so put it to good use.

In the eyes of the addressee, your facial expressions show how you feel about the topic, which gives the addressee a head start regarding what to expect as you begin to sign. People indicate their feelings all the time in English with their tone; you can do the same in signing with your expressions and how much you exaggerate them. If you watch the facial expressions of Deaf people as they sign, you will see that the exaggerated facial expression is harnessed to complement the thought.

Here's a sentence to help you practice using facial expressions and attitude to show your feelings:

English: The weather is awful!
Sign: WEATHER — AWFUL

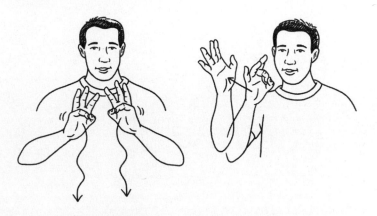

If you thought that weather is the subject, you're right. And what about the weather? It's awful. Sign **weather** with your eyebrows raised. As for the facial expression for awful, it's as natural as crunching your eyebrows close together. Also, when you sign awful, flick your middle finger and your thumb by your temple and throw in a sneer.

Here's another sentence that shows how to explain how you feel by using your facial expression:

English: The wedding was beautiful.
Sign: WEDDING — BEAUTIFUL — FINISH

Note: The sign *finish* shows it has already taken place.

Fun & Games

Using the following pictures, recall what each sign means and then fill in the blanks. If you need help, the answers are in Appendix A.

a.

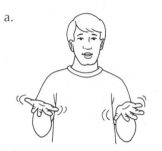

b.

c.

d.

e.

f.

g.

h.

(continued)

1. My picture won _____ place.

2. _____ that's interesting!

3. Our plane leaves at _____.

4. I _____ pizza at the mall.

5. We live on a _____ farm, with hundreds of acres of crops.

6. The _____ is broken, so I'm afraid to _____ on it.

7. I don't like to _____ in small _____; being inside clouds scares me.

8. _____?! That doesn't make any sense.

Chapter 3

Starting to Sign Basic Expressions

● ●

In This Chapter

▶ Starting or joining in a conversation

▶ Getting to know others

▶ Relaying information through Constructed Dialogue and Constructed Action

● ●

*T*his chapter sets you off on the right foot (or hand!) to meet and greet fellow signers and start signing basic expressions. You can acquaint yourself with American Sign Language by watching Deaf people sign. Being included in a conversation is a great transition for conversing in ASL. Don't worry about signing perfectly. Deaf people will know that you're a novice signer — just have fun with it.

Interacting with other signers is an important part of getting the basics under your belt. You'll find that all signers, Deaf and hearing, have different styles. Like English, the words are the same, but no two people talk alike. Setting a goal to be clear is a must. Your style will come naturally.

Initiating a Conversation

Most people who learn ASL look forward to signing with others. Attending functions with other signers gives ample opportunity to practice Sign. At Deaf functions, signed conversation happens everywhere. If you're invited by a Deaf person, allow the person to introduce you to others — great conversations start this way. If you're on your own and want to strike up a conversation, this section tells you how to properly get someone's attention and provides some ideas for conversation starters.

If Deaf people correct your signing, view this as a compliment and take no offense. They see you as a worthy investment.

When you initiate a conversation, you want to avoid *to be* verbs. These verb types set up ASL conversation in the passive form of speaking, and ASL must always be in the active form. So if you use *to be* verbs, Deaf people will have difficulty reading your ASL. In a nutshell, follow this rule: Never sign *am, are, was, were, be, being,* or *been.* They aren't used in ASL. You may see signs for these words as you're out and about, but they've been invented to teach Deaf children English, so don't use them.

Attracting someone's attention

Attracting someone's attention is easy in English. A simple yell turns many heads. To get a Deaf person's attention, tap the person on the shoulder or the back of the arm between the elbow and the shoulder. Waving at someone is another good way to get attention. A wooden floor is also a big help — stomping on the floor is an acceptable and popular attention-getter. Deaf people feel the vibration on the floor and turn to see its origination.

Another way to get someone's attention is to make and maintain eye contact. You can tell someone across a crowded room that you have something on your mind by catching the person's eye. And then, after eye contact has been made and you've approached each other, you can proceed with a conversation. Non-signers may view this action as staring and think that it's rude, but in the Deaf world, making and maintaining eye contact is a necessary common practice.

Never throw objects at a Deaf person to get the person's attention. Besides being just plain rude, it's also dangerous. ASL is a visual language, so Deaf people really value their eyesight. Accidentally hitting someone in the eye could be devastating, and you could get hit back!

Using greetings and closings

Asking questions is probably the most popular way to start a conversation. You can ask a person's name, sign yours, ask what school the person attended, and so on. Many Deaf people attended one of the residential schools for the Deaf that are located throughout the United States; you may have a city in common. You can also start a conversation with a simple **hi** or **hello,** followed by **nice to meet you.** These greetings work with Deaf people of all ages. Signing **What's up?** is a simple, informal greeting that's a great opener, too.

Shaking hands and giving hugs are also common additions to Deaf greetings. Hand-shaking is more formal than hugging, just as is true in the hearing world.

You can join a conversation easily by using one of the following openings:

HI/HELLO

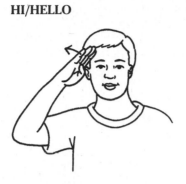

NICE TO MEET YOU

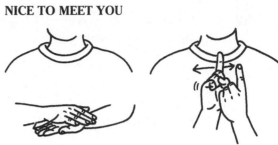

EXCUSE ME

PLEASE

HONORARY INTRO

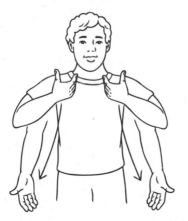

If you ask a question, raise your eyebrows and tilt your head forward; doing so shows others that your sentence is a question and that you're waiting for a response. Try these simple questions:

English: Do you sign?
Sign: SIGN YOU Q

English: Are you deaf?
Sign: DEAF YOU Q

English: How are you?
Sign: WHAT'S UP

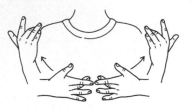

 When you see two people standing close together and signing small, don't stare. They may be having a private conversation.

Chewing gum is a no-no in Sign. Mouth movement is an important part of signed communications. Do everyone a favor and keep chewing and signing separate.

When you're ready to end a conversation, here are a couple signs that are sure to help:

GOODBYE

SEE YOU LATER

YOU'RE WELCOME

Signin' the Sign

 Buddy and Della are at the park. Buddy sees Della make a gesture that looks like a sign and decides to approach her.

Buddy: Do you sign?
Sign: SIGN YOU Q

Della: Yes, are you deaf?
Sign: YES — DEAF YOU Q

Buddy: No, my sister is deaf.
Sign: NO — MY SISTER — DEAF

Della: Oh, I see; you sign well.
Sign: OH I SEE — SIGN SKILL YOU

 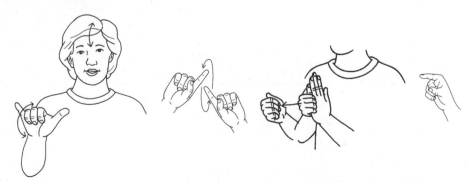

Getting Acquainted

Meeting new friends is always exciting. Getting acquainted with Deaf friends is very much like getting acquainted with people who hear, but you need to keep in mind a few important points. This section spells them out for you.

As you get acquainted with folks, keep these tips in mind:

- **During introductions, simply *fingerspell* (sign each letter individually) your name.** Deaf people are the only ones who give name signs. Those who can hear don't invent their own, nor do they give name signs to each other. (See the nearby sidebar for more on what exactly name signs are.)

  Keep in mind that when someone asks you your name, sign your first and last name — it's good manners.

  Titles, such as Mr., Mrs., and Ms., aren't used in ASL. Simply spell out the person's name.

- **Follow the conversation that's started and do your best to understand what you can.** If you don't catch something, don't interrupt the signer. Wait until she's finished.

- **Keep a steady hand.** Your signs are easier to read when your hand isn't shaking.

- **Ask questions for clarification.** Don't be embarrassed if you don't understand something. Asking questions is the best way to learn.

What's in a name sign?

Name signs aren't formal names; they're manual letters that express some characteristic of a person, or even just a manual letter or letters that represent someone's name. Having a name sign allows everyone in the Deaf community to know who you're talking about and helps avoid constantly having to fingerspell someone's name. You sign name signs on the signer's body or in front of the signer. You normally make the handshape of the first letter of a person's first name and, sometimes, last name(s).

Signin' the Sign

 Dee and Cameron are meeting for the first time. They're making their introductions.

Dee: Hi, I'm Dee.
Sign: HI — D-E-E ME

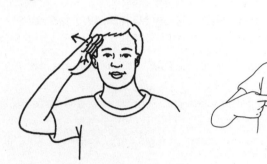

Cameron: Nice to meet you. I'm Cameron.
Sign: NICE MEET YOU (plural) — C-A-M-E-R-O-N ME

Dee: Nice to meet you, too.
Sign: NICE MEET TOO

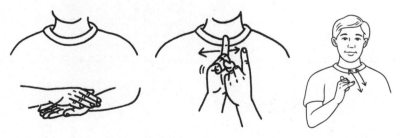

Sharing feelings and emotions

Sharing your feelings and emotions when signing is easy because Sign is naturally so expressive. Put your heart into what you're signing to genuinely express what you mean. You can express some feelings and emotions with minimal Sign and a lot of facial expressions because people already understand such expressions.

Take a look at some signs for feelings and emotions:

SAD

HAPPY

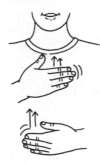

ANGRY

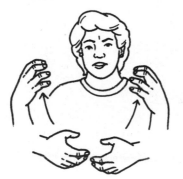

CURIOUS

Signin' the Sign

Dee and Buddy are at the store. Dee is shocked by the rising cost of everything. She shares her displeasure with Buddy.

Dee: Everything is so expensive!
Sign: EVERYTHING EXPENSIVE

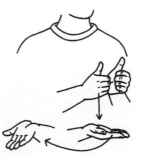

Buddy: Yes, and no sales.
Sign: TRUE — DISCOUNTS NONE

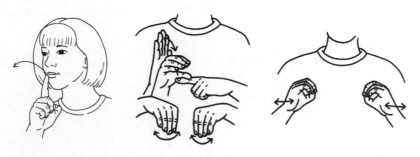

Dee: It's sad; even stamps are going up.
Sign: SAD — STAMP COST — INCREASE TOO

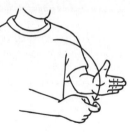

Buddy: It really makes me angry.
Sign: ANGRY ME

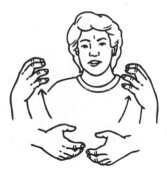

Dee: Me, too.
Sign: ME TOO

Connecting your thoughts

When you're ready to connect your thoughts in ASL, use the signs in this section for connectors. Remember that clarity is the key to a successful conversation, so as you add more information, look at the Deaf addressee and make sure that the person's facial expression is engaged. If the person asks you for clarification, don't shy away from your thoughts; the Deaf person is trying to follow along, so keep going!

ALSO

BUT

OR

OTHER

ADDITIONALLY

Talking about where you're from

Signing about where you're from is a great way to converse with a new friend. Because it can lead to other topics of conversation, it's a common icebreaker and will help you practice your Sign vocabulary. You can practice your fingerspelling — you may not know the sign of a particular location, or it may not have a sign — and expand your geographical knowledge. For example, you could sign about different famous landmarks and tourist sites.

Countries

Signing in every country is different. Although some countries have similar sign languages, no two are exactly alike.

When two Deaf people from different countries meet, their chances of communicating are pretty good because they're both skilled at making their points known in their respective countries. Although their sign languages are different, their communication skills may involve mime, writing, gestures, and pointing. People who can hear can also do those things, but their communication skills are usually more dependent on listening to the spoken language.

Some country name signs that are used in ASL are offensive to those respective countries. For instance, the ASL sign for Mexico also means "bandit," and the signs for Korea, Japan, and China are signed near the eye with a hand movement that indicates "slanted eyes." Many signers are now using the indigenous name signs that are politically correct and aren't offensive.

Here are the signs for the countries in North America:

CANADA

UNITED STATES/AMERICA

MEXICO

Here are the signs for some European countries:

ENGLAND

FRANCE

SPAIN

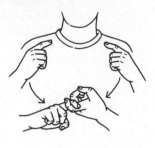

States, cities, and other locations

Many states and cities have name signs or abbreviations, but it's okay to ask someone to fingerspell a place if you don't understand.

Some common state and city signs are in Table 3-1.

Table 3-1		Signs for Various Cities and States	
English	*Sign*	*English*	*Sign*
ARIZONA		ATLANTA	
CALIFORNIA		BOSTON	
COLORADO		DENVER	

(continued)

Table 3-1 *(continued)*

English	Sign	English	Sign
FLORIDA		HOUSTON	
KENTUCKY		LOS ANGELES	
MINNESOTA		MIAMI	
NEW YORK		PITTSBURGH	
TEXAS			

Signin' the Sign

 Lindsey is telling Angie about a road trip he and Buddy are taking to visit friends in several states.

Lindsey: Buddy and I are taking a trip.
Sign: B-U-D-D-Y (point) ME — TRAVEL — WILL

Angie: Wow! Sounds like a fun time.
Sign: WOW — SEEMS FUN

Lindsey: We're going to Texas, California, and Colorado.
Sign: US TRAVEL WHERE — TEXAS CALIFORNIA COLORADO

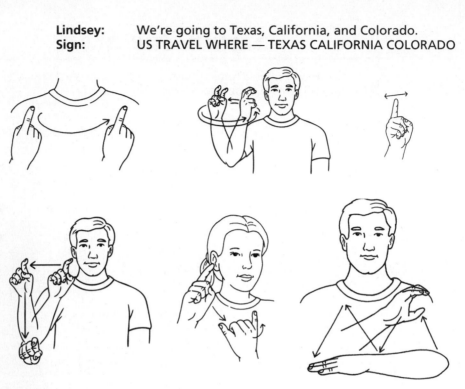

Angie: Will you see Chip?
Sign: YOU SEE C-H-I-P Q

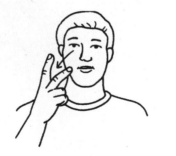

Lindsey: Yes, Chip's in Los Angeles.
Sign: YES — C-H-I-P LA

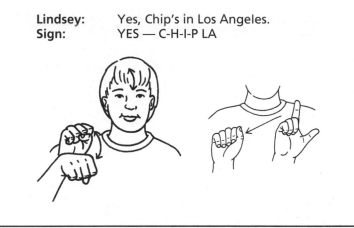

Locations add the details to what you're signing. Details are the key to clear and precise conversation. The following location signs will help:

BRIDGE

LAKE

CORNER

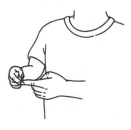

TREE

MOUNTAIN RIVER FLOWER

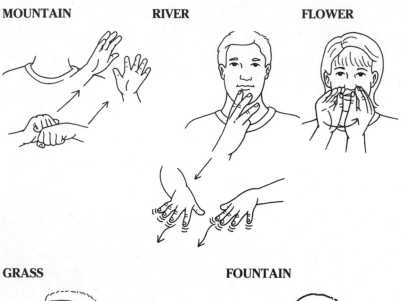

GRASS FOUNTAIN

Signin' the Sign

Dee and Ted are in Japan. They're in awe of the beautiful country and are sharing their feelings about the experience.

Dee: The trees are beautiful in Japan.
Sign: JAPAN — TREES — BEAUTIFUL

Ted: The mountains are so high.
Sign: MOUNTAINS HIGH

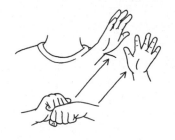

Dee: There are so many rivers.
Sign: RIVERS — MANY

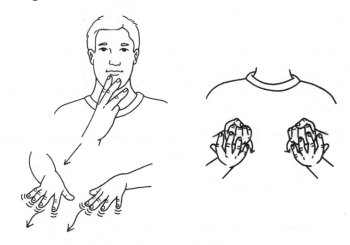

Acting the Part: Constructed Dialogue and Constructed Action

One thing people tend to do in English when they talk about a conversation is recall who said what to whom. Sometimes, the speaker has to clarify some things so the listener gets an accurate picture. In ASL, the picture is a lot clearer because you show, not tell. This type of communication has different names: *episodic signing, role shifting,* or *Constructed Action.* Constructed Action is the latest term because it has the latest research. Regardless of the term, the idea is to construct a picture for your addressee to convey what transpired in a conversation. Constructed Action describes the action of what occurred in a conversation, but there's also *Constructed Dialogue,* which focuses on what was said.

Constructed Dialogue

Constructed Dialogue is a way to communicate the details of what was said in a conversation. This technique requires your body to shift slightly from side to side so you can role shift. The purpose of this shift is to take on the character of the two people who had the conversation you're describing.

When you engage in Constructed Dialogue, keep a couple of things in mind: Make sure the person with whom you're signing knows the names of the people you're talking about and also what the gist of the conversation between the two people was.

Here's a scenario to show you how Constructed Dialogue works: Sheri and Buddy are talking about Sheri's upcoming wedding. Sheri wants to let Buddy know that her aunts can't agree on the color of the cake. Sheri has already shared with Buddy what the problem is, who is involved, and their general thoughts on the subject.

Sheri shifts her body/waist to the left slightly and takes on the role of Aunt Dee, signing Aunt Dee's name once. After the shift, Sherri doesn't need to sign Aunt Dee's name again; she can just shift her body to the left. Aunt Dee, when referred to, remains in this position for the duration of the conversation.

Sheri signs: *Orange and cream are too Halloween-like; people are going to think it's a costume party.*

Because only two people are involved in the dialogue and Buddy knows who they are, introducing the name of the other participant, Aunt Denni, isn't necessary, but Sheri may sign Aunt Denni's name just to make sure she is clear.

Sheri shifts her body slightly to the right and begins to respond as if she is Aunt Denni: *Don't be silly, orange is Sheri's favorite color, and it is her big day after all.*

Sheri shifts to the left again, assuming Aunt Dee's position, and signs: *I think we need another opinion.*

Sheri shifts to the right again, taking on the role of Aunt Denni, and signs: *That really isn't necessary.*

After you get the idea of Constructed Dialogue down, start practicing it with others. You'll find that recalling the past with others isn't that difficult and that doing so adds a little complexity to your signing, allowing you to follow others with more certainty as they use Constructed Dialogue.

Constructed Action

Constructed Action is similar to Constructed Dialogue except that you sign actions instead of words from a conversation.

Here's a scenario: Wanda is talking to Della about the new dress she purchased to wear to a dinner last week. Wanda is telling Della that the dress fit fine at the mall, but on the night she wanted to wear it, the dress was too short!

Wanda shows Della exactly how she reacted by signing *put on the dress* and then *mirror.* Wanda looks into the mirror and signs *short* on her legs, exactly on the spot where the dress comes to. Her facial expression is dumbfounded: open mouth and wide-eyed as she puts her hand on her forehead. Notice that Wanda doesn't sign any dialogue, only action.

You can use Constructed Action for any type of information — humorous, serious, or simply informative. As with Constructed Dialogue, Constructed Action takes some practice, but it will sharpen your signing prowess.

Fun & Games

Look at the following signs and try to find those words in the puzzle. The answers are in Appendix A.

1.

2.

3.

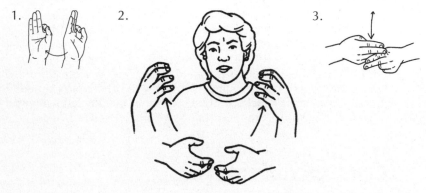

4.

5.

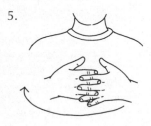

6.

7.

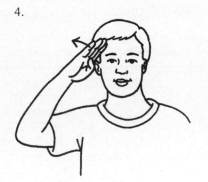

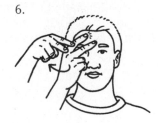

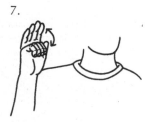

```
W   K   E   E   S   S   O
F   L   Y   M   T   U   C
R   D   F   Q   U   A   I
A   N   G   R   Y   I   X
N   A   M   E   X   M   E
C   E   Y   B   O   O   M
E   H   E   L   L   O   F
```

Chapter 4

Getting Your Numbers and Times Straight

....

In This Chapter

▶ Signing cardinal and ordinal numbers

▶ Using ASL to express numbers and time

....

*N*umbers are a big part of American Sign Language. This chapter gives you the lowdown on using numbers in all kinds of ways. We also cover expressions of time, which come up in conversation all the . . . time (see what we mean?). If you familiarize yourself with the various signs for numbers and time words, you'll be better able to converse with Deaf people, and they'll be impressed with your ability to use these signs in many different types of sentences.

Counting on Numbers

Did you know that you can count in ASL in 27 different ways? That's a pretty cool piece of trivia, but for this book, we concentrate on just two of those ways — cardinal numbers and ordinal numbers. If you'd like to check out some other ways to count, Gallaudet University and the National Technical Institute of the Deaf are great resources.

Cardinal (counting) and *ordinal* (ordering) numbers will get you through everyday situations, such as counting the millions you won on the lottery, giving your address and phone number to the movie star who wants to get to know you better, and telling your mom that you won the first Pulitzer Prize in your family.

When you want to specify more than one item — that is, express a plural — you sign the item first, followed by the quantity. Unlike English, you don't have to change the item to a plural by adding "s." A good way to remember this is to keep in mind that you need to show what the item is before you can tell someone how many items there are. For example:

English: Two books
Sign: BOOK TWO

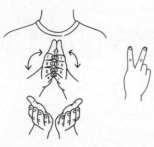

English: Four cars
Sign: CAR FOUR

To count as you're going through a list, whether you're using ordinal or cardinal numbers, notice whether the list goes straight down or in a row. Follow the pattern in the list when you sign; just count with a small motion either sideways or downward. This is extra information that allows your viewer to see the organization of the list.

Getting from one to ten with cardinal numbers

Being able to give numerical information in ASL opens many doors. You can give someone your phone number, make an appointment, and warn a potential guest that you have 12 — yes 12! — cats and two angry neighbors.

When you're indicating quantity and counting things, sign the numbers 1 through 5 and 11 through 15 with your palm facing you and the numbers 6 through 10 and 16 through 19 with your palm facing the person to whom you're signing.

Just as in English, there are exceptions to every rule, especially the one about which way your palm faces. To tell time in Sign, let your dominant (active) index finger touch your other wrist in the place where you'd wear a watch, and then use your dominant hand to sign the appropriate hour (number), with your palm facing toward the person you're signing (see the later section "Talking about Time" for more on signing time expressions). The same palm-facing-outward rule applies to addresses and phone numbers (see "Signing phone numbers and the like," later in the chapter).

Table 4-1 shows you how to sign the cardinal numbers 1 through 19.

Table 4-1		Cardinal Numbers		
English	*Sign*		*English*	*Sign*
ONE			TWO	
THREE			FOUR	
FIVE			SIX	
SEVEN			EIGHT	
NINE			TEN	

(continued)

Table 4-1 *(continued)*

English	Sign	English	Sign
ELEVEN		TWELVE	
THIRTEEN		FOURTEEN	
FIFTEEN		SIXTEEN	
SEVENTEEN		EIGHTEEN	
NINETEEN			

To sign decade numbers — 30, 40, 50, and so on — you sign the first number (3, 4, 5) followed by the sign for the number **0.** You sign hundreds — such as 600, 700, 800, and so on — by first signing the number (6, 7, 8) and then the sign for **hundred,** as the following examples show:

THIRTY (30)

FORTY (40)

FIFTY (50)

SIX HUNDRED (600)

SEVEN HUNDRED (700)

EIGHT HUNDRED (800)

Ordering ordinal numbers

Ordinal numbers show orderly placement: first cup of coffee, second chapter, and third base, for example. To indicate an ordinal number in ASL, twist your wrist inward while signing the respective number.

FIRST

SECOND

THIRD

Signing phone numbers and the like

As you meet more Deaf people and give out your phone number, sign the numbers with your palm facing outward, toward the person to whom you're giving the information. You'll also encounter some Deaf people who use their index fingers to sign *parenthesis* before signing an area code. Doing so does make the information clearer.

You sign Social Security numbers like phone numbers, with your palm facing the addressee.

Talking about Time

In ASL, telling time can be an important tool to make sure that you're never too late or too early. As you're learning this valuable piece of information, always remember that you should put the expression of time as close to the beginning of the sentence as possible; that is, you generally express the time before the subject. This part of a sentence in ASL allows the Deaf person with whom you're conversing to get a clear concept of when the event happened, effectively framing the information that you're about to share. If you forget to state the time factor early in the sentence, just add it when you can.

The time factor can be a date, a day, a month, "now," "dawn," "tomorrow," "immediately," and so on. However, at this *time,* the *idea* of "when" can be as simple as pointing to your watch and then expressing any given hour. If you want to say that something happened in the morning, sign **morning.** If you want to express nighttime, sign **evening.**

The signs in Table 4-2 help you express time. "Seconds" doesn't have a sign, but if you spell S-E-C after a number, your point will be clear — for example, **three S-E-C.** You sign the following time expressions with two signs: First touch your wrist to indicate a watch/time and then sign the number. Keep your hand with your palm facing outward and you'll be as clear as Big Ben on a sunny day!

Table 4-2		Time Signs	
English	*Sign*	*English*	*Sign*
ONE O'CLOCK		TWO O'CLOCK	
FOUR HOURS		FOUR HOURS (variation)	
TWO MINUTES		TEN MINUTES	

(continued)

Table 4-2 *(continued)*

English	Sign	English	Sign
DAWN		MORNING	
NOON		TWILIGHT	
NIGHT		ALL NIGHT/ OVERNIGHT	

English	Sign	English	Sign
ARRIVE		SHOW UP	
LEAVE (formal)		LEAVE (informal)	
STAY		ON THE DOT	

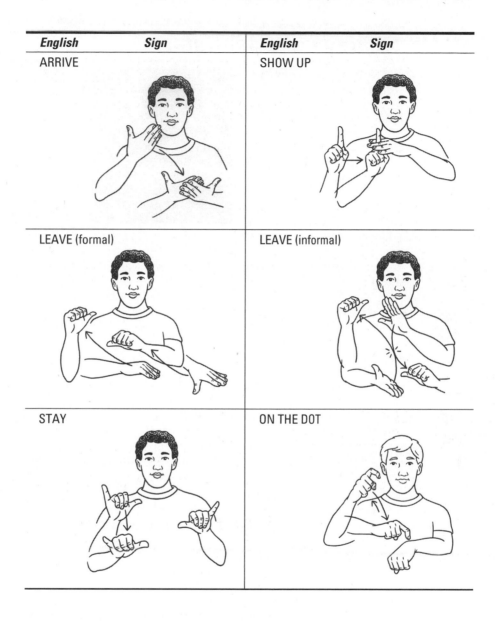

Signing calendar dates

We're all slaves to our day planners and schedules, and the Deaf are no different. They rely on their calendars like everyone else. To sign months of the year in ASL, you fingerspell them. You may see a person signing **calendar** while using the first letter of the month incorporated in the sign. This can get confusing because three months start with the letter "J," two start with the letter "M," and two start with the letter "A." This method isn't uncommon, but it's not formal signing either. Until you get your feet under you, fingerspell the months of the year.

Here are a couple of examples:

J-A-N 22, 2012

Here you fingerspell each letter of the month, sign 22, and then sign 2, 0, and 12.

When two numbers are the same, point your palm downward facing the ground and then sign the number from one side to the other.

N-O-V 17, 2012

Again, fingerspell the month, sign 17, then sign 2, 0, and 12.

The months that you can abbreviate are Jan., Feb., Aug., Sept., Oct., Nov., and Dec.

The months that you should completely spell out are March, April, May, June, and July.

Signin' the Sign

Ted is going to Della's house for a visit. Della is giving Ted directions in hopes that he'll arrive on time.

Della:	Can you come over to my house at 7 P.M.?
Sign:	7 P.M. — MY HOUSE — COME — CAN YOU — Q

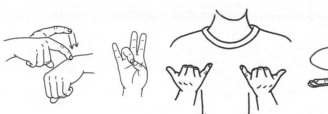

 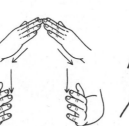 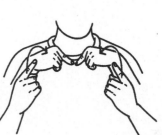

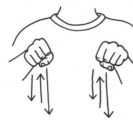 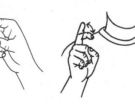

| **Ted:** | Yes, I can. |
| **Sign:** | YES — CAN ME |

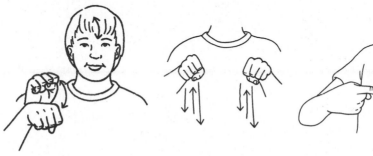

Della: Remember, it's 329 West Drive.
Sign: REMEMBER — HOUSE — WEST — D-R — 3-2-9

Ted: Can you give me directions?
Sign: DIRECTIONS — GIVE ME — CAN — Q

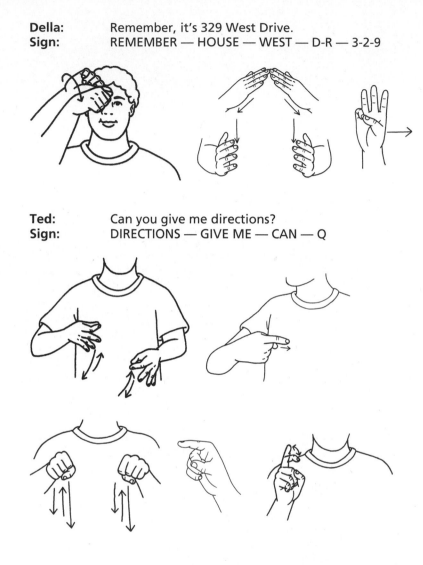

Della: Right on West Drive; the third house on the right.
Sign: HOUSE — THIRD RIGHT — STREET — WEST — D- R

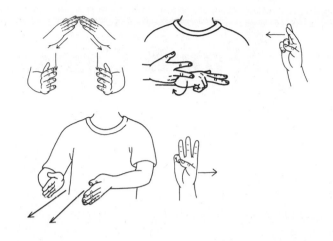

Fun & Games

Fill in the blank with the right sign.

1. In order to win you must come in _____ place.

2. A rooster wakes up at _____.

3. In the Christmas carol "The Twelve Days of Christmas," there are _____ golden rings.

4. We eat lunch at _____.

5. Command a dog to _____.

6. Revelers go out at _____.

c.

a.

b.

d.

e.

f.

Chapter 5

Signing at Home

· ·

In This Chapter

▶ Discovering signs for your house and furnishings

▶ Signing various holidays

▶ Using some signs for family life

· ·

*I*n this chapter you find things all around the house to identify using American Sign Language. As you go about your house, try to sign as many items as you can as you move from room to room. When you feel you've conquered several rooms, start stringing the signs into short sentences. Later in the chapter, you discover signs for holidays and signs to help you communicate with children.

Handling Signs about Your Home

You can give guests the grand tour of your home without uttering a sound. Notice how the signs in Table 5-1 let your fingers do the talking.

Table 5-1		Dwelling Signs	
English	*Sign*	*English*	*Sign*
DOOR		FLOOR	
GARAGE		HOME	
HOUSE		LIVE	
LOCK		OWN	
RENT		WINDOW	

English	*Sign*	*English*	*Sign*
YARD		UPSTAIRS	

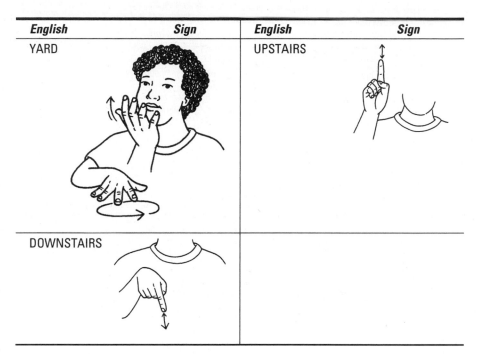

DOWNSTAIRS		

To sign **condo,** you fingerspell C-O-N-D-O, and to sign **apartment,** you use the abbreviation and fingerspell just A-P-T.

English: Do you own your home or rent?
Sign: YOUR HOME — OWN — RENT WHICH Q

English: The door is locked.
Sign: DOOR — LOCKED

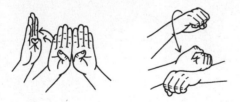

English: The garage has a window.
Sign: GARAGE — WINDOW HAVE

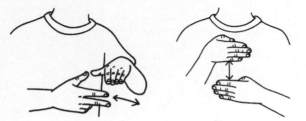

English: His house is big.
Sign: HIS HOUSE — BIG

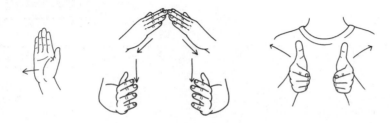

English: Can I go upstairs?
Sign: UPSTAIRS — GO ME CAN Q

Touring all the rooms

Touring a house room by room yields many surprises. One surprise is that each room has its own sign. (Well, maybe that's not so surprising.) Table 5-2 gives most of them.

The sign for **closet** has several motions, so here's some explanation: With your dominant hand, make a hook with your index finger. This finger acts as a hanger. Your passive index finger acts as a pole on which to put the hangers. Put several "hangers" onto the "pole."

Table 5-2		Rooms	
English	*Sign*	*English*	*Sign*
BASEMENT		BATHROOM	

(continued)

Table 5-2 (continued)

English	Sign	English	Sign
BEDROOM		CLOSET	
DINING ROOM		KITCHEN	
LIVING ROOM			

To get the attention of a Deaf person in a room you're entering, flick the light off and on — that will do the trick.

English: Can I use the bathroom?
Sign: BATHROOM — USE ME CAN Q

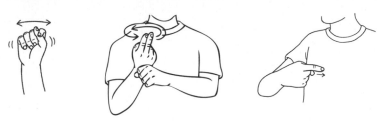

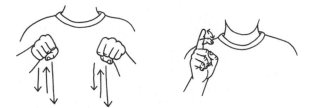

English: Is this your bedroom?
Sign: BEDROOM — YOURS Q

English: The kitchen is hot.
Sign: KITCHEN — HOT

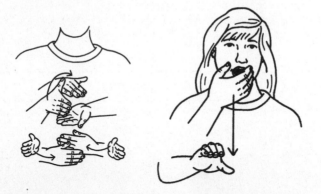

English: Don't play in the living room.
Sign: LIVING ROOM — PLAY THERE — DON'T

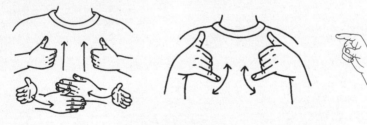

Furnishing your home

After you have rooms, you can start filling them with furniture. Table 5-3 shows you the signs for everything from window treatments to carpet.

After you have the sign for **chair** down, you'll have no problem with **love seat** or **couch.** To sign **love seat,** sign chair (double motion), and then, with the same handshape, put your dominant hand next to your passive hand to show a couch for two. To sign **couch,** make the sign for chair (single motion), and then move your dominant hand outward to show several seats.

Table 5-3	Home Furnishings		
English	*Sign*	*English*	*Sign*
BED		BLINDS	
CARPET		CHAIR	
COUCH		CURTAINS	

(continued)

Table 5-3 *(continued)*

English	Sign	English	Sign
LAMP		LOVE SEAT	
PICTURES		RECLINER	
TABLE		VASE	

If you're comfortable with these furnishings, try the following sentences.

English: Sit on the couch.
Sign: COUCH — SIT

English: Turn on the lamp.
Sign: LAMP O-N

English: My carpet is white.
Sign: MY CARPET — WHITE

English: The picture is crooked.
Sign: PICTURE — CROOKED

Signin' the Sign

Dave and Debbie have just purchased their first house. Here's what they have to say about it.

Dave: The house has a big yard.
Sign: HOUSE YARD — BIG

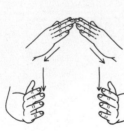  

Debbie: I want to see the kitchen.
Sign: KITCHEN — WANT SEE ME

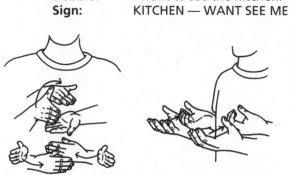 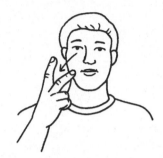

Dave: We need a couch, lamp, and pictures.
Sign: COUCH LAMP PICTURES — NEED US

Debbie: It's great to own, not rent, a house.
Sign: HOUSE — OWN GREAT — RENT NOT

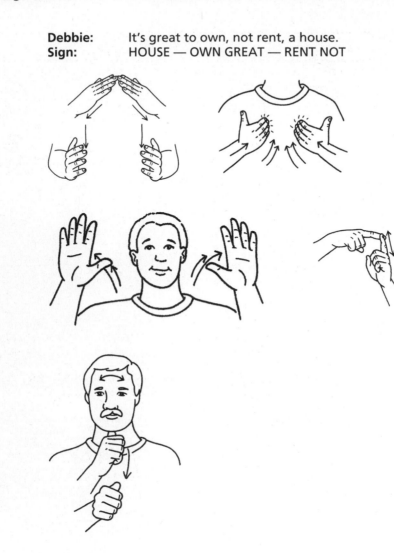

Hanging Out for the Holidays

The holidays and other yearly celebrations are an enjoyable time for family and friends to gather 'round and join in the festive good cheer. Partake in the festivities with your Deaf friends by practicing the signs in Table 5-4.

If you're gathered around a table with some Deaf folks and you want to propose a toast, knock on the table to create a vibration. You will then have the floor.

Table 5-4		Holiday Signs	
English	*Sign*	*English*	*Sign*
CHRISTMAS		EASTER	
VALENTINE'S DAY		THANKSGIVING	
MOTHER'S DAY		FATHER'S DAY	

(continued)

Table 5-4 *(continued)*

English	Sign	English	Sign

NEW YEAR'S

MEMORIAL DAY

HALLOWEEN

INDEPENDENCE DAY

HOLIDAY

CELEBRATION

Teaching the Tots

Raising a brood is quite a responsibility. Nothing is more impressive than teaching your children a second language like ASL. You can use the signs in Table 5-5 every day around the house. As you're hanging out with your Deaf chums, see which signs they use with their children and take note. These signs have to do with everyday life of the family, whether Deaf or hearing.

Table 5-5		Signs for Children and Family	
English	*Sign*	*English*	*Sign*
SLEEP		DREAM	
REST		PRAY	

(continued)

Table 5-5 *(continued)*

English	Sign	English	Sign
LAUGH		VACATION	
SCHOOL		COLLEGE	
BEDTIME		CHORES	

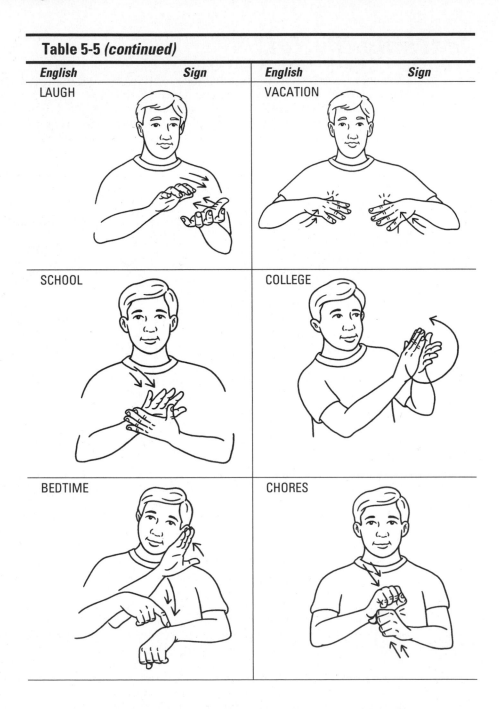

English	Sign	English	Sign
ACTIVITY		BABY	
CHILD			

Keeping Track of Your Subjects in Space

At home or out and about, you often talk about people who aren't right there with you. For instance, at work, you may discuss with one of your co-workers how much you like your boss. When using Sign, you don't have to be able to see someone (or something) to be able to talk about him, her, or it. (That's a good thing, too. How else could you plan a surprise party for your spouse?)

All you have to do to discuss someone who isn't physically present is assign that person a point in the space near your passive hand. You use the same sign for **he, she,** and **it** — your index finger extended in a pointing gesture (see Chapter 1). If the he, she, or it is nearby, you point your index finger at the person or thing, but if the person or thing isn't in your general vicinity, you select a specific place in the space in front of you to sort of stand in for the person or thing. In ASL, this sign isn't gender-specific. You point to the same space every time you refer to the absent one. So if you want to sign about Buddy, fingerspell his name and point to your passive hand area.

Fun & Games

Grab a friend, and then both of you make a list of 20 vocabulary signs from this chapter. Don't show each other your individual lists. Fingerspell the first item on your list and have your friend point to what you're spelling from the items around the house, or on the calendar if it's a holiday. With the first one wrong, the other takes a turn. The first person who catches all the fingerspelling and points to all the items correctly is the winner!

Part II
American Sign Language in Action

The 5th Wave   By Rich Tennant

"He's still wrestling with the ethical conundrum of a professional mime learning ASL."

In this part . . .

These chapters guide you through basic conversation with people who sign. Here you find information on asking for directions, dining out, shopping, hobbies and recreation, and more. You also find out how to get into those social circles of Deaf people, how to engage in common topics, and how to get a conversation started with small talk.

Chapter 6

Asking Questions and Making Small Talk

In This Chapter

▶ Introducing yourself in a conversation

▶ Using key question words to convey and elicit information

▶ Knowing the signs for family relationships, locations, and occupations

▶ Adding pronouns and possessives to your signing repertoire

Hearing people get to know one another by asking questions and making small talk. Deaf people are no different. You begin with the basics and build from there. This chapter gets you started conversing with your family and friends in American Sign Language by giving you the signs for various information-seeking questions. Then we cover signs for family relationships and signs to help you talk about where you live and work. Finally, we show you the signs for pronouns, including possessives.

Signing Key Questions: Six Ws, One H

When you want to sign a question, you simply put the question word at the end of the sentence — words such as **who, what, when, where, which, why,** and **how.** In this section, we explain these key signs and then show you how

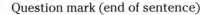

to ask questions. As a rule, after you sign your question, you repeatedly sign the manual question mark, which is shown here:

Question mark (end of sentence)

 Throughout this book, the letter **Q** follows all ASL examples and dialogues that are questions. Use the end-of-sentence manual question mark when you see the letter Q in this book.

You also have the option of placing the question mark at the beginning of the sentence:

Question mark (beginning of sentence)

 As you sign the question word, lean forward a little, look inquisitive, scrunch your eyebrows together, and tilt your head to one side.

Your dominant hand — the one that you write with — does the action.

Always maintain eye contact. That way, you and the other person can make sure that you understand each other.

You sign the following inquiry words at the beginning or at the end of a sentence:

Who? With your dominant hand, place your thumb on your chin and let your index finger wiggle from the joint. The other three fingers curl under.

What? Put your hands outward in front of you, with elbows bent and palms up. Shake your hands back and forth towards each other.

Where? Hold up the index finger of your dominant hand as if you're indicating "number one" and shake it side to side.

When? Put both of your index fingers together at a 90-degree angle at the tips. Your dominant index finger then makes a full circle around the passive index finger and returns to the starting position.

Which? Make both hands into fists with your thumbs pointing up; alternate each fist in an up-and-down movement.

Why? With your dominant hand, palm facing up, bend and wiggle the middle finger. Make this sign close to your temple.

How? With your fingers pointing downward and the backs of your fingers and knuckles touching, roll your hands inward to your chest and up so that the pinky sides of your hands are touching.

Check out the following examples of short questions:

English: Who is going?
Sign: GOING WHO Q

English: What do you mean?
Sign: MEAN WHAT Q (the word "you" is implied because you're talking to that person already)

Signin' the Sign

 Virginia and Mark are roommates. It's Saturday morning, and they're drinking coffee and signing about what they have planned for the day.

Mark: Are you working today?
Sign: TODAY — WORKING YOU Q

Virginia: Yes, for two hours.
Sign: YES — TWO HOURS — SHORT (this signed answer can be translated to mean, "I am only working briefly")

 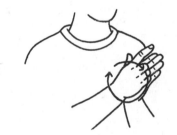

Mark:	I'm going to the movies.
Sign:	MOVIES — GO ME

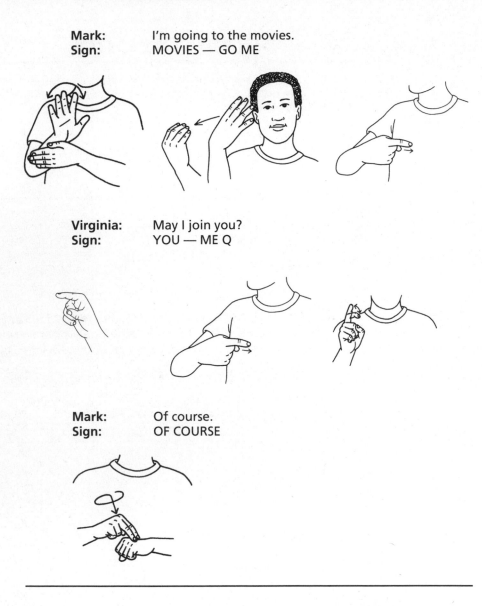

Virginia:	May I join you?
Sign:	YOU — ME Q

Mark:	Of course.
Sign:	OF COURSE

Discussing Family, Friends, and More

This section helps you confidently share information about yourself and your family. Understanding another person's signs is one thing, but responding to them is another. You already know all the ins and outs of who your relatives are and where you live and work, so here's where you find the most commonly used signs to convey that information.

Family and friends

Describing your family is one way to tell someone about yourself. Using the common signs in Table 6-1 can make your eccentric family seem almost normal.

Table 6-1		Family Members	
English	*Sign*	*English*	*Sign*
FATHER		MOTHER	
SON		DAUGHTER	

(continued)

Table 6-1 *(continued)*

English	Sign	English	Sign
BROTHER		SISTER	
AUNT		UNCLE	
MALE COUSIN		FEMALE COUSIN	
FAMILY			

To sign a male cousin or male nephew by your temple, form a manual **C** by your temple and shake it or an **N** and twist it. The same can be done by the jaw to indicate a female cousin or niece. Your hand should never touch your head.

Signs for some other members of your family, such as grandchildren and in-laws, are a bit trickier. To talk about your **grandchildren,** fingerspell G-R-A-N-D and then sign children.

For **in-laws,** sign the person and then sign **law.**

To sign **stepbrother, stepsister, stepfather,** or **stepmother,** sign the letter "L," thumb pointing upward and index finger pointing forward, and shake the hand subtly.

Sign a **half sibling** by expressing the manual ½ and then signing **brother** or **sister.**

Take a look at these examples:

English: Is this your sister?
Sign: (point) HER— SISTER — YOURS Q

English: No, my sister-in-law.
Sign: NO — SISTER LAW — MINE

English: He is my half brother.
Sign: MY 1-2 (as in ½) BROTHER — HIM (point)

To show "½" the palm must be facing the signer, and the 1 then moves in a downward motion (toward the ground) as you pop out your middle finger to join your already raised index finger making the 1 a 2 and, therefore, showing the over-under aspect of ½.

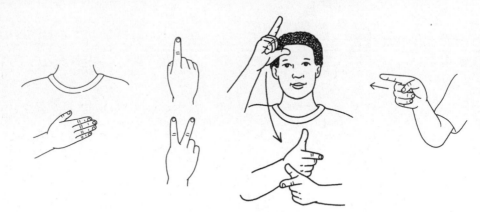

To sign a school friend or work colleague, simply sign the word and then sign **friend.** You may signify a close friend by signing **friend** with more intensity. You can also indicate that close friends are **like two peas in a pod** by signing crossed fingers and pursing your lips; this sign looks the same as when you cross your fingers to mean "good luck" or "I hope so."

Relating where you live and work

Giving others information about your workplace and home is easy — the information is already in your memory. Signing this info to others is a snap, but be careful because many other eyes can see what you sign.

Giving addresses and phone numbers

Exchanging addresses and phone numbers is a great way to make friends with other signers. Asking someone to repeat the information is okay; everyone does it in both English and Sign. You fingerspell most of this information, although the directional words "north," "south," "east," and "west" do have signs (see Chapter 7).

Here are some common abbreviations:

- **Avenue:** A-V-E
- **Circle:** C-I-R
- **Drive:** D-R
- **Street:** S-T
- **Apartment:** A-P-T
- **Way:** W-Y

You sign street addresses by fingerspelling the street name and then signing the house number, keeping your palm facing the addressee. Sign the city's name next, but only when you're sure that the addressee understands the sign.

Prominent cities may have name signs (refer to Chapter 3 for some examples). For less prominent cities, fingerspell the name. Deaf people will show you a local sign if it exists. Often, you sign cities that have two-word names by using the first letter of each word. As a general rule, sign cities the way the Deaf do. As they say, when in Rome. . . .

You sign zip codes with your palm facing outward. Sign all five numbers in succession.

When you sign phone numbers, all numbers face the addressee — outward. If you're not sure that the information you're giving is clear, sign an area code by making parentheses with both index fingers and then sign the numbers. Alternatively, just sign L-D (for long distance) before you give the number.

Signing the suffix part of phone numbers doesn't follow any set rule. Some people fingerspell all four numbers in succession, and others break up the phone number suffix into two sets of two numbers. For instance, if the last four numbers of a phone number are 1212, you can sign them as 1, 2, 1, 2 or 12, 12. You don't need to worry about putting a hyphen between the numbers like you would if you were writing the number down.

The signs in Table 6-2 may help you, too.

Table 6-2	Signs about Where You Live		
English	*Sign*	*English*	*Sign*
DOWNTOWN		COUNTRY	
CITY		TOWN	
STREET		PHONE	

English	Sign	English	Sign
LONG DISTANCE/ L-D		ADDRESS	
CELLPHONE		CALL (SUMMONS)	

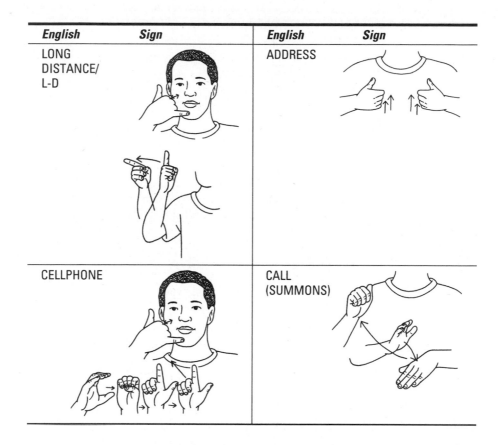

Signin' the Sign

Donna is moving to Chicago. Mike is hoping that the two of them can stay in touch; Donna feels the same way. Mike wants to get her new address so that he can write to her.

Mike: Where are you moving?
Sign: MOVING YOU — WHERE Q

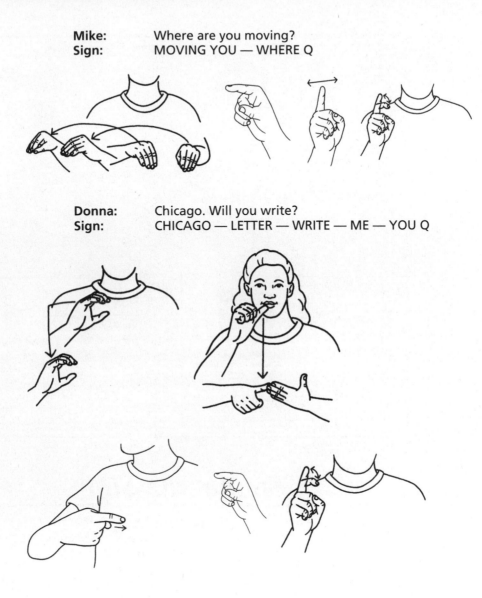

Donna: Chicago. Will you write?
Sign: CHICAGO — LETTER — WRITE — ME — YOU Q

Mike: Yes, what's your address?
Sign: YES — ADDRESS YOURS — WHAT Q

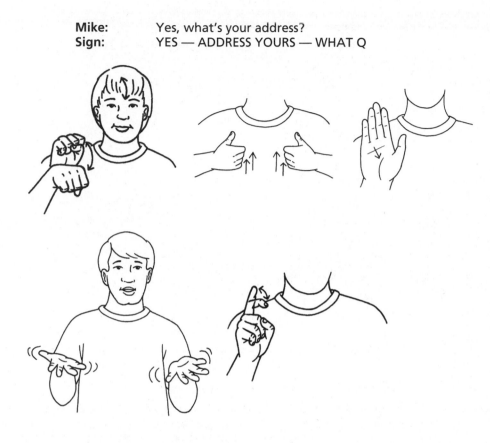

Donna: 171 Anywhere Lane, 98765.
Sign: 1-7-1 A-N-Y-W-H-E-R-E L-A-N-E 9-8-7-6-5

Mike:	Thanks. Phone me when you arrive.
Sign:	THANKS — ARRIVE YOU — PHONE ME

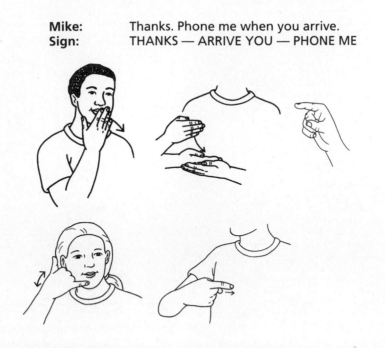

Jabbering about your job

When you want to tell someone where you work, you usually do it by finger-spelling. If the name of your company is an acronym, you fingerspell that as well. Few places have name signs that are understood by everyone. However, when sharing info about your profession, be it your job title or what your job entails, you can usually use signs. Table 6-3 lists just a few of the many job signs used today. (Check out Chapter 11 for more work-related signs.)

Table 6-3		Job Signs	
English	*Sign*	*English*	*Sign*
BOSS		COOK	

English	Sign	English	Sign
INTERPRETER		MANAGER	
DOCTOR		ACCOUNTANT	
POLICE		TEACHER	
PRESIDENT		TREASURER	

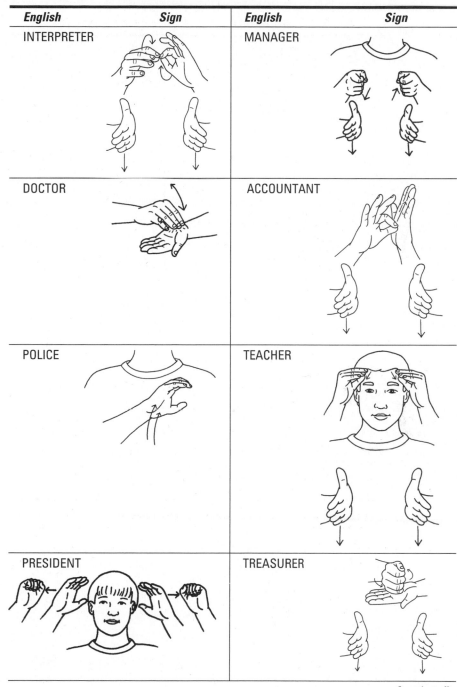

(continued)

Table 6-3 *(continued)*

English	Sign	English	Sign
SECRETARY		VICE PRESIDENT	
MECHANIC		SALESPERSON	
ASSISTANT		LAWYER	

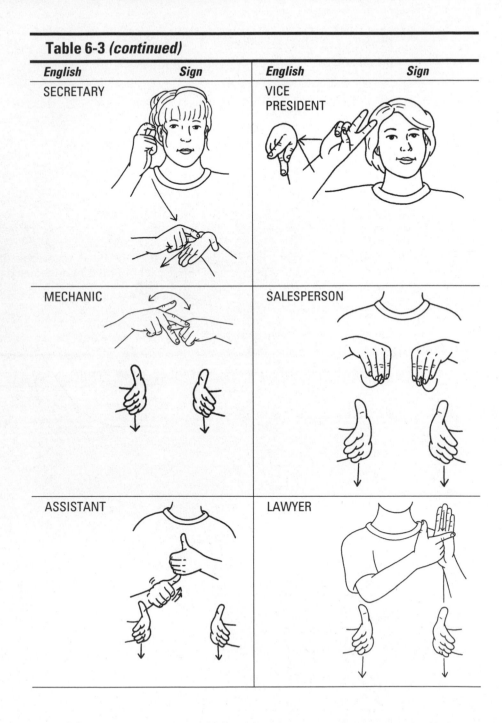

English	Sign	English	Sign
SERVER	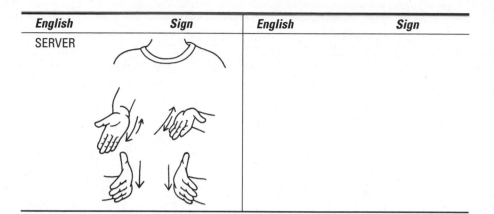		

 All vice presidents are signed V-P by the side of the head, regardless of whether you're talking about the vice president of the United States or the vice president of the local PTA chapter.

Signin' the Sign

 Juanita and Kim are seated next to each other at a dinner party hosted by Tom, a mutual friend. They strike up a casual conversation.

Kim: Hi, I'm Kim, Tom's accountant.
Sign: HI — K-I-M ME — ACCOUNTANT FOR T-O-M

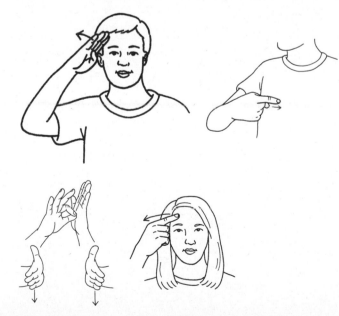

Juanita: I'm Juanita. Nice to meet you.
Sign: J-U-A-N-I-T-A ME — NICE MEET YOU

Kim: Do you work at Bailey & Sons?
Sign: B-A-I-L-E-Y S-O-N-S — YOU WORK Q

Juanita: Yes, I'm vice president of marketing.
Sign: YES — MARKETING — V-P — ME

Kim: What an interesting job.
Sign: JOB — INTERESTING — TRUE

Juanita: I sure meet a lot of different people.
Sign: DIFFERENT — PEOPLE — MEET ME

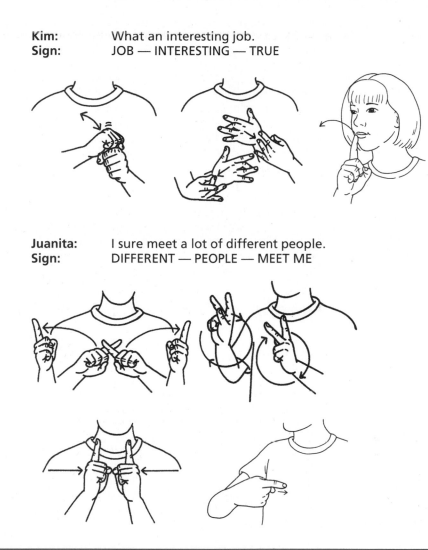

Using Possessives and Pronouns When Chatting

In the course of getting to know someone, especially when you're both asking questions about each other or mutual acquaintances, you'll find that using pronouns is probably easiest. You use pronouns in Sign the same way that you do in English; you need to refer to a noun before you use a pronoun. Of course, if you're using a pronoun to indicate someone or something nearby, you can point to that person or thing as you sign.

You may also use possessives during your conversation. Show possession by indicating whom you're talking about or what's being possessed and then showing an open palm facing the person. You can also use proper nouns (a person's name) to discuss possessives. Fingerspell the name of the person, point to the item you're talking about, and sign a question mark. For example, suppose that you're signing with someone and you want to know if the coat on the hook belongs to Tony. Fingerspell T-O-N-Y, point to the coat, and sign a question mark.

If you're signing *with* Tony, point to the object or fingerspell it if it's not in view, look at Tony, sign toward him with an open palm, and then make a question mark. You've now asked him, "Is that yours?" Remember to keep your eyebrows up and wear an inquisitive look.

Personal pronouns and possessives

Table 6-4 lists pronouns that refer to people and also gives you the signs for the possessive pronouns.

Table 6-4	Personal and Possessive Pronouns		
Pronoun	**Sign**	**Possessive**	**Sign**
I, ME		MY, MINE	
HE		HIS	
SHE		HERS	

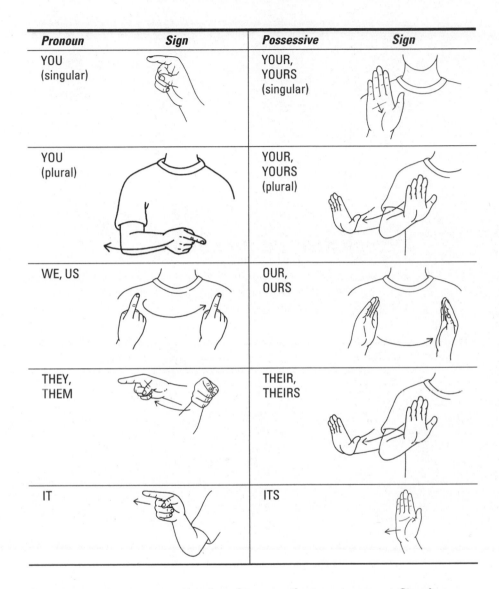

Pronoun	Sign	Possessive	Sign
YOU (singular)		YOUR, YOURS (singular)	
YOU (plural)		YOUR, YOURS (plural)	
WE, US		OUR, OURS	
THEY, THEM		THEIR, THEIRS	
IT		ITS	

As you can see, you use some signs for more than one pronoun. Simple sentences can follow English word order. Put the possessive pronoun sign before or after the person or thing you're signing; the order doesn't matter. For example:

English: My dog.
Sign: DOG MINE or MY DOG

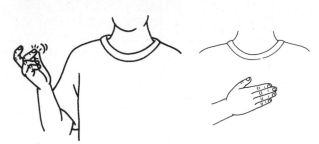

Demonstrative pronouns

As a group, four little pronouns — **this, that, these,** and **those** — get a big name, *demonstrative pronouns*. But you don't really need to know the names, just the signs, which are in Table 6-5.

Table 6-5	Demonstrative Pronouns		
Pronoun	*Sign*	*Plural*	*Sign*
THIS		THESE	
THAT		THOSE	

Sign the pronoun **that** by pointing to your subject with your dominant hand in the **Y** shape and bent at the wrist. Sign **this, these,** and **those** by pointing to the subject or subjects.

Sign singular possessives by holding your hand, palm outward, toward the person to whom you're referring. Sign plural possessives the same way, but also move your hand from side to side in front of each person in a sort of sweeping motion.

The following sentences give you some practice with pronouns and possessives:

English: He is rich.
Sign: RICH HIM

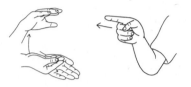

English: He has money.
Sign: MONEY HIS

English: She is wise.
Sign: WISE HER

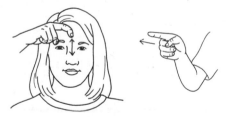

English: She has wisdom.
Sign: WISDOM HERS

English: They have gold.
Sign: GOLD HAVE THEM

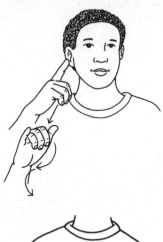

English: The gold is theirs.
Sign: GOLD THEIRS

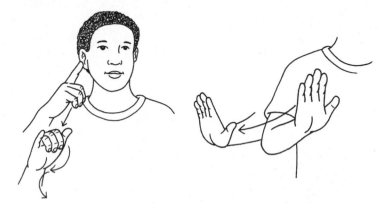

Fun & Games

Match the signs with the words. Feel free to go back through this chapter to find them. Your goal isn't necessarily to get the signs all correct but to get used to using them.

1. Uncle _____

2. Teacher _____

3. His _____

4. Call _____

5. Which _____

6. Sister _____

7. Mother _____

8. Work _____

9. City _____

10. My/mine _____

11. Why _____

12. Server _____

c.

f.

g.

d.

a.

e.

h.

b.

i.
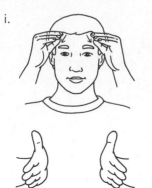

k.

l.

j.

Table 7-2 (continued)

English	Sign	English	Sign
FORWARD		IN FRONT OF	
STRAIGHT		TURN	

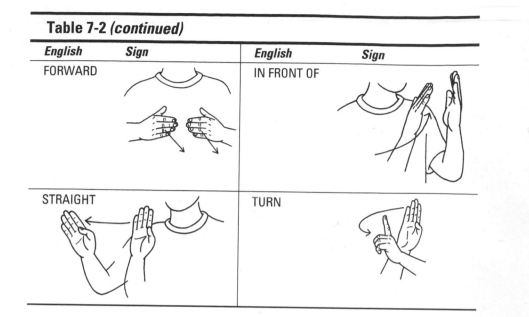

The following sentences put these signs in action.

English: Go straight; don't turn.
Sign: STRAIGHT — TURN — DON'T

English: The cross street is Maple Drive.
Sign: CROSS STREET WHAT — M-A-P-L-E D-R

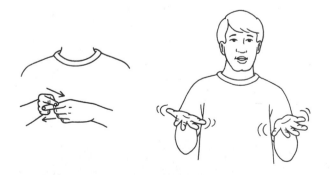

Chapter 7

Asking for Directions

• •

In This Chapter

▶ Giving and getting directions in Sign

▶ Making use of natural and urban landmarks in your directions

▶ Using signs for transportation

▶ Adding conjunctions to your directions

• •

Getting where you need to go can happen as quickly as a wave of your hand. You can go a long way by using the signs for directions and transportation that are included in this chapter.

Finding Your Way

REMEMBER

When giving or getting directions in American Sign Language, you need to keep two things in mind. Get these strategies down and you can tell people exactly where to go and how to get there:

✔ Try to start with a point of reference that's familiar to both of you, such as a store, restaurant, or bridge, and then give the directions.

✔ Go from big to small; from general to specific.

For example, in the United States, you go from state to city to neighborhood to street to house number.

Table 7-1 groups signs for compass points and other directional signals. Notice that the handshapes you use for the **compass points** and for **left** and **right** are the first letters of the words.

Table 7-1	Compass Points		
English	*Sign*	*English*	*Sign*
NORTH		SOUTH	
EAST		WEST	
LEFT		RIGHT	

The following examples show you how to sign directions in perfect order.

English: My house is west of the store.
Sign: STORE — MY HOUSE — WEST

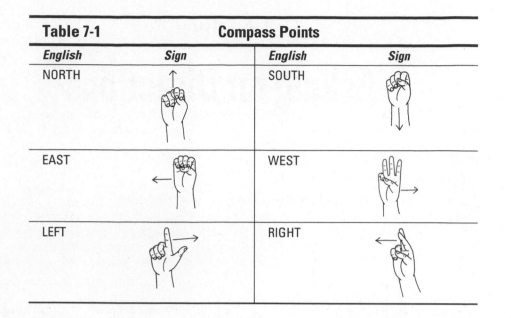

English: Turn right twice.
Sign: RIGHT — RIGHT

Notice that you don't sign the word *twice;* you simply sign **right** twice. Make sure you shift your body ever so slightly as you start to sign **right** the second time.

To give directions, you often establish relationships. Don't worry; you don't have to commit for very long. Table 7-2 lists the signs for the situational relationships you use to give directions as well as some landmarks and distances that you might use.

To sign **straight,** use the B manual handshape and then move it straight out in front of you, bending your wrist.

The sign for **straight** is also one sign for **sober** — the sentence's context tells you which word is being signed. Also, you use this same B handshape to sign the direction to turn left or right onto a street. Some people use the sign for **left** or **right** before this B sign. In many cases, it adds clarification.

Table 7-2	Directional Relationship Signs		
English	*Sign*	*English*	*Sign*
AFTER		BACK	
BEFORE		BEHIND	
BESIDE		CROSS STREET/ INTERSECTION	

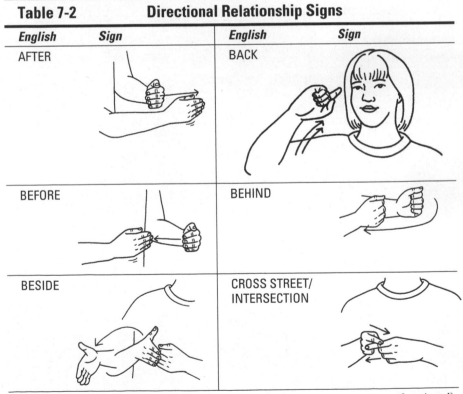

(continued)

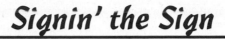

Signin' the Sign

Buddy is going to the mall. Although he knows the town of Pueblo, he isn't sure how to get to the mall from where he's located. He sees Linda; she knows the town well. Notice how she helps him while using a familiar reference point.

Buddy: How do I get to the mall?
Sign: M-A-L-L ARRIVE — HOW Q

  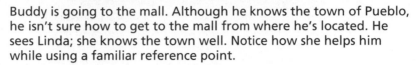

Linda: Do you know where the museum is?
Sign: MUSEUM WHERE — KNOW YOU Q

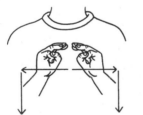 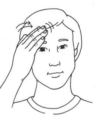

Buddy:	From this cross street I go north.
Sign:	HERE CROSS STREET — NORTH GO ME

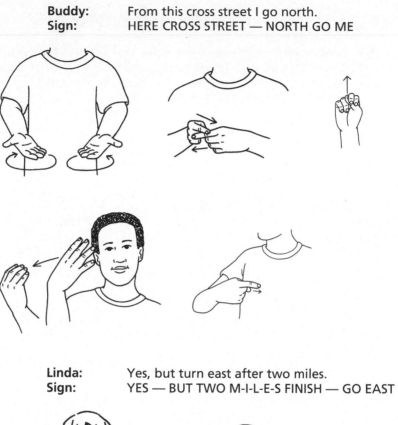

Linda:	Yes, but turn east after two miles.
Sign:	YES — BUT TWO M-I-L-E-S FINISH — GO EAST

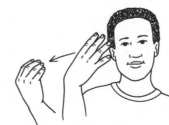

Looking to Natural Landmarks

Most people find landmarks to be helpful when giving or receiving directions. After all, telling someone to turn right at the bottom of the hill is much easier than telling someone to turn right after traveling 1.3 miles. The signs for natural landmarks in Table 7-3 are sure to help you.

Table 7-3		Natural Landmarks	
English	*Sign*	*English*	*Sign*
FIELD		HILL	
LAKE		MOUNTAIN	

(continued)

Table 7-3 *(continued)*

English	Sign	English	Sign
RIVER		TREE	
WATERFALL		ROCK/ STONE	

You may see some people fingerspell *field;* whether you fingerspell it or sign it, the goal is to be as clear as possible.

Take a look at the following sentences to see how you can use these landmark signs when giving directions.

English: When you get to the lake, turn right.
Sign: LAKE ARRIVE — RIGHT TURN

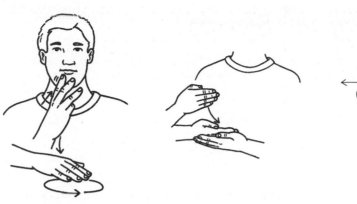

In ASL, you sign **get to** as **arrive.**

English: At the base of the mountain is a small store.
Sign: MOUNTAIN BASE — SMALL STORE — THERE

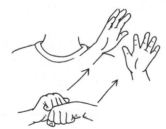

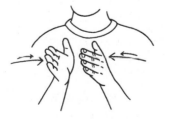

Searching the Streets

Going through town can be overwhelming unless you know how to get where you're going. Table 7-4 demonstrates the landmarks you can use to direct someone in the city.

You sign **building** with both hands in the H handshape, but don't tuck in your thumbs — leave them out. Place one hand on top of the other four times; then, with B handshapes, palms facing each other, go straight up — go high for a skyscraper.

You sign a **stop sign** by making the sign for **stop** and then making a square-cut line with your index finger. It would be great to make the octagon shape, but who can?

Table 7-4		Urban Landmarks		
English	**Sign**		**English**	**Sign**
BRIDGE			BUILDING	
GAS STATION			HIGHWAY	

English	Sign	English	Sign
ROAD/ STREET		STOPLIGHT	
STOP SIGN			

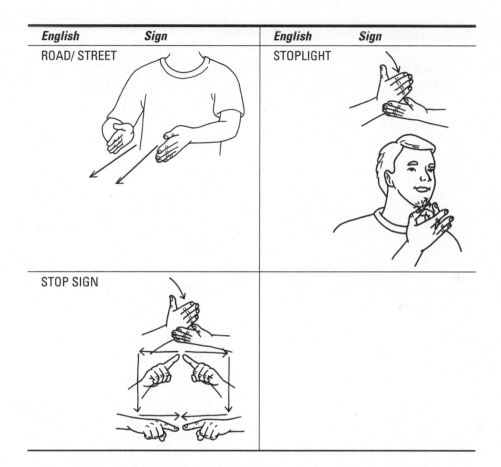

You've no doubt given directions similar to the ones in the following examples. Now, see how to do it in Sign.

English: Pass the park and go three miles south.
Sign: P-A-R-K PASS — SOUTH THREE M-I-L-E-S GO

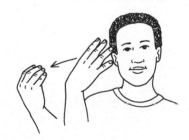

English: At the stop sign, go right.
Sign: STOP SIGN ARRIVE — RIGHT

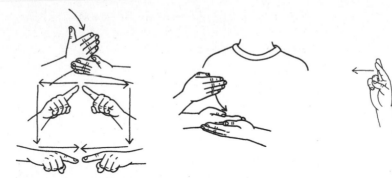

English: Go across the bridge.
Sign: BRIDGE — GO OVER

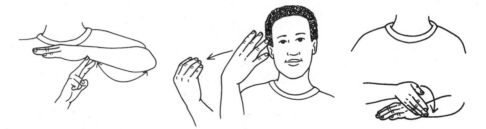

English: The gas station is near the highway.
Sign: HIGHWAY — GAS STATION — NEAR

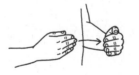

Transporting Yourself

Whether you just need to get around town or you decide to see the world, your travel requires wheels. This section gives you just that. Consider the signs in Table 7-5 for your free-wheeling adventures.

Table 7-5		Wheels	
English	*Sign*	*English*	*Sign*
BICYCLE		CAR	
MOTORCYCLE		PLANE	
SUBWAY		TRAIN	

Bus is fingerspelled B-S — leave out the "u." To sign **driving a bus,** mimic a truck-size steering wheel at the lower chest level, wrap your hands around the imaginary wheel, and steer back and forth. This motion also works for trucks, RVs (after you fingerspell R-V), or any large vehicle. Just fingerspell the big rig first.

Get the wheels in motion, so to speak, by using these automotive signs.

English: The car was in an accident.
Sign: CAR ACCIDENT

You sign **accident** by making a 5 handshape, palms facing you, fingertips facing each other. Crash them together, ending in an S handshape.

English: If I miss the train, I'll fly.
Sign: TRAIN MISS — FLY ME — WILL

 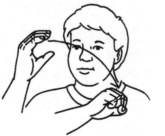 

English: You need a motorcycle helmet.
Sign: MOTORCYCLE HELMET — NEED YOU

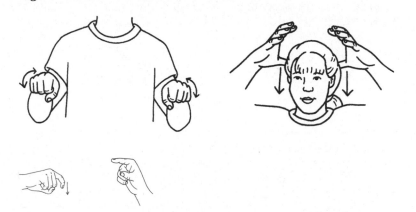

Directing Your Sentences with Conjunctions

As you probably remember from grammar classes of long ago, *conjunctions* join thoughts or phrases. One of the most common conjunctions is *but,* so we explain that one first.

To sign **but,** put your dominant hand on the dominant side of your head and flick your index finger twice, ending with your index finger up.

Check out the following example.

English: Go to the party but be home at midnight.
Sign: PARTY GO — BUT HOME MIDNIGHT — MUST YOU

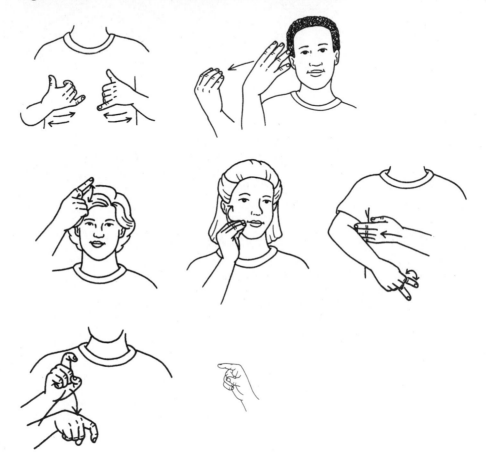

The either/or and neither/nor conjunctions are called *correlative conjunctions,* and you use your hands and head to convey these signs.

When signing **either . . . or** and **neither . . . nor,** keep in mind that you use these conjunctions to answer these types of questions, not to ask them. So although you don't use the facial expressions you use to ask questions, you keep your head still or nod "yes" for affirmation when you sign **either,** and you shake your head from side to side while signing **neither.**

English: Do you want apples or oranges?
Sign: APPLES ORANGES — WANT YOU — WHICH

English response: Either apples or oranges would be fine.
Sign response: EITHER FINE

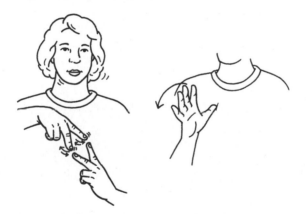

English: Do you want chicken or steak?
Sign: CHICKEN STEAK — WANT YOU — WHICH

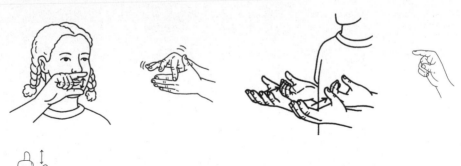

English response: I want neither chicken nor steak.
Sign response: NEITHER

Fun & Games

Turn these signed sentences into English.

1. **Sign:**

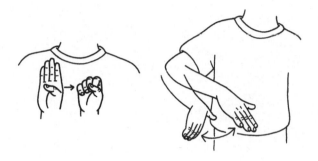

English:

2. **Sign:**

English:

3. **Sign:**

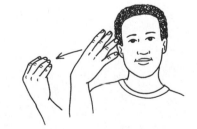

English:

(continued)

4. **Sign:**

English:

5. **Sign:**

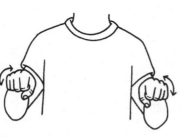 

English:

6. **Sign:**

English:

7. **Sign:**

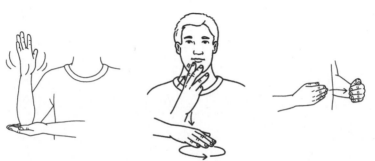

English:

8. **Sign:**

English:

9. **Sign:**

English:

Chapter 8

Dining and Going to the Market

· ·

In This Chapter

▶ Mastering the signs for meals

▶ Using signs in restaurants

▶ Showcasing signs while shopping

· ·

*W*hen dining out with Deaf people, who love to wine and dine like anyone else, you may want to ask them what's good on the menu, but perhaps you don't know how. This chapter covers signing three square meals, dining out and ordering drinks, and finding sales and specials in the grocery store.

Eating Three Square Meals a Day

When you're lucky enough to get an invitation to join other signers for brunch, take along these signs to get you through the event. In this part I go over signs for breakfast, lunch, and dinner, plus everything you'll see on the table — except your elbows. Before you dive into a dish of delights for any meal, check out Table 8-1 for a list of some necessary tools.

Table 8-1		Utensils and Dishes	
English	*Sign*	*English*	*Sign*
BOWL		CUP	

(continued)

Table 8-1 *(continued)*

English	Sign	English	Sign
FORK		GLASS (drinking)	
KNIFE		NAPKIN	
PLATE		SPOON	

These next sentences help you see American Sign Language in action. Here's how to sign the words for what you'll need at the table. A good host knows not only when to use the salad fork but also how to sign it. To sign **place setting**, sign **fork, knife,** and **spoon.** A great way to remember how to make the signs for tableware is pretty simple: what you do with the objects relates to the signs. For example, you sign **napkin** with a wiping motion on the mouth; you sign **spoon** using a scooping motion; you sign **fork** with a stabbing motion; and you sign **knife** using a cutting motion.

English: I need another place setting, please.
Sign: PLEASE — FORK — KNIFE — SPOON — NEED ME

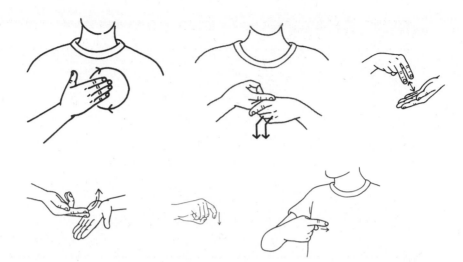

English: The plate and glass are broken.
Sign: PLATE — GLASS — BROKEN

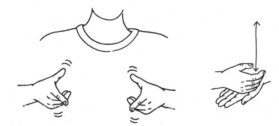

English: I need three bowls.
Sign: THREE BOWLS — NEED ME

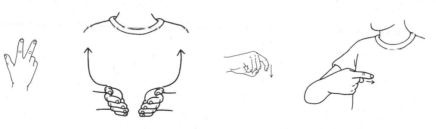

English: The napkin is dirty.
Sign: NAPKIN — DIRTY

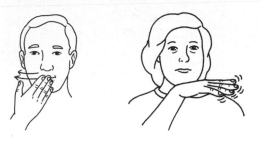

Table 8-2 shows you how to sign meal-related words.

Table 8-2	Mealtime
English	*Sign*
BREAKFAST	
LUNCH	

English	Sign
DINNER	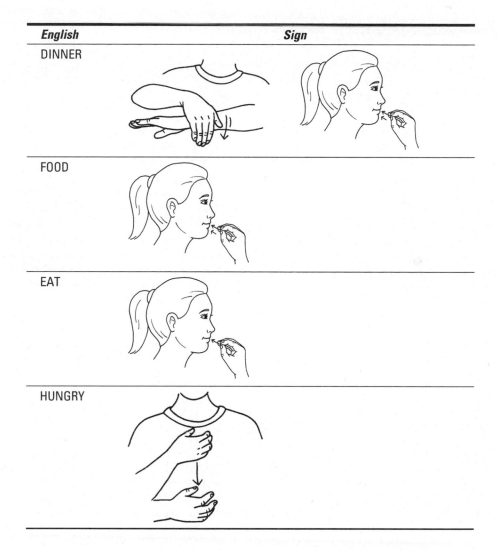
FOOD	
EAT	
HUNGRY	

If you want to show **gorging,** sign **food** with both hands alternately putting food in your mouth while your cheeks are puffed out or your mouth is wide open. The faster you sign, the more you gorge. To sign **starving,** just sign **hungry** faster, open your mouth a little, and look hungry. Don't forget your facial expression. It'll really show just how full or hungry you are!

Having breakfast

Because breakfast is the most important meal of the day, the signs for breakfast foods are the most important ones of the day. The signs in Table 8-3 certainly help at the breakfast table.

Table 8-3		Breakfast Foods	
English	*Sign*	*English*	*Sign*
BACON		CEREAL	
EGGS		SAUSAGE	
TOAST			

Even if you're still half asleep, you won't have any problems figuring out most of these signs. The sign for **bacon** mimics the waviness of a fried strip; **toast** lets you know that the bread is browned on both sides; **cereal** is the crunchy stuff you chew. Use the common abbreviations for **orange juice** and sign the letters **O** and **J** to convey this popular breakfast beverage. Get going on practicing your early-morning skills with the following examples:

English: I want eggs, not cereal.
Sign: EGGS WANT — CEREAL NOT — ME

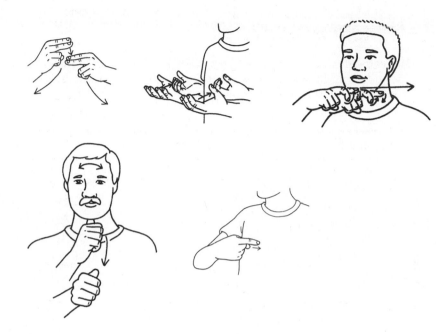

English: The orange juice is cold.
Sign: COLD O-J

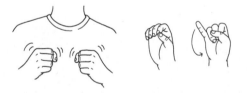

English: I'll have sausage and eggs.
Sign: SAUSAGE — EGGS — HAVE ME

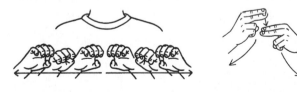

Munching on lunch

Doing lunch with friends is at your fingertips. The set of signs in Table 8-4 can hold you through the afternoon. Just don't get too excited about signing these items or you may end up eating them all in one sitting!

Table 8-4		Lunch Items	
English	*Sign*	*English*	*Sign*
BURGER		CHEESE	
SODA		FRENCH FRIES	
PIZZA		SALAD	
SANDWICH			

To order a hamburger, you imitate the motions of making a patty, but for other lunch signs, you use the manual alphabet. For example, you sign **French fries** by repeating the letter **F** from one side to the other side as if you are dipping them, and you sign **pizza** by bending your index and middle fingers and then making a manual **Z.** (Refer to Chapter 1 to see how to sign the letters of the manual alphabet.) Follow these examples:

English: I'm hungry, and it's time for lunch.
Sign: NOW TIME — NOON FOOD — HUNGRY ME

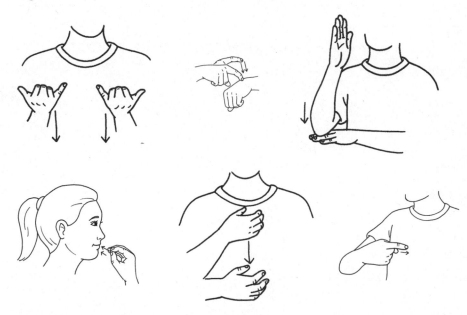

English: I want a cheeseburger and fries.
Sign: CHEESEBURGER — FRIES — WANT — ME

English: The soda is cold.
Sign: SODA — COLD

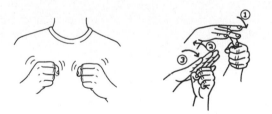

English: I want a sandwich and salad for lunch.
Sign: NOON FOOD — SANDWICH — SALAD — WANT ME

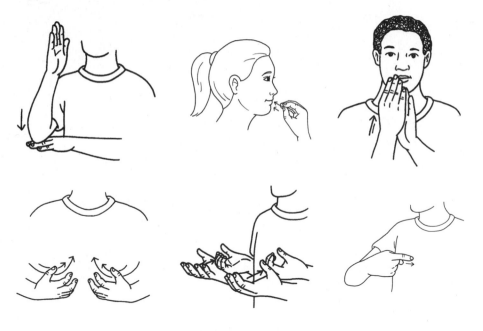

Signin' the Sign

 Two co-workers are going to lunch and are discussing what they're in the mood to eat. Here's what they each decide.

Dee: I'm hungry; I want a hamburger, French fries, and a soda.
Sign: HUNGRY ME — HAMBURGER FRENCH FRIES SODA — WANT ME

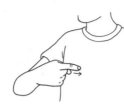

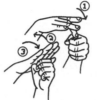
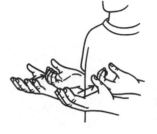

Ted: I want a fish sandwich and water.
Sign: FISH SANDWICH — WATER — WANT ME

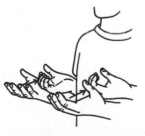

Dee:	They have chicken.
Sign:	CHICKEN — HAVE THEM (point)

Enjoying dinner

Supper is ready, and so are you. Putting the evening meal into conversation is a piece of cake. Follow the signs in Table 8-5 and you'll say a mouthful. (The signs for drinks are coming up in the "Don't forget the drinks!" section.)

Table 8-5		Dinner Terms	
English	*Sign*	*English*	*Sign*
BREAD		CHICKEN	
FISH		FULL	
HAM		POTATO	

English	Sign	English	Sign
SOUP		SPAGHETTI	
STEAK			

Fortunately, you sign **chicken, fish,** and **pig** like the food they provide. If you want to order steak or beef, you can use the same sign for either one.

Signing how you want it cooked is a breeze; just use the manual alphabet and give your hand a little shake: M for medium, but fingerspell M-E-D W-E-L-L and W-E-L-L D-O-N-E. If you want your steak rare, fingerspell R-A-R-E.

Don't sign rare with a shaken **R** — the untrained eye could mistake that motion for "restroom" or the direction "right."

Here are some dinner-related sentences to give you practice:

English: Soup and bread were served.
Sign: FINISH — SOUP — BREAD — SERVE

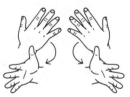  

Finish at the beginning of a sentence adds past tense to the whole sentence. (See Chapter 2 for more information on signing in past and future tense.)

English: Chicken and spaghetti are on special.
Sign: SPECIAL — WHAT — CHICKEN — SPAGHETTI

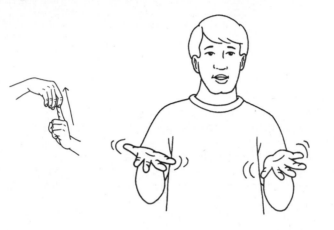

English: The steak is rare.
Sign: STEAK — R-A-R-E

English: I'd like a potato with my fish.
Sign: MY FISH — POTATO TOGETHER — WANT ME

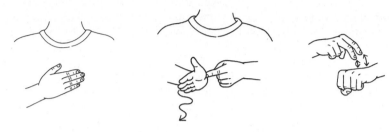

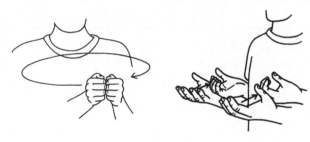

English: I'm full.
Sign: FULL ME

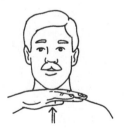

Dining Out

Everyone enjoys going out to restaurants from time to time. Take a look at the signs in Table 8-6, which you can use no matter what type of restaurant you go to. Bon appetit!

Deaf people usually point out to the server what they want on the menu. If you're dining out with Deaf people, don't try to take control when ordering. They've probably been eating in restaurants long before they met you.

Table 8-6		Words for Dining Out	
English	*Sign*	*English*	*Sign*
ORDER		RESERVATION	
RESTAURANT		SERVER/ WAITER/ WAITRESS	

Ethnic food around town

Restaurant row is just down the street. Many Deaf people enjoy eating at ethnic establishments, and I know you'd like to enjoy both the food and the company. The food signs in Table 8-7 are just the thing to get you going — come and get it!

ASL doesn't have established signs for ethnic foods. If the grub is popular, you may see a variety of ways to sign it if there isn't already an established sign from its country of origin. In the southwestern part of the United States, Mexican food is popular, and Mexican Sign Language for this ethnic food is pretty well established in the border states.

Table 8-7	Ethnic Foods		
English	*Sign*	*English*	*Sign*
LASAGNA		SUSHI	
TACO		TORTILLA	
TOSTADA			

The following sentences will work up an appetite for any eager signer:

English: We will eat dinner at a restaurant.
Sign: RESTAURANT — EVENING FOOD — EAT THERE — WE WILL

 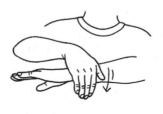

English: I like egg rolls.
Sign: EGG R-O-L-L-S — LIKE ME

English: Tostadas are cheap.
Sign: TOSTADA — CHEAP

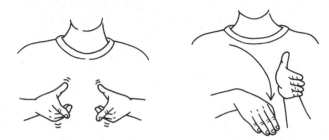

English: She likes tortillas.
Sign: TORTILLAS — SHE LIKES

Don't forget the drinks!

When dining out or going for a night on the town, drinks are often a big part of the occasion. Table 8-8 can help you when ordering common beverages.

Table 8-8	Common Beverages		
English	*Sign*	*English*	*Sign*
BEER		COFFEE	

(continued)

Table 8-8 *(continued)*

English	Sign	English	Sign
WHISKEY/ SHOT		WINE	
SODA/COLA		MILK	
WATER		TEA	

English: We need ice.
Sign: I-C-E — NEED US

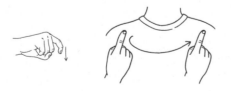

English: The water is warm.
Sign: WATER — WARM

English: I need a glass for my beer.
Sign: BEER GLASS — NEED ME

English: The coffee is strong.
Sign: COFFEE — STRONG

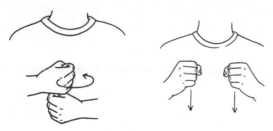

Signin' the Sign

Belinda and Denni are out on the town. Belinda wants to propose a toast and is asking about drinks when the waitress approaches.

Belinda: What would you like to drink?
Sign: DRINK — WANT WHAT Q

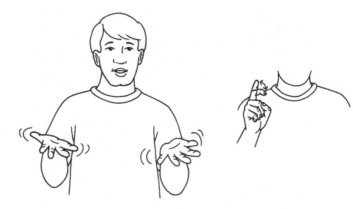

Denni: A cold beer.
Sign: COLD BEER

Belinda:	A glass of red wine.
Sign:	GLASS RED WINE

Attention, Shoppers!

Grocery shopping made simple — that's what you'll find when you do it in Sign. This section gives you a handle on going to the market and other food-related stores.

Signing specialty stores

Everyone at one time or another goes to the market. You'll be the guru of groceries, hands down, when using the signs from Table 8-9.

Table 8-9		Types of Stores	
English	*Sign*	*English*	*Sign*
BAKERY (BREAD STORE)		BUTCHER (MEAT STORE)	

(continued)

Table 8-9 *(continued)*

English	Sign	English	Sign
DISCOUNT STORE	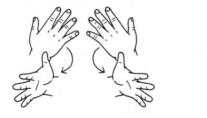	GROCERY (FOOD STORE)	

English: I went to the butcher's.
Sign: FINISH — MEAT STORE — GO ME

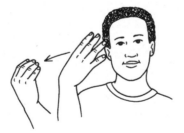

English: The bakery smells good.
Sign: BREAD STORE — SMELLS DELICIOUS

Getting a good deal

Few things are more satisfying than saving money when you're shopping for groceries. Signing specials from the marketplace, like those in Table 8-10, give you the upper hand as you finger your way through the fruit. Note that some signs mean several words, as in "two for the price of one."

Table 8-10		Sale Ad Words	
English	*Sign*	*English*	*Sign*
SAVE		SPEND/ BUY	
SELL		BARGAIN/ CHEAP	

(continued)

Table 8-10 *(continued)*

English	Sign	English	Sign
COUPON			

English: The meat is on sale today.
Sign: TODAY — MEAT — SALE

English: You can buy two steaks for the price of one.
Sign: TWO STEAKS — PAY — ONLY ONE

English: I saved money.
Sign: FINISH — MONEY— SAVE ME

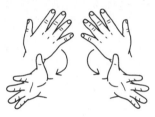

English: You spent too much.
Sign: FINISH — SPEND — (you is implied) TOO MUCH

Fun & Games

Sign the following words. You can look back in the chapter for help.

1. Sign three different utensils (worth 3 points).

2. Sign three different types of beverages (worth 3 points).

3. Sign one Italian food (worth 1 point).

4. Sign one Mexican food (worth 1 point).

5. Sign the words *full* and *hungry* (worth 2 points).

6. Sign the words *eggs* and *cereal* (worth 2 points).

7. Sign the word *salad* (worth 1 point).

Thirteen total points are possible. Let's see how you did:

10–13:   Thumbs up!

6–9:   You're getting there!

1–5:   Keep practicing!

Chapter 9

Shopping Made Easy

In This Chapter

▶ Signing various clothes and colors

▶ Paying for your goods

▶ Comparing costs

Signing and shopping fit together like hand and glove. This chapter focuses on fashions, colors, and seasons in American Sign Language. We throw in signs for money and comparing prices, too — at no cost to you.

Clothes for All Seasons

Dapper duds are all the rage. These signs show you how to ask for and get your garb in any season because everyone loves a well-dressed signer. Table 9-1 talks fabric. Although you fingerspell many fabrics, here are some fabrics that you sign.

Fabric signs bear a strong resemblance to what they represent. For example, the sign for **leather** is similar to cowhide, and the **cotton** sign is like tearing apart a cotton ball.

Table 9-1		Fabrics	
English	*Sign*	*English*	*Sign*
COTTON 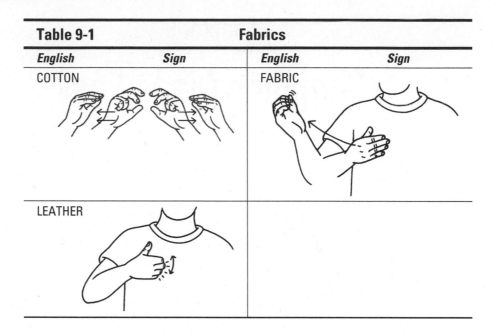		FABRIC	
LEATHER			

These words are the basics for all your clothing needs. You sign **wear** the same way as **use,** so don't worry that they look the same. The sign for **clothes** is the same as the sign for **costume** — try that on for size!

WEAR

CLOTHES

The winter look

Changing with the seasons is no problem. Winter wear signs are cool because they look like what they are. Check them out in Table 9-2.

Table 9-2		Winter Clothing	
English	*Sign*	*English*	*Sign*
BOOTS		COAT	
GLOVES		HAT	
SCARF			

ASL has a variety of signs for gloves because there are different kinds of gloves. Either way, you want to mimic putting on a pair of gloves. You sign **mittens** by making an outline of your thumb and four fingers with the index finger of your passive hand. Mittens aren't as common as gloves, so if people don't understand you, you can always rely on fingerspelling.

Hat and **scarf** are simple: Sign them like you're putting them on.

Men tend to sign **boots** by mimicking pulling boots on their legs. Women tend to sign boots on the arm. (This isn't a rule, only an observation.)

Try these sentences on for size:

English: Wear your coat.
Sign: YOUR COAT WEAR

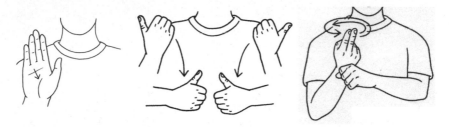

English: The scarf is white.
Sign: SCARF WHITE

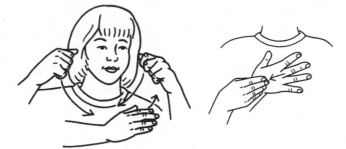

English: Are these your gloves?
Sign: GLOVES YOURS Q

Now, it's time to go undercover. You sign most underwear signs to look like what they represent. You can sign **men's briefs** like **panties**. You may often see **long johns** expressed by signing **long** and then fingerspelling J-O-H-N-S. One way to sign **T-shirt** is with the manual handshape **T** and then **shirt.** You fingerspell anything slinky or kinky. Take a look at Table 9-3 for clarification.

Table 9-3		Underwear	
English	*Sign*	*English*	*Sign*
PANTIES		BRA	
UNDERWEAR (men)		T-SHIRT	

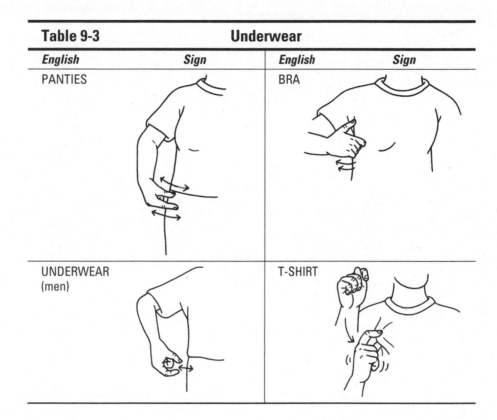

Fall fashion

You'll have no trouble with fall fashions when you know the basic signs for cool weather wear (see Table 9-4).

Table 9-4		Cool Clothing	
English	*Sign*	*English*	*Sign*
BELT		DRESS	

(continued)

Table 9-4 *(continued)*

English	Sign	English	Sign
HIGH HEELS		PANTS/ SLACKS	
SHIRT		SHOES	
SOCKS		SWEATER	

Be cool. Practice these sentences that feature cool-weather wear:

English: Your dress is pretty.
Sign: YOUR DRESS — PRETTY

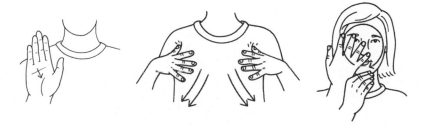

English: Her belt is leather.
Sign: HER BELT — LEATHER

English: If you wear pants, don't wear high heels.
Sign: IF PANTS WEAR — HIGH HEELS WEAR NOT

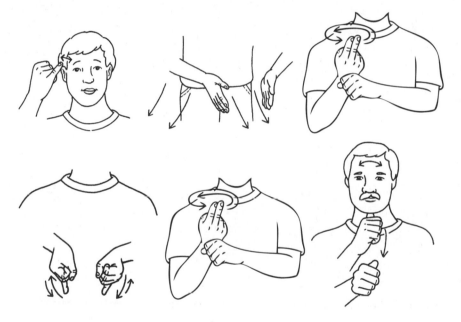

English: Where is my sweater?
Sign: MY SWEATER — WHERE Q

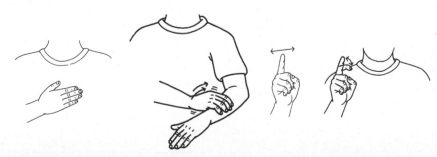

Spring style

Dressing for spring is a beautiful thing. The signs in Table 9-5 show you how to fit in all the fashionable circles when the weather begins to warm up.

Table 9-5	Spring Apparel and Accessories		
English	*Sign*	*English*	*Sign*
BLOUSE		PURSE	
SKIRT		NYLONS	
TIE		UMBRELLA	
WALLET			

Spring into action and take a look at the following sentences:

English: Where's my umbrella?
Sign: MY UMBRELLA — WHERE Q

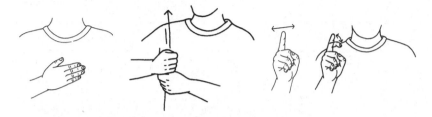

English: I want that skirt.
Sign: SKIRT — THAT (one) — WANT ME

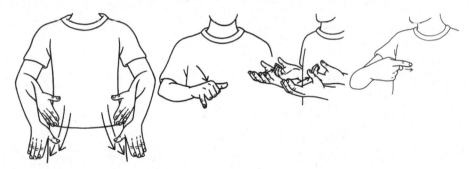

English: Where is my wallet?
Sign: MY WALLET — WHERE Q

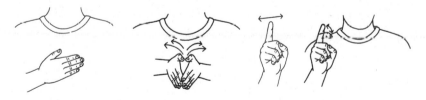

English: If you wear a blouse, I'll wear a tie.
Sign: IF BLOUSE YOU WEAR — TIE ME WEAR

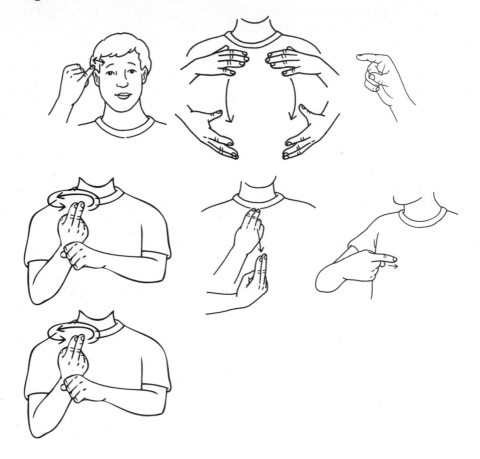

English: Her purse is nice.
Sign: HER PURSE —NICE

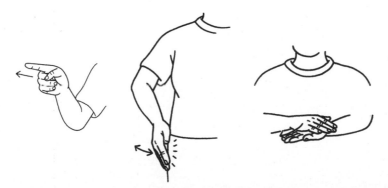

Summer suits

You can let everyone know your taste in summer wear with just a few bare-bones signs. Table 9-6 gives you the hottest signs for the coolest summer clothes.

To sign **sunglasses,** just put the sign for **sun** before **glasses.** For a **two-piece swimsuit** for women, you sign **bra** and **panties;** for a **one-piece swimsuit,** you sign **one piece.** You fingerspell **men's swimming trunks,** or you can sign **shorts.** But if you're talking Speedos, sign it like **panties.**

Table 9-6		Summer Sizzlers	
English	*Sign*	*English*	*Sign*
SHORTS		SUNDRESS	
SUNGLASSES			

Now that you have the summer basics, try these sentences:

English: Where did you buy those sunglasses?
Sign: SUNGLASSES — BUY YOU — WHERE Q

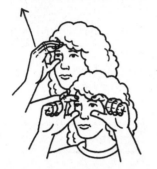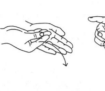

English: These shorts are old.
Sign: SHORTS (point) — OLD

English: When will the T-shirt shop open?
Sign: T-SHIRT SHOP — OPEN — WHEN Q

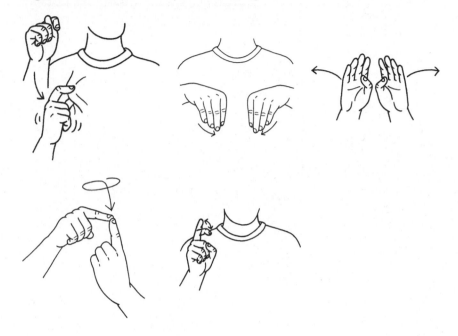

Clothing by color

Adding color to the canvas only brightens your repertoire of Sign. Time to bring it all home. This section gives you a start with your basic colors. Use the signs in Table 9-7 to mix and match your way throughout the year.

Table 9-7		Common Colors	
English	*Sign*	*English*	*Sign*
BLACK		BLUE	

(continued)

Table 9-7 *(continued)*

English	Sign	English	Sign
BROWN		GREEN	
ORANGE		PINK	
PURPLE		RED	
WHITE		YELLOW	

Following are some sentences that let you practice your newfound coloring skills:

English: Her dress is blue and white.
Sign: HER DRESS — BLUE WHITE

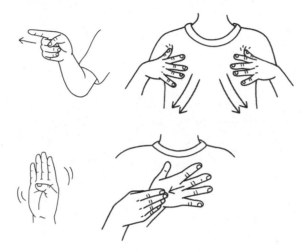

English: His tie is green.
Sign: HIS TIE — GREEN

English: He wore a yellow cotton shirt.
Sign: FINISH — HE WEAR SHIRT — YELLOW COTTON

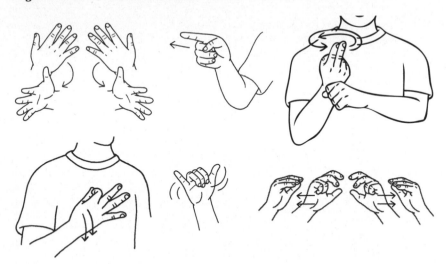

English: Her purse was black leather.
Sign: FINISH — HER PURSE — BLACK LEATHER

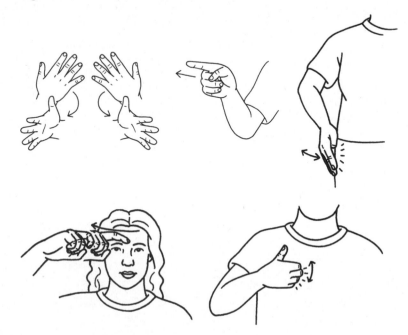

Signin' the Sign

 Aurora and David are going shopping. The stores have many sales, and they're looking for the best deals. Follow along as they move through the aisles.

Aurora: That blue dress is pretty.
Sign: BLUE DRESS — PRETTY

David: Those brown shoes are big.
Sign: BROWN SHOES — BIG

Aurora: Do you like the black slacks?
Sign: BLACK SLACKS — YOU LIKE Q

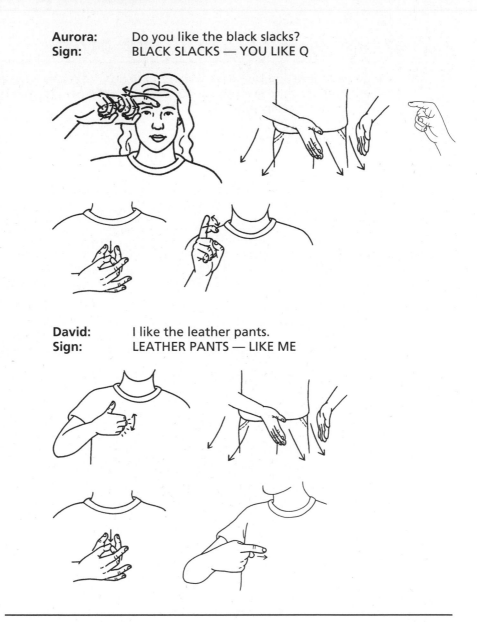

David: I like the leather pants.
Sign: LEATHER PANTS — LIKE ME

All about Money

Now comes the not-so-fun part — paying for all your new items. But because you have to fork over the money, the signs in Table 9-8 cover the variety of ways to pay for those purchases.

When signing **ATM/debit card** or **credit card,** outline a card shape after making the signs in Table 9-8.

Table 9-8		Payment Options		
English	*Sign*	*English*		*Sign*
ATM/DEBIT CARD		CASH		
CHARGE		CHECK		
CREDIT CARD				

Table 9-9 covers other money-related words.

Table 9-9		Financial Words	
English	*Sign*	*English*	*Sign*
BANK		BILLS/ DOLLARS	
CENTS		CHANGE	
MONEY		PAY	

Here are some financial-transaction sentences for you to practice money matters:

English: I'll pay with my credit card.
Sign: CREDIT (outline card) — PAY WILL ME

English: She wrote a $50 check.
Sign: FINISH — CHECK 5-0 DOLLARS — WRITE HER

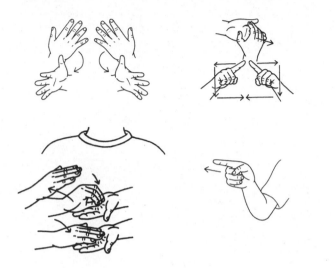

English: The bank gave me an ATM card.
Sign: A-T-M (outline card) — BANK — GIVE ME

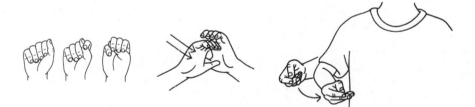

You can sign **credit card** two different ways. The old way is shown in Table 9-8. The new way: Outline a card shape and then show the motion of swiping it through a machine.

Signin' the Sign

Robert and Krista are going clothes shopping. They like to save money, so they're doing some comparison shopping.

Robert: I'm buying new clothes.
Sign: NEW CLOTHES — BUY ME

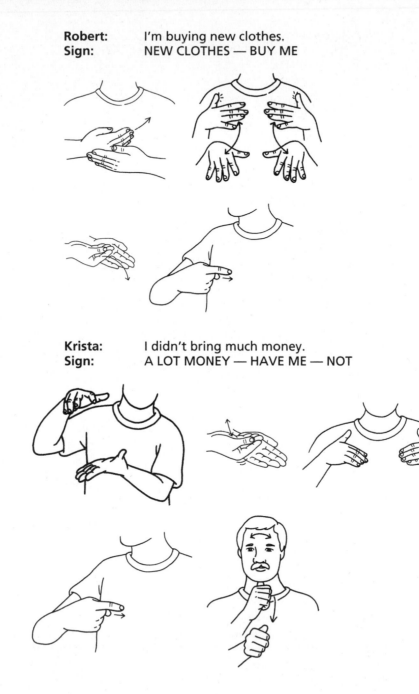

Krista: I didn't bring much money.
Sign: A LOT MONEY — HAVE ME — NOT

Robert: Buy a couple of blouses on sale.
Sign: TWO BLOUSES — SALE — BUY

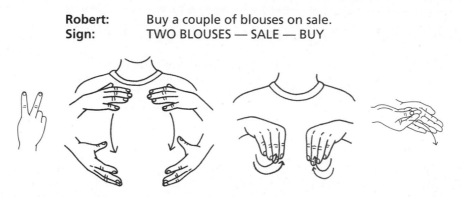

Krista: If I buy blouses, I'll need pants.
Sign: IF BLOUSES BUY — PANTS NEED ME

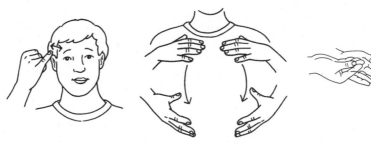

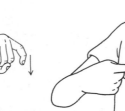

Robert: Use your credit card.
Sign: CREDIT (outline card) — YOURS USE

Shopping Superlatives and Comparisons

In English, you sometimes form words that compare by adding endings, such as "er" or "est." For comparatives and superlatives in Sign, you use the root (base) word and then add a modifier. For example, you sign **greatest** simply as **great,** and you sign **happier** as **happy.** After you decide which base word you want to use, sign it and then add one of the words from Table 9-10 — whichever one is the most appropriate.

Comparing costs is a pretty common thing to do. Here's how to sign the better bargain. If you're at the store, you can always point to what you're referring to; that way you can avoid fingerspelling. To sign that you found the cheapest or most expensive item, simply sign **cheap** or **expensive** and then sign the word **top.** This is a good way to compare several prices. You can also sign **cheap** or **expensive** and then sign **better.**

Table 9-10		Super Words	
English	*Sign*	*English*	*Sign*
GOOD		BETTER	
BEST		TOP	

(continued)

Table 9-10 *(continued)*

English	Sign	English	Sign
BOTTOM		BAD	
WORSE/ WORST			

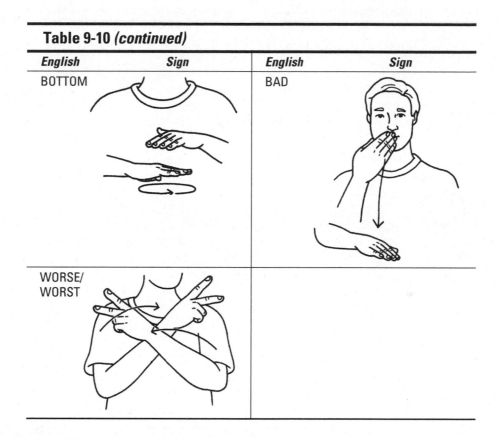

English: The red shirt is better than the green one.
Sign: RED SHIRT — GREEN SHIRT — RED BETTER

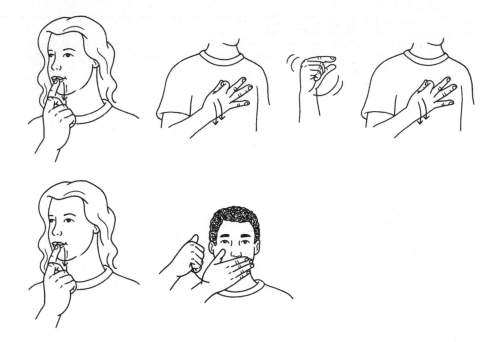

English: His coat is the warmest.
Sign: HIS COAT — WARM — TOP

English: Your shoes are the ugliest.
Sign: YOUR SHOES — UGLY — WORST

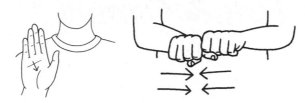

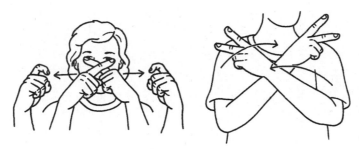

Fun & Games

Match the signs with their corresponding words by drawing a line between each pair. You can find the answers in Appendix A.

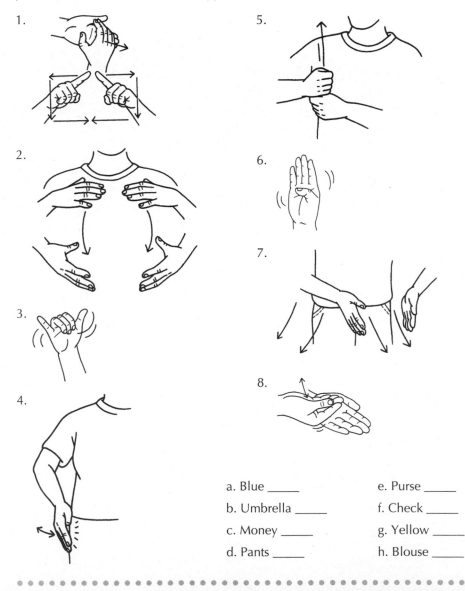

1.

2.

3.

4.

5.

6.

7.

8.

a. Blue _____   e. Purse _____

b. Umbrella _____   f. Check _____

c. Money _____   g. Yellow _____

d. Pants _____   h. Blouse _____

Chapter 10

The Signer About Town

In This Chapter

▶ Planning and conversing during a night on the town

▶ Signing about your social status

Going out on the town, you see Deaf people signing at every turn. Because you're reading this book and discovering ways to communicate in American Sign Language, stopping to chat with them is no longer difficult.

The signs in this chapter give you an edge on conversing with other signers about the world of culture and entertainment. After you familiarize yourself with this chapter, you can discuss movies, plays, the theater, and even exhibits in a museum. I also give you signs to communicate your social status.

Making Plans

Getting together with friends has never been so easy. The signs in Table 10-1 help get you on your way.

 Some timely tips to pencil in: **Appointment** and **reservation** are the same sign, so if you can sign one, you've got the other. The sign for **schedule** looks like the grid on a calendar page. You sign **socialize** with one thumb circling the other. **Write down** and **record** share the same sign. And the sign for **canceling an appointment or date** is exactly what you might expect — you make an **X** on your passive hand.

Table 10-1		Planning Signs	
English	*Sign*	*English*	*Sign*
APPOINTMENT/ RESERVATION		CALENDAR	
CANCEL		SCHEDULE	
EVENT		WRITE DOWN	
SOCIALIZE			

The following sentences are sure to help you make or break plans:

English: Write it down on your calendar.
Sign: YOUR CALENDAR — WRITE DOWN

English: What is your schedule for tomorrow?
Sign: TOMORROW — YOUR SCHEDULE — WHAT Q

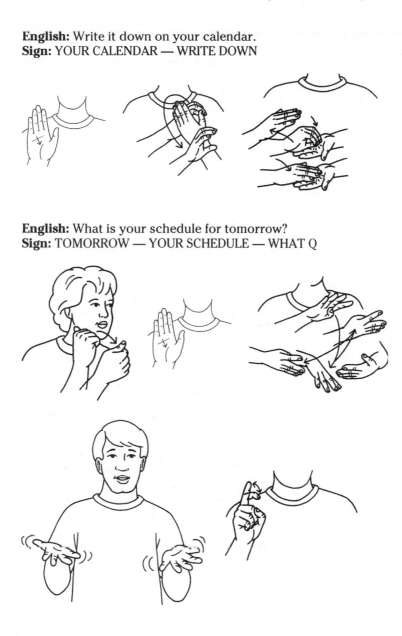

English: The event was cancelled.
Sign: FINISH — EVENT — CANCEL

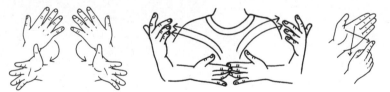

You sign **finish** to show that the sentence is in past tense (see Chapter 2 for a discussion of tenses).

When you're giving the time or you need to sign what time something occurs, you touch your wrist where you normally wear your watch and then sign the number. For example, if you want to tell someone that it's 2 o'clock, touch your wrist and then sign the number **2.** To distinguish between a.m. and p.m., you sign **morning, afternoon,** or **night** after the number. This rule has two exceptions: For **midnight,** you don't touch your wrist; you simply sign the number **12** straight down. And for **noon,** you sign **12 noon** straight up.

Check out the signs for numbers in Chapter 4. You can then make a date for a specific day and time with the cute Deaf guy or girl you just met.

Going to the movies

You can sit around the house and watch a good TV program with your Deaf friends if your TV has closed-captioning (CC), which displays the text on the screen. If the captioning doesn't come on, just give it a minute.

Open-captioning (OC) is different. This captioning is the subtitles you usually see on foreign films, either at home on a DVD or out in the theater. In case you were wondering, yes, Deaf people do attend movies. Many Deaf people go to the movies to see the latest flicks and then go to dinner afterward. Some theaters have an OC night for newly released movies. This is a good place to meet Deaf people. Call your local theater to see whether it has a captioning night for the Deaf.

Some theaters don't have OC but do have *rear window* captioning. This involves a device that plugs into the seat's cup holder and extends in front of you, near eye level, displaying the movie's captions. You can also sometimes find *assistive listening devices* as well.

To sign **open-captioning,** simply fingerspell O-C.

Communicating during a movie is common among signers. They converse about everything — the movie's plot, an actor, or even the lack of salt on the popcorn! Table 10-2 presents some signs to help you enjoy the show.

Table 10-2	Movie and TV Terms		
English	*Sign*	*English*	*Sign*

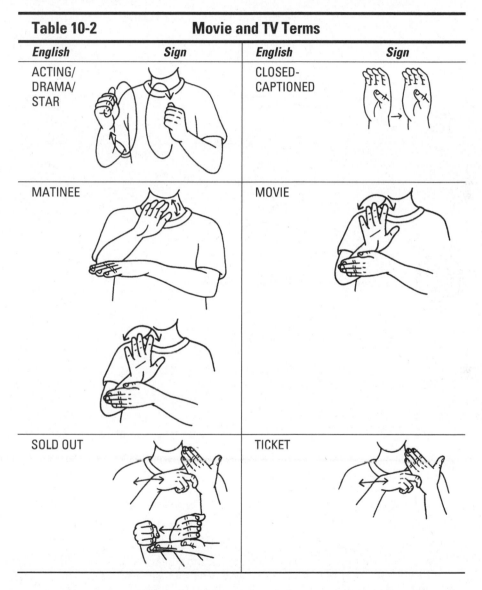

Are you feeling a bit like Bond, James Bond, or are you more in the mood for bonding in a romantic way? Table 10-3 shows you signs that indicate various types of movies.

Table 10-3		Movie Genres	
English	*Sign*	*English*	*Sign*
ACTION		COMEDY/ FUNNY	
MYSTERY		ROMANCE	
FANTASY			

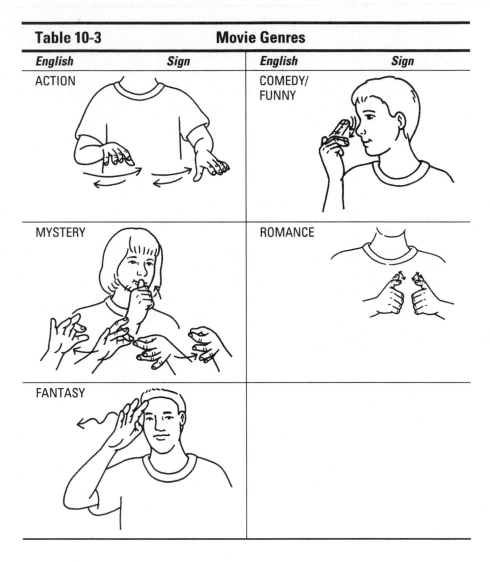

English: The movie sold out.
Sign: MOVIE — SOLD OUT

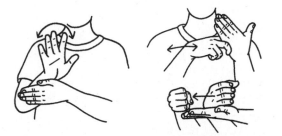

English: If the movie is open-captioned, I'll go.
Sign: IF MOVIE O-C — ME GO

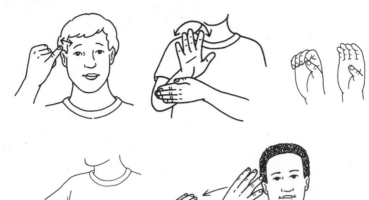

English: The matinee was a comedy.
Sign: AFTERNOON MOVIE — FUNNY

English: We went to see the new mystery.
Sign: FINISH — NEW MYSTERY — SEE US

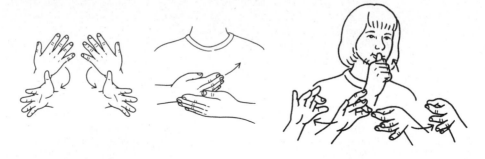

English: There's captioning Saturday at the movie.
Sign: SATURDAY MOVIE — O-C

Going to the theater

Attending plays is always a great way to improve your signing skills, especially if the actors also sign. Many plays provide an interpreter so that Deaf people can attend and enjoy the play along with hearing folks.

Table 10-4 shows you a few of the more well-known theatrical terms that you may want to know.

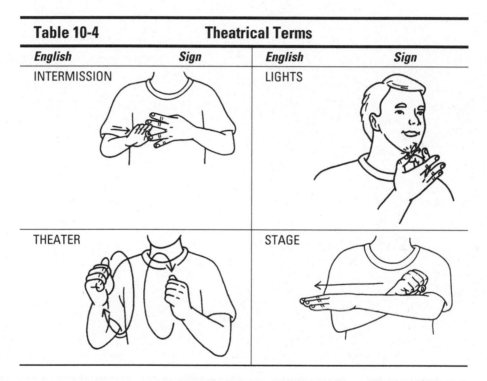

Table 10-4		Theatrical Terms	
English	*Sign*	*English*	*Sign*
INTERMISSION		LIGHTS	
THEATER		STAGE	

You sign **light** with a double **flick,** using your index finger and thumb under your chin and then mimicking the action of screwing in or taking out a light bulb. You can also sign **light** and mimic shining a spotlight or a flashlight.

The sign for **stage** doesn't allow your passive hand to move — only the active one outward.

English: When the lights go out, stop talking.
Sign: LIGHTS OUT — TALKING STOP

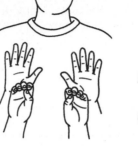
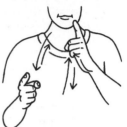

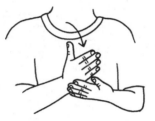

English: During intermission, I'm leaving.
Sign: DURING INTERMISSION — LEAVE ME

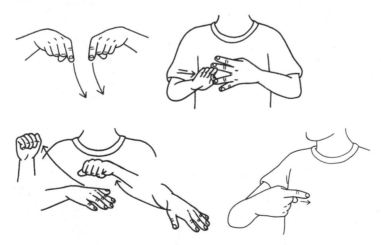

Going to the museum

Visiting a museum is quite an experience and one that many Deaf people can appreciate as easily as those in the hearing world. You don't have to be able to hear to enjoy all the wonderful things that are included in museums. However, being able to discuss what you see is nice.

Use the signs in Table 10-5 when you go back in time for a few hours.

Table 10-5	Museums and Museum Displays		
English	*Sign*	*English*	*Sign*
ART		DISPLAY/ EXHIBIT/ SHOW	
HISTORY		MUSEUM	
PHOTOGRAPHY		SCULPTURE	
TIME/ERA			

You sign **museum** like "house," only you use the manual **M** on both hands. You sign time periods by signing the manual **T** in a circular motion with your active hand on your passive hand. This means **time period** or **era.**

You sign **photography** by mimicking taking a picture. Make sure that you give it a double click because a single click means "to take a picture."

English: The museum is open.
Sign: MUSEUM — OPEN

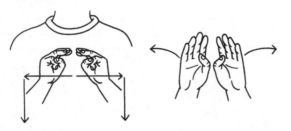

English: We saw the photography exhibit.
Sign: FINISH — PHOTOGRAPHY EXHIBIT SEE

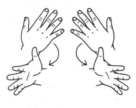  

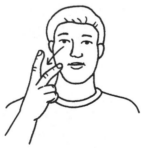

Selecting Your Social Station

Going out with the gang is a good time for those who like the night life. Deaf people enjoy their social bonds and can paint the town red with the best of them. Often, people go as singles, and other times, it's couple's night out. The signs in Table 10-6 will help you when you're planning that night out with your friends. At night, signs just seem to flow.

Table 10-6	Social Station Signs		
English	*Sign*	*English*	*Sign*
MARRIED		SINGLE	
DIVORCED		BACHELOR/ BACHELORETTE	

(continued)

Table 10-6 *(continued)*

English	Sign	English	Sign
DATE		FIANCÉ / FIANCÉE	
WIDOW/ WIDOWER			

Signin' the Sign

Denni and Wanda want to go to the movies, so they decide to schedule a time that works for both of them.

Denni: Want to go to a movie?
Sign: MOVIE — GO WANT Q

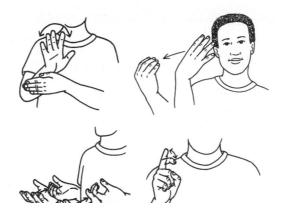

Wanda: Yes, I can go next Saturday — maybe a comedy.
Sign: YES — NEXT WEEK — SATURDAY — GO FUNNY MOVIE — MAYBE

Denni: I'll write it down on my schedule.
Sign: SCHEDULE — WRITE DOWN — ME WILL

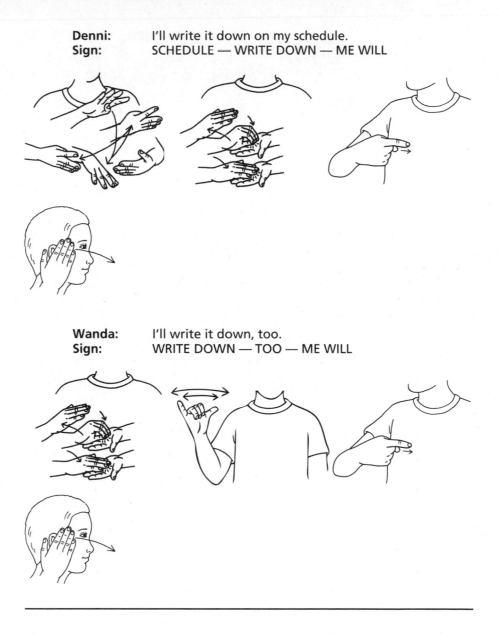

Wanda: I'll write it down, too.
Sign: WRITE DOWN — TOO — ME WILL

Fun & Games

Match the word with the clue and then sign it. (You can check back in the chapter to see if you're signing the words correctly.)

1. A place where you find relics   A. Bachelor

2. A place where you watch a movie   B. Socialize

3. A story of love   C. Reservation

4. Some restaurants require this   D. Art

5. A reason to go to a party   E. History

6. You read about it in books   F. Fiancé/fiancée

7. It can be a hobby   G. Museum

8. Dance and painting to many people   H. Theater

9. Soon to be married   I. Photography

10. A single man   J. Romance

Chapter 11

Takin' Care of Business

· ·

In This Chapter

▶ Talking about occupations

▶ Using signs for office equipment

▶ Knowing some general work signs

· ·

Many more Deaf people work in office jobs than ever before, so there's never been a better time to know some signs for around the office. The signs in this chapter can help you show Deaf visitors around the office or communicate with a Deaf colleague at your workplace.

Occupying Yourself with Occupations

The average American worker changes occupations many times in the course of a career. Table 11-1 gives you signs for some job position terms.

Table 11-1		Work Words	
English	*Sign*	*English*	*Sign*
ASSISTANT		BOSS	

(continued)

Table 11-1 *(continued)*

English	Sign	English	Sign
WORKER/ EMPLOYEE		DIRECTOR/ MANAGER	
SECRETARY		SUPERVISOR	

Here are some sentences that will surely come in handy at the office:

English: When is payday?
Sign: PAYDAY — WHEN Q

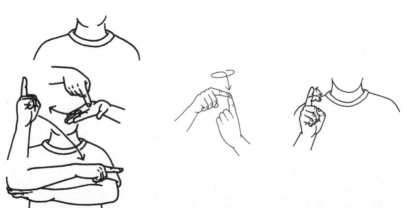

English: She was terminated by Human Resources.
Sign: H-R TERMINATE HER

Most people refer to Human Resources as "HR," so you sign this term by
fingerspelling H-R.

English: The boss has my time sheet.
Sign: TIME SHEET MINE — BOSS HAVE

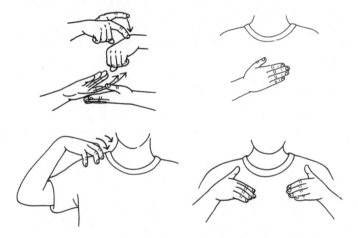

Signin' the Sign

Maria is a new office employee. Her trainer is George. She wants to
do well at her new job and asks George questions so she will know
what to do in her new work environment.

Maria: Is that the manager?
Sign: MANAGER — HIM (point) Q

George: No, he is the assistant manager.
Sign: NO — ASSISTANT MANAGER — HIM

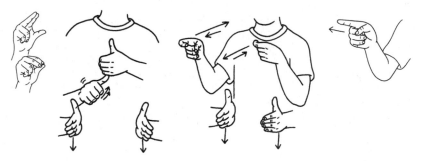

Maria: Where is the boss?
Sign: BOSS — WHERE Q

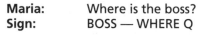

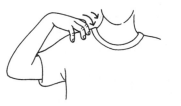
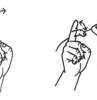

George: In a meeting.
Sign: MEETING

Maria: Who is my supervisor?
Sign: MY — SUPERVISOR — WHO Q

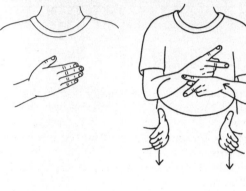

George:	Dee, she is a good boss.
Sign:	D-E-E — GOOD BOSS — TRUE (affirmation)

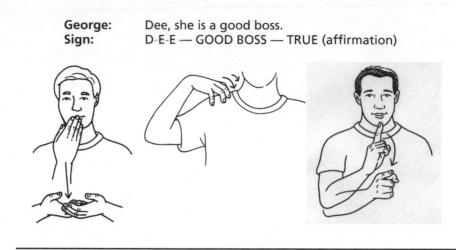

Sorting Office Supplies

Moving around the cubicle, you have many things to sign. Try the signs in Table 11-2 and you'll be the boss.

You may find the sign for **clock** to be a bit tricky, but it's really pretty simple. Touch your wrist where you wear your watch and then make both hands into manual L handshapes that are bent at the knuckle toward the wall or wherever the clock is located.

Table 11-2		Office Equipment	
English	*Sign*	*English*	*Sign*
CLOCK		OFFICE	

English	Sign	English	Sign
PAPER		COPY MACHINE	
PAPER CLIP		DESK/ TABLE	
PENCIL		EQUIPMENT	

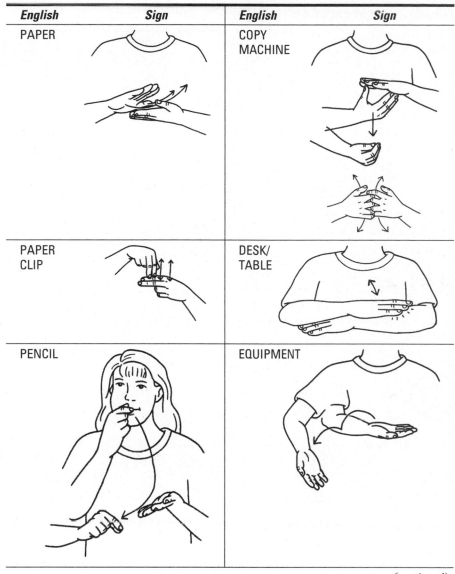

(continued)

Table 11-2 *(continued)*

English	Sign	English	Sign
PHONE		LAPTOP	
STAPLER			

The office is a great place to work these signs. The following sentences can give you a hand with some office items. And because office equipment doesn't always work, signs exist for that, too.

English: The copy machine is broken.
Sign: COPY MACHINE — BROKE

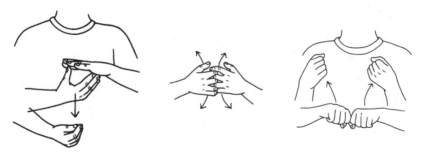

Sign **broke** or **broken** like you're breaking a stick with both hands in the manual S handshape.

English: My computer is frozen.
Sign: MY COMPUTER — FROZE

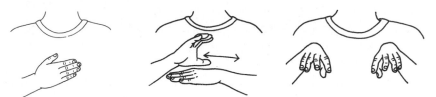

Sign **froze** or **frozen** like the word **freeze** (see Chapter 5).

English: Where is the stapler?
Sign: STAPLER — WHERE — Q

English: Do we have enough paper?
Sign: PAPER — ENOUGH — HAVE — Q

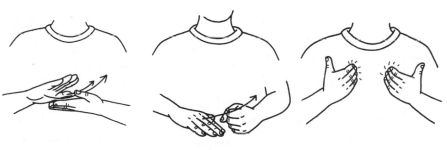

Getting to Work

The workaday world is full of tasks, from stocking shelves to attending meetings. The signs in Table 11-3 make work a little more fun; you can carry on a private conversation with another signer during a boring meeting.

Table 11-3		Business Terms	
English	**Sign**	**English**	**Sign**
BUSINESS		CLOSED DOWN (as in computer screen)	
DISCUSS		MEETING/ CONFERENCE	
PROMOTION		TRADING (stocks)	
WORK			

Put these work-related signs into action in the following sentences:

English: Are you going to the conference?
Sign: CONFERENCE — GO —YOU — Q

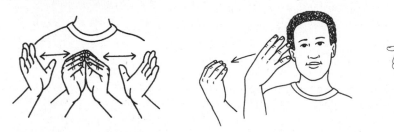

English: The managers meeting is upstairs.
Sign: MANAGERS MEETING — UPSTAIRS

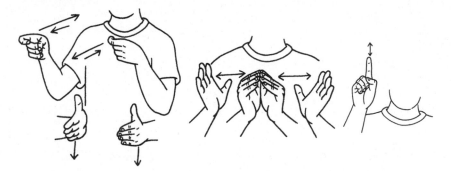

English: If you trade stocks, I will, too.
Sign: IF TRADE — YOU — ME — SAME

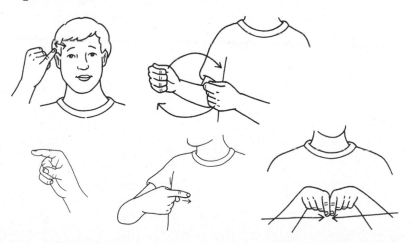

English: Where do you work?
Sign: WORK—YOU—WHERE — Q

English: The business is closed.
Sign: BUSINESS CLOSED

Fun & Games

Alice is a new supervisor at her job. She's at a meeting explaining what needs to be done tomorrow.

Fill in the gaps in her explanation.

Please use the (a)_____ only on Thursdays. Also, your (b)_____ is broken; it keeps crashing, but we're sending for someone to fix it. Please tell the other (c)_____ not to be late or they will be (d)_____. I will have my (e)_____ with me tomorrow. We will discuss a (f)_____ on Monday in my (g)_____. I want to (h)_____ more people.

1.

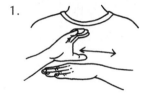

2.

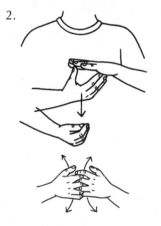

3.

4.

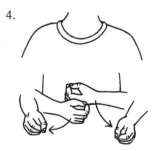

5.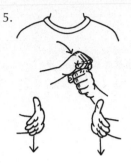

6.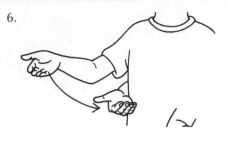

7.

8.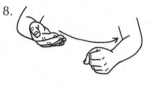

Chapter 12

Recreation and the Great Outdoors

· ·

In This Chapter

▶ Discovering the signs for various sports

▶ Signing words related to games and hobbies

▶ Knowing the signs for weather and the outdoors

▶ Playing around with rhetorical questions

· ·

You can relax in many ways. This chapter covers a few of the more active pastimes. We provide signs for sports, recreations, and hobbies in this chapter. And because you probably don't want to have a picnic in the rain, this chapter also deals with signs for the weather.

Exercising Your Right to Recreate

All work and no play makes Jack a dull boy — or so the saying goes. The point is that everyone loves to get out and play once in a while, whether on a team or individually. This section gives signs for various team sports first, and then, for those of you who are more independent, signs for solo sports. Have fun!

Getting into the competitive spirit

The majority of sports signs look like what they represent. For example, the signs for **tennis** and **baseball** mimic the swing of a racket and bat, respectively. Don't you just love it when signing is this easy? Check out Table 12-1 for more team sports signs.

Table 12-1		Competitive Team Sports	
English	*Sign*	*English*	*Sign*
BASEBALL		BASKETBALL	
BOXING		FOOTBALL	
HOCKEY		SOCCER	
WRESTLING		TENNIS	

Signing **ball** is easy: Mimic putting both hands on a ball; do it with a double motion. You can make the ball as small or as big as you want.

You sign wrestling and football the same way: Lock your fingers together but don't bend them. If you do this with a double motion, that's **football.** If you lock your fingers once and go side to side, that's **wrestling.**

Box and **boxing** are the same sign. Put your fists up like you're in a boxing stance. No two people hold up their fists the same way, so the sign varies from person to person.

Table 12-2 gives you signs for competitive terms. Some of these signs are a bit tricky, so allow us to give you some explanation.

You sign **match, game,** and **challenge** the same way, except the nouns **game** and **match** get a double motion while the verb **challenge** gets a single motion.

If you want to sign **versus,** use the same sign as the one for challenge.

You sign **compete, sports,** and **race** the same way. Make the manual **A** hand-shape with both hands, put your palms together, and then alternate them back and forth. If you want to show fierce competition, grit your teeth and alternate your hands rapidly.

Signing **referee** or **umpire** is as simple as putting your index and middle fingertips on your lips, like blowing a whistle (and don't forget that double motion). You'll probably see many signs for these two words, but this sign seems to be pretty common.

Here's a helping tip: You sign **score** just like **count.** You may see some Deaf people sign one team's score on one hand and the other team's score on the other hand.

To sign **tournament,** start with both hands in the same handshape — index and middle fingers bent, palms facing the addressee, with your dominant hand higher than your passive hand. Now, alternate your hands up and down like making a bracket for a round-robin tournament.

Lose and **lost** are the same sign. Make the manual **V** handshape with your dominant hand and allow it to hit your passive palm and bounce up again.

Table 12-2	Competitive Terms		
English	*Sign*	*English*	*Sign*
MATCH/GAME		CHAMPION/ CHAMPIONSHIP	

(continued)

Table 12-2 *(continued)*

English	Sign	English	Sign
RACE/ COMPETE/ SPORTS		REFEREE/ UMPIRE	
SCORE		TEAM	
TOURNAMENT		LOSE/LOST	
WIN/WON			

Here's how to put these signs into sentences:

English: The soccer game was good.
Sign: SOCCER GAME — GOOD

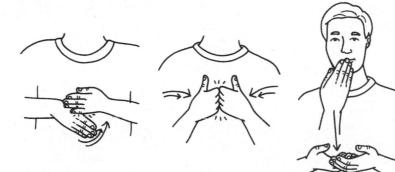

English: He can box and wrestle.
Sign: BOX — WRESTLE — BOTH CAN HIM

English: If you play soccer, you can't play basketball.
Sign: IF SOCCER PLAY YOU — BASKETBALL PLAY YOU — CAN'T

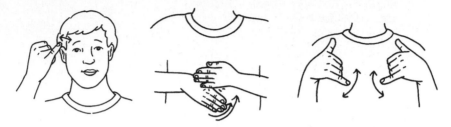

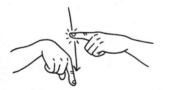

English: Our team won the race.
Sign: OUR TEAM — RACE — WON

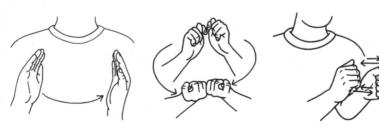

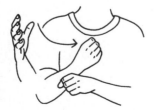

English: He's a football player.
Sign: FOOTBALL — PLAY HIM

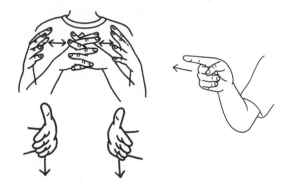

English: What's the score?
Sign: SCORE WHAT Q

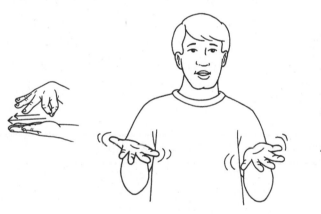

English: Did we win or lose?
Sign: WIN — LOSE — US WHICH Q

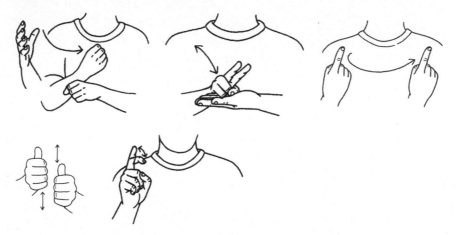

Setting out solo

You don't have to compete with a bunch of other people to be active and enjoy the great outdoors. Table 12-3 gives you the signs for sports that you can enjoy all by yourself if you want.

Table 12-3	Individual Sports		
English	*Sign*	*English*	*Sign*
CYCLING		GOLF	

English	Sign	English	Sign
HIKING		JOGGING	
SWIMMING		RUNNING	
WALKING			

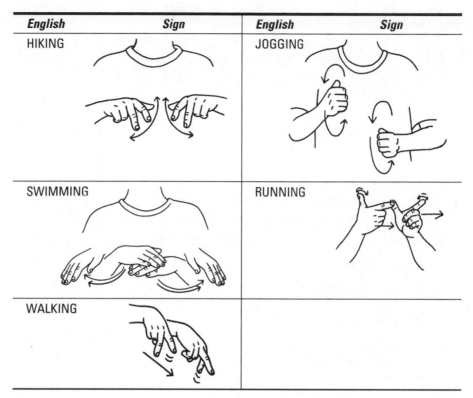

When you sign **jog,** make fists, put them beside your body, and move them as though you're jogging, while alternating your arms.

Here are a couple of signs that aren't really about sports but are handy to know for outdoor activities:

PICNIC   **CAMPING**

   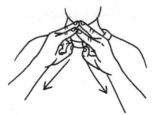

The following sentences show sports signs in action.

Glide your hands down the sides of your body after signing a sport to change from the sport to the player: golf to golfer, run to runner, and so on.

English: Mark is a good golfer.
Sign: M-A-R-K — GOOD GOLF (AGENT)

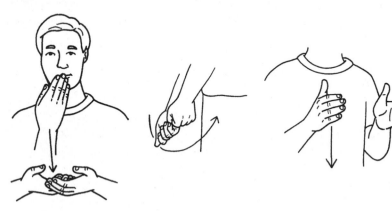

English: Do you like cycling?
Sign: CYCLING — YOU LIKE Q

English: Let's go hiking.
Sign: HIKING — US GO

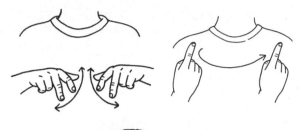

English: We're going on a picnic. Are you coming?
Sign: PICNIC GO US — COME YOU Q

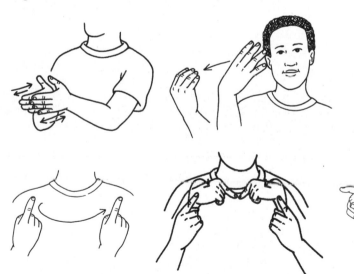

Playing Indoor Games

Not all games require a lot of physical activity. Nor do all of them have signs. For example, you fingerspell **cards, chess,** and **checkers.** You also fingerspell all board and card games. Mimic throwing dice for **gambling** and dealing cards for any **card game.** After you do this, fingerspell specifically what game you mean. Some indoor games do have signs, though, and you can find many of them in Table 12-4 — no cheating!

If your Deaf friends have a local sign for a game, just use that sign instead.

Table 12-4		Indoor Games	
English	*Sign*	*English*	*Sign*
BETTING		BOARD GAME	
DEAL CARDS		GAMBLING	
VIDEO GAMES			

English: Who wants to play poker?
Sign: P-O-K-E-R — PLAY — WANTS — WHO Q

English: Deal the cards.
Sign: DEAL CARDS

English: He likes playing chess.
Sign: C-H-E-S-S — HE LIKES

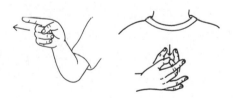

English: Do you gamble?
Sign: GAMBLE — YOU Q

Having Fun with Hobbies

From collecting to surfing the web, hobbies keep you busy, entertained, and sometimes even educated. The signs in Table 12-5 show you how to tell people about your hobby and make it come alive!

Table 12-5		Hobbies	
English	**Sign**	**English**	**Sign**
COLLECTING		BROWSING THE INTERNET	
KNITTING		READING	

English	Sign	English	Sign
SEWING		STAMP COLLECTING	

You sign **browsing the Internet** by showing the sign for **Internet** and then signing **search.** To sign **stamp collecting,** sign **stamp** and then **collect** — like gathering a bunch of stamps into the palm of your hand.

English: I collect stamps.
Sign: STAMPS — COLLECT ME

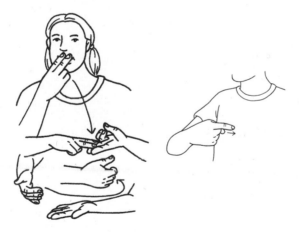

English: Knitting is relaxing.
Sign: KNITTING — RELAXING

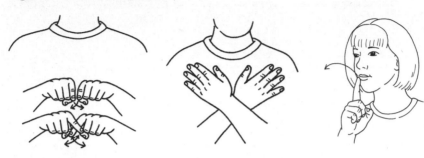

English: I like sewing.
Sign: SEWING — LIKE ME

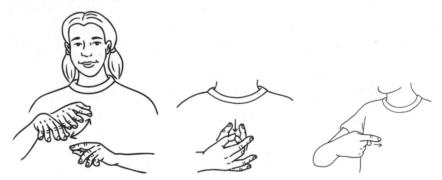

Seeing the Night Sky

Enjoying the serene beauty of the night sky is one of nature's most wonderful pleasures. Only one thing is better — having your new Deaf friends along to take in the view. Because American Sign Language is a visual language and the night sky is a visual phenomenon, it's fitting to see how these two awesome pleasures come together. The signs listed in Table 12-6 are fun to learn and fun to sign because there's movement involved — a shooting star, an eclipse of the moon, and a twinkling, star-filled sky are only a few examples.

Table 12-6		Celestial Signs	
English	*Sign*	*English*	*Sign*
STAR		SHOOTING STAR	
FULL MOON		CRESCENT MOON	
SKY		STAR-FILLED SKY	
ECLIPSE		HEAVENS	

English: Did you see the shooting star?
Sign: SHOOTING STAR — SEE — FINISH Q

English: The eclipse was red.
Sign: ECLIPSE — RED — TRUE (affirmation)

Getting the Weather Report

When isn't the weather a popular topic for discussion? Practice the basic weather signs in Table 12-7 and you'll be as right as rain. And because one should always be prepared, Table 12-8 provides signs for dealing with natural disasters.

Table 12-7		Weather Wise	
English	*Sign*	*English*	*Sign*
CLOUDY		DARK	
THUNDER		LIGHTNING	
STORM		SUNNY	

(continued)

Table 12-7 (continued)

English	Sign	English	Sign
WINDY		OUTSIDE	
WEATHER		RAIN	

Table 12-8   **Natural Disasters**

English	Sign	English	Sign
EARTHQUAKE		TSUNAMI	
FLOOD		FIRE	

English	Sign	English	Sign
DROWN		MUDSLIDE	
TORNADO/ HURRICANE (1)		TORNADO/ HURRICANE (2)	
WARNING		ALERT	
SAFE		ESCAPE	

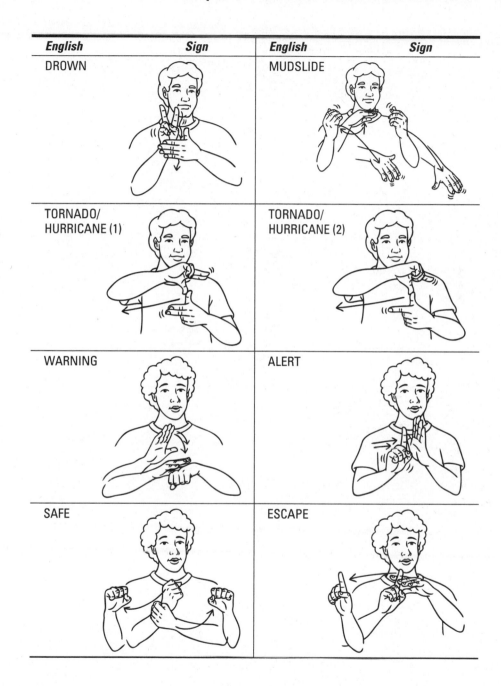

Check out these weather signs and give them a whirl. Try replacing them with other weather signs — it'll be smooth sailing.

English: It is cloudy today.
Sign: TODAY — CLOUDY

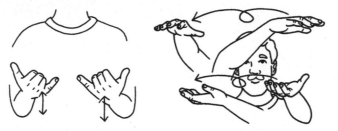

English: It's sunny outside.
Sign: OUTSIDE SUNNY

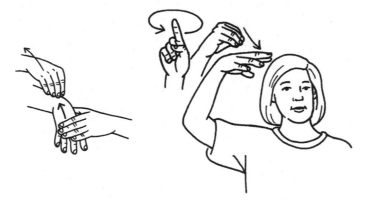

English: It's dark and windy this evening.
Sign: NOW NIGHT — DARK WINDY

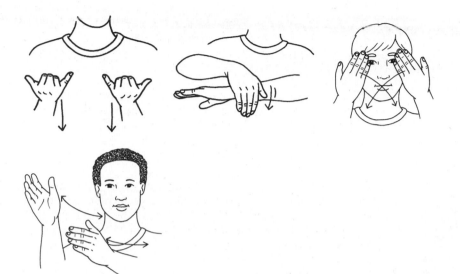

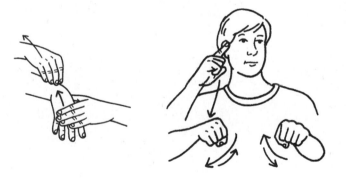

English: There is thunder and lightning outside.
Sign: OUTSIDE — THUNDER LIGHTNING

Having Fun with Rhetorical Questions in ASL

What you know about rhetorical questions in English is not the same as rhetorical questions in ASL. In English, a rhetorical question is a question that does not require an answer. In ASL, a rhetorical question is asked and the person who asks the question gives the answer as well. A rhetorical question is a way of making a point by providing the information for the very question you ask.

Keep your eyebrows up when you ask the question — that action tells everyone that you don't expect an answer. And if you're on the receiving end of a rhetorical question, you'll recognize it because the signer will barely pause before answering his own question. His hands won't go down to give you a chance to put your hands up to respond.

When you ask a rhetorical question, you use **who, what, why, where, when,** and **how** to make the sentence rhetorical, but you don't add a question mark because you aren't really asking a question. You are setting up the question to answer it yourself.

English: Brent is on my team.
Sign: MY TEAM WHO — B-R-E-N-T

English: The tournament is in Pueblo.
Sign: TOURNAMENT WHERE — P-U-E-B-L-O

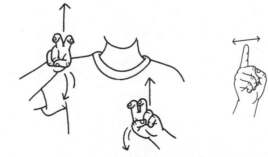

Signin' the Sign

Jason and Jesse can't decide what they want to do tomorrow — it just depends on the weather.

Jesse: I want to golf tomorrow.
Sign: TOMORROW — GOLF — PLAY WANT ME

 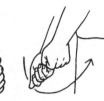 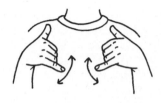

Jason: I'll go swimming tomorrow.
Sign: TOMORROW — SWIM ME

Jesse: If it rains, are you going swimming?
Sign: IF RAIN — YOU SWIMMING Q

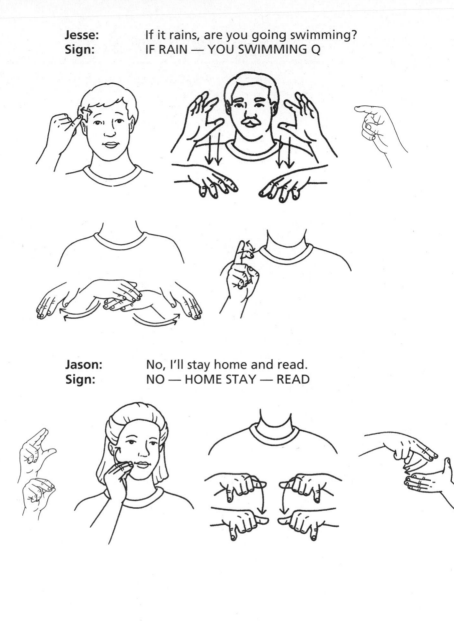

Jason: No, I'll stay home and read.
Sign: NO — HOME STAY — READ

Jesse: If it rains, let's play cards.
Sign: IF RAIN — CARDS US

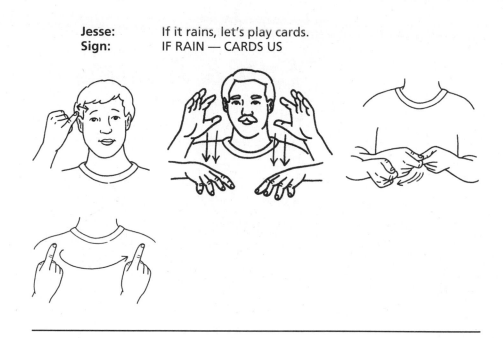

Fun & Games

Fill in the blanks with a sign. Go to Appendix A (or look through this chapter) to find out what the signs are.

1. Let's go to the park and have a _____. We'll invite the ants, too!

2. It is _____ outside. Did you bring a flashlight?

3. You need to _____. You seem stressed.

4. No _____ allowed. We're just playing for fun.

5. Do you play _____? I brought my bat and glove just in case.

6. The _____ is over; we won.

7. I don't like _____ and lightning during storms.

8. I went to a _____ match. Those guys are really strong!

a.

b.

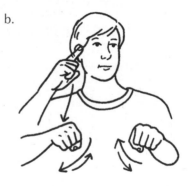

c.

d.

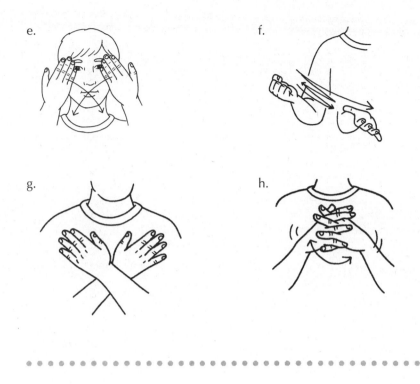

e.

f.

g.

h.

Chapter 13

Here's to Your Health

- -

In This Chapter

▶ Getting medical attention

▶ Using medical words

▶ Identifying body parts in Sign

▶ Managing emergencies in Sign

- -

*T*he medical field has many signs, and practicing them is fun. However, health and medicine are serious issues. Knowing the following medical signs doesn't automatically make you a medical interpreter, but that knowledge can go a long way in helping someone with an illness or emergency. In this chapter, we cover some of the main medical-related signs.

Going to the Doctor

Doctor visits ensure good health. In this section, we give you the signs to communicate successfully with medical personnel and tell them your symptoms. These signs are more helpful than an apple a day — try them and see.

Signaling medical personnel

The doctor is in! Table 13-1 shows the signs for various medical people.

Table 13-1		Medical Personnel	
English	*Sign*	*English*	*Sign*
CHIROPRACTOR		DENTIST	
DOCTOR		NURSE	
SPECIALIST		SURGEON	

The following sentences are sure to come in handy.

English: Do you need a nurse?
Sign: NURSE — NEED YOU Q

English: The doctor is in.
Sign: DOCTOR HERE

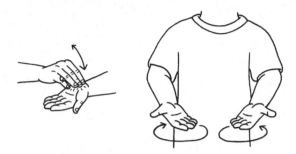

English: You need to see a chiropractor.
Sign: CHIROPRACTOR — GO — NEED YOU

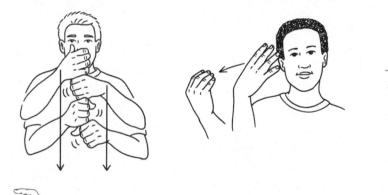

Figuring out how you feel

Knowing the signs for symptoms of an illness helps you figure out the best way to handle a medical problem. As with talking, signing is sometimes difficult when you don't feel well, but it's a necessary part of receiving help. The signs in Table 13-2 can take the sting out of communicating your problem.

Table 13-2		Feelings/Symptoms	
English	*Sign*	*English*	*Sign*
COLD		CONSCIOUS	
DIZZY		EARACHE	
HEADACHE		NAUSEA	
UNCONSCIOUS		TEMPERATURE	

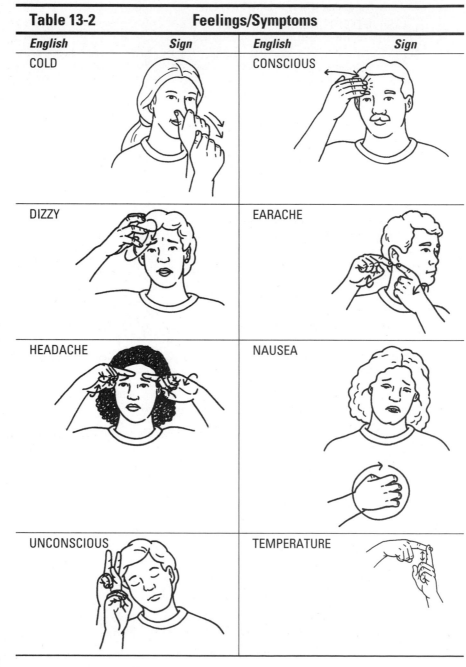

You sign **conscious** the same way as **know** and **familiar** or **aware**.

You sign **knocked out** as K-O. With your dominant hand, start the K handshape at eye level, with the O handshape ending at the side of your mouth. Complete the sign with your eyes closed while bending your head to the side or in front.

Feeling healthy, wealthy, and wise is great, but allow us to talk about the word *feel*. Sign **feel** by running your middle finger up your stomach, your chest, and outward. If you put your thumb up after signing feel, it means **feel good.**

FEEL

Expressing medical terms

Medical words are simple in Sign; they usually look like what they mean. For example, you sign **blood pressure** by making a C handshape with your dominant hand and then placing it on your arm muscle. You then mimic working a pump bulb. You sign **sutures** and **stitches** by mimicking that you're putting a needle in and out of the stitched area. Check out Table 13-3 to see for yourself.

Table 13-3		Medical Procedures	
English	*Sign*	*English*	*Sign*
BANDAGE		BLOOD PRESSURE	
DRAW BLOOD		INJECTION	

(continued)

Table 13-3 *(continued)*

English	Sign	English	Sign
SURGERY		SUTURE/ STITCH	
TEST		LIE DOWN	

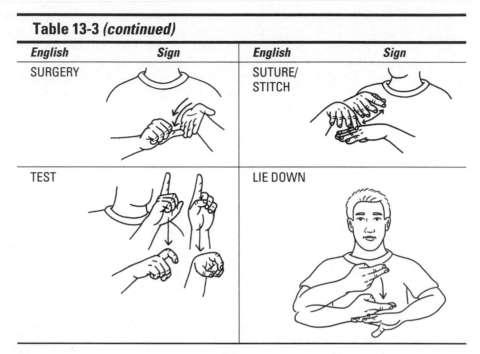

Some signs are similar in appearance. After you adjust to visually reading American Sign Language, you'll be comfortable in determining a sentence's context.

Try the following sentences for practice.

English: I need to check your blood pressure.
Sign: YOUR — BLOOD PRESSURE — CHECK — ME — MUST

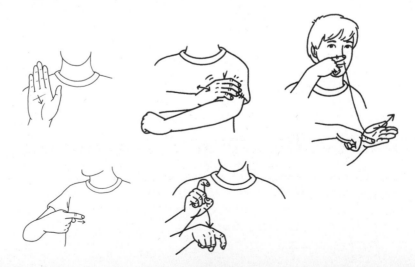

In ASL, you sign **I** and **me** the same way. Just point to yourself with your index finger.

English: He needs an injection.
Sign: INJECTION — NEED — HIM

English: How do I get blood drawn?
Sign: ME — BLOOD DRAWN — HOW Q

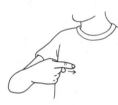

You fingerspell some medical terms, especially those that are abbreviations anyway. For example, you use the manual alphabet to sign **CPR, ER, OR, MRI, ICU, IV,** and **X-ray,** as well as the names of medications.

Describing Ailments and Treatments

The ailments in Table 13-4 are signs that many ASL users run into — that explains the bruises! Try these signs anyway.

Table 13-4		Ailments	
English	*Sign*	*English*	*Sign*
BREATHING PROBLEM (ASTHMA)		BRUISE	
COUGH		BROKEN BONE	
INFECTION		PAIN/HURT	
SICK/ DISEASE		SORE THROAT	

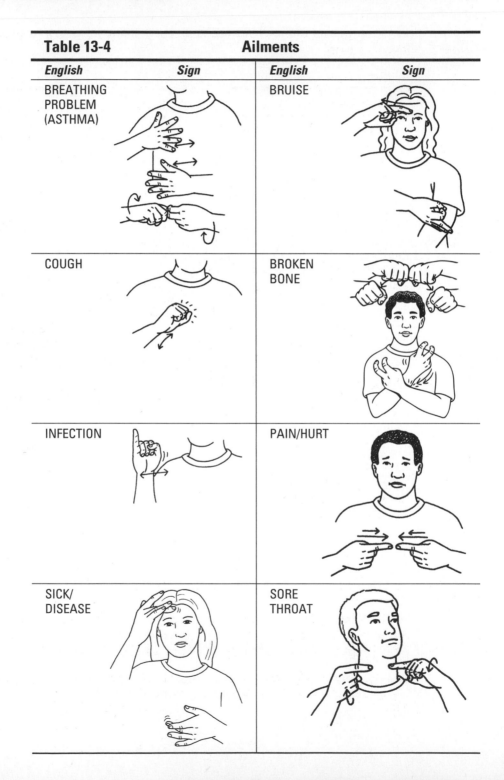

The signs in Table 13-5 are the perfect relief. Practice them and you'll feel a whole lot better!

Table 13-5		Remedies	
English	*Sign*	*English*	*Sign*
BED REST/ REST		CAST	
CRUTCHES		PRESCRIPTION	
WHEELCHAIR			

You sign **cast** by making the manual C handshape and placing it on your passive arm in a double sliding motion. If the cast is on a leg, point to the area. If it's a body cast, fingerspell B-O-D-Y C-A-S-T, or else you'll be pointing all day.

You sign **prescription** with the manual letters R-X and then a square with both index fingers starting at the top and meeting at the bottom — it means "slip."

If you're feeling up to it, try the following sentences.

English: She has an infection.
Sign: INFECTION — HAS — HER

English: Sit in the wheelchair.
Sign: WHEELCHAIR — SIT

English: You have a sprain.
Sign: SPRAIN — HAVE — YOU

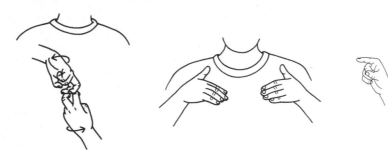

Pointing to Body Parts

If you're using ASL to describe ailments, it helps to be able to do more than point to the part that hurts, although in many cases, that's exactly how you sign different body parts. Tables 13-6, 13-7, and 13-8 illustrate the signs for body parts in three different groups. You sign most of the signs in these tables with a double motion; for example, for **ear,** tug twice on your earlobe.

Table 13-6		Parts of Your Head	
English	*Sign*	*English*	*Sign*
EAR		EYE	
HEAD		JAW	
MOUTH		NOSE	
THROAT		TEETH	

Table 13-7		Bendy Places: Joints		
English	*Sign*	*English*	*Sign*	

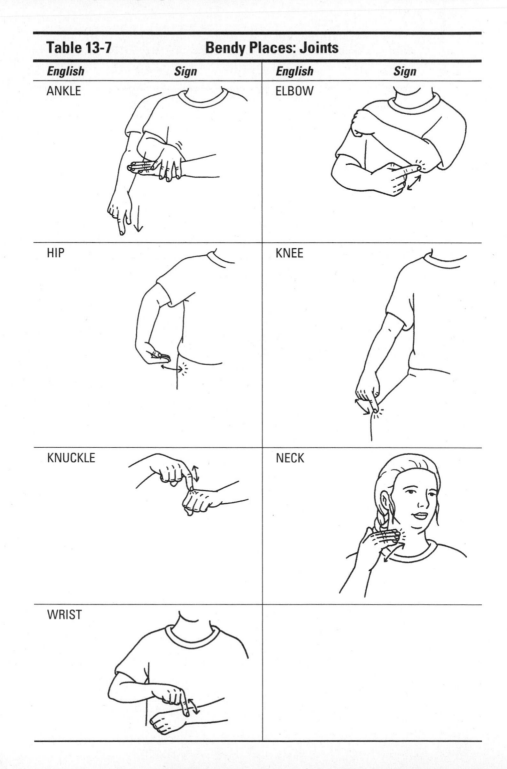

English	English
ANKLE	ELBOW
HIP	KNEE
KNUCKLE	NECK
WRIST	

Table 13-8		Larger Body Parts	
English	*Sign*	*English*	*Sign*
ARM		BUTTOCKS	
CHEST		FEET	
HAND		LEG	

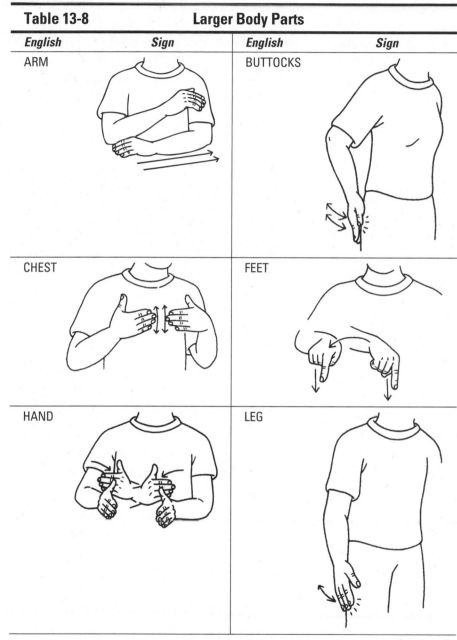

(continued)

Table 13-8 *(continued)*

English	Sign	English	Sign
STOMACH		TORSO/ TRUNK	

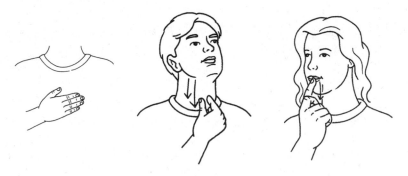

When you're not feeling that well, these sentences can help you get all the sympathy your hands can hold.

English: My throat is red.
Sign: MY THROAT — RED

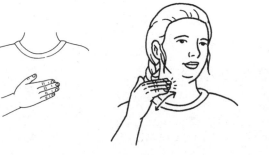

English: My neck is stiff.
Sign: MY NECK — STIFF

You sign **stiff** by using the same sign as **freeze.** With your hands in front of you, bend all your fingers slowly as if they're becoming frozen.

English: Can you cough?
Sign: COUGH — CAN YOU Q

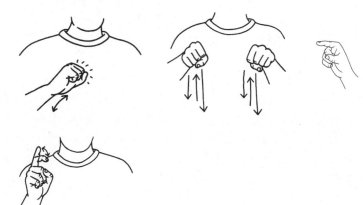

English: Her mouth is bleeding.
Sign: MOUTH BLEEDING — HER

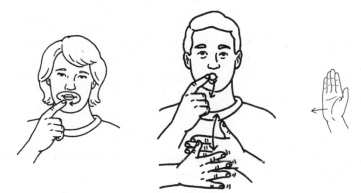

Handling Emergencies

Going to the hospital during an emergency is a scary thing. However, nothing is scary about these emergency-related signs (except having to use them). Table 13-9 may be your 9-1-1 when you need to help out in an emergency!

Table 13-9		Emergency Room Talk	
English	*Sign*	*English*	*Sign*
ADMIT/ ENTER	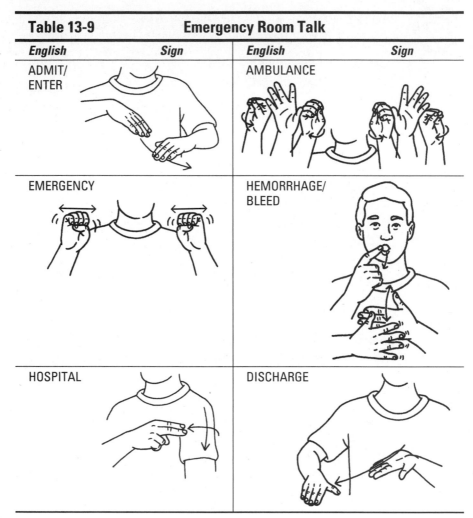	AMBULANCE	
EMERGENCY		HEMORRHAGE/ BLEED	
HOSPITAL		DISCHARGE	

Hemorrhage is the same sign as **bleed.** To sign bleed, move your dominant hand up and down rapidly. The faster you do it, the heavier the bleeding.

Signin' the Sign

Lily and George are going to the hospital; he is ill and needs medical attention. Read on and see how the story unfolds:

Lily: You need to get to the hospital.
Sign: HOSPITAL — GO — MUST YOU

 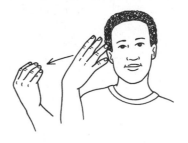

George: I'm dizzy and my stomach hurts.
Sign: DIZZY ME — STOMACH HURTS MINE

Lily: We'll go to the ER.
Sign: E-R — GO US — WILL

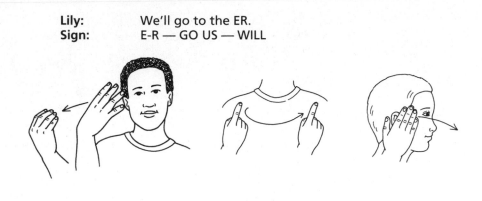

Fun & Games

· ·

This game focuses on signs that you're likely to need in a medical situation. Fill in the blank with the English word for each medical sign. The answers are in Appendix A if you need them.

1. Sit down when you're feeling _____.

2. Go to the _____ when you're sick.

3. Gargle when you have a sore _____.

4. Before the nurse _____, make a fist.

5. Don't eat or drink anything the night before _____.

6. When you break your arm, you'll need a _____.

7. A medical _____ needs immediate attention.

8. The doctor's _____ is usually his nurse.

1.

2.

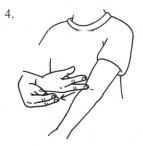

3.

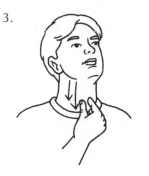

4.

5.

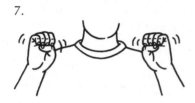

6.

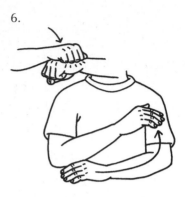

7.

8.

Part III
Looking into Deaf Life and Interpreting

The 5th Wave — By Rich Tennant

In this part . . .

These chapters allow you the opportunity to understand the Deaf experience through their history, their current challenges, and their view of themselves. You find out how to become an active member in the Deaf community by understanding Deaf culture and how Deaf people view the hearing world. Finally, you get the scoop on becoming an interpreter and talking with Deaf friends over the phone by using the latest technology.

Chapter 14

The Deaf Community and Deaf Etiquette

In This Chapter

▶ Viewing Sign through history

▶ Looking at the Deaf community and its culture

▶ Showing sensitivity to Deaf people

▶ Getting involved in the Deaf community

*Y*ou probably picked up this book because you want to find out how to sign and communicate with Deaf friends, family members, or colleagues. But there's more to the Deaf community than just American Sign Language (ASL). In this chapter, you find out the history of Sign, the challenges that Deaf people have faced both past and present, and what it means to live in two cultures and speak two languages. This information can help you better understand just what it means to be Deaf, which, in turn, can help you better communicate with the Deaf people you know.

Many people who can hear typically think Deaf people have a huge void in their lives because they can't hear. Nothing could be further from the truth. Even though Deaf people experience life a bit differently, they have a wonderful quality of life and enjoy the same things that hearing people do.

Digging into Sign's Past

The roots of ASL run fairly deep. Although early Greek writings refer to manual communication, no one knows whether those writings refer to just a few gestures or an actual alternative language using signs. Hippocrates studied deafness, and Socrates believed that it was a natural occurrence for Deaf people to communicate manually.

Juan Pablo Benet (1579–1629) wrote the first book, published in 1620, on how to teach Deaf people. He incorporated gestures, fingerspelling, writing, and speech.

You can find sign languages in every country throughout the world. Some countries, such as Canada and the United States, have similar sign languages, and their spoken languages are also similar. However, this isn't always the case. ASL is unique among the world's sign languages because it has had many influences and has influenced many sign languages of the world. This section explains the history of sign languages and the effect that these languages have had on the origins of ASL.

Exploring the two schools of thought on Deaf communication

Throughout history, people have attempted to teach Deaf people language. Many people believed that Deaf people would be enlightened by sound and speech reading. However, others — many of them Deaf — believed that manual communication was a more natural way to express ideas. Two schools of thought evolved regarding the communication methods of Deaf people:

✔ **Oralist method:** This method starts at childhood and relies on residual hearing, speech reading, and speech production in hopes of teaching verbal skills. In many cases, signing is forbidden. This school dates back to Europe. In Edinburgh, Scotland, the Briarwood Academy — perhaps the oldest oral school in Europe — emphasized speech; those who could afford it sent their children to this school. Their method of teaching was unknown because of their policy of secrecy. In the United States, oralists established themselves in the classroom after the Civil War. With the rebuilding of America, oralists wanted Deaf people to depend on speech rather than sign language.

Many forms of sign language, both early and modern, fall under the oralist method school of thought. This approach to sign language is closely tied to the spoken language of the land. When using the oralist method, the signed language adopts the properties of the spoken language. They share a common word order, and cultural implications and idioms are absent. In short, the signed language is a reflection of the spoken language.

Great Britain, Australia, and Russia are some of the countries that use oralist methods for communication. Efforts in the United States have had some success. Alexander Graham Bell was one of the American pioneers. His support of oralist methods of teaching gave credibility to oralism. His belief that Deaf children could learn to communicate verbally found a great deal of support from parents who wanted their Deaf children to speak. He was a contributor to schools that were established under this philosophy. A. G. Bell schools are well established in the United States even today.

✔ **Manualism:** Manualism, which emphasizes sign language over speech, dates back farther than oralism in the United States. It wasn't until the latter part of the 19th century that lip reading and speech were introduced into the classroom. Instructors of Deaf children believed that education should be done in sign language. Many of these instructors were religious people who believed that sign language was a gift from God. They believed that the oralists were depriving Deaf children of their natural language.

Examining when and how ASL began

Many people believe that ASL was strongly influenced by the work of Thomas Hopkins Gallaudet and Laurent Clerc in the early 1800s at the American Asylum in Hartford, Connecticut (see the nearby sidebar, "The origins of Deaf education").

Another influence of ASL's origin goes back long before the arrival of Gallaudet and Clerc. In the 17th century, Deaf people were living in the United States. They lived in their own communities on Martha's Vineyard and made their livings as farmers and fishermen. Most of these inhabitants were descendants of people who'd moved to America from England. Two hundred years later, their descendants were still living there and attending the American School for the Deaf under Clerc and Gallaudet. Many believe that the signs brought to America by these educators and the signs used by the Martha's Vineyard population are largely responsible for today's ASL.

The origins of Deaf education

Thomas Gallaudet (1787–1851) was a minister and an educator whose neighbor, Alice Cogswell, was a 9-year-old Deaf child. He traveled in Europe to study educational methods for teaching the Deaf. While in the British Isles, Gallaudet met Laurent Clerc and two of his companions, who invited him to France to study the educational methods of teaching the Deaf using manual communication. He sailed back to the United States with Clerc, and they raised money and established the American School for the Deaf in Hartford, Connecticut. Alice Cogswell was one of its first graduates.

ASL isn't related to English, although it borrows from English — as many spoken languages do. ASL has a word order that's different from English, and it has its own idioms, jokes, and poetry — all unrelated to English. People who support ASL believe that anything can be taught in ASL because it's a language guided by properties.

Sign is visually based. An object, such as a person, animal, or thing, needs to be understood by two parties before any information can be signed concerning the subject. Some people believe that this is the natural process for language. Many languages are based on this idea — it's the noun-verb rule. You need to name an object before you can discuss it.

Facing the Challenges of the Deaf Community

Through the years, Deaf people have had to face numerous challenges. In the past, they had little access to education and almost no opportunity for gainful employment. Although things have improved over time, Deaf people still face challenges. This section discusses challenges past and present and looks at how the Deaf community has made strides to overcome them.

Putting the past behind us

Sign language, like the Deaf people who use it, has had to fight for survival. Around the world, sign language — as well as those who communicate this way — has been viewed as lesser than languages of the hearing world. Many hearing people have dedicated themselves to changing the Deaf and their language.

For centuries, Deaf people had to undergo the treatment of being viewed as incomplete because of their absence of hearing. Some religious groups wanted to *save* Deaf people, while other groups wanted to *teach* them. Because of a lack of speech, Deaf people were viewed as deaf and dumb. This label, which Aristotle invented, has been attached to Deaf people since ancient Greece.

Deaf people have been associated with being demon-possessed because some of them can't speak. Because numerous biblical verses label Deaf people as dumb and/or mute, the Middle Ages — a dogmatic religious time — wasn't kind to them. Deaf individuals were hidden by family members, locked in asylums, or forced to try speaking, even though they couldn't hear themselves.

During World War II, Adolf Hitler's henchmen castrated Deaf men after they were locked up in concentration camps as part of various medical experiments.

Contemporary religious leaders have attempted to heal Deaf people of their "sickness" and accused them of lacking faith when miraculous hearing didn't happen.

Some people mock signing in front of Deaf people or tell them how sorry they are that they can't hear the birds singing or the phone ringing. Others are so rude as to talk about Deaf people right in front of them as though they aren't even there.

Many Deaf people and Deaf advocates have risen to challenge this oppression, and they seem to have been successful, because Deaf people are still signing to one another every day.

You've come a long way, baby

Although Deaf people are no longer viewed as being possessed by the devil, they still continue to face the challenges presented to them by a hearing world. Deaf people have fought for equal opportunities in education and employment and for cultural recognition, just to name a few things. Take a look at how the Deaf community has overcome modern obstacles.

The laws of the land

The Americans with Disabilities Act (ADA) has been a milestone, not only for Deaf people but for all Americans. Here's some basic information about the ADA. This isn't intended to be legal advice but general information. To find out more about the ADA, go on the Internet and search for "Americans with Disabilities."

- ✔ **Title I: Employment:** If 15 employees are deaf or disabled, the workplace must be modified to be accessible. For example, teletypes (TTY; see Chapter 16), ramps, and/or railings could be installed.

- ✔ **Title II: Public Services:** Programs, activities, and transportation can't discriminate against disabled people. Buses, taxis, and other public means of transportation need to accommodate the disabled population. Programs such as job training, educational classes, and other assistance to gainful employment must also be provided.

- ✔ **Title III: Public Accommodations:** All new construction of establishments such as hotels, grocery stores, retail stores, and restaurants are mandated to add physical assistance, such as ramps and railings.

✔ **Title IV: Telecommunications:** Telecommunication agencies that provide phone services must provide a relay service for TTY users.

✔ **Title V: Miscellaneous:** Prohibits any threats to disabled people or to persons assisting the disabled.

Getting classified as an "official" language

Although the Deaf population in the United States has had much progress through laws promoting civil equality and educational advancement of Deaf people, the road to total equality is still a long one. Not all states in America recognize ASL as an actual language.

The dispute over whether ASL is an actual language has been ongoing. Those who think that it should be considered a language often cite the following reasons:

✔ It syntactically contains properties like other languages, such as nouns, verbs, and adjectives.

✔ It maintains grammar rules that must be followed.

Presently, most states in the U.S. support this argument and recognize ASL as a foreign language. In addition, numerous colleges and universities offer credits for ASL as a foreign language.

On the other hand, many people don't buy the argument that ASL is a real language. Their argument goes like this:

✔ All countries, including the United States, use their own indigenous sign language. Therefore, if you were from Spain and traveled to Peru, your Spanish sign language wouldn't be compatible with Peruvian sign language, even though the hearing communities from both countries could speak Spanish and understand each other.

✔ At best, some countries, such as the United States, have had a profound impact educationally on other countries. Many foreign Deaf people come to the United States for schooling, and they take home many ASL signs.

Standardizing a sign language internationally has not happened with any one national sign language. However, a sign language system called International Sign Language (ISL), previously called *Gestuno,* is used at international Deaf events and conferences. It uses various signs from several national sign languages and was first used in the 1970s at the World Federation of the Deaf in Finland. To get more information about ISL, contact Gallaudet University.

Living and working as part of the silent minority

In a real sense, Deaf people living in the United States are a silent minority. Living in a world where one's language is known by few and understood by even fewer influences how Deaf people view themselves. (To categorize how Deaf people view themselves is too big a label to put on people who are individuals with various educational, economic, social, and deafness levels. Some people are more adaptable than others — in both the hearing and Deaf worlds.)

Being understood by few also influences Deaf people's feelings about how to exist as a people. This experience is often compared to living in a foreign country. Think about it: How would you feel if you were living in a foreign land where the language, customs, and culture weren't native to you? You'd probably go through each day with reluctance and uncertainty. You'd want to say what's appropriate, not something that would be viewed as ignorant. You'd feel frustrated when you wanted to state your opinion but couldn't make yourself understood. You'd feel isolated when everyone was laughing at a joke and you didn't understand the punch line. Deaf people often feel this way when they're surrounded by hearing people.

When speakers of a minority group come together, apart from the majority, they feel a certain sense of freedom to be able to speak — or sign — as fast as they want, and to converse, using idioms in their native language.

The Deaf as an Ethnic Group

Although Deaf people don't share a commonality of skin color, they share a common bond of culture. If culture is defined as shared knowledge, experience, language, beliefs, and customs, Deaf people are definitely an ethnic group.

This self-awareness of a Deaf ethnic group has only been in existence since the 20th century. Deaf pride has come from this identification. These people view themselves as whole people, not people with broken ears, as the label *hearing impaired* implies. When a person is culturally Deaf, he identifies and sometimes introduces himself as Deaf. To be a member of a Deaf community, the ability to communicate in ASL is a basic requirement.

Understanding Deaf culture

Just like any other culture, the Deaf community has its own customs, beliefs, and arts that are passed down from generation to generation. The culture of the Deaf community isn't arbitrary; it's a system of understandings and behaviors. This cultural group shares the characteristics of other cultural groups:

- The members share the commonalities of language and similar obstacles of daily life.

- The Deaf culture is based on a collective mind-set, not on an individual one. Many Deaf people feel a stronger tie to other Deaf people than to people who can hear.

- As Deaf people feel a strong bond to one another, they have a strong sense of cooperation.

- Deaf people come from all walks of life, from executives to construction workers, and as is true in English, those who are more educated than others are able to communicate more clearly by following the rules of their respective language.

- As with all cultures, time modifies and alters some aspects of the culture. This happens because culture is both learned and shared among a given group of people.

Culture teaches members of a community how they, as a people, respond to other ethnic groups and the world around them.

Knowing who falls into the Deaf cultural community

You may be thinking that the question of who fits into the Deaf community is a silly one — Deaf people, obviously! But the Deaf community includes these people, too:

- **Hearing people:** Those who can hear play important roles in the community of the Deaf as educators, ASL teachers, and interpreters for the Deaf. Many hearing people are also married to Deaf people or have Deaf children, making them part of the Deaf community.

- **Children of Deaf Adults (CODAs):** We say "children" because of the acronym, but obviously the term simply means people who have Deaf parents.

Living as bilingual/bicultural people

To be successful members of society, Deaf people have to be able to live and communicate in both the Deaf and the hearing worlds. They have to be comfortable navigating between the two — in other words, they have to be bilingual and bicultural. Proving that Deaf people can live as a bilingual, bicultural people, more Deaf people are attending college and working in white-collar jobs, and more interpreter training programs, which have Deaf instructors, are being established. Read the following examples to see this dual culture in action.

✔ Many Deaf people have felt the burden of not having the spiritual satisfaction that people desire because most churches don't have anyone who knows Sign to interpret and minister to a Deaf member of the congregation. Today, however, many Deaf people are going into the ministry and leading their own Deaf congregations. Many hearing ministries are also learning ASL.

The Los Angeles Church of Christ's evangelist, Ron Hammer, learned Sign from Deaf members of the church. He trained these members in leadership, and the interpreters began an interpreter-training program inside the church. Today, the Deaf membership of that church has increased dramatically to become one of the largest Deaf congregational regions in Los Angeles.

We should note that many Deaf people prefer to attend an all-Deaf church. The sermons and testimonials in these churches are in Sign, and interpreters aren't needed.

✔ Because Deaf people and hearing people share common interests and topics of conversation, they can use these commonalities to communicate and become closer. When a Deaf person is with his Deaf friends, he may talk about Deaf schools, but he can just as easily converse with a colleague at work about schools in general.

Topics such as the weather, sports, food, and entertainment are all popular (and are all discussed in various chapters of this book) with Deaf people as well as the hearing. Even topics that at first seem unique to the Deaf community are really similar to topics that are discussed by hearing people. For instance, Deaf people often discuss the nuances of ASL and "play on signs." Hearing people do the same when they play on words, making jokes and puns. Deaf people often converse about schools for the Deaf, discussing which ones they attended and their similar experiences with dorm life and residential supervision. Hearing people also talk about where they went to school, what they majored in, what dorm life was like, and so on.

✔ Politics is a topic of Deaf conversation, the same as with hearing people. Deaf people also try to make sense of political affairs as they, too, have family members who are in the military in these troubled times.

✔ Deaf people also enjoy the company of significant others. Conversations about dates, marriage, disagreements, and making up are topics most people, Deaf and hearing, have in common. Problems and solutions in relationships cross all cultural and linguistic barriers.

Sign language is not the same around the world. All countries have their own sign language. Interestingly, when two Deaf people meet and are from different countries, they have a higher chance of understanding each other as compared to two hearing foreigners who meet. Deaf people are used to being misunderstood or not understood at all and have to make extra efforts to get their point across.

Being Sensitive to Being Deaf

Being sensitive to Deaf people is a part of Deaf etiquette that's really for the hearing. Deaf people already know what it means to be Deaf, but those who can hear probably never think about the day-to-day struggles that the Deaf have to overcome in this world.

Getting close to a Deaf person requires a little vulnerability on both sides. Many Deaf people are just as insecure about not being understood as you are, but most of them are patient and incredibly skilled at getting their point across to you. Like all people, the Deaf come from all walks of life. Deaf men and women have the same careers that hearing people do — they're doctors, lawyers, teachers, homemakers, construction workers, and so on.

Living together in a hearing world

Here are some tips and hints to keep in mind when interacting with Deaf people:

✔ As your signing progresses, a Deaf person may ask if your parents are Deaf. This is a high compliment about your signing. It doesn't mean that you're fluent in ASL, but it does mean that your signing or facial expressions have characteristics of being influenced by someone who's a native signer.

✔ When visiting Deaf people, don't assume that you can just walk into the house because they can't hear the doorbell. Deaf people have strobe lights that are connected to the doorbell and the phone.

✔ If you're out having a meal with a Deaf person, don't feel obligated to order for the person unless you're asked, even if it's just to practice your Sign. Deaf people have been eating in restaurants longer than you've been friends, and they're accustomed to pointing to an item on the menu for the server.

✔ As you learn more signs, do your best to sign when you're talking with your hearing friends and a Deaf person joins the conversation. Signing what you're saying may be difficult, but you'll be able to do it in time with practice, and doing so helps the Deaf person feel included if he or she knows what you're saying.

Getting the Deaf perspective

After reading this book, no doubt you see that knowing Sign is just one piece (albeit a large one) of the puzzle to understanding the Deaf community. To really get a grasp on Deaf etiquette and culture, you have to get involved with the Deaf community. One sure way to get involved is to take an introductory ASL course from a Deaf instructor. Although you can find some awesome Sign instructors who can hear, a Deaf Sign instructor can teach from the Deaf perspective and is most likely a native signer.

An introductory class gives you exposure to signs, interaction with others and, hopefully, an opportunity to learn from Deaf guest speakers. You also get an understanding of the many signing styles that different people possess. An instructor can guide you as to where Deaf activities are taking place, who Deaf community leaders may be, and issues concerning the local community. Consider this class to be a segue to the Deaf community.

Participating in the Deaf Community

We can say a lot about the subject of participation in the Deaf community. A good rule to follow is, "When in Rome, do as the Romans do." In other words, when you're with Deaf people, respect their customs; what you don't know, you can figure out by observation and through asking questions. Basically, just watch and learn. Some of the things you may notice include the following:

✔ **A sense of unity:** Depending on the size of the Deaf community, Deaf people congregate at activities such as bowling leagues, Deaf clubs, Deaf plays, and fundraisers. In Los Angeles, the Deaf community is very large. Subgroups inside the community consist of Russians, Chinese, Italians, Hispanics, Jews, and many others. Each of these groups has its own respective traditions, customs, and celebrations. As a whole community, they come together for events such as the Lotus Festival, Deaf West Theater, and Deaf Awareness Month.

✔ **ASL pride:** Deaf people speak of ASL quite often in conversations. You may attend plays and parties where ASL is the main topic. The Deaf community is very proud and protective of this language, so it's often a hot topic.

✔ **Signing speed:** When you watch Deaf people in conversation and you can't understand anything that's signed, don't lose heart. Novice signers often don't understand Deaf nuances and abbreviations, and they often have a hard time keeping up. Stay with ASL; before you know it, you'll be signing like a pro.

And, just so you know, few things are more volatile in the Deaf world than a hearing person who, having taken a semester or two of ASL classes, proceeds to lecture a Deaf person because he or she doesn't sign the way the teacher instructed.

Finding your place in the Deaf community

As you find yourself with phone numbers of Deaf friends and invitations to Deaf socials, you'll be well on your way to being a constant student of ASL. Like everyone who studies, learning new ways of signing ideas will be commonplace. The possibility of going to school to professionally hone your skill and take classes in Sign may be an endeavor you soon realize.

Many people have no deafness in their families and learn ASL and Deaf culture at a rudimentary level. Time takes care of the rest as it gives way to proficiency through practice.

Some people have Deaf siblings or Deaf parents and know ASL through this avenue and understand Deaf culture because of them. These people have had deafness in their lives from the beginning.

All people who enter the Deaf world face a certain dynamic. Think of the dynamic as a bull's eye (see Figure 14-1). At the center is the core Deaf community leaders; these are the movers and shakers of the Deaf world. The next ring is the Deaf community as a whole. The next ring are Children of Deaf Adults, or CODAs, who are hearing people who choose to become interpreters. Following them are interpreters who have no Deafness in their respective families. On the outer ring are those who provide services to the Deaf community members but still have the ability to sign. These are teachers of the Deaf and can hear — vocational rehabilitation counselors, teachers at Deaf schools, and professional workers who provide services for the Deaf.

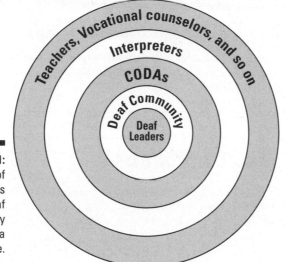

Teachers, Vocational counselors, and so on

Interpreters

CODAs

Deaf Community

Deaf Leaders

Figure 14-1:
Think of
the layers
of the Deaf
community
like a
bull's eye.

Communicating with new Deaf friends for the first time

Joining the Deaf community is not something that anyone can just decide to do. Attending your first Deaf function with the Deaf person who invited you is appropriate. Attending a Deaf social without first receiving an invitation is never a good idea. As you arrive, your host, the one who invited you, will introduce you to his or her friends, explain how you know each other, and mention that you're learning ASL. Saying both your first and last name is customary, and a good rule of thumb is to let people know that you can hear and that you're learning Sign. They'll know this already by watching your lack of fluidity in the language; however, through this admittance and vulnerability, bonds of trust are made.

As you walk through the social, you'll notice Deaf people signing in fluent ASL, but when they see you approaching, they'll revert to signing in an English word order while using their voices. They do this to accommodate you. They already know that you can't keep up with their pace or fluency, and they change their modes of communication to make sure you can understand the conversation. This is called *code switching*. After you depart from the conversation, you'll notice that the Deaf people will go back to turning off their voices and will converse in proper ASL. Don't take this personally as an offense. The gesture of using more English by the Deaf folks for your benefit — code switching — is something that all hearing people experience when they attend Deaf socials for the first time.

Someone's in the kitchen with Dinah

At social gatherings in someone's home, it's not uncommon for everyone to gather around the kitchen table. They do this because kitchens typically have good lighting, allowing everyone to see the signs clearly.

Questions you shouldn't ask

Never initiate a conversation about a Deaf person's hearing loss. Questioning someone about this implies that you don't view that person as whole, but broken, incomplete, or inferior. You'll find that the Deaf are comfortable talking about their hearing aids, batteries that need replaced, and ear molds, but it's best if you leave this subject to the individual who is Deaf. If you view a Deaf person with equality and respect, the hearing loss won't become a subject of any great importance. Often, as you become better friends, your questions will get answered in a passing conversation.

Just to satisfy your immediate curiosity, most Deaf people do not have a total hearing loss. They usually have what's called *residual hearing,* hearing that remains after deafness occurs, either at birth, after an illness or accident, or because of age. Deaf people have varying degrees of deafness; some are more profoundly deaf than others, so some Deaf people can speak clearly while others can't.

In your time with the Deaf, make it a growing experience; you're encountering a people with a rich history, a proud people with a bond of community. You aren't the first person to want to know their language, and you won't be the last.

Chapter 15

Interpreting: Are You Interested?

· ·

In This Chapter

▶ Seeing what kind of interpreting jobs are available

▶ Taking interpreting classes and getting other training

▶ Checking out certificate programs

▶ Choosing to work alone or with an agency

▶ Following the Code of Professional Conduct

▶ Honing your ASL and English skills

· ·

*1*t's not uncommon to go to a presentation and see an American Sign Language interpreter in the front, signing to Deaf audience members who came to see a speaker. Everyone's eyes tend to gravitate to the interpreter. Interpreters are fascinating to watch; what they do isn't something you see on a daily basis. Most folks are amazed that people actually understand all this gesticulation as a language.

This chapter provides information about the profession of ASL interpreting. I tell you how to train to become an interpreter, how to find work, and where *not* to interpret. Signing is fun, but signing and interpreting aren't the same thing. Interpreting isn't for everyone, and for those who do enter the field, it's done out of passion for the profession.

Knowing Where Interpreters Are Needed

The profession of interpreting isn't limited to one setting type, although you've probably seen interpreters in church, sitting up front with Deaf congregants watching. The profession follows Deaf people in their daily, weekly, and yearly activities. You can find interpreters in all sorts of places — on Deaf cruises to the Bahamas and Alaska, on game shows, at political rallies, and in classrooms.

Different establishments and settings have different rules, and it's always wise to find out this information prior to agreeing to accept an assignment. Some businesses pay biweekly and some pay monthly. You may be expected to pass a drug test and a background check (including fingerprinting), especially if you're interpreting in school settings, in military settings, or for companies that deal in sensitive information. And not every interpreter is comfortable in every environment. For example, psychiatric interpreting at a hospital or an institution has the potential to be emotionally taxing and isn't for everyone.

Here are some interpreting settings you may want to consider:

- Churches
- Colleges and universities
- Hospitals
- Mental health settings
- Military bases
- Residential schools for the Deaf
- School districts
- Social Security offices
- Social services
- Video relay service (VRS)
- Vocational rehabilitation

Most churches have interpreters who volunteer their services (though some churches do hire interpreters). If your church needs volunteer interpreters, this is a good place to meet Deaf people and hone your signing skills, as Deaf congregants will help you along.

Being wary of legal interpreting

Legal interpreting isn't just something you can do because you've honed your skills or are newly certified; legal interpreting requires special training. Your state may or may not require special certification, such as a Specialist Certificate: Legal (SC: L), but either way, it's best to leave this setting to those veteran interpreters who are specially trained for this environment. Even if someone in the court system invites you to interpret in a courtroom setting, refer the person to a list of qualified legal interpreters kept by the county court clerk or to a local interpreting agency. In some states you can be subpoenaed and must give an account of your rendered court work; novice interpreters aren't prepared for this. The bottom line on legal interpreting: Don't go there.

Getting the Proper Training with Interpreting Classes

As far as training goes, the first thing to consider is taking classes for interpreting. Some interpreters haven't taken any classes and have simply taken the test sanctioned by the Registry of Interpreters for the Deaf (RID) and received their certification. Although the fast track of skipping classes, taking the test, getting certified, and starting to work in the field may save you time, it is highly recommended that you take classes on interpreting. There's nothing like a solid foundation.

Sign language classes are offered in two-year programs. These two-year programs for studying to become an interpreter are called *Interpreter Preparation Programs* (IPP) or *Interpreter Training Programs* (ITP). The cost for these programs varies depending on the school. You don't have to be fluent in ASL before taking these classes. (However, if you have a degree of fluency but lack a solid educational foundation, talk to the instructors of the mentioned programs; their advice will be invaluable.)

In these classes you learn vocabulary, the history of the field of interpreting, the various strategies for interpreting, the history of deafness, and the implications of Deaf culture. You finish with a practicum and preparations for testing to become certified as a professional interpreter.

Upon completion of one of these programs, you receive a certificate. However, this certificate isn't the same thing as *certification* awarded by RID. See the upcoming section, "Certifying Your Success," for more on obtaining RID certification, as well as additional certifications.

Certifying Your Success

A certification that's sanctioned by RID is a lofty goal. To possess a RID certification, you must pass the RID certification test, which is comprised of a written exam and signing test.

In order to qualify to take the certification test, you must meet the following minimum requirements:

✔ Be at least 18 years of age

✔ Be able to hear (you can't be Deaf)

✔ Possess a bachelor's degree in any field (new regulation as of July 1, 2012)

When you're ready to take the certification test, contact RID through its website (www.rid.org) to set up a testing date and to pay the testing fee. You'll receive all necessary instructions through RID.

After passing both portions of the testing process, you'll receive your certification in the mail — a certificate for your wall and a card with your membership number for your wallet. You will also receive specific instructions for maintaining your certification, which will include attending professional development activities where *Continuing Educational Units* (CEUs) are offered. For more information, go to RID.org.

The RID offers numerous certifications. The following list contains certifications that are currently available, as well as ones that are no longer available but that are still honored by RID and that you may come across as you mix and mingle with veteran interpreters:

- **Nationalist Interpreting Certification:** This certification has three levels: NIC, NIC Advanced, and NIC Master. You must pass both a written examination and a performance examination to be awarded one of these certifications. Each level requires higher levels of proficiency. (***Note:*** This test is currently being revamped, and the testing procedure may be changed.)

- **Certification of Interpreting and Certification of Transliteration (CI/CT):** These certifications are no longer available for testing.

- **Comprehensive Skills Certificate (CSC):** No longer available for testing.

- **Master Comprehensive Skills Certificate (MCSC):** No longer available for testing.

- **Oral Transliteration Certificate (OTC):** You have to pass a written examination and a Sign performance examination to get this certificate. It's designed to show that a person satisfies the minimum requirements to work with people who rely on gestures, English, and lip reading, not so much on Sign.

- **Educational Interpreter Performance Assessment (EIPA):** This credential is honored in many states, and more states are adopting it as a standard for qualified educational interpreters. This certification is for educational interpreting only and isn't honored for community interpreting. It's designed for interpreters who work in a K–12 educational setting. You must pass a written component and a two-part performance evaluation. One part is based on receptive skills — how proficiently you can read the signing of a minor in an academic setting. The other part is based on expressive skills — how proficiently you can expressively interpret to a minor in an academic setting. For more information, go to www.classroominterpeting.org.

✔ **Reverse Skills Certificate (RSC):** This certificate was for Deaf individuals who work with hearing interpreters; the certificate was replaced by the CDI certificate and is no longer available.

✔ **Certified Deaf Interpreter (CDI):** This certification is for Deaf people only. These individuals help interpreters on assignment when the Deaf client is a juvenile, is elderly and hard to understand, suffers from a debilitating disease that affects the hands, has limited language skills, or is a foreign Deaf person and has limited knowledge of ASL.

After you're certified and ready to start interpreting, get business cards made with your name, certification, e-mail address, and phone number to help you network throughout your community.

Working for an Interpreting Agency

If you work through an agency or a school district, you'll work with an interpreter coordinator or a scheduler who will decide where your services are needed and who can intervene if you have professional issues that need to be resolved. If you hire yourself out and bypass an interpreting agency, you take on these responsibilities yourself.

Your best bet is to work with an agency when you're first getting started. Doing so helps you learn the ins and outs of the profession: when to invoice, how to invoice, how much to invoice, what to do if a client doesn't show up to the assignment, what to do if the client isn't satisfied with your performance, and so on. The agency will intervene on your behalf. Even veteran interpreters find benefits to working through an agency.

If you work for an interpreting agency, it may give you its business cards to distribute to first-time clients, as you are representing the agency on a given assignment. Be sure to give the agency's contact information in these instances, not your own. The client is the agency's client, and providing your personal business card instead of the agency's business card can be viewed as undermining the agency and its clientele. It's a trust issue; prove yourself trustworthy and professional.

Some veteran interpreters opt to freelance. They represent themselves as independent contractors for an agency rather than as subcontractors or staff interpreters. If you choose to be a freelance interpreter, keep in mind that you'll be responsible for maintaining your own tax deductions and records. It's also a good idea to register your *trade name* with the state where you reside. This is also called your "doing business as" name. You'll receive an *Employee Identification Number* (EIN), which you'll use on all your invoices and any other documentation in lieu of your Social Security number.

As you make your way into the world of interpreting, consider interpreters liability insurance. Although many interpreters don't carry it, some agencies require that you do. This is another reason to take classes on professional interpreting; your instructor can explain the rationale for having liability insurance for your work.

Regardless of where you work, try your best to meet other interpreters so that you can build a network and learn from others' expertise. You can find these professionals at state conferences and workshops for interpreters.

Abiding by the Code of Professional Conduct

The field of interpreting has a Code of Professional Conduct (CPC) set up for the appropriate professional behavior of ASL interpreters. Once called the Code of Ethics, the CPC is designed to ensure a high-quality service, maintain professionalism, and protect Deaf clients by guaranteeing the confidentiality of their personal information. All interpreters are required to know and abide by the CPC.

Following are the main tenets of the CPC (the RID website has a more detailed description):

- Interpreters must adhere to confidentiality.

- Interpreters must possess the knowledge and skills for each assignment.

- Interpreters must conduct themselves in a professional manner appropriate for any and all situations.

- Interpreters must demonstrate respect for the Deaf client.

- Interpreters must show respect for all colleagues, interns, and students of the profession.

- Interpreters must maintain ethical practices in business.

- Interpreters must continually strive for professional development.

Your certification is a guarantee to clients that you won't share any of their information or anything about the assignment where you interpreted for them. By breaking this confidentiality, you undermine the profession that all the other interpreters have made great strides to maintain. Even worse, you can develop a reputation among the Deaf community as someone who can't be trusted, and finding work may be difficult — it's that serious.

A business that solicits your skills pays you, trusts you, and assumes that you'll provide a high-quality service and represent the profession accordingly. Therefore, don't express your religious or political views while on assignment. You're hired to be neutral on all points.

Balancing Two Languages and Honing Your Skills

Going between two languages when interpreting — spoken English and ASL — is an exercise in mental gymnastics. Different situations have different registers: formal, informal, intimate, or casual. Also, you must take into account cultural considerations, nuances, and regional signs as you interpret.

You want to strive to always better your knowledge in both languages. Something as simple as going through an English dictionary and reviewing words is helpful. With today's technology, you can download a dictionary application on your phone and look up unfamiliar words or words whose meaning you've always assumed. This is a fast and simple way to review not just word meanings but also synonyms, homonyms, and spelling.

As for expanding your Sign vocabulary, discussing Sign with other interpreters and observing Deaf people as they sign are great ways to learn new terminology and see the terminology in context. Workshops, classes, and books on Deaf culture are also good ways to increase your knowledge on the subject. Remember, all languages are tied to a respective culture, so if you increase your understanding of a language, you may gain a better understanding of its culture.

Chapter 16

Using Technology to Communicate

In This Chapter

▶ Tapping the power of videophones

▶ Using a video relay service

▶ Trying other forms of communication

*A*t one time, Deaf people depended on the hearing world to help them place phone calls when the need arose. They had to use an interpreter, who stood in front of them and interpreted any and all information that the Deaf person required. Later on, the Deaf community could use a teletype machine, or TTY, to communicate information through an operator who had good typing skills but knew nothing of deafness, American Sign Language, or the role of an interpreter. Through the advancement of technology, however, Deaf people now have several options for communicating with friends, family, and business contacts (both Deaf and hearing), whether they're at home or out and about.

In this chapter, we acquaint you with the latest communication devices, such as videophones, that the Deaf community uses.

Can You See Me Now? Using Videophones

The videophone has replaced the TTY for talking to friends and family, making appointments, and attending to daily business needs. To set up a videophone, you generally need a computer, a webcam, and a phone service provider. Some videophones are available in hand-held models.

Videophone technology changes rapidly, so it's best to read up on videophones on the Internet to see what kind of phone and service would best fit your needs. In many cases, a videophone is free for Deaf people. Start your search at www.sorensonvrs.com.

Several companies provide videophones. These companies have their own equipment, technicians, and procedures for how they govern their operations. Any agency that operates a video relay service (VRS) must follow the Federal Communications Commission (FCC) guidelines for how it conducts its business.

Communicating with videophones

Deaf people can communicate using the videophone in one of two ways:

- **Communicating directly:** If two people have videophones, they can communicate directly with each other. Many Deaf people have videophones, so if Deaf friends want to talk to each other, they can just call without having to use any kind of relay service.

  The system can have glitches — the camera may freeze, a disconnection may occur, or the picture may not be as clear as it should be. These problems may be common, but they also happen when hearing people communicate with each other on any phone system or on a video device as well.

- **Communicating via a relay interpreter:** If a hearing person doesn't have a videophone but wants to talk to a Deaf person, the two of them need an interpreter who has the same device.

  These relay interpreters work for one of several companies that provide telecommunication services. To work for one of these businesses, an interpreter needs to be nationally certified to show that she has satisfied the minimum requirements of ASL competency. This requires being able to understand what a Deaf person is signing and to sign to the Deaf person what the hearing person is saying.

If two Deaf people want to converse but only one has a videophone, it's not uncommon for the person without the videophone to use one at the local library, a friend's home, or any agency that has a videophone. In short, two people must both have videophones to make contact to visually communicate.

However, a Deaf person can also use a TTY to call a videophone (for more on the TTY, see the nearby sidebar). The TTY caller dials the operator through a designated phone number, and the TTY operator calls the video relay service. The relay interpreter then contacts the Deaf person who has the videophone. This is a four way conversation: the Deaf person using the TTY, the TTY operator, the relay interpreter, and the Deaf caller on the videophone.

Hanging up the TTY

The TTY, or *teletype,* is becoming obsolete with the winds of technology. At one time, Deaf people held these devices in high esteem because they allowed the Deaf community to make calls and reach out to the world outside of their door. These machines were originally oversized boxes that would generate a text conversation between individuals. However, over time, they became portable, making it more convenient for Deaf people to transport and use them, provided a telephone was available. The Deaf community was thankful for this technology, but it wasn't enough. For one thing, the text was based in English. As you know from this book, American Sign Language is a completely different language, so the TTY required Deaf people to communicate all matters in a second language, whether or not they were fluent in English.

The functionality of the TTY was really quite simple: The Deaf person would place the phone's receiver on the TTY cradle and call an operator who also had a TTY. The Deaf person would tell the operator what number he wanted to call, and the operator would call it. The Deaf person would then communicate by typing, and the operator would read the words to the hearing person on the other line. The process worked in reverse for the hearing person to communicate with the Deaf person. This process was arduous and quite time-consuming. However, the TTY was an important precursor to the videophone.

What to expect when using a video relay service

Using a video relay service is pretty simple. A person calls the VRS, and the interpreter connects the call. When the other person answers, the interpreter notifies that person of the call and begins the interpreting process.

Keep in mind that this is a video relay, and the Deaf person and the interpreter can see each other. Because the process involves two modes of language — one verbal and one visual — there's a slight time delay to go from one language to the other.

The interpreter will speak as though she's the person on the other end of the line, so although it may feel strange at first, respond to the interpreter that way. Don't ask the interpreter to tell your friend something; just tell your friend, and the interpreter will take care of signing it for you. In a nutshell, act like the interpreter isn't there and talk directly to your party.

Being a video relay interpreter has several benefits: You get a lot of signing and voice practice, and you can pick up a lot of work year-round. For more on becoming an interpreter, flip to Chapter 15.

Don't get confused. The terms *operator* and *interpreter* are often used interchangeably on video relay; the relay interpreter/operator knows ASL, but a TTY operator is an operator who doesn't sign.

Keeping conversations private

A VRS interpreter who's certified by the Registry of Interpreters for the Deaf (RID) must abide by the Code of Professional Conduct. The most important part of the RID Code is the need to keep information confidential. This is a trust issue, and all Sign interpreters doing any type of interpreting work must follow the Code. So an interpreter can't repeat information obtained during an assignment (each videophone call is considered an assignment).

If an interpreter violates this trust, the violation may be reported to the RID in the form of a grievance. The RID takes this type of complaint very seriously.

Utilizing Other Communication Methods

Today, Deaf people can communicate with other Deaf people (and with hearing people as well) in numerous ways. With Skype, Fring, and other mobile applications, Deaf people are no longer tied to primarily using a VRS.

Texting 24/7

Today, many Deaf people use texting for everyday communication. Mobile phones are small and compact, which makes them easy to carry. Deaf people can text throughout the day to anyone who has the same capability. With this technology, Deaf people can send not only text messages but also photos and video clips.

Telecommunication businesses that sell phones and phone services have the capability to offer communication applications that allow Deaf people and hearing people to use video to communicate. Ask your phone company about this capability or just look through your phone applications.

Chatting visually

Deaf people can often communicate through text, e-mails, or even a fax, but these are still English-based modes and not the primary language of Deaf people. Deaf people welcome communication devices that are visually based and allow them the opportunity to communicate in Sign. The following are two means of technology that many members of the Deaf community use for their daily lives:

✔ **Fring** (which sounds like *spring*) is an application that can be downloaded to most phones from a phone service provider. Fring allows you to chat with your friends and family on your phone instead of your desktop computer or laptop computer. Fring will allow you to have a live chat, a video call, or a voice call. This application is capable of handling Sign chats, so it's Deaf user-friendly, but it can be used by hearing and Deaf alike. Go to www.fring.com to find out more about this application.

✔ **Skype** is a software program that allows users to see each other to communicate anywhere in the world. Communication can take place in spoken English or in Sign. With an Internet connection and a monitor, you can get Skype from your computer to chat with anyone. Deaf people can use Skype like a videophone without an interpreter. Skype can also be accessed through some televisions and mobile phones. By going to www.skype.com, you can learn more about this excellent communication feature.

Part IV
The Part of Tens

The 5th Wave   By Rich Tennant

"One of us has to tell her to put down the garden hose while she's signing."

In this part . . .

This part gives you tips on how to sign like a pro and how to pick up American Sign Language quickly. The book's final chapter sends you off with some popular expressions among Deaf people.

Chapter 17

Ten Tips to Help You Sign like a Pro

In This Chapter

▶ Practicing your signing and closely observing other signers

▶ Keeping a journal of your success

▶ Paying attention to facial expressions

*T*his chapter is all about providing you with ideas to practice and polish your signing skills. So if you're reading this, you're on the right track.

Watch Yourself and Others Sign

Watching yourself sign while standing in front of a mirror helps you see what others see when you sign. Watching interpreters lets you see how they make facial expressions and how they use signs in context. Watching others sign also gives you the opportunity to *read* how they sign. Try making a video of yourself signing and then playing it back. You can be your own best critic.

Discover Multiple Signs for Communicating One Thing

You can sign one thing in many different ways. The more ways you know, the more versatile you'll be. Even if a particular sign doesn't suit you, someone else may use it, so it's helpful to know it. For example, you can sign **do** in a number of ways. Ask a person who's been signing for a few years to show them to you.

Practice Your Signing — with Others

There's no substitute for practice. Use your time wisely by taking every opportunity to ask questions and fingerspell every advertisement sign. And go out of your way to meet as many Deaf people as possible. Sure, having a formal education in American Sign Language makes you a better signer, but practicing your skills with the Deaf person on the street can teach you things that a formal education can't.

Always Fingerspell a Name First

Name signs serve as identification and were originally used to talk about someone when the person wasn't present. The Deaf community — not hearing folks — gives name signs, which may be based on a person's initials, physical characteristics, or personality traits. However, a person's name must be established before you can use his name sign or talk about him. If you don't fingerspell a person's name first, you'll only cause confusion as to whom you mean.

Adjust Your Eyes; Everyone's Signing Is Different

Personalities tend to come out in Sign, just as they do in English. Some people talk fast and sign fast, and others want to give you all the details. Just as no two people talk alike, no two signers sign alike. By being open to the different ways that people sign, you can grow to understand the variety of signing styles as easily as you can understand most English speakers in the United States.

Use Facial Expressions like Vocal Inflections

Imagine talking without any high or low pitches — speaking only in a monotone, with few clues to emphasize your point. Your conversation would be boring and hard to understand. The same holds true when you sign. If you sign about someone being angry, look angry! If you want to convey your joy, you need to show that joy, and if something scary happened to you, look scared! As a general rule, the clearest facial expression is an authentic one. You achieve this by practicing actual expressions: Put on a big smile for joy, frown when you want to show sadness or unhappiness, and frown and scrunch your eyebrows together to convey a feeling of anger.

Journal Your Progress

Keeping track of your linguistic experiences — the good and the bad, the conflicts and resolutions — helps you map your progress and remember the ins and outs of Deaf culture. In your journal, maintain a separate section of terms and the various ways of signing different concepts; that helps you compare the similarities and differences among terms and concepts, expand your vocabulary, and see the bigger picture of the Deaf world. Sharing your journal with a certain Deaf person whose signing abilities you aspire to imitate is a great compliment to the person. But make sure you change the names in the conflicts and resolutions part to protect the innocent!

Get Some Signing Space

Signing and talking affect where you sit or stand. Because signing is manual, give signers a little room to converse. If you need privacy, go somewhere private to have your conversation. And make sure that you don't stand with bright light or the sun directly behind you, because whoever is watching you sign will only see your silhouette — a big giveaway that you're just a beginner.

Because ASL is a physical language, two signers having a conversation need more space than hearing people do. Also, walking right between two people who are signing is perfectly acceptable in the Deaf world; you don't need to say "excuse me."

Don't Jump the Gun

Sometimes, when you're watching someone sign, you may lose that person and not understand her meaning. Don't lose heart. Try to let the person finish the thought; you may put it all together at the very end, after she has finished signing all the information. Then, if you still don't understand, just explain that you didn't catch everything, and let the person know what you did catch.

(*Note:* Stopping someone and asking for clarification or waiting until the person is finished to see if you can make sense of things are two techniques used by many signers and interpreters. Both techniques have a place in Sign.)

Watch the Face, Not the Hands

You can find most of what you need to know on a signer's face. A person's face conveys moods, pauses, any information that can be demonstrated through mouth shapes, and how an action is done (slowly, quickly, sloppily, and so on). If you focus on a signer's hands, you miss a lot of crucial information; instead, focus on the signer's face and shoulders. Use your peripheral vision to watch the hands. By doing this, you see the whole signer, and you're apt to better understand the conversation.

Chapter 18

Ten Ways to Pick Up Sign Quickly

In This Chapter

▶ Volunteering at Deaf schools, clubs, social functions, and ministries

▶ Attending Deaf camps, silent weekends, and conferences

▶ Watching videos to improve your signing skills

igning with your friends has never been easier. You have natural signs and gestures to make your point. You also have this book to add to what you already know. This chapter is short, but it gives you great ideas for some of the things you can do if you want to pick up American Sign Language a little more quickly.

Volunteer at a Residential School for the Deaf

One way to immerse yourself in the Deaf world is to volunteer at a residential school for the Deaf. Deaf culture is the way of life at these schools, and by being exposed to the culture, you become intimately familiar with Sign. You can volunteer for after-school recreation programs or special-event preparations. Schools can never have too many volunteers to act as scorekeepers, coaches, assistants, ticket sellers, and other positions. By interacting with Deaf students, teachers, and parents, you'll measurably improve both your expressive (signing to others) and receptive (reading others' signs) signing.

Volunteer at Local Deaf Clubs

Many Deaf people tend to congregate at their own clubs for a variety of reasons. They socialize, play pool, go on trips, and watch TV, just to name a few activities. Many Deaf people bring their hearing children to these clubs so they can practice their signing and learn the ways of the Deaf culture. Some clubs even have photo albums of past members and guests. Deaf clubs also have fundraising events fairly often. Volunteering at one of these fundraisers is a great opportunity to practice signing while helping others. Volunteers are always needed to sell raffle tickets, take tickets during an event, keep score at games, or simply serve refreshments.

Attend Deaf Social Functions

Social functions are becoming more common since more Deaf people have started specialized organizations. These events vary from sports activities to Deaf camp-outs to raffles. People interested in helping with flyers and tickets are always welcome. You can find out about functions in your community by checking the community pages in the phone book, searching the Internet, or calling the local residential school for the Deaf, if your community has one.

It's customary to have a Deaf friend accompany you to one of these events, so that he or she can introduce you to Deaf people for the first time.

Make Deaf Friends

Having Deaf friends is really no different from having hearing friends. Many Deaf people enjoy watching and playing sports, going shopping, and surfing the Internet. A Deaf friend can help you a lot with ASL. Just think carefully about your friendship, though. Deaf people are sharing a language and culture with you that they hold in high regard; please try to do the same.

Assist Deaf Ministries

Attending Deaf churches and Deaf ministries is a sure way to meet Deaf people. Watching religious interpreters in these settings keeps you on the cutting edge of Sign vocabulary. Some churches that have large Deaf ministries have programs set up for members of their congregation who want to interpret for the Deaf. Church activities, such as picnics and Deaf Bible study groups, are enjoyable areas in which you can offer your assistance or simply watch the preaching in Sign.

Attend Conferences for Interpreters

Sign language interpreting conferences are held every year in each state. These conferences feature workshops and breakout sessions on various topics, incorporating the latest research on interpreting, ASL, and more. The conferences also usually have evening entertainment performances by Deaf people and hearing people alike. Attending one of these conferences is an excellent way to pick up information about interpreting, sharpen your ASL skills, and meet other people who are learning Sign. You'll also find booths with work opportunities, silent auctions, and mentoring opportunities by professional interpreters.

Work at Camps for the Deaf

Working at a Deaf camp gives the novice signer a relaxed atmosphere in which to work with Deaf children. Deaf camps are filled with fun activities such as games and hiking. You have ample opportunity to interact with Deaf people from different areas and to encounter a variety of signing styles and jargon. You may even get the opportunity to see both adults and children perform stories in Sign. Who knows, during a week of camp you may even form new friendships that last long after camp has ended.

Attend Silent Weekends

Silent weekends aren't as lengthy as Deaf camps. Beginning signers who can't miss time from work may find these weekends a perfect opportunity to mix with the Deaf community. These weekends vary as to how they're run. Some furnish cabins that allow people to talk in the evenings, usually after 4 or 6 p.m., while others allow no talking at all. In fact, you may even be fined — 10 or 25 cents per infraction — if you're caught talking! Entertainment is on hand, and an array of ASL teachers and interpreters are available to ensure that the weekend is filled with accurate signing.

You can obtain information about these silent weekends by going to www. rid.org. Each state has a chapter of the Registry of Interpreters for the Deaf (RID). Click your state's link for information.

Go to Deaf Workshops and Deaf Conferences

Many Deaf organizations exist, and one in particular is the National Association of the Deaf (NAD). Workshops and conferences take place through these organizations and offer a myriad of subjects — something to interest everyone. One popular subject is Sign itself. Many educators and veteran interpreters regularly present poetry in Sign or give in-depth analyses of particular properties of Sign. Attending one of these workshops may give you new insights into Deaf culture.

Watch Sign Language Videos

Videos are a sure way to improve your signing. Many companies specialize in ASL materials and are happy to send you their catalogs. Get together with a Deaf friend, grab a catalog, and let your friend help you decide which videos would be good to learn from based on your particular level of ability. The best way to find sources of these types of videos is to surf the Internet. Just enter the words "sign language" into your search engine and watch how many sites come up. Your local library is also a good source for videos. Although books are a big help, videos have the capacity to demonstrate three-dimensional signing, and you can also rewind them and view them in slow motion for easier learning. Besides, viewing one of these videos with a friend can be a lot of fun.

Chapter 19

Ten Popular Deaf Expressions

In This Chapter

▶ Practicing some common ASL expressions

▶ Knowing when to use certain idioms

American Sign Language uses expressions in much the same way that English does. This chapter describes some expressions that are commonly used in Sign. Practicing these expressions with people who've been signing for a while can be a shortcut to your success.

Some of the following signs have an exact English equivalent and some don't. The ones that don't, however, are quite similar to an English expression.

Swallowed the Fish

This idiom indicates gullibility. You use it in good humor after someone mistakenly places his trust in someone he shouldn't have. You can sign it about yourself or about another person. When you sign it, widen your eyes as if to show embarrassment due to the gullibility.

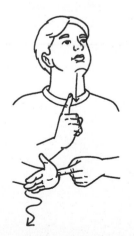

Train Gone

You don't normally direct this lighthearted idiom toward yourself but rather toward someone else. You often use this sign, which can be compared to the English idiom "missed the boat," when someone tells a joke and everyone laughs except one person, or when one person wants something repeated that everyone else understood the first time. In these moments, someone will look at the person who doesn't get it, smile, and sign **train gone.** The facial expression for this sign can be puffed cheeks (imitating a smokestack) or just a blank stare, whichever you prefer. Either way, everyone will know that someone didn't catch the information.

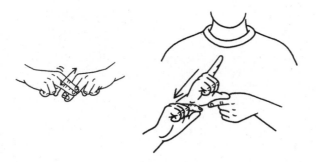

Pea Brain

Hearing people use this idiom as well, and just as in English, you shouldn't use this idiom very often because it's not polite. In fact, it's somewhat offensive, although perhaps in a group of good friends you can get away with it if you mean it in good fun. The facial expression that accompanies this sign determines the degree of meaning or, in this case, maybe the size of one's brain! Sticking out your flattened tongue while signing **pea brain** makes your meaning pretty clear. What's even meaner is crossing your eyes while showing the sign. So as a general rule, save this sign for people you know really well. You can also direct this sign at yourself in a self-deprecating manner when you do something stupid or state something that's obvious to everyone else.

Shucks/Darn!

If you've ever experienced a situation in which something doesn't go as expected, you probably already know how to use this expression. Like the illustration indicates, you open your passive hand facing up. Using your dominant hand, you start with the manual number 5 and, with the manual letter S, you act like you're catching a fly in the palm of your hand.

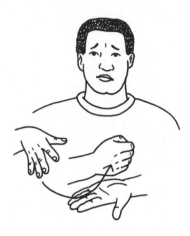

I Hope

To sign **I hope,** you cross your fingers on both hands. It's pretty simple and is generally understood in both the hearing and Deaf worlds alike. Just cross your fingers in R handshapes. You can add the facial expression of closing your eyes tightly and clenching your teeth or widening your eyes with your mouth slightly opened.

Your Guess Is as Good as Mine

This expression is used in English as well as Sign. In English, you use this expression only after someone asks a question. However, in Sign, you can ask a question and use this expression at the same time. A good facial expression to go with this sign is to smirk (smiling with just the corner of your mouth) and raise your eyebrows. Another way to emphasize this expression is to make the size of the sign bigger. Doing so tells whomever you're signing that you really don't have any idea whatsoever.

Cool!

This expression is also used in English as well as Sign. You can sign it in two different ways; both signs have pretty much the same meaning.

The first sign, shown in the following picture, is made by placing your index finger and thumb on your cheek and twisting your wrist in an inward motion. The facial expression can be a smile or pursed lips — as long as your attitude is positive, the facial expression will follow.

The second sign is made by putting your thumb on the center of your chest and wiggling the fingers, leaving your facial expression fully visible. Forming an "ooh" shape with your mouth means **really cool.** Opening your mouth wide can mean a **surprised cool.**

You will see Deaf people using both signs interchangeably.

Oh No!

Make this sign when you witness an embarrassing action or are explaining one of your own embarrassing actions to someone. Open your eyes wide; you can even put on a nervous smile as you express this sign. You make this sign with the manual 5 palm facing the signer and close it to make the manual S; it signifies a lump in your throat.

That's Pretty Straight-Laced

By making this sign, you're saying that someone is ultraconservative, close-minded, or just an old-fashioned square. For your facial expression, press your lips tightly together, perhaps paired with a snobbish-type expression.

Wow!

You can use this expression with a positive or a negative connotation. Your facial expression, along with the conversation's context, tells your friends exactly how you feel about the subject at hand. Your eyes should be wide open, accompanied by a partial smile. You fingerspell W-O-W right next to the side of your open mouth. If your response is less than favorable, you crunch up your eyebrows.

Part V
Appendixes

The 5th Wave   By Rich Tennant

ITALICIZING THE WORD "BABY"

In this part . . .

Appendix A contains all the answers to those tricky Fun & Games questions and puzzles. Appendix B provides detailed instructions for playing and using the CD.

Appendix A
Answer Key to Fun & Games

• •

Chapter 1

Refer to Chapter 1 for the manual alphabet.

Chapter 2

Answers: 1-g (first); 2-h (Wow); 3-e (six); 4-f (eat); 5-b (big); 6-c (chair, sit); 7-d (fly, planes); 8-a (What — the sign W-T)

Chapter 3

Answers: 1. France; 2. angry; 3. name; 4. hello; 5. U.S.; 6. Mexico; 7. bye

Chapter 4

Answers: 1-c (first); 2-d (dawn); 3-f (five); 4-a (noon); 5-e (stay); 6-b (night)

Chapter 5

Answers given in chapter.

Chapter 6

Answers: 1-d; 2-i; 3-e; 4-h; 5-a; 6-j; 7-c; 8-g; 9-k; 10-b; 11-f; 12-l

Chapter 7

Answers: 1. The bus is late. 2. Where is your car? 3. The train goes north. 4. I ride the subway. 5. Is that your motorcycle? 6. Drive two miles. 7. The tree is near the lake. 8. Turn left at the gas station. 9. Cross the bridge.

Chapter 8

Answers given in chapter.

Chapter 9

Answers: 1-f; 2-h; 3-g; 4-e; 5-b; 6-a; 7-d; 8-c

Chapter 10

Answers: 1-g; 2-h; 3-j: 4-c; 5-b; 6-e; 7-i; 8-d; 9-f; 10-a

Chapter 11

Answers: a-2 (copy machine); b-1 (computer); c-5 (employees); d-8 (terminated); e-3 (laptop); f-7 (promotions); g-4 (office); h-6 (hire)

Chapter 12

Answers: 1-a (picnic); 2-e (dark); 3-g (relax); 4-f (gambling); 5-c (baseball); 6-d (game); 7-b (thunder); 8-h (wrestling)

Chapter 13

Answers: 1. dizzy; 2. doctor; 3. throat; 4. draws blood; 5. surgery; 6. cast; 7. emergency; 8. assistant

Appendix B

About the CD

In This Appendix

▶ System requirements

▶ Using the CD with Windows and Mac

▶ What you'll find on the CD

▶ Troubleshooting

*N**ote:** If you are using a digital or enhanced digital version of this book, this appendix does not apply.*

This appendix walks you through the video CD that accompanies this book and also gives you the system and other technical specs you may need to play it.

System Requirements

Make sure that your computer meets the minimum system requirements shown in the following list. If your computer doesn't match up to most of these requirements, you may have problems using the software and files on the CD. For the latest and greatest information, please refer to the ReadMe file located at the root of the CD-ROM.

- A PC running Microsoft Windows
- A Macintosh running Apple OS X or later
- A CD-ROM drive

Note: Videos are only viewable from within the interface.

If you are reading this in an electronic format, go to `http://book support.wiley.com` for access to the additional content.

If you need more information on the basics, check out these books published by John Wiley & Sons, Inc.: *PCs For Dummies,* by Dan Gookin; *Macs For Dummies,* by Edward C. Baig; *iMacs For Dummies,* by Mark L. Chambers; and *Windows XP For Dummies* and *Windows Vista For Dummies,* both by Andy Rathbone.

Using the CD

To install the items from the CD to your hard drive, follow these steps.

1. **Insert the CD into your computer's CD-ROM drive.**

    The license agreement appears.

    Note to Windows users: The interface won't launch if you have autorun disabled. In that case, choose Star⇨Run. (For Windows Vista and Windows 7, choose Start⇨All Programs⇨Accessories⇨Run.) In the dialog box that appears, type *D*:**Start.exe**. (Replace *D* with the proper letter if your CD drive uses a different letter. If you don't know the letter, see how your CD drive is listed under My Computer.) Click OK.

    Note to Mac Users: When the CD icon appears on your desktop, double-click the icon to open the CD and double-click the Start icon. Also, note that the content menus may not function as expected in newer versions of Safari and Firefox; however, the documents are available by navigating to the Contents folder.

2. **Read through the license agreement and then click the Accept button if you want to use the CD.**

    The CD interface appears. The interface allows you to browse the contents and install the programs with just a click of a button (or two).

What You'll Find on the CD

Note: Shareware programs are fully functional, free, trial versions of copyrighted programs. If you like particular programs, register with their authors for a nominal fee and receive licenses, enhanced versions, and technical support. *Freeware programs* are free, copyrighted games, applications, and utilities. You can copy them to as many computers as you like — for free — but they offer no technical support. *GNU software* is governed by its own license, which is included inside the folder of the GNU software. There are no restrictions on distribution of GNU software. See the

GNU license at the root of the CD for more details. *Trial, demo,* or *evaluation* versions of software are usually limited either by time or functionality (such as not letting you save a project after you create it).

Following is a list of the clips that appear on this book's video CD:

Clip 1: The manual alphabet (Chapter 1)

Clip 2: Chatting in simple sentences (Chapter 2)

Clip 3: Signing an exclamation (Chapter 2)

Clip 4: Approaching someone new (Chapter 3)

Clip 5: Making initial introductions (Chapter 3)

Clip 6: Signing feelings and emotions (Chapter 3)

Clip 7: Discussing travel and locations (Chapter 3)

Clip 8: Example of Constructed Dialogue (Chapter 3)

Clip 9: Example of Constructed Action (Chapter 3)

Clip 10: Signing numbers (Chapter 4)

Clip 11: Signing times and directions (Chapter 4)

Clip 12: Signing about the house (Chapter 5)

Clip 13: Making plans (Chapter 6)

Clip 14: Giving one's address (Chapter 6)

Clip 15: Making small talk (Chapter 6)

Clip 16: Giving directions around town (Chapter 7)

Clip 17: Discussing what to eat for lunch (Chapter 8)

Clip 18: Ordering drinks (Chapter 8)

Clip 19: Going shopping (Chapter 9)

Clip 20: Finding sales and paying for items (Chapter 9)

Clip 21: Asking questions on the job (Chapter 11)

Clip 22: Making plans based on the weather (Chapter 12)

Clip 23: Handling a medical emergency (Chapter 13)

Troubleshooting

The two likeliest problems are that you don't have enough memory (RAM) for the programs you want to use or you have other programs running that are affecting installation or running of a program. If you get an error message such as Not enough memory or Setup cannot continue, try one or more of the following suggestions and then try using the software again:

- **Turn off any antivirus software running on your computer.** Installation programs sometimes mimic virus activity and may make your computer incorrectly believe that it's being infected by a virus.

- **Close all running programs.** The more programs you have running, the less memory is available to other programs. Installation programs typically update files and programs, so if you keep other programs running, installation may not work properly.

- **Have your local computer store add more RAM to your computer.** This is, admittedly, a drastic and somewhat expensive step. However, adding more memory can really help the speed of your computer and allow more programs to run at the same time.

Customer Care

If you have trouble with the CD-ROM, call Wiley Product Technical Support at 800-762-2974. Outside the United States, call 317-572-3993. You can also contact Wiley Product Technical Support at http://support.wiley.com. John Wiley & Sons, Inc., will provide technical support only for installation and other general quality control items. For technical support on the applications themselves, consult the program's vendor or author.

To place additional orders or to request information about other Wiley products, call 877-762-2974.

Index

• Numerics •

1, sign for, 75
2, sign for, 75
3, sign for, 75
4, sign for, 75
5, sign for, 75
6, sign for, 75
7, sign for, 75
8, sign for, 75
9, sign for, 75
10, sign for, 75
11, sign for, 76
12, sign for, 76
13, sign for, 76
14, sign for, 76
15, sign for, 76
16, sign for, 76
17, sign for, 76
18, sign for, 76
19, sign for, 76
30, sign for, 77
40, sign for, 77
50, sign for, 77
600, sign for, 77
700, sign for, 77
800, sign for, 77

• A •

accountant, sign for, 125
acting, sign for, 219
action, sign for, 220
active hand, 14–15
ADA (Americans with Disabilities Act), 303–304
additionally, sign for, 59
address, sign for, 121
addresses
  about, 119–121
  country/city, 59–62, 120
  zip codes, 119

adjectives, 24–25
admit, sign for, 292
adverbs, 24–25
after, sign for, 139
agency (interpreting), 317–318
ailments, 283–286
alert, sign for, 267
all night, sign for, 80
alphabet, 12–13
also, sign for, 58
a.m., sign for, 13
ambulance, sign for, 292
America, sign for, 60
American Sign Language (ASL)
  about, 1
  ASL pride, 310
  classes in, 309, 310
  college credit, 304
  indigenous sign languages, 304
  origins, 300
  standardization, 304
  word order, 311
Americans with Disabilities Act (ADA), 303–304
ankle, sign for, 288
answer key, for Fun & Games activities, 345–346
apartment, sign for, 89
appointment, sign for, 215, 216
Arizona, sign for, 61
arm, sign for, 289
arrive, sign for, 81
art, sign for, 225
ASL (American Sign Language)
  about, 1
  ASL pride, 310
  classes in, 309, 310
  college credit, 304
  indigenous sign languages, 304
  origins, 300
  standardization, 304
  word order, 311

assistant, sign for, 126, 233
assistive listening devices, 218
asthma, sign for, 284
Atlanta, sign for, 61
ATM card, sign for, 205
attention, attracting, 48
aunt, sign for, 116

• B •

baby, sign for, 105
bachelor(ette), sign for, 227
back, sign for, 139
bacon, sign for, 164
bad, sign for, 211
bad movie, sign for, 24
bakery, sign for, 181
bandage, sign for, 281
bank, sign for, 206
bargain, sign for, 183
base hand, 14–15
baseball, sign for, 247, 248
basement, sign for, 91
basic expressions
  about, 47
  Constructed Action, 69
  Constructed Dialogue, 68–69
  Fun & Games activity, 70–71
  getting acquainted, 53–62
  initiating conversations, 47–52
  Signin' the Sign dialogue, 63–67
basketball, sign for, 248
bathroom, sign for, 91
bed, sign for, 95
bed rest, sign for, 285
bedroom, sign for, 92
bedtime, sign for, 104
beer, sign for, 177
before, sign for, 139
behind, sign for, 139
belt, sign for, 191
Benet, Juan Pablo (author), 300
beside, sign for, 139
best, sign for, 210
better, sign for, 210
betting, sign for, 258
bicultural people, living as, 307–308

bicycle, sign for, 149
bilingual people, living as, 307–308
bills, sign for, 206
black, sign for, 199
bleed, sign for, 292
blinds, sign for, 95
blood pressure, sign for, 281
blouse, sign for, 194
blue, sign for, 199
board game, sign for, 258
body language, 16–17
body parts, 286–291
book, sign for, 16
boots, sign for, 189
boss, sign for, 124, 233
Boston, sign for, 61
bottom, sign for, 211
bowl, sign for, 174
boxing, sign for, 10, 248, 249
bra, sign for, 191
bread, sign for, 170
bread store, sign for, 181
breakfast, 162, 164–165
breakfast, sign for, 162
breathing problem, sign for, 284
bridge, sign for, 65, 146
briefs, sign for, 190
broke(n), sign for, 240
broken bone, sign for, 284
brother, sign for, 116
brown, sign for, 200
browsing the Internet, sign for, 260, 261
bruise, sign for, 284
brush teeth, sign for, 10
building, sign for, 146
burger, sign for, 166
business
  Fun & Games activity, 245–246
  getting to work, 242–244
  occupations, 233–238
  office supplies, 238–241
  Signin' the Sign dialogue, 235–238
business, sign for, 242
but, sign for, 58, 151
butcher, sign for, 181
buttocks, sign for, 289
buy, sign for, 15, 183

• C •

calendar, sign for, 216
calendar dates, 82, 216
California, sign for, 61
call, sign for, 121
camping, sign for, 255
camps (Deaf), 335
Canada, sign for, 60
cancel, sign for, 216
car, sign for, 22, 149
cardinal counting, 73
cardinal numbers, 74–77
carpet, sign for, 95
cash, sign for, 205
cast, sign for, 285
CD
    contents, 348–350
    customer care, 350
    system requirements, 347–348
    troubleshooting, 350
    using, 348
CDI (Certified Deaf Interpreter), 317
celestial signs, 262–264
cellphone, sign for, 121
cents, sign for, 206
cereal, sign for, 164
Certificate of Transliteration (CT), 316
certification (interpreting), 315–317
Certification of Interpreting (CI), 316
Certified Deaf Interpreter (CDI), 317
chair, sign for, 22–23, 95
challenge, sign for, 249
challenges of the Deaf, 302–305
champion(ship), sign for, 249
change, sign for, 206
charge, sign for, 205
chats (visual), 325
cheap, sign for, 183
check, sign for, 205
cheese, sign for, 166
chest, sign for, 289
chewing gum, 50
chicken, sign for, 170
children, teaching, 103–105
Children of Deaf Adults (CODAs), 306

chiropractor, sign for, 278
Christmas, sign for, 101
CI (Certification of Interpreting), 316
circumstance, 40–41
cities
    addresses, 119
    city of origin, 59–62
    directions, 146
    fingerspelling, 61
    landmarks, 143–145
    signs for, 61–62, 120
city, sign for, 120
Clerc, Laurent (educator), 301
closed down, sign for, 242
closed-captioning, sign for, 219
closet, sign for, 91, 92
closings, 48–51
clothes, sign for, 188
clothes shopping
    about, 187–188
    by color, 199–202
    fall, 191–193
    Signin' the Sign dialogue, 203–204,
        207–209
    spring, 194–196
    summer, 197–199
    winter, 188–191
cloudy, sign for, 265
coat, sign for, 189
CODAs (Children of Deaf Adults), 306
Code of Professional Conduct, 318–319
code switching, 311
coffee, sign for, 177
Cogswell, Alice (Deaf child), 301
cola, sign for, 178
cold, sign for, 280
collecting, sign for, 260, 261
color, clothing by, 199–202
Colorado, sign for, 61
come one, sign for, 36
comedy, sign for, 220
comparisons, 210–213
compete, sign for, 249, 250
competitive sports, 247–254
Comprehensive Skills Certificate (CSC), 316
conditional sentences, 40–41

condo, sign for, 89
conference, sign for, 242
conferences, 335, 336
conjunctions, 151–154
conscious, sign for, 280
Constructed Action, 69
Constructed Dialogue, 68–69
conventions, explained, 2–3
conversation starters. *See also* getting
   acquainted
  about, 47–48
  attracting attention, 48
  closings, 48–51
  greetings, 48–51
  initiating conversations, 47–52
  private conversations, 324
  Signin' the Sign dialogue, 51–52
cook, sign for, 15, 124
cool!, sign for, 37, 340
copy machine, sign for, 239
corner, sign for, 65
cotton, sign for, 188
couch, sign for, 95
cough, sign for, 284
count, sign for, 249
countries, 59–60, 120
country, sign for, 120
coupon, sign for, 184
credit card, sign for, 205
crescent moon, sign for, 263
cross street, sign for, 139
crutches, sign for, 285
CSC (Comprehensive Skills Certificate), 316
CT (Certificate of Transliteration), 316
cultural issues
  bicultural people, 307–308
  bilingual people, 307–308
  CODAs, 306
  Deaf culture, 306
  hearing people, 306
Cultural Wisdom icon, 5
culture (Deaf), 306
cup, sign for, 174
curtains, sign for, 95
customer care, 350
cycling, sign for, 254

• D •

dark, sign for, 265
darn!, sign for, 339
date, sign for, 228
daughter, sign for, 115
dawn, sign for, 80
Deaf camp, 335
Deaf communication. *See also* Deaf
   community and etiquette
  Bell, Alexander Graham, 300–301
  manualism, 301
  oralist method, 300–301
  relay services, 323–324, 336
  TTYs, 322–323
Deaf community and etiquette
  about, 299
  ADA laws changed, 303–304
  ASL as official language, 304
  ASL pride, 310
  attracting attention, 48
  bilingual/bicultural living, 307–308
  challenges, 302–305
  clubs, volunteering at, 333–334
  code switching, 311
  compliments on signing, 308
  conversations with hearing and Deaf
   people, 309
  cultural issues, 306–308
  Deaf Awareness Month, 310
  Deaf camps, 335
  Deaf West Theater, 310
  dining out, 309
  entering homes, 308
  as ethnic group, 305–308
  existence as people, 305
  eye contact, 18, 48, 110
  feelings about self, 305
  gum chewing, 50
  history, 299–302
  interrupting, 53
  isolation feelings, 305
  Lotus Festival, 310
  manualism, 301
  Martha's Vineyard residents, 301
  ministries, 334

oralist method, 300–301
participating in, 309–312
pointing, 11, 59, 105, 286–291
private conversations, 324
questioning hearing loss, 312
residual hearing, 312
sensitivity, 308–309
signing speed, 310
silent weekends, 335
social function attendance, 334
unity of, 309–310
volunteering at schools, 333
who belongs, 310–311
Deaf conferences, 336
Deaf friends, 334
Deaf ministries, 334
Deaf workshops, 336
Deaf/deaf, 2
deal cards, sign for, 258
deals (shopping), 183–185
debit card, sign for, 205
demonstrative pronouns, 132–134
dentist, sign for, 278
Denver, sign for, 61
desk, sign for, 239
dining
  breakfast, 162, 164–165
  dinner, 163, 170–173
  drinks, 177–179
  ethnic food, 175–177
  Fun & Games activity, 186
  lunch, 166–168
  meals, 159–173
  restaurants, 174–181
  Signin' the Sign dialogue, 168–170,
    180–181
dining room, sign for, 92
dinner, 163, 170–173
dinner, sign for, 163
direct object, 29
directions
  compass points, 138
  conjunctions, 151–154
  directional relationship signs, 139–140
  finding your way, 137–140
  Fun & Games activity, 155–157
  natural landmarks, 143–145

  searching streets, 146–148
  Signin' the Sign dialogue, 141–142
  transportation, 149–151
director, sign for, 234
discharge, sign for, 292
discount store, sign for, 182
discuss, sign for, 242
disease, sign for, 284
display, sign for, 225
divorced, sign for, 227
dizzy, sign for, 280
doctor, sign for, 125, 278
doctor visits, 125, 277–283, 278
dollars, sign for, 206
dominant hand, 14–15
don't know, sign for, 17
door, sign for, 88
downstairs, sign for, 89
downtown, sign for, 120
drama, sign for, 219
draw blood, sign for, 281
dress, sign for, 191
drinks, 177–179
drive, sign for, 10, 22, 29, 31
drowning, sign for, 267

• E •

ear, sign for, 287
earache, sign for, 280
earth, sign for, 266
east, sign for, 138
Easter, sign for, 101
eat, sign for, 10, 29, 30, 163
eating
  breakfast, 162, 164–165
  dinner, 163, 170–173
  drinks, 177–179
  ethnic food, 175–177
  Fun & Games activity, 186
  lunch, 166–168
  meals, 159–173
  restaurants, 174–181
  Signin' the Sign dialogue, 168–170, 180–181
cclipse, sign for, 263
Educational Interpreter Performance
  Assessment (EIPA), 316

eggs, sign for, 164
eight, sign for, 75
eight hundred, sign for, 77
eighteen, sign for, 76
EIPA (Educational Interpreter Performance
    Assessment), 316
either, sign for, 152
elbow, sign for, 288
eleven, sign for, 76
emergencies
    attracting attention, 48
    medical, 291–294
emergency, sign for, 292
emotions
    facial expressions, 17–18, 330–331
    sharing, 55
    TTY communications, 322–323
employee, sign for, 234
England, sign for, 60
enter, sign for, 292
equipment, sign for, 239
era, sign for, 225
escape, sign for, 267
ethnic food, 175–177
ethnic group, Deaf as an, 305–308
etiquette and Deaf community
    about, 299
    ADA laws changed, 303–304
    as an ethnic group, 305–308
    ASL as official language, 304
    ASL pride, 310
    attracting attention, 48
    bilingual/bicultural living, 307–308
    challenges, 302–305
    clubs, volunteering at, 333–334
    code switching, 311
    compliments on signing, 308
    conversations with hearing and Deaf
        people, 309
    cultural issues, 306–308
    Deaf Awareness Month, 310
    Deaf camps, 335
    Deaf West Theater, 310
    dining out, 309
    entering homes, 308
    as ethnic group, 305–308
    existence as people, 305

eye contact, 18, 48, 110
feelings about self, 305
gum chewing, 50
history, 299–302
interrupting, 53
isolation feelings, 305
Lotus Festival, 310
manualism, 301
Martha's Vineyard residents, 301
ministries, 334
oralist method, 300–301
participating in, 309–312
pointing, 11, 59, 105, 286–291
private conversations, 324
questioning hearing loss, 312
residual hearing, 312
sensitivity, 308–309
signing speed, 310
silent weekends, 335
social function attendance, 334
unity of, 309–310
volunteering at schools, 333
who belongs, 310–311
event, sign for, 216
exclamations, 35–37
excuse me, sign for, 49
exhibit, sign for, 225
expressions and gestures
    about, 11, 337–342
    basic expressions, 47–41
    body language, 16–17
    darn!, sign for, 339
    facial expressions, 17–18, 330–331
    fingerspell, 11–14, 53, 330
    handshapes, 14–16
    I hope, sign for, 339
    oh no! sign for, 341
    pea brain, sign for, 338
    popular expressions, 337–342
    shucks!, sign for, 339
    swallowed the fish, sign for, 337
    that's pretty straight-laced, sign for, 341
    train gone, sign for, 338
    your guess is as good as mine, sign for,
        339–340
eye, sign for, 287

• F •

fabric, sign for, 188
face, watching, 332
facial expressions, 17–18, 330–331
facial grammar, 43–44
fall clothing, 191–193
family, sign for, 116
family and friends, 114–118
fantasy, sign for, 220
father, sign for, 115
Father's Day, sign for, 101
feelings, sharing, 55
feet, sign for, 289
female cousin, sign for, 116
fiancé(e), sign for, 228
field, sign for, 143
fifteen, sign for, 76
fifty, sign for, 77
fingerspelling
  about, 11–14
  calendar dates, 82
  dining, 171
  Fun & Games activity, 20, 106
  games, 258
  getting acquainted, 53
  medical terms, 283, 285
  movies, 218
  names, 53, 105, 130, 330
  origins of, 300
  practicing, 330
  shopping, 187, 189, 190, 197, 210
  transport, 149
  where you're from, 59, 61, 119–120
  workplace, 124, 235
  wow!, sign for, 341
finish, sign for, 26, 36
fire, sign for, 266
first, sign for, 77
fish, sign for, 170
five, sign for, 75
flick, sign for, 37
flood, sign for, 266
floor, sign for, 88
Florida, sign for, 62

flower, sign for, 66
fly, sign for, 22–23
food, sign for, 163
food store, sign for, 182
football, sign for, 248
fork, sign for, 175
forty, sign for, 77
forward, sign for, 140
fountain, sign for, 66
four, sign for, 75
four hours, sign for, 79
fourteen, sign for, 76
France, sign for, 60
freeware programs, 348
French fries, sign for, 166
friends and family, 114–118
Fring, 325
full, sign for, 170
full moon, sign for, 263
Fun & Games activities
  about, 2
  answer key, 345–346
  basic expressions, 70–71
  basics, 20
  business, 245–246
  dining, 186
  directions, 155–157
  grammar, 45–46
  health, 294–296
  home, 106
  nightlife, 231
  questions and small talk, 135–136
  recreation and outdoors, 274–275
  shopping, 214
  time, 86
funny, sign for, 220
furnishings (home), 94–98

• G •

Gallaudet, Thomas Hopkins (minister and
    educator), 301
gambling, sign for, 258
game, sign for, 249
garage, sign for, 88

gas station, sign for, 146
Gestuno, 304
gestures and expressions
 about, 11, 337–342
 basic expressions, 47–41
 body language, 16–17
 darn!, sign for, 339
 facial expressions, 17–18, 330–331
 fingerspell, 11–14, 53, 330
 handshapes, 14–16
 I hope, sign for, 339
 oh no! sign for, 341
 pea brain, sign for, 338
 popular expressions, 337–342
 shucks!, sign for, 339
 swallowed the fish, sign for, 337
 that's pretty straight-laced, sign for, 341
 train gone, sign for, 338
 your guess is as good as mine, sign for,
  339–340
getting acquainted. *See also* conversation
  starters
 about, 53
 connecting thoughts, 58–59
 name sign, 53
 sharing feelings/emotions, 55–57
 Signin' the Sign dialogue, 54, 63–67
 where you're from, 59–62
gift, sign for, 16
glass, sign for, 175
gloves, sign for, 189
GNU software, 348–350
golf, sign for, 254
good, sign for, 210
good dog, sign for, 25
goodbye, sign for, 51
grammar
 adjectives, 24–25
 alphabet, 12–13
 conditional sentences, 40–41
 conjunctions, 151–154
 demonstrative pronouns, 132–134
 exclamations, 35–37
 facial grammar, 43–44
 Fun & Games activity, 45–46
 nouns, 28

 noun/verb pairs, 22–23
 parts of speech, 21–25
 personal pronouns/possessives, 130–132
 personification, 41–43
 possessives, 129–134
 sentence structure, 28–33
 Signin' the Sign dialogue, 33–35, 37–40
 tenses, 26–27
 verbs, 28
Grammatically Speaking icon, 5
grass, sign for, 66
green, sign for, 200
greetings, 48–51
grocery store, sign for, 182
gum chewing, 50

• *H* •

ham, sign for, 170
hand, sign for, 289
hands, watching, 332
handshapes
 alternating, 15–16
 dominant hand, 14–15
 fingerspelling and, 12
 natural, 14–15
 passive hand, 14–15
 shared, noun/verb pairs, 22–23
hat, sign for, 189
he, sign for, 130
head, sign for, 287
headache, sign for, 280
health
 ailments and treatments, 283–286
 body parts, 286–291
 doctor visits, 125, 277–283, 278
 emergencies, 291–292
 Fun & Games activity, 295–296
 Signin' the Sign dialogue, 292–294
hearing impaired, 305
hearing people, in Deaf cultural
  community, 306
heavens, sign for, 263
hello, sign for, 49
hemorrhage, sign for, 292
hers, sign for, 130

hi, sign for, 49
high heels, sign for, 192
highway, sign for, 146
hiking, sign for, 255
hip, sign for, 288
his, sign for, 130
history, sign for, 225
hobbies, 260–262
hockey, sign for, 248
holidays, 100–102
home
    about, 87–91
    children, 103–105
    Fun & Games activity, 106
    furnishings, 94–98
    holidays, 100–102
    rooms, 91–94
    Signin' the Sign dialogue, 98–100
    subjects, 28–33, 105
home, sign for, 88
honorary intro, sign for, 49
hospital, sign for, 292
house, sign for, 88
Houston, sign for, 62
hungry, sign for, 163
hurricane, sign for, 267
hurt, sign for, 284

• I •

I, sign for, 130
I hope, sign for, 339
I see, sign for, 35
iconic signs, 9–10
icons, explained, 5
in front of, sign for, 140
Independence Day, sign for, 102
indirect objects, 31–33
indoor games, 258–259
infection, sign for, 284
initializations, 13–14
initiating conversations, 47–52
injection, sign for, 281
intermission, sign for, 223
International Sign Language (ISL), 304
interpreter, sign for, 125

Interpreter Preparation Programs (IPP), 315
Interpreter Training Programs (ITP), 315
interpreting
    about, 313, 319
    agencies, 317–318
    certification, 315–317
    Code of Professional Conduct (CPC), 318–319
    conferences for, 335
    legal, 314
    needs for, 313–314
    training, 315
intersection, sign for, 139
IPP (Interpreter Preparation Programs), 315
ISL (International Sign Language), 304
Internet resources
    Fring, 325
    RID, 316
    silent weekends, 335
    Skype, 325
    videophones, 321
    Wiley Product Technical Support, 350
it, sign for, 131
ITP (Interpreter Training Programs), 315
its, sign for, 131

• J •

jaw, sign for, 287
jobs, 124–127
jogging, sign for, 255
journaling, 331

• K •

Kentucky, sign for, 62
kitchen, sign for, 92
knee, sign for, 288
knife, sign for, 175
knitting, sign for, 260
knocked out (KO), sign for, 281
knuckle, sign for, 288

• L •

lake, sign for, 65, 143
lamp, sign for, 96
landmarks, natural, 143–145
laptop, sign for, 240
lasagna, sign for, 175
laugh, sign for, 104
lawyer, sign for, 126
leather, sign for, 188
leave, sign for, 81
left, sign for, 138
leg, sign for, 289
legal interpreting, 314
lie down, sign for, 282
lightning, sign for, 265
lights, sign for, 223
live, sign for, 88
living room, sign for, 92
local Deaf clubs, 333
lock, sign for, 88
long distance, sign for, 121
long johns, sign for, 190
Los Angeles, sign for, 62
lose, sign for, 249, 250
lost, sign for, 249, 250
loudly talk, sign for, 25
love seat, sign for, 96
lunch, 166–168
lunch, sign for, 162

• M •

male cousin, sign for, 116
manager, sign for, 125, 234
manual alphabet, 14
manualism, 301
married, sign for, 227
Master Comprehensive Skills Certificate
    (MCSC), 316
match, sign for, 249
matinee, sign for, 219
maybe, sign for, 16
MCSC (Master Comprehensive Skills
    Certificate), 316
me, sign for, 130

meals
    breakfast, 162, 164–165
    dinner, 163, 170–173
    drinks, 177–179
    ethnic food, 175–177
    lunch, 166–168
    restaurants, 174–181
    Signin' the Sign dialogue, 168–170,
        180–181
meat store, sign for, 181
mechanic, sign for, 126
medical terms, 281–283
meeting, sign for, 242
Memorial Day, sign for, 102
Mexico, sign for, 60
Miami, sign for, 62
milk, sign for, 10, 178
mine, sign for, 130
Minnesota, sign for, 62
mittens, sign for, 189
money, 205–207
money, sign for, 206
morning, sign for, 80
mother, sign for, 115
Mother's Day, sign for, 101
motorcycle, sign for, 149
mountain, sign for, 66, 143
mouth, sign for, 287
movie, sign for, 219
movies
    about, 218–222
    bad movie, sign for, 24
    closed-captioning, sign for, 219
    open-captioning, sign for, 218
mudslide, sign for, 267
museum, 225–226
museum, sign for, 225, 226
my, sign for, 130
mystery, sign for, 220

• N •

NAD (National Association of the Deaf), 336
name signs, 53, 330
napkin, sign for, 175
National Association of the Deaf (NAD), 336

Nationalist Interpreting Certification, 316
natural handshapes, 14–15
natural landmarks, 143–145
natural signs, 9–10
nausea, sign for, 280
neck, sign for, 288
neither, sign for, 152
New Year's Day, sign for, 102
New York, sign for, 62
nice to meet you, sign for, 49
night, sign for, 80
nightlife
  about, 215
  Fun & Games activity, 231
  making plans, 215–226
  movies, 218–222
  museum, 225–226
  selecting social stations, 227–228
  Signin' the Sign dialogue, 228–230
  theater, 223–224
nine, sign for, 75
nineteen, sign for, 76
no, sign for, 17
noon, sign for, 80
north, sign for, 138
nose, sign for, 287
nouns, in simple sentences, 28
noun/verb pairs, 22–23
numbers. *See also* time
  about, 73
  cardinal, 74–77
  counting, 73–78
  ordinal, 77–78
  phone, 78, 119–121
nurse, sign for, 278
nylons, sign for, 194

● *O* ●

objects, placing, 28–33
occupations, 233–238
office, sign for, 238
office supplies, 238–241
oh, sign for, 35
oh my gosh, sign for, 36
oh no! sign for, 341

on the dot, sign for, 81
one, sign for, 75
one o'clock, sign for, 79
ooh, sign for, 37
open-captioning, sign for, 218
or, sign for, 58
Oral Transliteration Certificate (OTC), 316
oralist method, 300–301
orange, sign for, 200
order, sign for, 174
ordinal counting, 73
ordinal numbers, 77–78
OTC (Oral Transliteration Certificate), 316
other, sign for, 58
our(s), sign for, 131
outdoors and recreation
  celestial signs, 262–264
  competitive sports, 247–254
  Fun & Games activity, 274–275
  hobbies, 260–262
  indoor games, 258–259
  rhetorical questions, 270
  Signin' the Sign dialogue, 271–273
  solo sports, 254–257
  weather, 265–269
outside, sign for, 266
overnight, sign for, 80
own, sign for, 88

● *P* ●

pain, sign for, 284
panties, sign for, 190, 191
pants, sign for, 192
paper, sign for, 239
paper clip, sign for, 239
parenthesis, 78
parts of speech
  about, 21
  adjectives, 24–25
  adjectives and adverbs, 24–25
  alphabet, 12–13
  conditional sentences, 40–41
  conjunctions, 151–154
  demonstrative pronouns, 132–134
  exclamations, 35–37

parts of speech *(continued)*
  facial grammar, 43–44
  Fun & Games activity, 45–46
  nouns, 28
  noun/verb pairs, 22–23
  personal pronouns/possessives, 130–132
  personification, 41–43
  possessives, 129–134
  sentence structure, 28–33
  Signin' the Sign dialogue, 33–35, 37–40
  tenses, 26–27
  verbs, 28
passive hand, 14–15
pay, sign for, 206
pea brain, sign for, 338
pencil, sign for, 239
personal pronouns/possessives, 130–132
personification, 41–43
phone
  relay services, 323–324
  text-messaging, 324
  TTYs, 323
phone, sign for, 120, 240
phone numbers, 78, 119–121
photography, sign for, 225, 226
picnic, sign for, 255
pictures, sign for, 96
pink, sign for, 200
Pittsburgh, sign for, 62
pizza, sign for, 166
plane, sign for, 22–23, 149
plate, sign for, 175
Play This! icon, 5
please, sign for, 49
p.m., sign for, 13
police, sign for, 125
popular expressions, 337–342
possessives, 129–134
potato, sign for, 170
practice, importance of, 330
pray, sign for, 103
prescription, sign for, 285
president, sign for, 125
pretty girl, sign for, 24
privacy, 331
private conversations, 324
promotion, sign for, 242

pronouns, 129–134
purple, sign for, 200
purse, sign for, 194

• *Q* •

Q, sign for, 2, 110
questions and small talk
  facial expressions, 17–18, 330–331
  family and friends, 114–118
  Fun & Games activity, 135–136
  key questions, 109–112
  living and working, 119–121
  possessives and pronouns, 129–134
  rhetorical questions, 270
  Signin' the Sign dialogue, 113–114, 121–129
  signs for question words, 109–114

• *R* •

race, sign for, 249, 250
reading, sign for, 260
reading signs, 11
recliner, sign for, 96
recreation and outdoors
  celestial signs, 262–264
  competitive sports, 247–254
  Fun & Games activity, 274–275
  hobbies, 260–262
  indoor games, 258–259
  rhetorical questions, 270
  Signin' the Sign dialogue, 271–273
  solo sports, 254–257
  weather, 265–269
red, sign for, 200
referee, sign for, 249, 250
relay interpreter, 322
Remember icon, 5
rent, sign for, 88
reservation, sign for, 174, 215, 216
Residential School for the Deaf, 333
rest, sign for, 103, 285
restaurant, sign for, 174
restaurants, 174–179
Reverse Skills Certificate (RSC), 317

rhetorical questions, 270
RID Certification test, 315–317
right, sign for, 138
river, sign for, 66, 144
road, sign for, 147
rock, sign for, 144
romance, sign for, 220
rooms (house), 91–94
RSC (Reverse Skills Certificate), 317
run very fast, sign for, 25
running, sign for, 255

• S •

safe, sign for, 267
salad, sign for, 166
sale, sign for, 183
salesperson, sign for, 126
sandwich, sign for, 166
sausage, sign for, 164
save, sign for, 183
scarf, sign for, 189
schedule, sign for, 215, 216
score, sign for, 249, 250
sculpture, sign for, 225
second, sign for, 77
secretary, sign for, 126, 234
see you later, sign for, 51
sell, sign for, 29, 30, 183
sensitivity, to being Deaf, 308–309
sentence structure, 28–33
server, sign for, 127, 174
seven, sign for, 75
seven hundred, sign for, 77
seventeen, sign for, 76
sewing, sign for, 261
shareware programs, 348
sharing feelings and emotions, 55
she, sign for, 130
shirt, sign for, 192
shoes, sign for, 192
shooting star, sign for, 263
shopping
   clothes, 187–204
   comparisons, 210–213
   deals, 183–185

Fun & Games activity, 214
   money, 205–207
   Signin' the Sign dialogue, 203–204, 207–209
   specialty stores, 181–183
   superlatives, 210–213
shorts, sign for, 197
shot, sign for, 178
show, sign for, 225
show up, sign for, 81
shucks!, sign for, 339
sick, sign for, 17, 284
sign language videos, 336
Signin' the Sign dialogues
   about, 2
   basic expressions, 63–67
   basics, 18–19
   business, 235–238
   clothes shopping, 203–204, 207–209
   dining, 168–170, 180–181
   directions, 141–142
   grammar, 33–35, 37–40
   health, 292–294
   home, 98–100
   icon, 5
   nightlife, 228–230
   questions and small talk, 113–114, 121–129
   recreation and outdoors, 271–273
   time, 82–85
signing, 9. *See also specific topics*
Sign/sign, 2. *See also specific topics*
silent weekends, 335
single, sign for, 227
sister, sign for, 116
sit, sign for, 22–23
six, sign for, 75
six hundred, sign for, 77
sixteen, sign for, 76
skirt, sign for, 194
sky, sign for, 263
Skype, 325
slacks, sign for, 192
sleep, sign for, 103
small talk and questions
   expressions, 17–18, 330–331
   family and friends, 114–118

small talk and questions *(continued)*
Fun & Games activity, 135–136
key questions, 109–112
living and working, 119–121
possessives and pronouns, 129–134
rhetorical questions, 270
Signin' the Sign dialogue, 113–114, 121–129
signs for question words, 109–114
soccer, sign for, 248
social functions, attending, 334
social station, selecting, 227–228
socialize, sign for, 215, 216
socializing
about, 215
Fun & Games activity, 231
making plans, 215–226
movies, 218–222
museum, 225–226
selecting social stations, 227–228
Signin' the Sign dialogue, 228–230
theater, 223–224
socks, sign for, 192
soda, sign for, 166, 178
sold out, sign for, 219
solo sports, 254–257
son, sign for, 115
sore throat, sign for, 284
soup, sign for, 171
south, sign for, 138
spaghetti, sign for, 171
Spain, sign for, 60
specialist, sign for, 278
specialty stores, 181–183
spend, sign for, 183
spoon, sign for, 175
sports
competitive, 247–254
solo, 254–257
sports, sign for, 249, 250
spring clothing, 194–196
stage, sign for, 223
stamp collecting, sign for, 261
stapler, sign for, 240
star, sign for, 219, 263
star-filled sky, sign for, 263

start, sign for, 15
states, 61–62
stay, sign for, 81
steak, sign for, 171
stitch, sign for, 282
stomach, sign for, 290
stone, sign for, 144
stop sign, sign for, 146, 147
stoplight, sign for, 147
store, sign for, 16
storm, sign for, 265
straight, sign for, 139, 140
street, sign for, 120, 147
streets, 146–148
subjects, 28–33, 105
subway, sign for, 149
summer clothing, 197–199
sundress, sign for, 197
sunglasses, sign for, 197
sunny, sign for, 265
superlatives, 210–213
supervisor, sign for, 234
surgeon, sign for, 278
surgery, sign for, 282
sushi, sign for, 175
suture, sign for, 282
swallowed the fish, sign for, 337
sweater, sign for, 192
swimming, sign for, 255
swimming pool, sign for, 10
system requirements, 347–348

• T •

table, sign for, 96, 239
taco, sign for, 175
talk loudly, sign for, 25
tea, sign for, 178
teacher, sign for, 125
teaching
Benet, Juan Pablo, 300
Briarwood Academy, 300
manualism, 301
oralist method, 300–301
team, sign for, 250

technology
  about, 321
  texting, 324
  videophones, 321–324
  visual chat, 325
teeth, sign for, 287
teletype (TTY), 322–323
temperature, sign for, 280
ten, sign for, 75
ten minutes, sign for, 79
tennis, sign for, 247, 248
tenses, 26–27
test, sign for, 282
Texas, sign for, 62
texting, 324
Thanksgiving, sign for, 101
that, sign for, 132
that's pretty straight-laced, sign for, 341
theater, 223–224
theater, sign for, 223
their(s), sign for, 131
them, sign for, 131
these, sign for, 132
they, sign for, 131
third, sign for, 78
thirteen, sign for, 76
thirty, sign for, 77
this, sign for, 132
those, sign for, 132
three, sign for, 75
throat, sign for, 287
thunder, sign for, 265
ticket, sign for, 219
tie, sign for, 194
time. *See also* numbers
  about, 78–81
  a.m./p.m., sign for, 13
  calendar dates, 82, 216
  Fun & Games activity, 86
  Signin' the Sign dialogue, 82–85
time, sign for, 225
Tip icon, 5
toast, sign for, 164
toothbrush, sign for, 10
top, sign for, 210

tornado, sign for, 267
torso, sign for, 290
tortilla, sign for, 175
tostada, sign for, 175
tournament, sign for, 249, 250
town, sign for, 120
trade, sign for, 242
train, sign for, 149
train gone, sign for, 338
training, interpretation, 315
transportation, 149–151
treasurer, sign for, 125
treatments, 283–286
tree, sign for, 65, 144
troubleshooting CD, 350
trunk, sign for, 290
T-shirt, sign for, 191
tsunami, sign for, 266
TTY (teletype), 322–323
turn, sign for, 140
twelve, sign for, 76
twilight, sign for, 80
two, sign for, 75
two minutes, sign for, 79
two o'clock, sign for, 79

• *U* •

umbrella, sign for, 194
umpire, sign for, 249, 250
uncle, sign for, 116
unconscious, sign for, 280
underwear, sign for, 191
United States, sign for, 60
upstairs, sign for, 89
us, sign for, 131

• *V* •

vase, sign for, 96
verbs, in simple sentences, 28
versus, sign for, 249
vice president, sign for, 126
video games, sign for, 258
video relay service, 323–324, 336

videophones, 321–324
videos of sign language, 336
visual chats, 325
vocal inflections, 330–331
volunteering, 333–334

• W •

waiter, sign for, 174
waitress, sign for, 174
walking, sign for, 255
wallet, sign for, 194
warning, sign for, 267
Warning icon, 5
water, sign for, 178
waterfall, sign for, 144
we, sign for, 131
wear, sign for, 188
weather, 265–269
weather, sign for, 266
websites
  Fring, 325
  RID, 316
  silent weekends, 335
  Skype, 325
  videophones, 321
  Wiley Product Technical Support, 350
west, sign for, 138
what, sign for, 36
wheelchair, sign for, 285
whiskey, sign for, 178
white, sign for, 200
widow(er), sign for, 228

Wiley Product Technical Support
    (website), 350
will, sign for, 26–27
win, sign for, 250
window, sign for, 88
windy, sign for, 266
wine, sign for, 178
winter clothing, 188–191
won, sign for, 250
work, sign for, 242
worker, sign for, 234
workplace information
  Fun & Games activity, 245–246
  getting to work, 242–244
  occupations, 233–238
  office supplies, 238–241
  Signin' the Sign dialogue, 235–238
worse/worst, sign for, 211
wow!, sign for, 36, 341–342
wrestling, sign for, 248
wrist, sign for, 288
write down, sign for, 216

• Y •

yard, sign for, 89
yellow, sign for, 200
you, sign for, 131
your guess is as good as mine, sign for,
    339–340
you're welcome, sign for, 51
your(s), sign for, 131

John Wiley & Sons, Inc.
End-User License Agreement

READ THIS. You should carefully read these terms and conditions before opening the software packet(s) included with this book "Book". This is a license agreement "Agreement" between you and John Wiley & Sons, Inc. "WILEY". By opening the accompanying software packet(s), you acknowledge that you have read and accept the following terms and conditions. If you do not agree and do not want to be bound by such terms and conditions, promptly return the Book and the unopened software packet(s) to the place you obtained them for a full refund.

1. **License Grant.** WILEY grants to you (either an individual or entity) a nonexclusive license to use one copy of the enclosed software program(s) (collectively, the "Software") solely for your own personal or business purposes on a single computer (whether a standard computer or a workstation component of a multi-user network). The Software is in use on a computer when it is loaded into temporary memory (RAM) or installed into permanent memory (hard disk, CD-ROM, or other storage device). WILEY reserves all rights not expressly granted herein.

2. **Ownership.** WILEY is the owner of all right, title, and interest, including copyright, in and to the compilation of the Software recorded on the physical packet included with this Book "Software Media". Copyright to the individual programs recorded on the Software Media is owned by the author or other authorized copyright owner of each program. Ownership of the Software and all proprietary rights relating thereto remain with WILEY and its licensers.

3. **Restrictions on Use and Transfer.**

   (a) You may only (i) make one copy of the Software for backup or archival purposes, or (ii) transfer the Software to a single hard disk, provided that you keep the original for backup or archival purposes. You may not (i) rent or lease the Software, (ii) copy or reproduce the Software through a LAN or other network system or through any computer subscriber system or bulletin-board system, or (iii) modify, adapt, or create derivative works based on the Software.

   (b) You may not reverse engineer, decompile, or disassemble the Software. You may transfer the Software and user documentation on a permanent basis, provided that the transferee agrees to accept the terms and conditions of this Agreement and you retain no copies. If the Software is an update or has been updated, any transfer must include the most recent update and all prior versions.

4. **Restrictions on Use of Individual Programs.** You must follow the individual requirements and restrictions detailed for each individual program in the "About the CD" appendix of this Book or on the Software Media. These limitations are also contained in the individual license agreements recorded on the Software Media. These limitations may include a requirement that after using the program for a specified period of time, the user must pay a registration fee or discontinue use. By opening the Software packet(s), you agree to abide by the licenses and restrictions for these individual programs that are detailed in the "About the CD" appendix and/or on the Software Media. None of the material on this Software Media or listed in this Book may ever be redistributed, in original or modified form, for commercial purposes.

CAPÍTULO 14

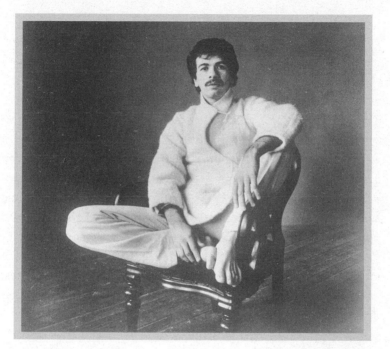

Me gustaría compartir algo con ustedes: realmente me embriago de gratitud. La gratitud es una de las cosas más importantes a las que el ser humano puede aspirar porque, cuando uno es agradecido, uno va más allá del bien y del mal. Bien y mal son solo palabras que se utilizan para referirse a la energía que se relaciona con la culpa. Ángeles y demonios te dan una ovación de pie cuando haces tu mejor esfuerzo para ser agradecido. Los invito en este segundo, en este momento, a abrazar el amor incondicional. El amor incondicional es un tipo de amor que es más grande que tus problemas, más grande que tu equipaje, tus cargas y tus

ilusiones. El amor hace que tú y yo seamos necesarios en contraposición a innecesarios. El amor resuelve la distancia y la separación. El amor convierte todas las banderas del mundo en un río de colores. El amor es esa luz que todos tenemos dentro, cada uno de nosotros. Saludo la luz que eres y que llevas dentro del corazón. Te saludo.

Todo aquel que haya visto un espectáculo de Santana en los últimos años sabe que me gusta inyectar una dosis de realidad en el concierto. Después de cuatro o cinco temas musicales, tal vez, después de tocar "Black Magic Woman" y "Oye Como Va" y justo antes de "Maria Maria", los cantantes hacen un receso y yo comienzo a hablar con la multitud. Les doy la bienvenida y les cuento sobre la luz que cada uno de ellos lleva dentro, que ellos *son* luz; *luminoso* es la palabra que me gusta utilizar. Les pido que piensen en la posibilidad de aceptar la nobleza y la grandeza de sus vidas. Siempre les digo "Evalúen la posibilidad de reconocer que no están separados de su propia luz, que es lo que gran parte de la cultura y de la religión quiere que crean: que no son dignos, que son horribles pecadores, que llegaron a este mundo como pecadores, incluso antes de que abrieran los ojos por primera vez. Que deben reparar y que están solos".

En ocasiones, en ese momento, alguna persona grita o algunas personas gritan que quieren rocanrolear y gritan el nombre de la canción que quieren escuchar; entonces, digo: "Oye, hombre, escucha unos minutos. Agradezco que hayan pagado la entrada y sé qué canciones quieren escuchar, pero tal vez necesiten más escuchar esto. ¿Qué tal un nivel superior de consciencia durante un minuto?".

Siento que ahora, en esta parte del libro, quiero detenerme, como hago en los conciertos, y decir algunas cosas que conectan puntos. Quiero volver a explicar por qué escribo este libro, para hablar sobre el Tono Universal, y recordarles a todos que no es tan solo un dicho, realmente somos todos uno. Baso todas mis creencias en esa única nota.

Yo soy muchas cosas: un padre, un esposo, un guitarrista, el líder de una banda y un creyente. También soy un orador y un maestro, esa es una gran parte de lo que soy ahora, y es el resultado del trabajo que he hecho en mí mismo, que comenzó hace muchos años con los maestros que elegí seguir. Una de las lecciones más importantes que aprendí es a escuchar lo que decían y tomarme el tiempo para detenerme y escucharme a mí mismo. Existe un concepto muy noble de los budistas orientales: eres el jardinero de tu propia mente. Es la idea de que uno debe responsabilizarse por sus pensamientos, detenerse y evitar tener pensamientos que sean inadecuados o dañinos.

Deberíamos escribir en grandes letras mayúscula: EL EGO NO ES TU AMIGO. El ego ama la duda, te criticará y te hará sentir culpable hasta la muerte. Te condenará, juzgará y tirará a una zanja, y luego se reirá de ti. Esa es la razón por la que la meditación puede ser muy difícil. Es fácil *hacer* nada, pero es muy, muy difícil *pensar* en nada. Realmente uno nunca puede hacerlo. De todas formas, lo que hay que hacer es apartarse de esos pensamientos, como salir de un río que corre, y simplemente sentarse en la orilla, observarlo y dejar que el río siga su camino. La meditación es el primer paso para controlar toda esa charla, charla que continúa dentro tuyo para que, finalmente puedas decidir en quién confiar, en tu luz o en tu ego. ¿Sabes cuál es la diferencia?

Hace ya bastante tiempo que pienso en el intercambio entre la filosofía oriental y la mente occidental en la década de 1960 y la relación entre ambas. Había muchos gurús y maestros espirituales que surgían en esa época y cada uno tenía una prioridad y un camino diferentes que podías seguir, incluso cuando el mensaje fundamental era el mismo. No existía una guía o un sitio web que podías leer para saber cuál era el mejor para ti. Tenías que escuchar a cada uno de ellos con el corazón y el sentido común, analizar quienes pasaban el tiempo con ellos y decidir si la forma de hablar, la disciplina y los requisitos tenían sentido para ti. Si eran verdaderos gurús, sus mensajes hablaban sobre amor y conexión.

Era una época emocionante y las ideas que nos traían estos gurús nos mostraban el camino en un mapa que siempre estuvo allí, pero que nunca pudimos ver. De repente, existían todos estos caminos que podíamos tomar que no sabíamos que existían. Incluso, en la actualidad, pienso que la filosofía oriental es como un viejo tío sabio que intenta ayudar a la mente occidental, que puede quedar inmersa en la adolescencia, actuar como un adolescente malcriado, que quiere divertirse y que huele a media sucia y a cerveza. Esos gurús entraron en escena y nos enseñaron cómo ser espirituales. Me enseñaron a enfrentar esa parte de mi vida con madurez en el momento en que lo necesitaba.

Existe una gran diferencia entre religión y espiritualidad. Ahora sé que solo se puede creer en ambas si estás dispuesto a asumir la responsabilidad personalmente. Si en vez de verte a ti mismo como una gota de agua, te ves como parte de un océano entero, una parte de todos y de todo. Si puedes dominar esa idea y si puedes dominar el ego (muchas religiones cuentan con que no lo puedas hacer), entonces, sabes que tu responsabilidad no es solo para contigo mismo sino que para con todo y todos. Amarte a ti mismo es amar a otros, y lastimar a los otros es lastimarte a ti mismo. Si crees en esto, entonces, no tiene sentido que exista solo una religión, que vas a ver a Dios y que aquellos que se equivocan se irán al infierno.

No creo en la idea de que solo un tipo de persona pueda caminar por la alfombra roja, ¿sabes? Puedes quedarte con el tipo de cielo que es selectivo. Yo quiero el cielo que es para todos. En ese aspecto, Sri Chinmoy fue quien más me ayudó. Solía decir que solo existe una meta pero que existen diversos caminos y que cada religión tiene razón, a su manera. En Occidente, tenemos una forma de pensar que se resume en lo siguiente: el diablo me obligó a hacerlo pero Jesús me defiende. También se puede expresar de esta manera: el diablo me obligó a hacerlo pero de todas formas Jesús me ayudará a cruzar el río de la vida.

Maldita sea. ¿Qué tipo de responsabilidad es esa? Incluso si no hiciste nada que el diablo te haya dicho que hicieras, ¿a cuántas personas debe cargar Jesús? ¿Qué les parece bajarse y caminar un poco por sus propios medios?

Incluso antes de 1972, de grabar *Caravanserai*, de juntarme con

Deborah y de conocer a Sri, había tomado la decisión, conscientemente, de alejar mi vida de conflictos y de los juegos del ego. Fue
uno de esos planteos que uno se hace una vez cada tanto, pero este
era algo certero; no importaban las consecuencias, lo que dijeran
las personas, si se unían a mí o no, e incluso si estaba solo.

La razón de ser de los gurús es que uno no lo puede hacer solo
todo el tiempo, definitivamente no al principio. Necesitas que
alguien más sostenga la luz para iluminar tu camino y así poder
ver hacia dónde te diriges. Un verdadero gurú ilumina y disipa la
oscuridad. Jesús fue un gurú. En ocasiones, no es lo que los gurús
dicen o hacen, sino la forma en que cambian las cosas con su sola
presencia. En la década de 1970, cuando Miles subía al escenario
junto con todos sus músicos, sin decir nada y sin siquiera soplar la
trompeta, podía cambiar por completo el foco de la música con tan
solo mirar de cierta manera o lograr que alguien dejara de tocar
puras porquerías con tan solo acercarse. Así funciona un gurú.

John McLaughlin solía contarme que Miles le decía: "No lo olvi-
des; *yo* fui tu primer gurú". Miles podía ser raro, pero no estaba
equivocado.

Creo que esa es la razón por la que los gurús y los maestros
orientales buscaban acercarse a los músicos, porque las personas
les prestan atención. Esos gurús eran inteligentes, sabían lo que
hacían. No iban a publicar anuncios ni emitir spots publicitarios en
la radio. Hablaban y muchas personas escuchaban, muchas de las
cuales eran músicos a quienes, a su vez, otras personas escuchaban. No estoy seguro de por qué muchos músicos tomaban aquel
camino. Lo que sí sé es que a todos les llega el momento en el que
deben tomar una decisión para mejorar. Incluso la tortuga más
vieja con el caparazón más duro tiene que sacar la cabeza de vez en
cuando y creo que era más fácil hacerlo en esa época que hacerlo
ahora. The Beatles sacaron la cabeza con el Maharishi. Antes que
ellos, John Coltrane leía a Krishnamurti, hablaba sobre él con las
personas y aprendía principios espirituales.

Es posible que las personas todavía se pregunten sobre este
asunto: a quién seguía cada músico y durante cuánto tiempo lo

hicieron. Pero eso es una distracción, lo importante no es quién estudió con quién, sino el porqué. En cuanto a mí, se trataba sobre mi deseo de evolucionar, elevarme y compartirlo con otros seres humanos, enviar cartas a casa desde el frente mientras luchaba mi propia batalla contra el ego. Seguí a Sri Chinmoy durante casi diez años, pero mi camino espiritual nunca se detuvo.

Creo que, a esta altura, puedes adivinar que la batalla contra el ego nunca se gana por completo. Implica diligencia, paciencia y voluntad, y desde el principio debe ser una transformación suave. Si quieres progresar y ganar la batalla contra el ego, no puedes simplemente cortar cabezas o tirarte en la parte más profunda del mar sin saber nadar. El camino debe ser delicado y comenzar en un lugar seguro. Incluso después de que aprendes a meditar o a concentrarte todos los días en el amor, la devoción y la entrega, todos los días también existe la posibilidad de volver a caer en los hábitos antiguos. Incluso, ahora, debo recordar dejar ir a mi ego y dejar de invertir en la ilusión de separación e indignidad. Es algo que debe hacerse día a día.

Sri solía decir que en cada momento debemos decidir si queremos tener la mente que desea la división o el corazón que aspira a la unión. Solía interpretarlo de la siguiente manera: cuando Santana volaba por el mundo en los 70 y los 80, estábamos muy por encima de las nubes. Miraba por la ventana hacia una gran manta suave donde todo era soleado y tranquilo; todo se veía perfecto. Pero sabía que en aproximadamente una hora, debíamos pasar nuevamente a través de las nubes y enfrentarnos a lo que pasara abajo, a lo que nos estuviera esperando.

Ser humano no es fácil para nadie. Cada uno debe lidiar con su propia condición de humano. Si tan solo todos pudiéramos repetir, una y otra vez, que la chispa de la divinidad en nuestro interior le ganará a nuestros pies de barro; sería genial. Los gurús y los guías no serían necesarios. Si solo fuera así de simple.

Tardé años en decir eso con confianza sobre mí mismo y ser capaz de hablar sobre mis convicciones en público y sobre el escenario. Pero no existe una poción mágica que funcione para todos, no existe un maestro perfecto al que se pueda acudir, que pueda resolver todos los problemas. Aprendí muchas cosas de Sri Chinmoy. Después llegó el momento de aprender de mí mismo y de otros. En la actualidad, existen dos maravillosos ajustadores de pensamiento, Jerry Jampolsky y Diane Cirincione, que con su delicada sabiduría me ayudan a no desviarme del camino. También leo el libro *A Course in Miracles* (traducido al español como Un curso de milagros) todos los días, discuto su mensaje con Jerry y Diane, y me esfuerzo por aplicar sus principios espirituales.

En definitiva, creo que cada uno tiene sus propias experiencias y sus propias emergencias. Debemos evaluar nuestras opciones, escuchar los mensajes que las diversas personas nos entregan y elegir un camino nosotros mismos. Creo que todos están destinados a encontrar su propio camino a casa.

Creo que soy un tipo de persona espiritual equilibrada y armoniosa. Me gusta reír y no cargar con esto como si fuera un mensaje esencial que debe pesarse y entregarse con cuidados especiales. Ser iluminado significa ser luz en todos los sentidos de la palabra.

Existe una historia que escuché sobre dos monjes que habían jurado nunca tocar a una mujer. En su camino, llegan a un río en el que una hermosa muchacha les pide ayuda para cruzar al otro lado. Uno de ellos le permite subirse a sus hombros y la cruza. Un poco más tarde, el monje que ayudó a la mujer nota que el otro está enojado y molesto. Le preguntó qué pasaba. "¿Y nuestros juramentos? ¿Cómo pudiste cargarla?", le preguntó el otro monje. El primer monje lo miró. "Oye, la bajé hace mucho tiempo; tú eres el que todavía la carga".

Seguiré compartiendo mis convicciones durante los espectáculos, es parte de quien soy, y creo que las personas deben escuchar lo que tengo para decir. Y si prestas atención, si *realmente* prestas atención a mi música, entonces podrás escuchar el mensaje, el Tono Universal del que hablo.

Tampoco es solo mi música. El Tono Universal se encuentra en ciertas canciones que transmiten el mismo mensaje de amor y conexión, que eliminan los filtros y muestran lo mejor de cada uno de nosotros y quiénes podemos ser. Canciones como "A Change Is Gonna Come" de Sam Cooke. "What's Going On" de Marvin Gaye. "Imagine" de John Lennon. "One Love" de Bob Marley. "A Love Supreme" de John Coltrane. Incluso la canción para niños "Rema, rema, rema tu barco" y cuando dice "Feliz, feliz, feliz, feliz / La vida es solo un sueño". Estas son canciones que el tiempo no puede borrar ni aplacar.

Gracias por estar aquí. Amamos llegar a ustedes con nuestra música. Cuando se vayan de este lugar y despierten mañana y tengan que lidiar con ustedes mismos, los invito a mirarse en el espejo y decir: "Este va a ser el mejor día de mi vida". Díganlo con claridad, con el alma y sinceridad. Cuando puedan hacerlo, entonces, serán realmente seres divinos y los saludo porque puedo ver a Cristo en ustedes. Veo a Buda, Krishna, Allah, Rama, Shangó. Veo santidad en ustedes. Si recuerdan algo de la noche de hoy, que sea esto. Díganse a sí mismos: "Oye, ese mexicano dijo que era mi elección. Solo mía. Puedo crear el cielo en la tierra". Que Dios los bendiga y sean bondadosos. "A Love Supreme", "One Love", "Imagine", gracias. Buenas noches.

CAPÍTULO 15

Santana, 1973: (Arriba, de izq. a der.) Tom Coster, Richard Kermode, Armando Peraza; (centro) Leon Thomas, Michael Shrieve, Chepito Areas; (abajo) yo, Dougie Rauch.

Seguimos a Sri Chinmoy entre 1972 y 1981, y creo que ambos, Deborah y yo, sentimos que obtuvimos lo que necesitábamos, que nos benefició su estilo de disciplina espiritual, y eso era exactamente lo que era, una disciplina. En una entrevista en la que participé a fines de los 70, dije que era un "un buscador con Sri Chinmoy. Incluso la música es secundaria para mí, no importa cuánto la ame". Creo que muchas personas se sorprendieron cuando leyeron eso en aquel momento, y todavía lo siento de este modo. Era un buscador; ahora, siento que soy un guía.

Debo ser claro: no se trata de música o de espiritualidad. Para mí, la música es parte de ser espiritual, una extensión de mis aspiraciones en esta vida. Si despertara para tan solo ser un músico, tan solo ir a trabajar o tan solo hacer esto o aquello, entonces, no podría ver todo el panorama y perdería la perspectiva. Pero si despierto y mi primer pensamiento es que estoy aquí para ser una mejor persona, en ese caso, el músico que hay en mí surgirá naturalmente.

La música es la fusión de sonido, intención, emoción y sabiduría. Hasta el día de hoy, mi canto es el mismo: "Soy lo que soy. Soy la luz". Y eso canto cuando me siento disperso, cuando siento que me alejo de mi centro, si siento que el Tono Universal se separa en varias notas. Necesito todo lo que soy para alcanzar esa sola nota y estar afinado. Esa nota está compuesta de cinco elementos: alma, corazón, mente, cuerpo y cojones.

Sabía que había tomado la decisión correcta de ser discípulo de Sri Chinmoy cuando no desapareció ese sentimiento que surgía cada vez que cerraba los ojos y lo escuchaba hablar y cantar. La alegría, la luz, la claridad. Cuando regresaba a San Francisco y visitaba el centro de meditación que Sri había abierto allí, podía sentirlo. Cuando despertaba para meditar a las cuatro de la mañana, me sentía de la misma manera.

El amor, la devoción y la entrega, ese es el nombre del camino de Sri Chinmoy. Muchas personas piensan que es el nombre del álbum que grabé con John McLaughlin. Algunos incluso piensan que me uní a Sri para poder tocar con John. Es cómico. Primero, no es fácil convencerse de tocar la guitarra junto a alguien como John y, además, es mucho, mucho más difícil estar al lado de Sri. No era como unirse al club de jardinería y reunirse todos los miércoles por la noche.

Todos los gurús y guías concuerdan con la parte que se relaciona con el amor: el amor es la fuerza unificadora del universo, es lo que nos mantiene unidos y nos da vida. El amor es el aire que fluye en nosotros y nos conecta. La devoción es el compromiso a vivir con prioridades espirituales, que era la dirección en la que ya me encaminaba cuando comencé a alejarme de las drogas y hacia la idea del trabajo interior. Ese comenzaba a ser mi camino cuando conocí a Deborah, que se movía en la misma dirección. La devoción no consiste solamente en la dedicación interior, sino que también implica escuchar y aprender un nuevo vocabulario para poder expresar aquello que nacía dentro de mí.

La entrega, esa parte era completamente propiedad de Sri. La entrega implicaba disciplina, la disciplina de Sri. No se trataba solamente del cabello corto y de que los hombres llevaran camisas y pantalones blancos, y estuvieran prolijos; y que las mujeres se vistieran con saris. No era solamente abstenerse y mantenerse alejado de las drogas y el cigarrillo. La entrega se trataba de mantener una dieta y un cronograma muy estrictos: dejar de comer carne, levantarse a las cinco de la mañana y meditar durante una o dos horas seguidas, aun cuando el cuerpo y la mente quieren hacer otras cosas, cualquier cosa menos eso. Sri era de los pocos gurús que incluían el ejercicio como parte de su camino. Sri era saludable y esto se notaba físicamente.

Una de las lecciones más importantes que aprendí de Sri era su audacia. Él creía tan firmemente en lo que hacía, que incluso antes de que este asunto de los gurús se popularice, ya lo ponía en práctica justo en el medio de la ciudad de Nueva York. Quería que sus discípulos fueran saludables, entonces nos hizo trotar. Luego comenzó con el tenis; armó equipos y jugó con profesionales. Quería que sus discípulos fueran vegetarianos, pero no había muchos establecimientos que sirvieran ese tipo de comida en esa época, entonces inspiró a las personas para que abrieran restaurantes. John McLaughlin y su esposa, Eve (Mahavishnu y Mahalakshmi) invirtieron y dirigieron un establecimiento llamado Annam Brahma en Queens, ubicado cerca del ashram de Sri. Más tarde, Deborah, su hermana Kitsaun, y yo inauguramos uno de los primeros restaurantes vegetarianos en San Francisco, Dipti Nivas. Creo que, al final, había más de treinta en todo el mundo. Sri había ayudado a crearlos.

La astucia de Sri para lograr que todo esto suceda en un mundo que, en términos generales, no entendía cuál era su intención era una de las cualidades que más respetaba. No tomó a todos sus discípulos y se mudó a una jungla en el extranjero, como hizo Jim Jones en Guyana. Jonestown era sinónimo de autoengaño y oscuridad. Sri, en cambio, se concentraba en el autodescubrimiento y en la luz, justo en el medio de Jamaica Hills, Queens.

Si alguien me preguntara dónde vivíamos Deborah y yo entre 1973 y 1981, hubiera dicho primero Queens y después San Francisco. La verdad es que entre todas las giras, las grabaciones y la administración del restaurante, que abrimos en septiembre del 73, viajábamos y nos quedábamos en Queens unas tres o cuatro veces por año. Nuestra estadía allí era como una peregrinación; duraba unas dos semanas y destinábamos aquel tiempo a la meditación y el ejercicio. Si bien íbamos varias veces al año, en determinadas fechas no podíamos faltar, como en el cumpleaños de Sri y en Navidad. Por eso, yo me aseguraba de que el cronograma de Santana no interfiriera con esas fechas.

Cuando estábamos en Queens, Deborah y yo podíamos relajarnos y adaptarnos a la rutina que Sri nos había preparado: la mayoría de los días, nos despertábamos a eso de las cuatro de la mañana, nos duchábamos y luego íbamos a la casa de Sri porque éramos dos de los pocos privilegiados (el primer círculo de discípulos) que meditaban en la galería con él, lo cual era un gran honor. Luego caminábamos o dormíamos una siesta y más tarde desayunábamos juntos. Deborah trabajaba en la cocina o en algún otro negocio, como en la tienda vendiendo libros y saris hindúes. Yo la ayudaba o pasaba el tiempo hablando con Sri.

Más tarde, Sri hablaba con sus discípulos, tocaba un poco de música en un órgano de juguete y hacía que todos canten con él. En ocasiones, cantaba canciones que había escrito él mismo, en otras, las inventaba en el momento y les enseñaba a todos la letra y la melodía. Cuando parábamos y cerrábamos los ojos, hablaba sobre la música y su poder especial que nos ayudaría a aspirar más rápido, a alcanzar el sentimiento universal de unidad y a conectar el exterior (la música que crea el hombre) con la música que todos llevamos dentro pero que no siempre escuchamos. Un tipo de música ayuda a alcanzar al otro, desde una nota hacia el Tono Universal.

Mi relación con Sri era muy diferente a la que Deborah tenía con él, porque yo no pasaba tanto tiempo con él como ella. Ella pasaba mucho tiempo con él mientras yo estaba de gira. Yo regresaría con miles de preguntas, con el deseo de saber cómo funcionaban las cosas en el camino de búsqueda de la luz y si esto o aquello estaba bien, y qué pensaba ella sobre diversas cosas. Durante el tiempo que pasé con Sri, nunca lo llamé Gurú o Maestro, ni nada por el estilo, pero le demostraba respeto. Por sobre todas las cosas, él era un guía y me hacía sentir parte de una hermandad. Y yo necesitaba regresar a esta hermandad para poder estar con almas que aspiraban transitar mí mismo camino, así como determinadas personas que desean escalar el monte Everest o explorar África necesitarán pasar tiempo juntas, hablar y respaldarse entre sí. Las energías iguales se atraen.

Requería un gran compromiso de tiempo y energía de nuestra parte, mío y de Deborah, y gracias a Sri estábamos preparados para hacerlo; un compromiso de energía hacia la excelencia. Durante varios años en la década de 1970, nuestro trabajo con Sri nos brindaba más satisfacción que cualquier otra cosa que el mundo nos ofrecía; más que el dinero, que los elogios y que las otras recompensas que eran el resultado de ser parte de Santana.

Sabía que para superar los juegos del ego, salir de mi encierro y tener una visión diferente de mi propia imagen debía entregarme y hacer lo que Sri decía. Era un compromiso parecido al de estar en las Fuerzas Armadas. Una vez que te pones el uniforme, llevas el uniforme. Esto era un campo de entrenamiento espiritual, las 24 horas del día, los 7 días de la semana. No era como ir a misa los domingos. Mantuve mi convicción y mi conciencia en un estado superior, y sentí como gran parte de mí cambiaba. Todo comenzó a cambiar.

Ahora lo pienso y estos cambios eran razonables. Era como si hubieran sido programados. Un cambio de vida llevaba a otro y a otro y después a otro: alejarme de las drogas y del loco estilo de vida del rock and roll; hacerme preguntas espirituales y cambiar mi alimentación; la banda separándose; aceptar finalmente que no podía resolver la brecha entre Gregg y yo; dirigirme en una dirección distinta con la música; conocer a Deborah; conocer a Sri. No puedo imaginar estos cambios si no hubiera dejado de fumar tabaco o marihuana, ni de comer comida chatarra. Parecía que todo estaba escrito, que todo eso debía suceder; más tarde comprendí, en mi interior, que era el reino invisible que se habría camino dentro de mí.

Era mi propio camino interior. Pero para los admiradores de Santana y las personas que se relacionaban con la banda, yo aún era aquel mexicano que cada noche se subía al escenario con su guitarra y, con ella, alcanzaba aquellas notas. No sabían lo que estaba atravesando hasta el día que aparecí vestido de blanco, sin mi largo cabello. Absolutamente nadie se lo imaginaba, ni siquiera las personas más cercanas a mí, y esto incluía a los miembros de Santana. Cuando Deborah y yo llegamos a Londres a fines de 1972 para las presentaciones que Santana daría en Europa, todos pensaron que había enloquecido, que había ido demasiado lejos. Todos menos Shrieve, por supuesto, que se había unido a Swami Satchidananda.

Cuando regresé a San Francisco, todos, incluida mi madre, pensaron que había perdido la razón o que simplemente, me había entregado. Mi familia y mis amigos de The Mission eran los que estaban más seguros de ello. "Te han lavado el cerebro. Esas personas te lavarán el cerebro; no hay nada más que Jesucristo. Todo lo demás es el diablo". Mi papá fue el único a quien no lo molestó. Me honró con no decir nada, respetar mi decisión y permitir que yo mismo lo descifrara y descubriera de qué se trataba.

Para los tipos más grandes que se habían separado de la banda y, por supuesto, para Bill Graham y Clive Davis, esto era un elemento más que demostraba que yo no sabía lo que hacía, que yo estaba dispuesto a destruir mi carrera. La mayoría no dijo nada pero yo podía sentirlo, y sus sospechas no desaparecieron hasta 1975 cuando volvimos a tocar la música original de Santana, el tipo de música que tocábamos cuando comenzamos. Hasta ese momento, de vez en cuando, las personas apuntarían a otras bandas de rock latino, como Malo y Azteca, y dirían: "Hombre, tocan Santana mejor de lo que lo hace Santana, ¿entiendes lo que digo?". Yo entendía *perfectamente* lo que querían decir, pero de todas formas los miraba y respondía: "No, ¿qué quieres decir?".

El único que siguió insistiendo fue Bill. Vino a casa varias veces y no bien lo saludaba, comenzábamos a hablar. En una ocasión, fue muy cortés. "¿Puedo entrar?".

"Por supuesto".

"Sabes que te quiero como a un hermano, como a mi hijo", dijo y comenzó a llorar.

Le pregunté qué le sucedía. Negó con la cabeza. "Las decisiones que tomas me rompen el corazón porque sé todo lo que has trabajado a lo largo de tu vida y siento que lo estás tirando todo por la borda".

Bill se había estado tomando las cosas muy a pecho no solo por mi decisión de seguir a Sri Chinmoy y de cambiar el sonido de Santana, sino también porque había un gran problema financiero. Al parecer, nuestro negocio no se había administrado de la mejor manera, se habían *mal administrado*. Ya no quedaba más dinero, todo había desaparecido, y como los impuestos no se habían pagado, se tuvo que involucrar el Servicio de Impuestos Internos (IRS). Casi todo el dinero que pensábamos que habíamos ahorrado, se había esfumado. Ese año, para recuperar el dinero perdido, Santana tocó más conciertos que nunca, estábamos continuamente de gira.

Sí, nuestra música había cambiado, pero de todas formas, las personas querían salir y ver a Santana, aún compraban las entradas para vernos tocar. Dije: "Bill, ahora voy a llorar yo. Pero si hago lo que todos me dicen que haga, hombre, no seré yo. Sé que tu intención es ayudarme a que tome decisiones mejores, pero no voy a destruir mi carrera y tampoco voy a permitir que maten quien realmente soy. Debo seguir adelante con mi búsqueda junto a Sri Chinmoy y estoy trabajando en esto con Deborah". Le dije: "Bill, es así de simple".

En ese momento, Deborah y yo vivíamos juntos. Recuerdo el

día que sentí que habíamos cruzado esa línea y que ya éramos una pareja. Me pidió que me acerque; tenía las llaves del Excalibur en su mano. Tenía una expresión particular en su rostro y sostenía las llaves hacia arriba con tan solo dos dedos como si sostuviera una rata muerta. "¿Qué?", pregunté. No tenía idea qué estaba haciendo. Dijo: "Ahora que estás conmigo, no vas a necesitar esto". Le pregunté: "¿Qué quieres decir?". Luego lo entendí.

Yo pensaba: "¿Quién se piensa que es? Eso se llama audacia, hombre". Pero me gustó cómo lo hizo; yo la respetaba y supe de inmediato cuál sería mi respuesta. Le dije: "Hagamos lo siguiente: como a ti no te gusta, tu deberás deshacerte de él". Creo que solo le tomó media hora venderlo.

En ese momento, supe que estaríamos juntos hasta el final. En abril, Sri nos estaba hablando y dijo que podía darse cuenta de que estábamos bien juntos, y que nos ayudábamos mutuamente en el camino espiritual. Dijo: "Ustedes dos deberían casarse". Nos miramos con duda en los ojos porque en esa época los jóvenes ya no eran tan formales, al contrario, la gente se alejaba cada vez más de esas costumbres antiguas y tradicionales. Yo tenía veinticinco y Deborah tenía veintidós. Estábamos enamorados, pero todavía no hacía un año que estábamos juntos. Creo, que en ese momento, podríamos haber vivido juntos eternamente, pero Sri nos convenció de que él veía algo más. "Creo que sus almas deben unirse; esto los ayudará a ambos con sus aspiraciones".

Cuando Deborah y yo regresamos a nuestro hogar, me preguntó: "¿Qué piensas?". Como quería conocer primero su reacción, respondí: "¿Qué piensas tú?". Así estuvimos un buen rato, ninguno de los dos quería dar el primer paso. Admito que no fue una propuesta muy romántica, pero insisto, no había recibido ningún tipo de capacitación en romanticismo. Realmente nos amábamos y queríamos estar juntos; queríamos recorrer el camino espiritual juntos y Sri nos había explicado cómo debía suceder, entonces, decidimos hacerlo.

Instantáneamente, Deborah se lo comunicó a sus padres. Volvimos a San Francisco, y al poco tiempo, el 20 de abril de 1973, fuimos todos al ayuntamiento para firmar los formularios. Luego, realizamos una pequeña ceremonia y recepción en Oakland, en la casa del hermano de SK, que era pastor así que también fue quien nos casó. Recuerdo que llevaba unos modernos zapatos blancos con plataforma, lo que me hacía mucho más alto que Deborah. También recuerdo que usé una corbata. Creo que solo me había afeitado la mitad del rostro. Todos me preguntaban por mi familia y si mis padres vendrían.

De hecho, no invité a nadie cuando me casé, a nadie. Ni familia ni amigos. La mamá de Deborah preguntó: "¿Dónde están tus padres, tus hermanos y tus hermanas?".

"No van a venir".

El resto de los invitados me miraron boquiabiertos. "¿No vienen?".

"No".

"¿Por qué no vienen?".

"Porque no los invité".

En los 60, cuando las cosas sucedían sin problemas ni sobresaltos, como se suponía que debían suceder, casi sin siquiera planearlo, decíamos que era un *groove*. Así fue nuestro casamiento y esa era mi prioridad; muy rápido y simple, sin complicaciones. Deborah y yo estábamos enamorados y vivíamos juntos, y en ese momento, solo eso me importaba. También planeamos una ceremonia espiritual en Queens con Sri.

La complicación que quería evitar era mi mamá; creo que nunca antes habíamos estado tan separados como en esa época y hacía bastante tiempo que no nos veíamos. Todavía no podía olvidarme ni superar el dolor que me había causado con todo lo que me había hecho cuando aún vivíamos en México, como gastar el dinero que había ahorrado para comprar una nueva guitarra. Cuando pensaba en todo este asunto, sentía una gran tensión en todos los músculos de mi cuerpo. Pasaron muchos años antes de que comenzara a liberar este dolor. De todas maneras, así me hacía sentir la idea de la ceremonia. Cuando Jo me preguntó por qué mi mamá no estaba aquel día, no sabía qué más decir. Le dije: "Mi mamá es muy dominante y querría cambiar todo".

Sí llamé a mi mamá después, con Deborah a mi lado, y le dije que nos habíamos casado. Me daba cuenta de que estaba herida. Se produjo un silencio y después de cortar el teléfono no sabía qué decirle a Deborah. Cuando celebramos nuestro matrimonio por segunda vez en Queens con Sri Chinmoy, Deborah me convenció de que invitara a mi familia. Organizamos, otra vez, una ceremonia muy simple y nada pretenciosa. Recuerdo volar a Nueva York con mi padre, mi madre y mi hermana Laura en el avión. Durante todo el camino, mi madre me dijo todo lo que tenía para decir, lo hizo muy difícil, y no le importó quién escuchaba. Solo podía quedarme sentado allí y escucharla. Esta vez no podía huir; me tenía atrapado. Recuerdo mirar a Laura y ella solo movía su cabeza y trataba de mirar en otra dirección.

Nunca había visto a mi mamá tan herida; nunca la había visto reaccionar de ese modo. Durante todo el viaje su mirada se perdía, luego comenzaba a llorar y se volvía a enojar. Laura intentaba intervenir y actuar como mediadora. Eso era exactamente lo que no quería que sucediera en la boda en San Francisco. Si bien no habría hecho nada intencionalmente para lastimar a mi mamá, lo había hecho al ignorarla y mantenerla alejada de mi vida. Para aquel entonces, tenía una relación más estrecha y cercana con la familia de Deborah que con la mía. Recuerdo que, después de casarnos, pasamos nuestro primer día de acción de gracias en Oakland, cortando el pavo y mirando como O. J. Simpson rompía otro récord de fútbol americano en Buffalo. Para mí, era natural. Su familia siempre me recibió con los brazos abiertos: "Vamos, ¿quieres una porción más de pastel de batata? ¿Y un poco más de esto?". Así de simple.

Yo todavía era joven y estaba creciendo y evolucionando, y todavía tenía el hábito de alejarme si veía venir un conflicto verbal, especialmente con una mujer. Sentía que se cerraba una puerta, y yo me iba. Era automático. Esa fue una de las cosas que tuve corregir en el trabajo interior que hice. Lo diré aquí: todas las oraciones y el entrenamiento espiritual, todos los ajustes internos y externos... ahora puedo ver que fueron realmente por mi mamá, y es por eso que le dedico este libro principalmente a ella, con mis agradecimientos por ser tan fuerte y paciente.

Fueron necesarios algunos años más para que mi mamá y yo realmente hiciéramos las paces y volviéramos a estar bien, pero lo logramos, y en los últimos treinta años de su vida nuestra relación fue óptima. Antes de eso, durante un tiempo hubo algunas asperezas. Fue un período bastante alocado, y yo estaba muy confundido con ciertos pensamientos y emociones. Lo diré de esta forma: no estaba del todo presente.

Incluso en nuestra primera boda, cuando solo estábamos Deborah, su familia y yo en Oakland, le dije a su familia que no podía quedarme para la recepción porque tenía un ensayo con la banda. Una vez más, me miraron sin poder creer lo que escuchaban. "Gracias a todos por este excelente día de bodas, pero tengo que ir a prepararme para la próxima gira". Deborah ya lo sabía, pero creo que no me anoté muchos puntos a mi favor ese día. Fui al coche y, como ya no era el Excalibur, olvidé lo que tenía que hacer y me había dejado las llaves adentro.

Recuerdo estar parado allí con Deborah mientras SK trataba de pasar una percha por la ventanilla para destrabar la puerta, mientras miraba a su hija de una forma tan intensa que se podía oír lo que estaba pensando: "¿Estás segura de que quieres casarte con este tipo mexicano?". Con el pasar de los años, cada vez que Deborah y yo discutíamos, ella decía: "Debería haberme dado cuenta en ese momento que esto no iba a funcionar". Pero aguantamos.

En abril del 73 empezamos a trabajar en el siguiente álbum de Santana, la continuación de *Caravanserai*, manteniendo el mismo sabor de jazz y la misma onda espiritual. Para ese entonces, nos valíamos por nuestros propios medios. ¿Quedaba alguien para decirnos qué hacer? Quizá Bill, pero CBS había despedido a Clive Davis más o menos por la época en la que empezamos el nuevo álbum, que se llamó *Welcome,* y no teníamos una conexión estrecha con nadie más en esa compañía discográfica; no como la teníamos con Clive. Las personas que vinieron después de él hicieron lo que tenían que hacer, pero realmente nunca trabajé con otra persona de la industria discográfica que comprendiera a los músicos y supiera hablarles como él, salvo por Chris Blackwell, de Island Records.

Tampoco quedaba nadie en la banda para quejarse de que estuviéramos cambiando nuestro estilo o yendo en otra dirección; Shrieve, Chepito y yo éramos los únicos que quedábamos de la formación original. No obstante, eso no me ayudó con la transición; el cambio en la banda y el paso a una nueva etapa de mi vida todavía me daban vueltas en la cabeza. Tocaba la música de John Coltrane una y otra y otra vez, para concentrarme. Todavía lo hago.

Esta vez, la pista que daba nombre al álbum, "Welcome", era en realidad una melodía de Coltrane. Shrieve y yo hablamos sobre quién debería estar en el álbum. Nos gustaba la idea de tener dos teclados y también dos percusionistas, como tuvimos en *Caravanserai*, así que conservamos a Richard Kermode y Tom Coster, y también estaba Chepito, que era el Tony Williams de los timbales, y Armando, que... bueno, ¡él era el Armando Peraza de las congas! Dougie, por supuesto, siguió con nosotros en bajo, aportando esa consistencia agradable y funky, e invitamos también a algunos amigos especiales (algunas de las mismas personas de Bay Area que tocaron en *Caravanserai*), además de John McLaughlin, el saxofonista Joe Farrell en flauta, Jules Broussard en saxo, y otros.

Por alguna razón, no le presté tanta atención al guitarrista como debería haberlo hecho en ese álbum. En *Welcome,* me centré en el estado de los tecladistas, de las congas y los timbales, y cosas como esas. La única melodía que realmente pensé para mi guitarra fue "Flame-Sky", en la que toca McLaughlin. El título proviene de algo que dijo Sri cuando le toqué la canción.

"Son tan buenos muchachos, tú y John", dijo afectuosamente. "Si tan solo pudieran ver cómo afectan al público... ustedes inflaman sus corazones haciendo que aspiren de nuevo a ser uno con Dios. La mayoría de las personas se olvidan, e invierten en una pesadilla de separación y distancia del Creador, y desempeñan los distintos roles que van creando, pero el único rol que es verdadero es la relación innegable con el Creador, y estar en tu propia luz.

Cuando las personas escuchen esta canción, saldrá una llama de su corazón directo al cielo, indicándole a los ángeles: 'Este está listo. Este está aspirando, y no deseando'".

Otra cosa que recuerdo sobre esa melodía: cuando John y yo hicimos nuestra gira juntos más adelante ese año, durante dos semanas, tocábamos "Flame-Sky" para abrir nuestros espectáculos y siempre cerrábamos con "Let Us Go into the House of the Lord". Qué estupenda banda: John trajo a Larry Young y Billy Cobham, y yo traje a Dougie y Armando. Recuerdo que Armando aceptó el desafío de Cobham en un ensayo después que Billy le dijera que nunca había conocido a un músico de conga que pudiera seguirle el ritmo: conga versus batería. Creí que había terminado en un empate, pero Armando aún no estaba impresionado. Levantó las manos y dijo: "Yo no necesito ninguna baqueta".

Los tres primeros conciertos fueron realmente rápidos y a mucho volumen, y pude ver gente que bostezaba, se cubría los oídos y se iba. En Toronto le dije a John que necesitábamos tener una reunión con todos. "A ver, hermanito. ¿Qué sucede?".

"Creo que necesitamos hacer algunas pruebas de sonido y realmente ensayar algunas de las introducciones, los finales y los temas, porque todas nuestras canciones están sonando igual. Necesitamos analizar las canciones, bajar el volumen y poner ritmo en algunas partes. Hacer un poco más lentas algunas canciones y agregar un poco de variedad. No estoy acostumbrado a ver que la gente bostece y se vaya de nuestros conciertos".

Tuvimos la reunión, y quizá yo fui un poco inmaduro en la forma en que convoqué al grupo por ser poco profesional, lo cual hirió los sentimientos de algunos. Más adelante me enteré de que John dijo que ni siquiera Miles le hablaba de esa forma. Pero yo estaba sorprendido de que nadie más hubiese planteado el problema. Sentía que, si íbamos a llenar un lugar con miles de personas, como lo hacíamos, por respeto al público no podíamos tocar como si fuese martes a la noche en un pequeño bar. Algo bueno trajo el haber expresado mi opinión, porque empezamos a tocar diferentes pasando por diferentes estados de ánimo, creando valles, praderas y montañas. Tuvo mucho éxito. Y sí, yo estaba trabajando en cómo hablarle a la banda. Todavía estoy aprendiendo.

La gran pregunta para el álbum *Welcome* era el tema voces: ¿quién iba a cantar ahora que Gregg se había ido de Santana? Miramos de nuevo nuestra colección de discos, y pensamos en Flora Purim, y la invitamos a unirse a nosotros. Ella venía de Return to Forever y cantó "Yours Is the Light". A mí me gustaba mucho el álbum *Karma*, de Pharoah Sanders, donde estaba la canción "The Creator Has a Master Plan", cantada por Leon Thomas, a quien a veces le gustaba cantar al estilo tirolés. Leon en ese momento estaba haciendo sus propios álbumes; escribió la letra de la canción "Gypsy Queen" de Gábor, y tenía el mismo productor que John Coltrane: Bob Thiele. Invitarlo a grabar y salir de gira con nosotros fue idea de Shrieve: "¿Y si conseguimos que Leon Thomas cante 'Black Magic Woman'? ¿Te imaginas esa canción con él?". Yo le dije: "De acuerdo, ¡hagámoslo!", y Leon aceptó. Me encanta cómo canta Leon en *Welcome*, en las canciones "When I Look into Your Eyes" y "Light of Life", con arreglo de cuerdas de Greg Adams.

Mi amigo Gary Rashid, Rashiki, justo había empezado a trabajar con nosotros en ese momento. Su primer trabajo fue ir al aeropuerto a buscar a Leon, y preguntaba: "¿Cómo lo voy a reconocer?". Leon llegó usando un traje tipo safari con un gran sombrero y un bastón. No hubo problema. Leon se convirtió en una parte importante de Santana. Grabó y luego salió de gira con nosotros desde la primavera del 73 hasta fines de ese año. Pero al principio creo que no tenía mucha fe de que lo tratáramos bien. Él vio que todas las noches yo cenaba comida vegetariana preparada especialmente, así que le dijo al coordinador de la gira que quería algo especial. "Está bien, ¿qué te gustaría?", preguntó el representante.

"Hígado y cebollas", que yo creo que era como pedir un bife: un menú caro. Así que nuestro coordinador de gira se aseguró de que en cada comida (en el hotel y en el detrás de escena) hubiese un plato de hígado y cebollas para Leon. ¿Y adivina qué pasó? Al tercer día ya estaba harto: "¿No comen otra cosa más que hígado, muchachos?".

La primera melodía en *Welcome* es "Going Home", que está

inspirada en la *Sinfonía del Nuevo Mundo* de Antonín Dvořák, con arreglos de Alice Coltrane. Le pedí a Richard Kermode que tocara ese arreglo en el mellotron, y a Tom Coster que tocara el órgano Yamaha como ella tocaba su Wurlitzer. Te seré honesto: Shrieve y yo presionábamos a Tom todo el tiempo, diciéndole que escuchara a Alice Coltrane, a Larry Young, a Miles tocando el Yamaha... y Dios lo bendiga, porque Tom podría habernos dicho "¡Váyanse al diablo!" e irse, pero no lo hizo. Su actitud en cambio fue: "De acuerdo, lo intentaré". Y una vez que consiguió entender el tono, todo fue más fácil.

"Going Home" surgió después de conocer a Alice Coltrane ese año, que para mí fue quizá la mayor concreción de mi sueño espiritual: pasar de ser un lavaplatos a reunirme con la viuda de John Coltrane y luego poder hacer música con ella.

Nos conocimos en la primavera del 73, cuando Alice me invitó a ir a su casa en Los Ángeles para conocerla a ella y a su amigo Swami Satchidananda. Para ese entonces, ella había adoptado el nombre hindú Turiya. Satchidananda me cayó bien, y quizá era otro gurú que podría haber seguido, pero yo soy de naturaleza apasionada, y creo que el propio poder y pasión de Sri estaban bien para mí. Si existe algo así como la disciplina en el romance, entonces eso es Sri Chinmoy, porque es un amante de lo supremo, y yo me siento atraído hacia los amantes. Cuando te abrazan, es un abrazo realmente estrecho. No te dejan ir fácilmente.

Deborah y yo vivíamos nuestra vida en dos hogares: uno en Marin County y el otro en Queens, en un lugar que rentábamos en Parsons Boulevard, cerca del ashram de Sri. Íbamos y veníamos de uno a otro, y confiábamos lo suficiente en nuestro matrimonio como para que ella fuera a Nueva York a meditar mientras yo me quedaba y grababa en San Francisco. Así que, cuando Turiya me invitó a pasar un tiempo con ella, después de escuchar mi álbum *Love Devotion Surrender*, Deborah supo que era una oportunidad para que yo estableciera una importante relación musical y espiritual; una que debía desarrollar. Así que Deborah fue a ver a Sri en Queens mientras yo iba a Los Ángeles.

De todos modos, estábamos todos interconectados, pero yo me sentía más abierto que nunca a tocar música y aprender. Traté de aprender *todas* las lecciones que pude de todos los maestros que pude encontrar. Podría decirse que en este período, toda la meditación, las charlas y la escucha que hacía eran como pelar una alcachofa, quitando las capas más externas hasta llegar al corazón de quien yo realmente era, quien seré siempre, sin jugar a las escondidas conmigo mismo, como suele hacer la gente.

Pasé casi una semana con Turiya. Ella me abrió su casa y yo me sentí muy agradecido. Recuerdo escucharla hablar sobre música y sobre su camino espiritual y, por supuesto, sobre John, aunque ella nunca lo llamaba así. Le decía Ohnedaruth (su nombre espiritual), o unas pocas veces lo mencionó como el Padre. Me contó que él nunca dejaba de tocar, incluso cuando estaba en casa, mucho tiempo después de un concierto. Cuando tenía el día libre, seguía tocando; me contó que podía pasar una hora solo mirando el saxo, y luego otra hora moviendo sus dedos hacia arriba y hacia abajo por todo el instrumento. Finalmente se lo llevaba a la boca y comenzaba a tocar. ¡Aleluya! Así que primero él visualizaba la música, luego pasaba a la mecánica. Creo que Coltrane nunca dejaba de pensar en tocar el saxo porque no quería que el fuego se apagara; si dejas que se apague, tienes que volver a empezar de cero.

También pasé algo de tiempo con los hijos de Turiya. Los observaba saltar en la piscina durante el día, y cada noche después que los niños se iban a dormir, ella y yo charlábamos un rato. Después ella iba a su habitación y yo descansaba en el sofá. A eso de las tres y media de la mañana nos levantábamos, y ella tocaba el arpa y el piano. Yo escuchaba, y luego los dos meditábamos un rato más.

Una mañana, casi al final de la semana, empezamos a meditar. Cuando meditas a las tres de la mañana, la primera media hora es como estar en un avión que pasa por una zona de turbulencia. Tienes los ojos enrojecidos, sabes que todo a tu alrededor está oscuro, intentas mantenerte despierto y tiemblas. Y entonces, de repente, las cosas se vuelven realmente agradables. Esa mañana pude ver una hermosa llama en la vela que estaba ardiendo: era como una llama dentro de la llama. Así que, en mi mente, entré allí, como lo había hecho muchas veces antes. Pero esta vez comencé a sentir la presencia de alguien más en la habitación, además de Turiya. Era John Coltrane. Entonces él se materializó en mi visión. Me miraba directamente a mí, y sostenía dos conos de helado, ¡cada uno con tres bochas!

Lo miré, él sonrió y dijo: "¿Te gustaría probar un poco?". Entonces fue como si Turiya hubiese entrado en la visión por el rabillo de mi ojo izquierdo, y me dijo: "Adelante, prueba uno". Así que, interiormente, tomé uno de los conos y lo lamí, y se sentía dulce y cremoso: simplemente delicioso. "Está bueno, ¿eh?", me dijo John.

"Sí, gracias. Está muy bueno".

"Bien, ese es un acorde de séptima disminuida en si bemol".

"¿Qué? ¿En serio?".

Luego escuché que Turiya decía: "Prueba otro". Solo que esta vez me pareció que me lo estaba diciendo en voz alta desde la habitación contigua, como si supiera lo que estaba sucediendo en mi meditación.

Hombre, eso sí que *me asustó*. ¿Cómo sabía? No tengo duda de que cuando la gente lea esto va a pensar algo como: "Oh, claro, este tipo tomó demasiado LSD y todavía tenía alucinaciones". Pero del 72 al 81 dejé de tomar drogas. Quizá una vez, un año después, por curiosidad probé un poco de mescalina, pero en ese momento en el 73 estaba totalmente sobrio, no había consumido nada.

Tienes que comprender que, hasta el día de hoy, cuando escucho la música de John Coltrane, siento la certeza de que Dios nunca me suelta la mano. No importa cuán oscuras se vuelvan las cosas, no importa lo que pase, Dios sigue en mí. Para mí, su música es la forma más rápida de salir de la oscuridad del ego: de la oscuridad, la culpa, la vergüenza, el prejuicio, la condena, el miedo, la tentación, de *todo*.

Y no me refiero solo a *A Love Supreme* y *Meditations* y sus álbumes más espirituales. Si escucho "Naima" o "Central Park West" o "Equinox" o "The Night Has a Thousand Eyes", o cualquiera de las baladas más viejas que grabó, descubro que cada nota está surcada de matices espirituales. Hay una oración constante allí que cualquiera puede escuchar.

Incluso cuando Coltrane toca una canción, es mucho más que eso; y me gustan las canciones. Me gusta "Wild Thing". Me gusta "Louie Louie" y cualquier cosa de The Beatles o de Frank Sinatra. Pero lo de Coltrane no eran solo canciones; al menos, no para mí. Su música es sobre la luz, y su sonido era un lenguaje de luz. Es como el solvente que colocas en el agua sucia y turbia: lo revuelves, e instantáneamente el agua vuelve a quedar limpia. El sonido de John Coltrane es un solvente que limpia la turbiedad de la distancia y la separación de uno mismo. Por eso es que todos amamos a Trane, Wayne Shorter, John McLaughlin, Stevie Wonder y tantos otros, porque su sonido nos recuerda que todo es redimible. Eso es lo que Coltrane le estaba diciendo a la gente: cristaliza tus intenciones, tus motivos y tu propósito para el bien superior del planeta.

Nunca pude conocer a Coltrane, ¡pero lo siento a través de tantas otras personas! Alice Coltrane, por supuesto; Albert Ayler; John Gilmore... especialmente a través de su práctica espiritual y su música intergaláctica. Hoy todavía puedes escuchar a Coltrane en Wayne Shorter y Herbie Hancock, y en la música de Charles Lloyd, Pharoah Sanders, Sonny Fortune y muchos otros.

Sé que algunas personas se rascan la cabeza cuando les digo que la música de John Coltrane tiene el poder de reorganizar las estructuras moleculares. Una vez me encontraba en una ceremonia de los Juegos Olímpicos; estaba hablando sobre el poder sanador de la música y a mi lado estaba Wynton Marsalis. Él sacudió la cabeza e hizo una mueca. Yo me largué a reír. Quizá Wynton haya cambiado su perspectiva, pero en ese entonces pude darme cuenta de que lo yo estaba diciendo le resultaba una incoherencia. Es una bendición tan grande poder tocar desde tu alma y llegar a tanta gente... pero también es una bendición poder escuchar y percibir el poder sanador que viene de la música de otras personas. A eso me refiero cuando hablo del Tono Universal.

CAPÍTULO 16

Deborah y yo, en el espectáculo Day on the Green en el
Oakland Coliseum, 4 de julio de 1977.

*Alrededor del año 2004, tuve un sueño muy muy detallado. En este
sueño, yo estaba en un edificio en Milán, de noche. John McLaughlin
también estaba allí, y podíamos ver afuera a través de una ventana
hacia un parque que, en el medio, tenía luces muy brillantes. Eran como
luces para un interrogatorio, así que todo lo demás estaba oscuro, salvo
donde iluminaban esas luces, y allí había unos muchachos jugando al*

fútbol, pero no podían ir muy lejos porque tenían que mantenerse dentro del área iluminada. John y yo estábamos viendo este partido de 'fútbol a la luz' y, de repente, veía a Todd Barkan (el tipo que dirigía el club de jazz Keystone Korner en San Francisco) cruzando por el parque, y con él iba alguien que llevaba unos saxos y empujaba una bicicleta. ¡Era John Coltrane!

John y yo veíamos que los dos hombres venían hacia el edificio donde estábamos nosotros, y nos sentíamos más y más emocionados. Coltrane dejaba la bicicleta afuera, venía con sus instrumentos de viento y algunas partituras, y Todd nos presentaba. "Oye, Carlos, John está trabajando en una canción y creo que quiere que la toques con él".

"¿Qué? ¿En serio?".

Coltrane me miraba. "Hola, ¿cómo estás?".

"Eh, hola, John". Yo estaba tan nervioso, que solo pensaba: "Oh, Dios mío, estoy con John Coltrane ¡y quiere que toque algo con él!" Mientras Coltrane sacaba los instrumentos yo miraba la partitura, y era una canción de iglesia afroamericana, algo como "Let Us Go into the House of the Lord". Yo pensaba: "¡Oh, sí! No hay problema. Puedo hacer esto". Y empezaba a trabajar en mi parte.

Pero cuando miraba hacia arriba, Coltrane se había ido. Le preguntaba a Todd: "¡Ey! ¿qué le pasó a John?".

"Oh, alguien acaba de robarle la bicicleta, así que salió corriendo, pero creo que el ladrón se escapó". Así que yo decidía ayudarlo y salía del edificio, y de repente me encontraba en la carretera entre Nassau Coliseum y Jones Beach. Veía la bicicleta de Coltrane, pero la habían desmantelado; le faltaban las ruedas y el asiento. Yo la recogía de todos modos y la traía de vuelta, y encontraba a John. Y allí me desperté de golpe.

Ese sueño me dejó una profunda impresión. Todavía era de madrugada, pero tenía que contárselo a alguien, así que llamé a Alice: "Turiya, lamento llamarte a esta hora". Ella dijo: "Descuida; ya he hecho mi meditación. ¿Cómo estás?". Le conté sobre el sueño, y me dijo que para ella tenía perfecto sentido. Lo interpretó de este modo: creía que los chicos jugando en el parque eran los chicos que escuchan música hoy, entrando y saliendo de la oscuridad, buscando una música que los traiga a la luz, como la de John Coltrane. La bicicleta robada y sin ruedas representaba cuán difícil era hacer que esa música llegase a las personas. Ya no había ningún vehículo que ayudase a llevar la música de Coltrane a quienes necesitan escucharla. Su música tiene tan poca difusión y tan poca prensa, pero es importante sacar a la gente a la luz de su música: hacer de Coltrane un nombre reconocido en todas partes.

Desde 1972 he estado tratando de ponerle de nuevo las ruedas a la bicicleta, grabando "A Love Supreme" y "Naima" con John McLaughlin, grabando "Welcome" y "Peace on Earth", sugiriéndole a la gente la música de John y también la de Alice Coltrane que, a mi criterio, lamentablemente no se tiene en cuenta, pero creo que su música también es atemporal.

Tengo muchas otras ideas. Hice una cruzada para que la gente de los Grammy designara su premio anual a la trayectoria con su nombre: el premio John Coltrane a la trayectoria. Quisiera armar un álbum completo de Coltrane interpretando "Naima": tres o cuatro discos que incluyan algunas de las mejores interpretaciones que hizo de esa hermosa canción, en vivo y en el estudio. Apoyo a Ravi Coltrane, hijo de John y Alice, y a su esposa, Kathleen, en todo lo que están haciendo para preservar el hogar de Coltrane en Dix Hills, en Long Island, donde Coltrane escribió A Love Supreme y donde empezó su familia con Alice.

Hay otra cuestión sobre ese sueño con John Coltrane y la bicicleta, y la gente es libre de decir que estoy alucinando. No estarían del todo equivocados, tampoco; en cierta forma ¡creo que nací alucinando! Pero muchas veces es difícil distinguir entre los sueños y la imaginación. En cualquier caso, la misma mañana en la que Alice Coltrane interpretó el sueño, recibí una llamada telefónica de mi amigo Michel Delorme de Francia. Le conté sobre el sueño, le di todos los detalles, y él le restó importancia a su modo típico: "¡Puf! Claro, Carlos. Estoy viajando con McLaughlin. Anoche estábamos en Milán, hablando sobre tú y John Coltrane".

El año 1973 fue un año de disciplina espiritual, y también un año de extremada locura, que puso a prueba nuestra resistencia. Con Santana estábamos más de gira que en casa; algunas noches hasta hacíamos dos funciones. Según mis cálculos, creo que hicimos más de doscientos espectáculos. ¿Por qué trabajábamos tan duro? Una gran parte era la sensación de que mientras la gente pagara, teníamos que seguir tocando. No teníamos la suficiente confianza en nosotros mismos como para creer que el público seguiría allí si nos tomábamos un tiempo de descanso y luego volvíamos a Nueva York o Londres o Montreux. Tampoco sabíamos que había otra opción. Si nuestro representante nos decía que necesitábamos hacer cierta cantidad de dinero, y si la estábamos pasando mal por culpa del Servicio de Impuestos Internos (IRS), ¿quién de nosotros tenía la experiencia como para rebelarse ante eso? Éramos jóvenes, estábamos ansiosos y creíamos en nuestra nueva música. Fue nuestra decisión. Nadie nos puso un revólver en la cabeza.

Lo que me ayudó fue que meditaba, mi dieta era saludable y no andaba de juerga, y Shrieve estaba en el mismo camino que yo. Fue entonces cuando comenzamos a usar incienso en el escenario y cuando puse en mi amplificador una foto de Sri Chinmoy en meditación profunda. No creo que hubiera podido atravesar ese año sin la fortaleza espiritual necesaria para sostener lo que estábamos haciendo en la gira. Habíamos viajado mucho antes, pero puedes preguntarle a cualquiera que haya estado en Santana ese año; había momentos en los que era como ir a la guerra. Y yo sentía que Shrieve y yo éramos compañeros en el campo de batalla. Fue duro, pero estábamos enamorados de la música, y nunca nadie se quejó.

Cuando pienso en esos tiempos, me doy cuenta de que no siempre fui el tipo más afable para tener alrededor. Era como un ex fumador juntándose con un grupo de fumadores y diciéndoles que tenían que cambiar. Creo que, como la mayoría de las personas que no aún no están maduras de espíritu, yo tendía a ponerme muy quisquilloso y a actuar como un engreído. Quizá daba la impresión de tener un sentido de superioridad y cierta rigidez acerca la espiritualidad. Lo diré de esta forma: aún tenía mucho por crecer, y me llevó algún tiempo darme cuenta de ello.

Creo que algunos de los que seguíamos a Sri Chinmoy en ese entonces sentíamos que teníamos alguna especie de llave de los cielos, y que todos los demás eran unos tontos. Ojalá Sri en sus enseñanzas también hubiera dicho: "Mira, si vas a estar en un camino espiritual, debes ser amable con la gente que no está en el mismo camino". Yo no lo sabía, pero tenía que crecer mucho: todavía estaba muy muy verde en el asunto de manejarme con delicadeza con los demás. Por contraste, me daba cuenta escuchando las entrevistas a John Coltrane que él era muy considerado con el desarrollo espiritual de las personas (o con su carencia de este) cada vez que hablaba. A eso necesitaba aspirar yo; no solo a su música. Estaba aprendiendo muchas cosas en 1973.

La otra cosa que hizo que ese año fuera más fácil para mí, fue que la banda estaba en su versión óptima: quizá una de las mejores versiones en toda la historia de Santana. Lo diré de esta forma: en retrospectiva, esa banda de 1973 (con Leon Thomas, Armando y Chepito, TC y Kermode, Dougie, Shrieve y yo) fue, musicalmente, la mejor banda y la más desafiante en la que haya estado jamás. Y la cuestión es que, cuando tocábamos entregando lo mejor de nosotros, en realidad solo estábamos tratando de encontrarnos a nosotros mismos.

Esa formación fue lo más cerca que alguna vez estuvo Santana de ser una banda de jazz. En las pruebas de sonido probábamos cosas nuevas, y era muy divertido. Recuerdo que nos inspirábamos en pequeños segmentos musicales escritos por un tecladista llamado Todd Cochran, que escribía para Freddie Hubbard y otros, y también grababa su propia música. Tenía una canción llamada "Free Angela" que empezamos a hacer, y que para mí sonaba como salida del álbum *Crossings* de Herbie. Hasta el día de hoy, hacemos pruebas de sonido y ensayamos cosas nuevas todo el tiempo, incluso si estamos en el mismo lugar por dos o tres noches y ya hemos probado el sistema. "¿Igual quieren hacer una prueba de sonido?".

"Sí, claro. Probemos algo nuevo…".

Creo que la mejor forma de explicar ese año es comenzar con Japón: esa fue nuestra primera vez en ese país y esa parte del mundo. Como Suiza, se convirtió en un país al que Santana volvió una y otra vez, y donde encontramos otro amante de la música iluminado (como Claude Nobs en Montreux, que allí se había convertido en un gran promotor musical), el Sr. Udo. Algunos lo llaman el Bill Graham de Japón, porque fue quien realmente empezó a llevar grandes espectáculos de rock allá. Estoy de acuerdo con eso, pero él también se ganó su nombre porque respeta la música y trata bien a los músicos. Nunca dejó de creer en Santana y en lo que hacíamos; nunca. Siempre ha sido circunspecto y elegante en su forma de vestir, y siempre tiene algunas muy buenas historias para contar; cuando se ríe, lo hace abiertamente y sin reprimirse. Él es otro de los custodios de la llama, uno de esos ángeles que llegó en el momento adecuado para guiarnos y cuidarnos. El Sr. Udo es el único promotor con el que he trabajado en Japón.

Cuando fuimos en el 73, Japón todavía era muy tradicional; podías ver tanta gente por la calle en kimonos como en trajes. Todavía no había llegado McDonald's, ni Kentucky Fried Chicken. El Sr. Udo se aseguraba de que comiéramos bien, y siempre era el anfitrión perfecto, nos llevaba afuera a cenar; y todavía lo hace, y yo todavía me aseguro de reservarnos tiempo para ello cuando Santana va a Japón. En nuestra última visita, le regaló a Cindy el kimono más bello y alucinante que vi, lleno de bordados, que la hizo derretirse; ¡fue muy gracioso ver a mi esposa convertirse en una nena de seis años!

Japón siempre ha sido el mejor lugar para conseguir los sistemas electrónicos más nuevos, especialmente estéreos. Los japoneses tenían videos en formato analógico (Betamax) apenas salieron, y discos compactos y cintas de audio digital cuando nadie más los tenía. Esa primera vez que estábamos en Tokio, descubrimos Akihabara, el distrito donde estaban todas las tiendas de productos electrónicos, y allí fue cuando descubrí que Armando, con su estupenda confianza en sí mismo, era también un estupendo regateador.

Salir de compras con él y observarlo negociar era asombroso. Armando tenía una rutina donde él entraba a una tienda y tomaba un pasacintas o algo, lo volvía a poner en su lugar como si oliera mal, se iba, y después volvía como si se hubiese arrepentido.

Entonces le decía al vendedor: "¿Se acuerda de mí? Me llamo Armando Peraza y estoy aquí con Santana. Esta... *cosa*... ¿precio especial para mí? ¿Cuánto?". El vendedor era lo suficientemente inteligente como para saber qué decir. "Cuesta trescientos noventa y cinco dólares. Pero, para usted, trescientos cincuenta dólares. Y quizá un buen descuento en auriculares". Armando decía entonces: "Hmm. No está mal. Deme eso anotado, por favor".

A menudo me daba cuenta de que era la primera vez que alguien le pedía al vendedor que hiciera eso. Así que el hombre escribía su oferta, e inmediatamente Armando cruzaba la calle e iba a otra tienda, donde había estado apenas diez minutos antes. "¡Oiga! ¿se acuerda de mí? ¿Armando Peraza, de Santana? Mire esto: lo mismo que usted tiene aquí. Enfrente me lo dejan a trescientos cincuenta dólares. ¿Qué puede hacer usted por mí?". Y así le rebajaban el precio a trescientos veinte dólares. "¿Es esa su mejor oferta? Porque todos en Santana quieren esta cosa también; los voy a traer a todos a comprar aquí. Solo anóteme el precio así se los muestro". Y puedes adivinar lo que ocurría después. Armando volvía a la otra tienda y salía con algo así como un 40 por ciento de descuento. Luego los dos vendedores hablaban por teléfono entre ellos comentando sobre ¡ese loco cubano!

Armando no hacía esto solo con los productos electrónicos; le encantaban los sacos buenos, y también era un adicto a los zapatos. Era divertido verlo haciendo su trabajo de regateo; yo aprendí mucho.

En Tokio, el Sr. Udo arregló que tocáramos durante toda una semana en el Budokan, un hermoso estadio que había sido construido para competencias de judo. The Beatles habían estado allí en 1966, y se convirtió en otra joya en el mundo de las giras de rock, uno de esos lugares donde todos los grupos querían tocar, y grabar, si tenían suerte. Nuestros espectáculos se grababan en cinta para pasarlos por televisión y estaban llenos de gente todas las noches. Pensé que quizás era hora de sacar el primer álbum en vivo de Santana, y el Sr. Udo estaba de acuerdo. Así que también grabamos nuestros conciertos en Osaka en otro hermoso teatro llamado

Koseinenkin Hall. Fue una experiencia increíble: el amor y el respeto del público, el apoyo del Sr. Udo, el nivel en el que estábamos tocando. Cuando nos fuimos de Japón para ir a tocar a Australia y Nueva Zelanda, supe que habíamos grabado la mejor música que habíamos interpretado jamás.

Hicimos la gira de Extremo Oriente y Australia en un avión que rentamos: un viejo avión de hélice que Chepito apodó la Tortuga voladora, porque todos nuestros viajes parecían llevar una eternidad. Recuerdo que ir de Hong Kong a Perth se sintió como un vuelo de veinticuatro horas. Pero en ese entonces no importó; ¡estábamos tan felices con la aventura! Terminábamos de dar un gran espectáculo y, todavía mareados de la emoción, subíamos al avión. Yo cerraba los ojos y cuando despertaba, estábamos en un país nuevo que nunca antes había visto: Indonesia, Malasia, Australia. También estaba realmente feliz porque la prensa hablaba muy bien de nosotros, a pesar de que podrían haberse sentido desilusionados por no haber escuchado la banda Santana original y el tipo de conciertos que hacíamos antes.

El último concierto de la gira fue en Nueva Zelanda, en Christchurch, y recuerdo que la banda funcionando tan bien, como si hubiésemos llegado a la cima de una montaña. Realmente se sintió como el mejor concierto de la gira, lo mejor que había sonado jamás la banda. No grabamos todos nuestros espectáculos en ese entonces, pero sabía que los admiradores podían grabar a Santana en concierto, o encontrar a alguien que lo hiciera. Sabía que había videos piratas dando vueltas, si bien no era algo tan extremo como el caso de Grateful Dead, con todas esas grabaciones y comercio piratas. Por alguna razón, sin embargo, no pude encontrar una grabación de nuestro espectáculo en Christchurch hasta el 2013, cuando conseguimos una copia a través de uno de nuestros fervientes seguidores de Santana. Los llamamos los guardianes, porque saben más sobre la banda y su historia que cualquiera de nosotros. Tuvimos que arreglar la grabación en el estudio porque la cinta se había deteriorado y estaba floja. Pero, una vez reparada, pudimos escuchar la ejecución con nitidez, y validaba todo lo que yo recordaba haber sentido sobre el espectáculo. Había un sentido de aventura en lo que tocábamos; extendíamos nuestros límites y probábamos cosas nuevas, incluso en la última fecha de la gira, y no había más turbulencia, ningún problema con la estructura de las canciones o las transiciones. Sentí que el espectáculo se había hecho solo; así de bueno fue. Todavía no lo puedo creer.

De allí volvimos a los Estados Unidos y seguimos de gira otras cinco semanas. Fue durante este período que Deborah y yo recibimos nuestros nombres espirituales de Sri; nombres que nos había prometido el año anterior. Devadip, que significa "lámpara de Dios" y "ojo de Dios", era mi nuevo nombre; y el de Deborah era Urmila, que significa "Luz del Supremo". En ese mismo momento, Deborah y Kitsaun se estaban preparando para abrir Dipti Nivas, el restaurante vegetariano que Sri nos había pedido que abriéramos en San Francisco porque él no aceptaba donativos. Prefería que sus seguidores hicieran el tipo de cosas que difundían su mensaje de amor. "No trates de cambiar el mundo", decía. "El mundo ya está cambiado. Trata de amar al mundo". Un nuevo restaurante vegetariano aspiraba a ese objetivo espiritual y era el tipo de contribución que él deseaba.

El restaurante se abrió en el distrito Castro, que se estaba volviendo conocido como centro de la comunidad gay de San Francisco, y a medida que el vecindario crecía, esto ayudaba a los negocios locales. Al principio yo no estaba seguro de si podríamos llevar adelante un restaurante, pero vi cómo Deborah se hacía cargo, y dado que Kitsaun también era un discípulo, supe que entre los dos estarían bien. Recuerdo cómo Deborah una vez se acercó a un drag queen muy alto y le dijo: "Lo siento, señor. No está permitido fumar aquí". Él se veía como si hubiese pasado la mitad del día arreglándose. La miró y apagó el cigarrillo. Deborah era firme y eficiente cuando se trataba de estas cosas.

Pronto, cualquiera que fuera vegetariano o estuviera pensando en dejar la carne, o simplemente sintiera curiosidad, venía. Las frittatas y los guisados y los jugos frescos eran deliciosos, y el lugar recibía excelentes críticas. Deborah y Kitsaun comenzaron a dar clases de meditación allí, y bandas como la de Herbie Hancock venían a comer cuando estaban en la ciudad. Lo que estábamos haciendo allí, como lo definió Sri desde el principio, era una ofrenda de amor. La gente podía saborear nuestras intenciones y sentir lo que teníamos para ofrecer a nivel espiritual. Dipti Nivas siguió siendo popular durante un largo tiempo.

La segunda etapa en nuestra gira fue el primer recorrido real de Santana por América Central y América del Sur: diez países, incluido México. Fue mi primera vez tocando allí desde que me había ido, en 1963. De hecho, el primer espectáculo fue en Guadalajara, en mi estado natal de Jalisco, así que puedes imaginarte la atención que recibía. Seré honesto: creo que no estaba preparado para eso. Todavía estaba tratando de ordenar mi vida espiritualmente, de encontrar mi identidad. Y, musicalmente, era mucho más estadounidense que cualquier otra cosa, todavía estaba enamorado del blues y el jazz de Miles y de Coltrane. En mi mente, incluso antes de reunirme con la prensa en México, yo pensaba que iban a querer reivindicarme como suyo. ¿Sabes cuáles fueron las primeras preguntas cuando comenzamos a dar entrevistas? "¿Por qué no tocas música mexicana? ¿No te gusta la música de tu país natal? ¿Por qué no hablas español?".

Hacerme ese tipo de preguntas era como agitar una bandera roja frente a un toro. Los periodistas hicieron la conferencia de prensa de un modo muy polémico. Mi mente daba vueltas con todo tipo de respuestas posibles, como: "Yo no soy mexicano, soy indio yaqui, como mi padre". O "¿Sabes? Lo que crees que es música mexicana, en realidad es europea: ritmos de dos tiempos y de vals. Incluso la palabra *mariachi* viene de la palabra francesa para 'casamiento'". Pero los entrevistadores tenían tanto interés en una lección de historia musical como yo en un interrogatorio.

Las cosas no arrancaron bien entre esos escritores mexicanos y yo. Hubo una especie de guerra entre nosotros que perduró durante años: incluso mi mamá, que estaba viviendo en San Francisco, se enteró de ello. Sus amigos le enviaban los periódicos, y ella me llamaba diciéndome: "¿No puedes suavizar un poco las cosas? Sé que lo que dices es verdad, pero los estás haciendo encabronar como locos". Ella leía todo. "¿Por qué estás tan enojado?", me preguntaba. Todos en mi familia siempre se han portado así (Tony, Jorge y ahora María), preguntándome cómo estaba y pidiéndome que cuidara mis palabras. Ese comportamiento ya es una tradición familiar; incluso cuando a veces tengo decirles respetuosamente que no estoy de acuerdo, los amo aún más por preocuparse tanto por mí.

Las cosas mejoraron con la prensa mexicana en el transcurso de los años, no obstante, ese malestar nunca me impidió ir y hacer el mismo tipo de espectáculos que en el resto del mundo. Llevó tiempo; cuando volví después del éxito de *Supernatural*, creo que fue la primera vez que realmente me sentí a gusto con el hecho de ser mexicano y de estar en México, incluso con todo el interrogatorio que recibía. Una cosa es cierta: nunca hubo un momento en que no sintiera el amor de la gente cuando tocaba ahí. El público mexicano siempre me hizo sentir en casa, incluso esa primera vez en el 73.

Un hecho destacado de esa gira me hizo sentir incluso más orgulloso de ser mexicano. Cuando llegamos a Nicaragua, hogar de Chepito, acordamos hacer un concierto de beneficencia para los sobrevivientes del gran terremoto que había golpeado allí justo antes de Navidad, el año anterior. En realidad, este era el segundo concierto de beneficencia que hacíamos; el primero fue en California, el mes de enero anterior, junto con The Rolling Stones y Cheech y Chong. Esta vez tocamos en un estadio de fútbol en Managua, donde había sucedido el terremoto. ¿Y quién fue el maestro de ceremonias del espectáculo? Yo no podía creerlo: Mario Moreno o, como lo conocen todos los mexicanos, ¡Cantinflas!

Todos en América Central y América del Sur conocían las películas de Cantinflas y lo amaban. Era como todos los hermanos Marx en uno: le tomaba el pelo a la alta sociedad, se escapaba de los policías; se sobreponía sin dejar de ser quien era. Los admiradores llenaron el aeropuerto cuando él llegó. Cuando subió al escenario

en el estadio, el lugar estaba atestado de gente. Él fue hasta el micrófono y dijo: *"¡Hermanos, hermanas!* Recibí una llamada telefónica
mientras estaba en Barcelona, diciendo que me necesitaban aquí
como maestro de ceremonias esta noche, y en seguida dije: '¡Por
supuesto! Para mis hermanos y hermanas de Nicaragua, ¡claro que
sí!' ". El estadio estaba lleno hasta arriba, y todos aplaudían y grita-
ban con entusiasmo. Entonces Cantinflas se puso serio. "Solo tengo
una cosa para pedirles". Todos hicieron silencio.

"Quien sea que haya tomado mi cartera, ¿me la podría devolver?".

Nunca escuché tal explosión de risa. No era solo el sonido;
podías sentir la energía. En un solo momento, cincuenta mil personas que habían sido afectadas por el terremoto y llevaban meses
esperando ayuda, de golpe soltaron su tensión y sus preocupaciones y estaban riendo juntas. Realmente fue algo espiritual. Con
una sola frase, con apenas unas palabras, Cantinflas se conectó con
cada persona que estaba en ese lugar. Esa fue una enorme lección
para mí: el poder de la risa.

También me recordó que en la iglesia, cuando era chico, vi una
pintura de la gente en el Día del Juicio Final: los que eran condenados e iban al infierno, y los otros, que tenían suerte e iban al cielo.
Yo era todavía un niño: ¿se suponía que esto debía inspirarme? Yo
pensaba: "Esto no tiene nada que ver conmigo", y tomaba el poco
dinero que tenía y me iba al cine a ver a Dean Martin y Jerry Lewis
haciéndose los tontos. Me reía hasta morir. Siempre me han gus-
tado mucho las comedias y los cómicos, especialmente aquellos
que saben cómo reírse de sí mismos sin ser racistas o vulgares.

La risa puede ser algo muy espiritual; si me preguntas, creo que
pasar unas horas desternillándose de risa es más efectivo que todo
un mes de meditación. Puede sacarte de ti mismo y ayudarte a soltar muchas capas de miedo y enojo. Si haces que alguien se ría, que
realmente se ría, estás tratando con la consciencia del Cristo y la
consciencia del Buda y la iluminación divina. Para mí, Rodney
Dangerfield, Bill Cosby, Richard Pryor y George Lopez son todos
hombres santos, en el sentido de que cada uno de ellos mira la vida
y busca un modo de reírse de ella. Todavía me río cuando recuerdo

cómo Mel Brooks dejaba a Count Basie y su banda en medio del desierto en *Blazing Saddles* y tenía un sheriff afroamericano que cabalgaba con una montura Gucci: eso es ser un genio cómico y espiritual. Hay tantas cosas sucediendo en ese preciso momento. La risa es liviandad, y si no tienes sentido del humor, las cosas pueden ponerse negras muy rápidamente.

Otra de las lecciones que aprendí en esa gira por América del Sur en el 73 fue que, como yo hablaba español, pude practicar mucho dando entrevistas y hablando con el público desde el escenario. Estaba hablando más y más en nombre de la banda en público, incluso cuando Shrieve y yo todavía tomábamos las decisiones musicales en forma conjunta.

Bill Graham produjo ese primer concierto en Nicaragua para ayudar a los damnificados por el terremoto en enero del 73, y creo que esa era otra razón por la cual él y yo éramos tan compatibles. Siempre creí que la música podía ayudar a las personas que necesitaban ayuda, y todavía lo creo. De hecho, así es como empezó Bill: produciendo conciertos para recaudar dinero para la San Francisco Mime Troupe, luego para ayudar a algunas personas que habían sido arrestadas, y si hay algo que nunca cambió en él, es que nunca dejó de organizar conciertos de beneficencia y funciones para recaudar fondos para buenas causas, sin importar cuán grande fuera ya su reputación personal. Estando rodeado de hippies y en ese ambiente tan particular de San Francisco, no podría haber terminado de ninguna otra manera: haciendo lo que podía para ayudar a la gente y para protestar por lo que consideraba incorrecto.

¿Recuerdas el concierto S.N.A.C.K. que organizó Bill en 1975 con Bob Dylan y Neil Young y otras bandas, para recaudar dinero para programas después de la escuela? ¿O cuando ayudó a recaudar dos millones de dólares después del terremoto de California del 89 con todas esas bandas de rock e incluso Bob Hope? Cada vez que me llamaba a mí para cosas como esa, yo siempre decía "sí: anota a Santana en la lista". De hecho, le decía que nos pusiera al comienzo de la lista, porque sabía que así podría usar nuestro nombre para conseguir otras bandas importantes.

Justo antes de que Bill muriera en el 91, estábamos hablando sobre un concierto a beneficio para los indios americanos en el Shoreline Amphitheatre en Mountain View, para conmemorar el aniversario de 1492. Lo íbamos a llamar "500 Años de Supervivencia a Colón". El último mensaje de teléfono que me dejó fue sobre ese proyecto: "Que estés bien, amigo. Nos vemos mañana".

A fines del 73, todos estábamos cansados de estar de gira, y Ray Etzler era nuestro representante. Bill todavía supervisaba la parte comercial de Santana, y si bien realmente nos auto-administrábamos, contratamos a Ray para que se ocupara de cosas que necesitaban un manejo especial, como las negociaciones con Columbia Records, que parecía estar cada vez menos de nuestro lado.

Welcome salió en noviembre de ese año, y queríamos que nuestro próximo álbum fuera nuestro concierto de Japón. Habíamos escuchado las cintas de nuestros conciertos en Osaka y eran excelentes; habían capturado a la banda en su mejor desempeño, y estábamos realmente orgullosos de ellas. Teníamos un excelente plan para sacar esa música al mercado, convirtiéndola en una experiencia completa del concierto de Santana: tres elepés, con un folleto e imágenes de Japón, incluida una del Buda, todo hecho por talentosos artistas japoneses. El álbum incluía una melodía que creamos durante esos conciertos y a la que le pusimos el nombre en homenaje al Sr. Udo.

Era un plan hermoso y ambicioso, y la música era nueva, pero no era algo que Columbia pudiera manejar. Con la portada, la presentación y los tres discos del álbum, era demasiado caro para ellos. No creían que se iba a vender lo suficiente. Incluso después de que los japoneses finalmente lanzaran *Lotus* en el verano de 1974 y éste se convirtiera en el álbum importado de mayor venta, Columbia no cambió de opinión; ni siquiera Bill pudo persuadirlos. Así de diferentes eran las cosas después de que Clive hubiera sido obligado a irse. Yo estaba aprendiendo cuán burocráticas podían ser las cosas en los Estados Unidos y cuán diferente se manejaban las compañías discográficas en Europa y en Japón. ¿Sabes qué hizo Columbia alrededor de la época en la que salió *Lotus*? Armó un álbum de grandes éxitos de un solo disco, como si hubiésemos sido un grupo ya pasado de moda, y lo lanzó aproximadamente al mismo tiempo. Eso nos cayó muy mal.

Nos habíamos esforzado tanto para dar lo mejor de nosotros en ese álbum, para ofrecer cientos de espectáculos ese año, que si miras la agenda de Santana en la primera mitad de 1974, te darás cuenta de que ese tiempo lo usamos para recuperarnos. Hubo unos pocos espectáculos de Santana, pero la mayor parte de mi energía e intención estuvo enfocada en la meditación y en estar con Deborah en Queens. Hice unos pocos conciertos espirituales con Deborah y John y Eve Mclaughlin, y a veces con Alice Coltrane y su grupo, y a veces, cuando estaba Sri, él arrancaba la noche leyendo su poesía.

Compartir tiempo con Turiya me inspiró a escribir algunas melodías espirituales y, cuando ella las escuchó, me sorprendió con la creación de algunos arreglos para acompañarlas: océanos sinfónicos de sonido, olas que iban y venían. Esas primeras melodías se convirtieron en "Angel of Air / Angel of Water" en el álbum *Illuminations*, que fue el primer álbum espiritual con mi nombre en la portada. Todos los planetas se alinearon para hacer que eso sucediera: En ese entonces, Turiya estaba decidiendo entre compañías discográficas, y Columbia aceptó producirlo pero no esperaba que fuera a tener ningún éxito en la radio, así que la actitud era que verían qué hacer con él cuando estuviera listo. Básicamente, Columbia nos dijo: "Vayan y diviértanse". El álbum fue como *Abraxas* (en el sentido de que no trajo ninguna complicación en absoluto), pero la música realmente me llevó más lejos del sonido clásico de Santana que casi cualquier otra grabación; más lejos, pero más cerca de donde estaba mi corazón.

Hicimos las sesiones en Capitol Studios en Los Ángeles, donde solía grabar Frank Sinatra, porque Turiya lo conocía y allí había espacio para una sección completa de cuerdas. Todo se hizo en vivo, y fue increíble estar en la misma sala con Jack DeJohnette y Dave Holland (quienes habían tocado con Miles), Armando y Jules

Broussard, y Tom Coster. Había una onda excelente: Armando contaba una historia y todos nos reíamos a carcajadas, luego Turiya decía algo que nos hacía reír aún más. Todos imaginan a Alice Coltrane como una persona profundamente espiritual y seria que, de algún modo, estaba cerca de lo divino y no podía estar haciendo bromas. Pero a ella le encantaba reírse y divertirse.

Recuerdo que una vez íbamos en una limusina y me dijo: "Carlos, tengo que decirte algo, pero por favor no te rías".

"De acuerdo, Turiya, no lo haré".

"Quiero hacerte escuchar mi nueva canción favorita", me dijo, mientras se reía como una niñita. La hizo sonar, y era "Supernatural Thing", de Ben E. King. Y le dije algo como: "¿Esta es tu número uno ahora? Está buena, es una excelente melodía". Era maravilloso ver esa parte de ella, ver cómo disfrutaba de la música sin prejuicios, sin necesidad de que fuera un estilo u otro.

Me encanta el arreglo de cuerdas en *Illuminations* y lo que tocaba Turiya en arpa y órgano, especialmente en "Angel of Sunlight" que, como muchas otras canciones de ella, iniciaba con tabla y tamboura, que tocaban dos discípulos de Sri Chinmoy. Yo toqué mi solo, y los ingenieros consiguieron un tono increíble de mi guitarra, lo cual creo que se debió en parte a la habitación, pero también a que el amplificador Boogie que llevé tenía una segunda perilla de volumen que me permitía tocar suavemente pero con mucha intensidad. Hay un chiste que dice: "¿Cómo consigues que un guitarrista baje el volumen? Ponle una partitura enfrente". Bueno, en esa sesión yo andaba de puntillas, actuando con mucho cuidado por las figuras que me rodeaban, así que no iba a tocar mi guitarra a todo volumen, pero el Boogie me ayudó a mantener el volumen bajo pero tocar fuerte, de mi propio modo.

Mi momento favorito en todo el álbum llegó después de que terminé ese solo. De repente, Turiya despegó como una nave espacial tocando ese Wurlitzer, doblando las notas con sus rodillas (tenía un aparato que sobresalía al costado del órgano), y Jack, Dave y yo nos mirábamos como diciéndonos "si nos tropezamos con eso, nos matamos". Fue una de las cosas más intensas que le escuché tocar jamás.

Fue idea mía invitar a DeJohnette y a Holland para el álbum; Turiya había querido traer a un baterista joven de Los Ángeles, Ndugu Chancler. Ella me lo presentó y él me dijo que había tocado con Herbie, Eddie Harris y muchos otros. Tenía un sonido que me gustó inmediatamente, muy parecido al de Tony Williams. De hecho, Ndugu también había tocado con Miles durante un breve tiempo. No tocó en *Illuminations*, pero pude escucharlo tocar y memoricé su nombre porque definitivamente quería reunirme con él en algún momento. Todavía hago eso con los músicos que escucho y me gustan. Agendo el nombre en mi archivo mental, y a veces pasan años hasta que vuelvo a pensar en ellos y los llamo.

Al comienzo del verano, Shrieve y yo empezamos a trabajar en las sesiones que se convirtieron en *Borboletta*, que considero como la tercera parte de una trilogía, junto con *Caravanserai* y *Welcome*. Les digo "las bandas sonoras"; esos tres álbumes eran como un grupo. Los tres tenían el mismo estilo suelto y jazzístico, y el mismo humor espiritual. Las sesiones fueron en mayo y junio, y TC se volvió muy importante para nosotros en el estudio (obtuvo parte del crédito de la producción, junto con Shrieve y conmigo) y mantuvimos parte de la misma banda que teníamos en *Welcome*, con unos pocos cambios. Flora Purim y su esposo, Airto Moreira, fueron muy importantes en ese álbum. Leon Patillo (que cantaba y tocaba teclados) se unió también a la banda, aportando una onda tipo gospel, diferente a la que había aportado Leon Thomas. Le pedimos a Stanley Clarke, que tocaba el bajo con Return to Forever, que nos ayudara en algunas de las pistas, y lo hizo. Dougie se fue para trabajar en otros proyectos, como tocar con David Bowie. David Brown volvió a la banda y también tocó en algunas de las pistas.

Fueron sesiones divertidas. Yo me estaba acostumbrando a ver caras nuevas para cada álbum, y disfrutaba viendo cómo reaccionábamos cuando ellos tocaban con alguien nuevo por primera vez. Siempre había alguno que escuchaba al otro con espíritu crítico, evaluándolo. Estábamos tocando "Promise of a Fisherman" cuando miré a Armando y Airto, y realmente parecía que estaban enfrentándose musicalmente, presionándose uno al otro. Airto me miró como diciendo: "¿Qué le pasa a este tipo?". Después me preguntó: "¿Siempre es tan competitivo? Tiene todas esas congas, y yo lo único que tenía era un triángulo, pero aun así parecía que quería darme una paliza". Yo me acostumbré a ese tipo de sorpresas.

¿Otra sorpresa? Casi habíamos terminado con el nuevo álbum y estábamos preparándonos para nuestra primera gira en seis meses cuando Shrieve se enfermó y tuvo que ir al hospital. Tenía cálculos renales. Lo llamé a Ndugu (él había tocado en una de las pistas de *Borboletta* porque parecía que Shrieve necesitaba más tiempo para recuperarse) y le pedí que se uniera a nuestra gira.

Me di cuenta inmediatamente de que Ndugu era la persona correcta: era especialmente bueno haciendo un ritmo de fondo funky, y también podía manejar los números con ritmo de jazz. Muchos bateristas solo saben hacer o uno o lo otro, y su ritmo de fondo puede volverse realmente rígido y agobiante. Ndugu no tenía nada de rigidez; era abierto y nada sofocante. También estaba bendecido con la capacidad de saber qué tipo de ritmo era mejor y podía recrear esa sensación que producían las canciones de Marvin Gaye y Stevie Wonder, lo cual ayudó a Santana a moverse a una especie de funk de los 70. Michael Shrieve tenía un estilo más parecido a Elvin Jones y Jack DeJohnette, y tenía su propio sentido del funk, pero no estaba tan ligado al estilo de los 70 como el funk de Ndugu. Eran simplemente dos formas de tocar diferentes.

A mí no se me había ocurrido sacar a Michael Shrieve de la banda cuando se enfermó, pero eso fue lo que ocurrió naturalmente. Yo sabía que no íbamos a cancelar la gira, y me daba mucha curiosidad ver cómo podría cambiar nuestro sonido y desarrollarse en una nueva dirección. Así que tenía estos motivos para seguir adelante, y sé que él no estaba de acuerdo con todos. Nunca decidimos formalmente que iba a dejar la banda, y nunca hicimos oficial o pública su salida. Cuando pienso en eso ahora, creo que no lo manejamos de la mejor forma o con la debida caballerosidad, al estar Michael en el hospital. Pero la decisión de seguir con la gira fue lo que nos hizo darnos cuenta de que necesitábamos tomar caminos separados.

No puedo hablar por Michael, pero creo que la separación le dio la libertad de reasignar el tiempo que iba a dedicar a la gira, a explorar algunas ideas musicales diferentes, porque eso es lo que hizo. Es un baterista súper talentoso que hizo música en otras bandas y para películas; hasta el día de hoy todavía aporta canciones a Santana. Se mudó a la Ciudad de Nueva York y vivió allí durante los años 70 y 80, y yo lo visité allí casi todas las veces que fui a la ciudad. Siempre fue muy amable y amistoso; creo que habíamos pasado por demasiadas cosas juntos en la música y en nuestro camino espiritual como para que el sedimento del enojo o el resentimiento pudieran embarrar las cosas entre nosotros.

El hecho de que Shrieve dejara Santana fue el paso final de la banda en su evolución de ser una cooperativa a ser un grupo con dos líderes, y finalmente un grupo donde solo yo estaba a cargo. Shrieve era la última conexión con la vieja banda, la última persona con quien yo podía consultar y a quien a veces podía delegar autoridad. Chepito todavía estaba en Santana, pero todavía tenía sus propias motivaciones; era más como un músico acompañante contratado en la banda, y creo que pasar tanto tiempo de gira en el 73 lo había distanciado un poco de mí y había generado un poco de tensión en la relación que teníamos, como nos pasó a todos.

Si quieres saber la fecha en que asumí todas las obligaciones de liderar Santana y realmente se convirtió en mi banda, sería a fines de junio del 74. Desde entonces he tratado de hacer lo mejor para mantenerme fiel al espíritu original de la banda y a la música. Y desde entonces ha sido una bendición y también una obligación. Tengo la libertad de no tener que rendir cuentas a otras personas, pero al mismo tiempo está la responsabilidad diaria de tomar decisiones y hacer planes, y todavía estoy haciendo lo mejor que puedo para conducir a Santana con honestidad a un lugar donde todo salga de maravilla.

En ese entonces yo tenía casi veintiocho años, y cuando miro atrás no recuerdo que fuera difícil el cambio a ese rol de ser el líder.

No me sentía demasiado joven o demasiado ingenuo o carente de experiencia. Ya habíamos pasado por ese gran cambio que nos colocó a mí y a Michael al mando. Lo sentí como algo natural: en mi opinión, Santana era yo incluso antes de que hubiera una banda Santana. Lo difícil era resistir las interpretaciones de otras personas de lo que consideraban que Santana era o debía ser, tanto desde afuera como desde adentro de la banda. Las personas más cercanas a mí que me alentaron a ser yo mismo y a confiar en mí fueron Bill Graham, Deborah y, especialmente, Armando. Él fue el único dentro de Santana que estuvo siempre de mi lado con una confianza suprema que era contagiosa. Me decía: "Hay un solo Santana en esta banda, y eres tú, Carlos. Diles que ahora tú eres el capitán".

A mediados de los años 70 se sentía estupendo ser joven y estar liderando una de las bandas de rock más importantes del momento. La música y los éxitos de nuestros tres primeros álbumes, y la película de Woodstock, fueron como una gran ola de energía que no dejó de llevarnos durante esos años. La bendición fue que podíamos estar tan ocupados como quisiéramos, incluso sin que tuviéramos ningún éxito de radio nuevo (si bien sí teníamos algunos éxitos más en nosotros, que vendrían más adelante en los 70).

La otra bendición fue que teníamos un equilibrio interno y un enfoque que, durante gran parte del tiempo, nos mantenía alejados de las tentaciones y excesos de la era. Estábamos empezando a tener un lenguaje con el cual abordar el mundo espiritual y las "realidades" que nos rodeaban. Había un puente entre los reinos de lo visible y lo invisible que era importante si queríamos seguir adelante con nuestra música y seguir siendo relevantes, conectarnos con el pasado y continuar hacia el futuro.

Cuando pienso en esos años en la década de los 70, pienso en los muchísimos músicos y leyendas que pude conocer por el lugar que ocupaba Santana en el mundo de la música. Algunos eran héroes, otros eran amigos, y otros no lo eran; y siempre había algo que aprender de todos ellos.

Recuerdo sentirme incómodo porque Muddy Waters actuara como banda soporte para nosotros. Nosotros deberíamos haber sido la banda soporte para él, siempre. Su música de blues era tan importante para tanta gente, y él era la única leyenda del blues con quien me sentía demasiado intimidado como para presentarme, incluso en 1974 y 75. Me encantaba ver cómo armaba sus espectáculos; quién tocaba primero y quién le seguía. Por ejemplo, me preguntaba por qué Muddy necesitaba tres guitarristas en su banda. Pero entonces, en medio del recital, él señalaba a uno de ellos, que tocaba un solo al estilo de B. B. King. Luego Muddy señalaba al siguiente muchacho, que tocaba un solo al estilo de Freddie King. Finalmente le tocaba al último muchacho, que sonaba un poco como Albert King. Luego Muddy se paraba con su guitarra slide y la remataba, les demostraba a todos quién estaba a cargo, y el lugar reventaba de aplausos.

Hacia el final del espectáculo, el público se quedaba con la boca abierta, preguntándose cómo era posible que este hombre mayor tuviera tanta energía y alma. Entonces Muddy lo demostraba una vez más en el bis. Decía: "Muchísimas gracias. Es tan maravilloso tocar para todos ustedes. Y ahora quiero presentarles a una persona muy especial: por favor, ¡reciban con un cálido aplauso a mi nieta!" Y hacía salir a una joven dama de unos veintitantos años. Gran aplauso. "Bien, y ahora quiero que saluden con otro aplauso a mi hija". Por supuesto, todos esperaban una mujer en sus cincuenta, pero en cambio, salía una niñita de seis años. De repente todos comprendían, y en el momento perfecto, Muddy decía: "Ahora ven que mi herramienta *todavía* funciona... uno, dos, tres, ¡va!" Y hacía su último número.

Son cosas que no se pueden inventar. Admiro tanto la mentalidad y el espíritu de ese tipo.

Este fue otro momento especial del 75: el mismo día que conocí a Bob Dylan, ¡también hice una improvisación con The Rolling Stones! Yo me estaba alojando en el Plaza Hotel, al otro lado de Central Park, y Bob también. Conocía su música de los 60, por supuesto, pero en los años siguientes realmente había comenzado a admirar su genialidad. Recuerdo que una vez me senté con "Desolation Row", escuchando la letra y tratando de desglosar su significado: "Einstein, disguised as Robin Hood / With his memories in a trunk / Passed this way an hour ago / With his friend, a jealous monk" (Einstein, disfrazado de Robin Hood / Con sus memorias en un baúl / Pasó por aquí hace una hora / Con su amigo, un monje celoso"). Quiero decir, este tipo es como Charlie Parker o John Coltrane en cuanto a cómo fluye su imaginación: absolutamente asombrosa.

Nos presentaron y nos quedamos un rato en una suite, charlando y conociéndonos, cuando recibí una llamada diciendo que la gente de CBS Japón estaba allí. Recordé que tenía una reunión con ellos. Estaban allí para mostrarme el álbum *Lotus*, y le pregunté a Bob si quería verlo. Así que la gente de la discográfica vino y comenzaron a mostrar los detalles del álbum, esparciendo las imágenes en el piso y desplegando las páginas del libro. Realmente era una presentación increíble. Vi que a Bob se le agrandaban los ojos.

Sonó de nuevo el teléfono, y esta vez era la gente de The Rolling Stones: la banda estaba en la ciudad, tocando en el Madison Square Garden. Preguntaban si yo quería ir e improvisar con ellos. "Bueno, estoy aquí con Bob Dylan".

"¡Entonces tráigalo también a él, por favor!"

Así que, un rato después, subimos a un taxi: Bob, mi amplificador Mesa/Boogie con la cubierta de piel de serpiente, y yo. Nadie envió una limusina ni nada, lo cual no fue problema hasta que llegamos al Garden, le dijimos al personal de seguridad del detrás de escena quiénes éramos, y fue obvio que no nos creyeron. Probablemente pensaron: "¿Bob Dylan y Carlos Santana juntos? ¿Y llegan en un taxi? No, no". Llamamos a la gente de The Rolling Stones y ellos vinieron a buscarnos.

El concierto fue increíble; creo que era la última noche de conciertos de la banda allí, y el ambiente era electrizante. Hubo una banda soporte que usaba tambores metálicos y Billy Preston estaba allí dando vueltas; iba a tocar con The Stones, así que pude conocerlo. Hicieron su espectáculo y, cerca del bis, vinieron hasta mí y me pidieron que subiera y tocara en "Sympathy for the Devil". Mick cantó su parte, luego giró hacia mí, yo puse mi dedo sobre la cuerda y... ¡*zas!*

De repente noté que las cabezas giraban y los ojos me miraban a mí. No sé si la banda había puesto un micrófono en mi amplificador demasiado alto o algo, pero de algún modo creo que no estaban listos para el sonido del amplificador Boogie: la distorsión y la intensidad. Yo pensaba: "¡Sí! *Así* es como debe sonar".

No voy a decir que lo que sucedió después de esa noche fue por mí, pero sí diré que si alguien recuerda la siguiente gira de los Stone en el 77, el escenario estaba lleno de amplificadores Mesa/Boogie. Y al año siguiente Dylan tocó en Japón, e hicieron un hermoso álbum doble del concierto.

Ese mismo verano, finalmente pude improvisar con Eric Clapton. Cuando tocamos juntos no escucho a Eric Clapton o a Santana. Con Eric, es una conversación sobre a quién amamos más. "Oh, ¿tú tienes algo de Otis Rush? ¿Qué tal algo de Muddy Waters?". Cuando tocamos no se trata de cruzar espadas y hacer un duelo, que es como muchas personas piensan en la improvisación. No es Fernando Lamas versus Errol Flynn. Es: "Tú tienes a Robert Johnson y yo tengo a Bola Sete".

Creo que los mejores guitarristas son los que más héroes tienen; algunos británicos tienden a limitarse a un tipo de estilo, pero no Clapton ni Jeff Beck ni Jimmy Page. Ellos escuchan música marroquí y africana; hace poco, Jeff Beck ha estado escuchando coros rumanos. George Harrison escuchaba música de sitar indio. Creo que Stevie Ray Vaughan podía ser muy intrépido a la hora de escuchar música: no escuchaba solo a T-Bone Walker, sino también a Kenny Burrell, Grant Green y Wes Montgomery. No sería justo llamar a Stevie un guitarrista de blues. Te das cuenta de eso en "Riviera Paradise": su vocabulario iba más lejos, mucho más allá de Albert King. Todos estos muchachos que mencioné están abiertos a muchas influencias, pero siempre estarán enraizados en algo. Para mí, cada músico es como un aeropuerto: hay una cantidad de aviones diferentes que llegan, aterrizan y se van. Nunca es solo una aerolínea.

Es algo que siempre cambia: ahora quiero escuchar algo de Manitas de Plata, porque él es blues y flamenco juntos. Quiero algo de *Guitar Forms,* de Kenny Burrell, con arreglos de Gil Evans y Elvin Jones en batería (podría vivir con eso en una isla desierta para siempre). Aún con lo mucho que me gusta John Lee Hooker, a veces tengo que decir: "Quédate ahí, vuelvo enseguida. Tengo que ir a escuchar algo elegante, como 'Las Vegas Tango'".

Últimamente noté que todos los muchachos del heavy metal (al menos los que tocan muy rápido, como Eddie Van Halen y Joe Satriani) me recuerdan al tipo de audacia de Frank Zappa, que se inclina más hacia una onda Paganini que a una onda B. B. King o Eric Clapton. Quizá allí ya no haya una conexión con el blues, pero eso no es ni bueno ni malo: hay un hermoso contraste en el conjunto. Son manzanas, naranjas, peras y bananas. Santana no va a ser la música favorita de todo el mundo, todo el tiempo.

"No estás hecho de oro", me decía mi mamá.

"¿Ah, sí? ¿Qué significa eso?".

"No puedes gustarle a todo el mundo. No puedes ser el niño mimado de todos".

Tenía razón. Esa fue otra de las lecciones que aprendí unos años más tarde. En 1980, tocamos en un programa doble en Colonia, Alemania, con Frank Zappa: dos espectáculos, uno que él abrió y nosotros cerramos, y otro que nosotros abrimos y él cerró. Yo no pensaba que esta iba a ser otra situación como las que tuvimos con Rahsaan Roland Kirk y Wilson Pickett, pero cuando fui a la habitación de Frank para agradecerle por la música, pude darme cuenta de que era alguien que no me permitiría entrar en su consciencia. No recuerdo qué me dijo, pero me dio la sensación de que no debía estar allí.

Le hablé rápidamente de mi admiración y gratitud por su música, y me fui. Se lo dije con sinceridad; me gustaba su música, especialmente "Help, I'm a Rock" de *Freak Out!* y ese *blues* puro y sucio, "Directly from My Heart to You" de *Weasels Ripped My Flesh.* Lo que fuera que no le gustaba a Frank de mí, salió a la luz unos años después cuando hizo "Variations on the Carlos Santana Secret Chord Progression", y con escucharlo solo una vez me di cuenta de que no se trataba de un halago. Aunque, de algún modo, lo era, porque hizo un esfuerzo y dedicó tiempo y energía a desarrollar un argumento sobre mi música. ¿Sabes cómo lo descubrí? Yo aún compraba los álbumes de Frank, incluso después de ese encuentro en el 77. Me encantó el título *Shut Up 'n Play Yer Guitar*, así que lo compré y ahí estaba.

Mi respuesta a alguien que está tan dedicado a ese tipo de críticas, odios o sentimientos tóxicos nunca ha cambiado con el correr de los años. Sonaba el teléfono, y era Miles u Otis Rush. Hoy el teléfono todavía suena, y es Wayne Shorter o Buddy Guy. ¿Me importa lo que pienses sobre mí?

A comienzos del 75, había muchos llamados de Miles, especialmente cuando yo me encontraba en la Ciudad de Nueva York. Volviendo al 71, en cierta ocasión Miles me llamó a mi hotel en Nueva York y me invitó a ir a un concierto algo extraño en The Bitter End. "Anota esta dirección. Quiero que vengas con tu guitarra".

"Está bien, Miles", le respondí. Fui, pero no llevé la guitarra. Cuando llegué al lugar, Miles le estaba gritando al dueño del club, con esa voz ronca que tiene. En medio de todas esas palabrotas, de repente giró hacia mí y me dijo con toda amabilidad: "Eh, Carlos, ¿cómo estás? Gracias por venir". Luego se dio vuelta nuevamente hacia el propietario, y volvió a la carga con los gritos y el lenguaje soez.

Richard Pryor recién comenzaba su función. Era el encargado de la apertura y estaba haciendo reír a todos. Después Miles dijo: "¿Dónde está tu guitarra?". Me encogí de hombros. "Ah, ya veo". No dije nada, pero esta era la banda con Jack, Keith y Michael Henderson en bajo. Por la forma en que estos muchachos estaban mezclando todo, no fui capaz de encontrar nada. Comenzaron a tocar, pero Miles seguía enfadado con el dueño y había decidido hacer una especie de huelga. Dejó su trompeta en el suelo y seguidamente se acostó, ahí mismo, frente al escenario, mientras la banda seguía trabajando con colores, no realmente canciones.

Se debe haber resuelto lo que debían resolver, porque finalmente Miles se levantó, se colocó la trompeta en la boca y todo se encaminó. De pronto hubo un tema, un enfoque y una sensación de estructura. Fue sorprendente: cambió la música sin tocar siquiera una nota.

Pienso que Wayne y Herbie estarían de acuerdo en que una gran parte de aquello que los hizo como son ahora se debe al tiempo que pasaron con Miles. Creo que eso pasaba con todos los que tocaban con Miles: incluso al día de hoy Keith Jarrett, Chick Corea, Jack DeJohnette, Dave Holland, Gary Bartz y muchos otros hacen la mejor música de jazz y producen una música que hace que todo lo demás suene a música de fácil escucha. Recuerdo una vez que Branford Marsalis mencionó esto después de tocar en el álbum *Decoy* de Miles. Dijo que con Miles podía tocar música que nunca había pensado en tocar, pero apenas volvió al ruedo con su propia banda comenzó a tocar de la manera anterior. Le reconocía a Miles el mérito de haber sacado cosas nuevas de él.

Sé cómo se sentía Branford, porque la consciencia de Miles contagia a muchos músicos; no solo a los que tocaron con él. Me contagió a mí incluso antes de haberlo escuchado en vivo, tan solo por escuchar sus álbumes, leer las notas de la funda y tocar junto con John McLaughlin en *In a Silent Way*. En realidad Miles nunca me lo preguntó, pero a veces tenía la sensación de que me hacía preguntas para ver si me gustaría unirme a su banda. En ocasiones me preguntaba: "¿Así que te gusta vivir en Frisco?". Eso era lo más cercano a una invitación que me manifestaba, pero luego se me hacía un nudo en el estómago y me decía a mí mismo: "No, no lo hagas". Terminará una amistad". Con Miles sabía bien que no debía acercarme demasiado. También era un honor pensar que eso era posible, pero nunca pensé que podría relacionarme con la música que él hacía en ese entonces.

La otra característica de Miles era uno no se podía guiar por lo que él había hecho en el pasado. Eso puede ser intimidante. Él avanzaba con su música sin mirar atrás. Tengo el recuerdo de una sola vez en que cambió de parecer, solo por un momento. Miles estaba en el Keystone Korner en el 75 y su banda comenzó con algo de funk profundo. Miles estaba tocando el órgano; ni siquiera había sacado la trompeta de su hermoso estuche de cuero. La música sonaba como un gato aullando en un callejón, con un altavoz para sonidos graves que solo podían escuchar las ardillas, muy, muy bajo. Yo pensaba: "Ay, maldición, ¿esa es la canción de apertura?". De repente, una mujer corpulenta que estaba ubicada en el frente gritó: "¡Miles! ¡Miles! ¡Toca la trompeta!"

Todo el lugar la estaba observando y su compañero trataba de hacerla callar, pero ella ni se percataba. "¿Qué? Pagué tu maldita entrada y también, la mía. Miles, ¡toca la condenada trompeta! No queremos oír esta mierda".

La decisión a continuación dependía de Miles. Miró a la mujer, abrió el estuche, sacó la trompeta e hizo bajar a toda la banda. Luego se hincó sobre una sola rodilla frente a ella y le dio un pequeño gusto con *Sketches of Spain*. Solo una mujer podría haber conseguido eso, y me encantó la manera en que Miles lo manejó.

En aquella época empecé a observar algunas cosas de Sri que apartaban mi cariño hacia él. Seguía tratándome con favoritismo, pero a veces hacía comentarios que no me hacían sentir bien. Yo sentía que un hombre santo no debería quejarse de sus discípulos y mofarse de sus imperfecciones. Mi sensación era que como discípulos se suponía que nosotros éramos los humanos, los que necesitábamos un trabajo interno, y que él debía ser quien nos mostrara cómo ser compasivos.

Mi alejamiento de Sri fue gradual, pero eficiente y tangible, ya que para mí todo lo que solía ser miel se convertía en vinagre. En el año 77, sentí que era hora de irme. Tanto Larry Coryell como John McLaughlin ya se habían ido, pero Deborah quería quedarse. Estaba empezando una larga gira con Santana a principios de ese año y fue ahí cuando le comenté a ella que lo dejaría. "Si tú quieres te puedes quedar con Sri, pero yo me voy".

La gira de Santana en la primera mitad del 77 continuó durante meses y meses. Yo estaba desconectado y apartado de mi vida en muchos sentidos. Deborah y yo estábamos en la misma frecuencia cuando me fui y sentí que nuestros caminos espirituales debían estar juntos, con la orientación de Sri o sin ella.

Pero cuando esa extensa gira llegó a su fin, en abril, me di cuenta de que era el momento de volver a casa y estar con Deborah, o todo se terminaría. Volvimos a estar juntos y ella se puso muy, muy inflexible; entonces supe qué debía hacer para no perderla. Le pedí a Bill que viniera a nuestra casa de Marin. Había reservado a Santana para que se presentara en algunas fechas en el Radio City Music Hall. Después de una gira por los EE. UU. en la que se habían agotado todas las entradas, este sería el broche de oro de aquellos cuatro meses. Yo reconocía y respetaba eso. Sabía lo que estaba arriesgando, pero le dije a Bill: "No puedo hacer esos conciertos, viejo. Tengo que dedicar un tiempo a reconciliarme con Deborah y a recomponer la relación. Y tiene que ser ahora, ya mismo".

Lo primero que Bill dijo fue: "Carlos, estás completamente loco. ¡Las entradas ya están a la venta!" Le respondí: "Bueno, probablemente me haya vuelto loco, pero siento que en este preciso momento esto es lo más importante para mí y no hay nada que pueda hacerme cambiar de opinión". Lo puse en palabras que sabía que él entendería. "La máquina Santana no es más importante que mi relación con Deborah". Bill me miró y en su rostro pude ver cómo atravesaba lentamente una mezcla total de emociones: enojo, dolor, frustración y, finalmente, abatimiento y una profunda tristeza. Seguidamente exclamó: "Carlos, espero que alguna vez en mi vida conozca un amor como ese".

CAPÍTULO 17

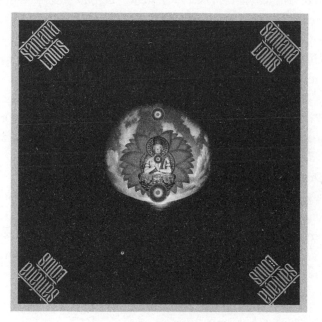

¿Alguna vez te cansas del olor a pan recién horneado cuando sale del horno temprano por la mañana, aunque sea siempre la misma vieja receta? El agua no se cansa de ser agua; el sol no se cansa de ser sol. El ego es el que se cansa. Ahí es cuando tengo que decirle a mi ego: "Aquí mando yo, no tú". Si el ego pasa a tener el control, todo envejecerá o tendrá colocado un sello de fecha. Entonces tengo que decirme a mí mismo: "No. No tengo miedo de tocar 'Black Magic Woman' u 'Oye Como Va' y hacerlas nuevas otra vez".

    La buena música no tiene fecha de vencimiento. En los 70 comenzaba a sentir que alguna música de la radio se estaba volviendo bastante desechable, y esa sensación nunca se me fue. A esas canciones que van y vienen las llamo "fragmentos de audio": son como las citas irrelevantes que se incluyen en los noticiarios de la noche. ¿Cómo se puede obtener un significado, atemporalidad o elegancia de un fragmento de audio? Para mí, un fragmento de audio es lo opuesto a algo "por siempre inolvidable". "Light My Fire", de The Doors: eso no es un fragmento de audio. "No Woman No Cry" y "Exodus", de Bob Marley: esos son por siempre inolvidables.

En los 70 teníamos a The Bee Gees y a Tony Orlando. Disco y punk. El público glorificaba a The Ramones y a The Sex Pistols, mientras yo me decía a mí mismo: "Está bien, déjenme ver esa energía". La sentí; fue válido. Al mismo tiempo estaban Jaco Pastorius y Tony Williams, para mí eso era punk. Mi opinión es que, independientemente de la intensidad que tenga, no conozco ninguna música punk que sea más intensa que la de The Tony Williams Lifetime.

¿Qué me estaba sucediendo realmente en ese entonces? Marvin Gaye y Al Green. Creo que siempre existirán un momento y un lugar en que escucharé a Led Zeppelin o AC/DC y me encantarán. Pero cuando necesito recargarme de verdad, cuando siento que he estado debajo del agua demasiado tiempo y necesito salir a la superficie a tomar aire, siempre están Coltrane o Miles.

A fines de los 70 no me permitía a mí mismo pensar que algún otro tipo de música "estaba de moda" y que la mía era anticuada. Pero cuando leo las entrevistas que hice para *Creem* o *Rolling Stone*, mis valores parecían de otra generación. En un sentido, lo eran: los 60 se trataban de "Cambiemos el mundo". Lo escuchas en la música: ayudemos a las personas y seamos amables. Seamos *este* tipo de gente: gente buena. Era una consciencia de sanación.

Bob Marley era el corazón, la consciencia y el alma de los 70. No hay duda al respecto. Creo que él es el artista más importante de los 70. Cuando todo se estaba convirtiendo en disco o en discordia, él fue el aglutinante que hizo de la música algo significativo. Su música tenía un objetivo: difundir la misión rastafari de unidad: el yo y el yo. Esta no difería de la filosofía de alcanzar nuestra propia luz, que es de la que hablaba Sri. "One Love", "A Love Supreme"; no me canso de decir que esas dos canciones se complementan entre sí. Bob Marley tenía un objetivo, y su música poseía belleza, movimiento, sexo y verdad.

Comencé a escuchar a Jimmy Cliff y *The Harder They Come* allá por el 73, lo que despertó mi interés por la música de Trinidad y Brasil. Hazlo y verás que empezarás a escuchar todos los sonidos que vinieron de África. Pero volvía a pensar: ¿Qué es esta música de Jamaica? Está bien, reggae. Al principio la llamaban calipso; ahora es roots reggae".

Third World, Burning Spear, The Abyssinians: Bob Marley tenía toda otra forma de hacerlo. En el primer álbum que tuve de él, *Catch a Fire*, lucía como algo similar a un gran mechero que podías usar para encender un churro. Yo pensaba: "¡Guau!, esta música es realmente diferente. Muy, muy diferente; ¿dónde está el 1? ¿Cómo funciona ese ritmo?". Él tenía a dos hermanos en la banda, Carlton y "Family Man" Barret, en batería y bajo. Se los robó a Lee Perry, que había sido productor de Marley, y no creo que Perry alguna vez lo haya perdonado. Creo que yo tampoco lo hubiera hecho.

No conocí a Bob Marley; nuestros caminos nunca se cruzaron. Pero una vez que dejé a Sri, volví a fumar marihuana y lo escuché muchas veces. Él fue la redención de los 70: cada álbum que producía era aún mejor que el anterior.

Lo que era sorprendente, sin embargo, es que no había muchos afroamericanos que fueran admiradores de Bob Marley. Particularmente las personas afroamericanas estrictas que iban a la iglesia y eran muy rectas: no les gustaba su filosofía, ni sus cabellos, ni su marihuana. Algunos intentaron cambiar eso cuando tomaron la decisión de que Marley actuara como artista soporte para los Commodores, y él tocó en el Madison Square Garden. Lo mismo ocurrió con Jimi Hendrix: nunca tuvo un público afroamericano muy grande, y creo que eso le preocupaba.

Toda esa música de reggae me hizo conocer el tipo de vida isleña. Me ayudó a ver que algún día podía disminuir el ritmo, relajarme y vivir en un lugar como Maui. Cruzas la calle y el océano es tu tina de baño. El cielo es tu techo; la comida es lo más fresca que puede existir. Es mejor que el Ritz-Carlton. Esto me hizo llegar a la conclusión de que el reggae se trata de esto y me permitió descubrir a qué lugar se supone que te lleva: donde no hay problemas, hombre, ni preocupaciones. Muy lejos del "¿Qué me pasa? ¿Por qué no puedo aprender a relajarme?". Escuchar a Bob Marley te transporta a un flujo natural, místico. Estos tipos nunca estaban apurados. Eso aún suena muy bien.

Te diré las mejores bandas que surgieron de ese ámbito. Una era The Police. Eran totalmente punk y gracias a Sting escribían canciones inteligentes con esa energía punk. Otro grupo era The Clash: escribían canciones con inteligencia, un mensaje y un objetivo, y les encantaba la música latina. Los conocí detrás de escena en el 82, cuando ambos grupos fuimos la banda soporte de The Who en Filadelfia. Tocaban cumbias en un radiocasete que tenían; Joe Strummer tarareaba las líneas y a toda la banda le gustaba esa música. También tocaban música afroamericana, como el hip-hop de los primeros tiempos. Me vi gratamente sorprendido. Su música contenía una simetría de la africanidad.

A veces la música de los 70 y los 80 era sorprendente, como, por ejemplo, la fusión del rock con el hip-hop. Estaba Afrika Bambaataa con Johnny Rotten y James Brown; y unos años más tarde Run-DMC se agrupó con Aerosmith y luego apareció el rock afroamericano y el hip-hop blanco: Living Colour y The Beastie Boys. Eso tuvo lugar en los 80, pero ese tipo de mezcla inesperada estaba desde antes; por ejemplo, en lo que Miles hizo en The Fillmore. Así es como cambian las cosas en la música: un tipo de música sigue a otra y de repente, ¡se modifica nuevamente! Eso es lo importante para mí.

Columbia Records nos dio su apoyo de mala gana. Dado que ya hacía un largo tiempo que Clive Davis se había ido, nadie me presionaba para producir éxitos de radio, pero yo sabía que querían otro *Abraxas* de Santana. No lo decían, pero podía sentirlo. Yo estaba listo para volver. Había ido tan lejos y había avanzado tanto con Santana, Alice

Coltrane y John McLaughlin, que imaginé que debíamos intentar llevar a Santana en una dirección de canciones más de tipo radial. Era como recorrer nuevamente un camino familiar. *Amigos*, con las canciones "Europa" y "Dance Sister Dance", surgió de allí.

Greg Walker es un cantante que tiene mucho, mucho sentimiento y necesitábamos a alguien nuevo en 1975, cuando Leon Patillo se fue. Ndugu trajo a Greg a un ensayo al SIR en San Francisco, y así empezó todo. Llegó a Santana en el momento preciso, justo cuando comenzábamos *Amigos*. La primera canción que cantó con nosotros fue para el álbum. La voz de Leon tenía un sonido de *gospel* nítido, pero la voz de Greg venía de Luther Vandross. Greg posee esa misma destreza y forma de presentación del soul.

Lo que recuerdo haberle dicho a Greg fue que no *vendiera* una canción. No es lo mismo que decir: "Eh, compra este neumático". Bríndame tu corazón. Sigo diciéndoles eso a los cantantes de Santana, porque son la parte frontal del espectáculo. Trata la canción como si estuvieras ofreciendo amor; no te muestres ni suenes obvio.

Greg tenía cierta valentía en él; muchos músicos que se unen a la banda y suben al escenario por primera vez dicen: "¡Mi Dios!, no sabíamos que iba a ser así. Es como un 747 que despega; estoy tratando de agarrarme lo mejor que puedo". Luego deben decidir si prefieren estar colgados de la cola o ir en la cabina de vuelo. Greg estuvo al frente desde el principio, sin problemas. Por un tiempo, ayudó a definir a Santana. Salvo cuando Leon volvió para cantar en *Festival*, Greg estuvo al frente y fue el centro de tres importantes álbumes: *Amigos*, *Moonflower* e *Inner Secrets*.

Retomamos el contacto con Dave Rubinson a través de Bill Graham, y esta vez todos teníamos más experiencia y trabajábamos mejor juntos. Escribió "Dance Sister Dance" con Ndugu y TC; para mí, sonaba como la versión de lo que ellos habían imaginado que era Spanish Harlem. Cuando la escuché por primera vez, pensé: "Bien…". Pero lo que más me gusta es el final, con sus acordes de sintetizador. Pudimos trabajar con sintetizadores y otras tecnologías desde el principio porque Weather Report ya había sentado el camino, y a mí me encantaban Jan Hammer, George Duke y Herbie, claro está.

Yo no tenía temor ni me daba vergüenza usar esa tecnología: probé con un ARP Avatar por un tiempo, tocando la guitarra directamente a través del sintetizador. Pero siempre sentí que apenas tocaba la guitarra, todas las demás cosas eran simplemente cosas. Es decir, si tocas algo de Albert King comparado con cualquier cosa en el sintetizador, ¿qué puedo decirte? Es como comparar una ballena con un pez de colores.

Pienso que el mejor tributo a Santana es una canción que Sonny Sharrock compuso justo antes de morir. Me habló de ella una noche en San Francisco, en Slim's. Fui a verlo y me dijo: "Escribí una canción sobre ustedes, viejo. Se llama 'Santana'". La busqué por un tiempo hasta que finalmente la encontré. Recuerdo que dije: "El hermano Sonny debe haber estado escuchando el final de 'Dance Sister Dance'".

Columbia nos informó que *Amigos* era un éxito, así que todos estaban felices y amaban a Santana otra vez. Hicimos otro álbum con Rubinson, *Festival*, en el cual Paul Jackson se unió a la banda para tocar el bajo y Gaylord Birch, la batería. Ndugu se fue y recomendó a Gaylord.

Generalmente, cuando alguien se marcha de Santana se debe a que es momento de crecer en direcciones diferentes. En ciertos casos el músico se da cuenta por sí solo, pero otras veces es mi tarea comunicarle que es hora de partir, crecer, ser exitoso... y quizá volvamos a vernos; gracias por todo. Esto ocurre la mayoría de las veces. En raro que los músicos se vayan por su propia voluntad. Pero Ndugu tenía otros planes y fue él quien decidió marcharse.

Ndugu es un perfecto músico con sentimiento. Tocaba "Europa" hermosamente. Podía tocar con nosotros y luego con Marvin Gaye, George Benson o Michael Jackson. ¡Y antes de hacerlo con nosotros había tocado con Miles! Se puede escuchar en el comienzo de "Billie Jean"; ese ritmo es cadencioso. En 1988 Ndugu volvió como integrante de la Santana-Shorter Band.

Santana seguía siendo una banda de *rock*, pero estaba creando su propia identidad: estaba cambiando, creando nueva música, surgiendo con nuevos modelos para presentarnos—. Acerca de "Dance

Sister Dance": no estoy tratando de mentirles o hacerme el chistoso, pero siempre me sorprende cuando una canción de Santana se convierte en un éxito. Incluso cuando presentamos "Black Magic Woman" y "Oye Como Va", una voz interior me decía que tal vez esto era un error, que quizá no teníamos el rock and roll suficiente para ser populares.

Después otra voz me respondía: "Discúlpame: ¿por qué tú mismo te pones limitaciones? No querrás ser prisionero de ti mismo, levantando la mano y explicando 'Hola, soy Carlos Santana, el del *rock* latino'".

En 1977 *Lotus* estaba vendiendo copias con la trascendencia suficiente como para que Columbia quisiera un álbum en vivo: eso fue parte de la inspiración para *Moonflower*. Una mitad del álbum eran pistas en vivo y la otra, canciones de estudio. Bill Graham es reconocido en el álbum por su "dirección" y, además, fue él quien quiso que hagamos un cover de una canción de The Zombies. Nos insistió y nos pidió que eligiéramos entre "Time of the Season" o "She's Not There". Bill estuvo involucrado más directamente esta vez, a veces incluso en el estudio.

Eso era un desafío, porque Bill podía tener opiniones muy firmes adondequiera que fuese, aunque no fuera realmente el productor. En una oportunidad estábamos grabando una canción y por alguna razón tuvo la idea de que necesitaba intervenir, como lo haría un productor. Tom estaba tocando un solo y Bill comenzó: "Detente, detente". ¡Detuvo la toma!. TC le preguntó: "¿Qué ocurre?". Bill comenzó a explicarle que debía hacer el solo nuevamente y concentrarse en este cuando entrara, mientras describía: "Estoy imaginando un helicóptero que sobrevuela una playa, de este cuelga una soga a la que va aferrada una mujer desnuda; por la playa corre un caballo sin montura y ella debe aterrizar justo arriba del caballo, ¿entiendes? Tu solo debe entrar así, por lo que debes hacerlo de vuelta".

Todos se quedaron en silencio. Pregunté: "Bill, ¿por qué

simplemente no le dices que entró demasiado pronto?". Me respondió: "Eso acabo de hacer, idiota".

Lo otro que le encantaba hacer a Bill en las sesiones de grabación era contar historias. Cuando lo hacía, sabíamos que estaríamos allí por un rato, al menos hasta que alguien dijera: "Eh, ¿quién va a pagar todo este tiempo en el estudio?". Valía la pena. Decidimos hacer "She's Not There", y fue otro éxito. A lo largo de los años, Bill escogió dos canciones para Santana y ambas se convirtieron en éxitos.

Me gustan los diseños de los dos álbumes que hicimos con Bill; hombre, he tenido la bendición de que pocas personas intentaran detenerme una vez que tomé una decisión con respecto a la portada de un álbum. La portada de *Moonflower* es una foto que me encanta, tomada desde la cima de una montaña, en la que se ven nubes teñidas por el dorado del atardecer. La encontré en un libro de fotografías sobre el Himalaya. La foto de la portada de *Inner Secrets* fue tomada por Norman Seeff, el fotógrafo que hizo la portada de *Rumours*, de Fleetwood Mac. En la imagen aparezco bailando mientras la banda aplaude. No recuerdo qué canción estábamos bailando, tal vez una del álbum, pero sí me acuerdo de que Norman me hizo sentir más cómodo de lo que me había sentido en cualquier otra sesión fotográfica.

Puede verse en las portadas y en la música: las cosas estaban cambiando nuevamente en el interior de Santana. Hicimos *Amigos;* un año después Gaylord Birch se fue y entró Graham Lear en batería, otra recomendación de Ndugu. Él había escuchado a Graham con Gino Vannelli y exclamó: "¡Este tipo es maravilloso!" Tenía razón: al igual que Steve Gadd, Graham tenía precisión y sentimiento. Se quedó con nosotros casi siete años, mientras ingresábamos en los 80, y aprendí mucho de él. A Chepito también le caía bien y solía llamarlo "refugiado", porque era de Canadá: esto viniendo de un nicaragüense. Sobre el escenario lo presenté como "Graham Lear, el grande". Si quieres oír lo bueno que podía ser el estilo que Graham podía aportar a una pista, escucha "Aqua Marine" de *Marathon* del 79 o cualquier otro tema instrumental de esa época. ¡Precisión llena de sentimiento!

*   *   *

Cerca de la época en que *Inner Secrets* estaba por salir, en el 78, Greg Walker estaba listo para dejar Santana y trajimos a Alex Ligertwood, otra persona que estaba en mi archivo musical. La primera vez que lo escuché fue cuando cantaba en la banda de David Sancious, Tone; y actuaron como nuestra banda soporte en el Beacon Theatre, en 1975. David es un tipo estupendo. Toca la guitarra y los teclados; venía de la banda de Bruce Springsteen y usaba sombreros del Zorro como los que solía tener Lenny White: un auténtico músico del *rock* de fusión. Noté que el cantante de David tenía una maravillosa voz de R&B, aunque casi no se le entendía cuando hablaba debido a su notable acento escocés. Llamé a Alex e hizo algunos conciertos en los que Greg también cantó; ahí descubrí que me gustaba la idea de tener dos cantantes. Podían complementarse mejor: uno más alto y nítido; el otro, más bajo, más tosco, y con estilo de *blues*.

A lo largo de los años lo intenté una y otra vez. Así lo hacemos hoy, con dos cantantes: Tony Lindsay, Andy Vargas y, en ocasiones, Tommy Anthony, que toca la guitarra pero que también puede llegar a notas altas y nítidas con su voz. Es como el baloncesto, algunos tipos aportan su fuerza y otros son como guepardos. Y también están los que son como las anclas de una canción. Necesitamos versatilidad, pero yo necesito que no dejen caer la pelota. Los músicos de mi banda son como los jugadores, y nuestra meta es llegar al corazón, de la forma que podamos.

En la primavera del 79 Greg nos dejó y Alex vino a ocupar su lugar. Se convirtió en la voz de Santana en muchos de nuestros álbumes, y en la mayoría de nuestras giras entre los 80 y los 90. Cuando canta, puede hacerte sentir a Dios, como lo hizo cuando cantó "Somewhere in Heaven" en el álbum *Milagro*, en el 92. Simplemente le crees.

Una cosa no había cambiado: yo seguía siendo Devadip. Cuando hice mis propios álbumes a fines de los 70, utilicé ese nombre porque esos eran álbumes entre álbumes: por un lado estaba la banda Santana y por el otro, la persona Devadip Carlos Santana. *Oneness* y *The Swing of Delight* son dos de mis álbumes más personales. Hice

Oneness en 1979 y mis influencias fueron Weather Report y los sonidos de sintetizadores, así como su excelente álbum, *Mysterious Traveller*.

También hice *The Swing of Delight* un año después. Dave Rubinson también me ayudó a persuadir a Columbia para hacerlo, a fin de que pudiera conseguir que Herbie Hancock, Wayne Shorter, Ron Carter y Tony Williams tocaran. Esa era la banda de Miles de los 60.

Eché una mirada al estudio y estaba muerto de miedo, pensando: "¿Qué diablos estoy haciendo?". Eso hace que un guitarrista baje la intensidad; la reduzca y entre muy, muy profundamente en su interior. En medio de la grabación Wayne tuvo un momento de duda, lo que era verdaderamente inusual en él. Detuvo la canción. Todos se alejaron de los micrófonos y Tony dejó las baquetas a un lado. Wayne solo movió la cabeza, y dijo: "Ese no soy yo. Nunca toco en forma desesperada o frenética. Empecemos de nuevo".

Me sentía muy bendecido de que hayamos logrado todo lo que me había propuesto hacer con ese álbum en un nivel alto. La revista *DownBeat* le dedicó una excelente reseña. Imagino que pudieron sentir el propósito. Ese álbum nació de mi deseo de honrar a Sri por lo que había hecho por nosotros: por Deborah y por mí. Él realizó el dibujo de la portada, en el que se ve un diseño de cerezas, color dorado.

Comencé a hacerme cada vez más amigo de Wayne y Herbie durante la producción del álbum. Ahí logré conocerlos verdaderamente, al sentarme y conversar con ellos. Wayne estaba mucho más indulgente y relajado de lo que había estado ocho años antes, cuando nos encontramos por primera vez. Se sinceró y empezó a contarme historias sobre Miles, así como perspectivas acerca de la música, cuya explicación llevaría unos diez minutos. O me mostraba cosas de un libro de ilustraciones grande y grueso que tenía. Una vez me mostró la imagen de una mujer de Venus. Le pregunté a Wayne por qué tenía cuatro pies. Me respondió: "No es que tenga cuatro pies, es que se mueve muy rápido". Bien, gracias por aclararlo. Algo que puedo mencionar sobre mi relación con Wayne es que a menudo tengo que disminuir el ritmo para alcanzar su velocidad. Él siempre se mueve rápido.

Wayne nunca se toma nada demasiado en serio; y menos a sí

mismo. Esto me dijo una vez: "Voy a salir de gira como un acto cómico, solo yo y mi saxo soprano. Y voy a ser el hombre recto".

Desde la primera vez que pasé el tiempo con Wayne y Herbie, pude ver que ellos seguían principios y observaciones espirituales, y se morían de risa juntos. Se enfocaban en ser ellos mismos, sin la influencia de ninguna forma particular de comportamiento, como niños íntegros e inmaculados.

Herbie es un genio supremo, y además, dulce como el helado con pastel, como lo describía Elvin Jones. Nos conocimos cuando actuó como banda soporte de nuestro grupo en el Boarding House, en el 72, y desde ese día nos veíamos con frecuencia; él me hablaba de su canto y de que le gustaba comer en Dipti Nivas, que a fines de los 70 llegó a convertirse en el restaurante vegetariano más famoso de San Francisco. En el 70 él estaba grabando en San Francisco con Ndugu, cuando Chepito me dijo que Herbie quería que yo fuera y participara. Era un honor para mí, pero no tenía tiempo para tocar, puesto que al día siguiente partíamos rumbo a Brasil.

Herbie es de Chicago y eso se nota en su sonido, a través del *blues*. Una vez le dije que escuchara algo de Otis Spann y me comentó que no estaba familiarizado con él. Ahí me di cuenta: "¡Claro! Existen dos caras de la ciudad, dos, por lo menos. De un lado está el sentimiento del blues de Otis Spann, Sunnyland Slim y Jimmy Johnson, que secundaban a Chuck Berry. Al otro lado se encuentran Wynton Kelly, Red Garland y John Lewis. Sin embargo, Herbie puede brindarte todo esto a la vez.

Nadie es más moderno ni valiente que Herbie con los pianos eléctricos y los sintetizadores: los verdaderos artistas no le temen a la tecnología. A partir de la época en que estuvo con Miles, descubrió una forma de utilizar esos instrumentos de modo tal que no sonaran ofensivos o extraños. Años más tarde, cuando él y yo fuimos recibidos conjuntamente en el Kennedy Center Honors, Snoop Dogg le agradeció a Herbie por haber dado a luz al hip-hop. No estoy seguro de cuánta gente comprenda lo enorme y verdadero que es eso. Solo hay que escuchar su álbum *Sunlight*, que salió incluso antes que "Rockit": todos usan esas ideas ahora.

* * *

En la actualidad, si pongo *Oneness* y escucho esas pistas me acuerdo de que en aquel tiempo Deborah y yo habíamos vuelto a estar juntos y yo solía pasar mucho más tiempo con SK. Algunas canciones surgieron de eso, incluida "Silver Dreams Golden Smiles". SK tocó la guitarra y cantó en ella, mientras que Clare Fischer hizo los arreglos de cuerdas.

En 1981 Deborah estuvo de acuerdo en que ambos debíamos dejar a Sri: era hora de quitarnos el polvo de los pies y de seguir avanzando. Un día nos fuimos de nuestra casa en Queens tarde por la noche y dejamos todas nuestras pertenencias; así de simple. Después supe que Sri quería sacarme mi nombre y que le había dicho a algunos discípulos que no nos vieran más, puesto que Deborah y yo íbamos a ahogarnos en un mar de ignorancia. No me gustó oír eso porque no quería retornar a lo que me había hecho acudir a él en primer lugar. No dejé de creer en los principios, la divinidad y la luz interior, pero esas palabras fueron algo oscuro.

El Sri que conocí decía frases como: "Cuando el poder del amor supere el amor al poder, el hombre tendrá un nuevo nombre: Dios". No sé bien cómo ocurrió, pero mucha gente piensa que Jimi Hendrix dijo eso. No fue él; fue Sri.

Sri me ayudó a ser algo más que simplemente Santana, el guitarrista. Me ayudó a lograr una consciencia más profunda de mi propia luz; una consciencia más profunda de mi propia conexión con la divinidad, la humanidad y el reino invisible. Es Dios, independientemente de cómo lo llames, y está más allá de todo enaltecimiento. Él no necesita una cartelera; no precisa que lo veneremos ni que lo adoremos. Tenemos que venerarnos, adorarnos y trabajar en nosotros mismos para cristalizar nuestra existencia a través de la disciplina. Eso es lo más importante que aprendí de Sri y aún me guío por ese principio.

CAPÍTULO 18

Miles Davis y yo en el Savoy, ciudad de Nueva York, 5 de mayo de 1981.

En los 80, Santana podía hacer todas las giras que quisiera. Viajábamos por todo el país, tocando en los mismos sitios de las mismas ciudades; de Detroit a Chicago, de Cleveland a los lugares típicos del área de Nueva York: Nassau Coliseum, Jones Beach. Sonábamos en las estaciones de radio de rock clásico y de éxitos de antaño. Estoy orgulloso de que esas canciones mantuvieran una buena música de guitarra durante muchos años en el aire, aun cuando hubiera pocos solos de guitarra en las canciones populares. Podían escucharse éxitos de antaño en el elevador o en Starbucks con un solo de Eric Clapton o de Jimmy Page, y a veces el solo en sí mismo era más memorable que la canción.

Uno de los mejores halagos que recibí después de Supernatural vino *de Prince. Me dijo: "Carlos, gracias a ti puedo tocar un solo de guitarra en una de mis canciones, y estará en la radio". Nunca había pensado en eso. Le respondí: "Sí, durante un tiempo no estaba bien recibido tener solos de guitarra en las canciones".*

En los 80, la radio no hacía ni deshacía a Santana. Creo que nuestra reputación siempre estuvo basada más en nuestros espectáculos, ya que la gente necesita sentir emociones. Cuando sientes algo, de inmediato te vuelves presente en el ahora. Y debido a ello, nuestros públicos pueden sentir que el propósito y el objetivo de la banda es mucho más que solo entretener. Es recordarles a todos en un nivel molecular su propio significado, transmitir la idea de que cada uno de nosotros tiene el poder de traer abundancia desde el universo ahora mismo. Santana es una experiencia en vivo que regala más momentos que memorias. Eso nunca cambiará.

El año 1981 era el momento de un nuevo comienzo y de un nuevo hogar: un hogar familiar. Deborah y yo dejamos la costa este y nos trasladamos desde el condado de Marin a Santa Cruz. Fue la primera casa que compramos juntos desde que nos conocimos, y al poco tiempo sus padres y los míos vinieron de visita. Empezamos a pasar más tiempo con nuestros amigos; Carabello y yo nos reencontramos porque él se había casado con Mimi Sanchez, que era una de las mejores amigas de Deborah. Comenzaron a venir con frecuencia a nuestra casa. En ese entonces todos estábamos más viejos e inteligentes.

Ver a Carabello crecer hasta convertirse en un hombre digno, positivo y respetable ha sido muy gratificante para mí, ya que mi deseo es que la gente comprenda que necesitamos creer los unos en los otros. Nos vuelve más fuertes que si estuviéramos solos, y puede hacernos cambiar. Siempre hay alguien en cada vecindario que finalmente se redime. En el mío fue Carabello; tenemos una larga historia vivida juntos que se remonta a mis días en Mission High, y estoy muy feliz de ellos.

Al igual que yo, Carabello siguió siendo amigo de Miles; este lo alojó en su casa cuando visitó la Ciudad de Nueva York. En el 81 Miles estaba regresando después de haber dejado de tocar en el 76. Nadie tenía noticias de él desde hacía unos cinco años. Todas las historias señalaban que se encontraba en un lugar oscuro, con las cortinas cerradas. De vez en cuando le enviaba tarjetas y flores. Herbie y Dave Rubinson me contaban de él porque solían visitarlo. Sé que él pensaba en mí y yo pensaba en él.

Santana tocó en Buffalo ese año; y mientras nos preparábamos para partir rumbo a la Ciudad de Nueva York y tocar en el Savoy, escuchábamos la música de Miles. Recuerdo que Rashiki me preguntó si pensaba que Miles volvería a llevarse la trompeta a los labios y tocar una vez más. Aún no lo sabíamos. Le respondí: "Nada es imposible; quizá cuando se aburra".

Efectivamente, cuando llegamos a Nueva York unos días después, me enteré de que Carabello vendría a nuestro espectáculo en el Savoy y traería a Miles. No lo podía creer. Terminamos la prueba de sonido, y ahí estaban detrás de escena. Miles vestía un traje que lo hacía ver algo desaliñado, como si estuviera viviendo una vida un tanto particular.

No importaba. Era hermoso verlo. Bill Graham producía esa gira y estaba tan eufórico como un niño. "Miles, ¡qué bueno verte! Gracias por venir. ¿Cómo estás? ¿Cómo te sientes?".

Miles pareció haber pensado que Bill lo estaba controlando. "¿Qué?", le respondió.

"¿Cómo te sientes, hombre?".

Miles le dijo: "Levanta una mano así". Bill levantó la mano y Miles le dio un puñetazo bien fuerte; un golpe corto al estilo de Sugar Ray Robinson, recto y rápido. "Me siento bien, muchachito judío". El mismo Miles de siempre.

Me dirigí a mi habitación para meditar, como hago antes de subir al escenario, y Miles me siguió. Le expliqué lo que tenía que hacer y seguidamente cerré los ojos, mientras me relajaba y entraba en mi interior. Quería hacer eso durante al menos diez o quince minutos. Miles se comportó muy respetuosamente. Él no hablaba, pero yo podía sentir sus ojos como dos láseres enfocados en el medallón que yo usaba. Podía oír su respiración; y abrí los ojos. Estaba observando el medallón como si fuera a perforarlo con la mirada, así que le pregunté: "Miles, ¿lo quieres?". Me respondió: "Solo si tú me lo colocas". Me lo quité, se lo colgué, y él siguió: "Yo también rezo, ¿sabes?".

"¿Tú rezas, Miles?".

"Por supuesto. Cuando quiero comprar unas líneas de cocaína, digo: 'Dios, por favor, haz que este cabrón esté en su casa'".

Yo pensé: "¡Rayos!"

Hay algo que yo solía hacer cada vez que tocábamos y Miles estaba cerca; todavía lo hago cuando estamos en la Ciudad de Nueva York. Toco un fragmento de "Will o' the Wisp", de *Sketches of Spain*. La tocamos en el concierto que dimos en el Savoy y luego de este Miles la mencionó por primera vez. "Sí, me gusta cómo la tocan. Muchos no saben cómo hacerlo bien". Le dije: "Miles, tenemos una limusina. ¿Quieres que te llevemos a tu casa?". Así es que los cinco nos metimos en la limusina: Miles, Carabello, el saxofonista Bill Evans, Rashiki y yo. Cuando Carabello subió a la parte delantera, deslizó el asiento hacia atrás y le pegó a Miles en el pie, a quien por alguna razón ya le dolía previamente. Miles se puso muy violento y de inmediato estalló contra Carabello.

Empezamos a dar vueltas en el coche, cuando de repente Miles me miró y exclamó: "Carlos, una perra portorriqueña intentó meterme cortisona para ayudarme con esto que tengo en el pie. Me decía: 'cortisona esto, cortisona aquello'". Pensé en eso y me empecé a reír. "Miles, te estaba diciendo 'corazón'. Te quiere".

Dios ama a los personajes, y Dios ama a Miles. Toda esa noche fue increíble y loca. Parecía como si estuviésemos en una versión diferente y extraña del País de las Maravillas; como si hubiésemos caído por la madriguera del conejo hasta llegar a otro mundo oscuro, aterrador. Miles nos indicaba hacia dónde ir. Él tenía el control, y adondequiera que fuéramos podías ver que las personas lo conocían. Que estuvieran contentas de verlo o no, eso era otra cosa. Él trataba de salirse con la suya en muchos aspectos: probar a la gente, hacer su actuación callejera.

Miles nos llevó a uno de esos clubes nocturnos que parecían salidos de *Escape from New York*. Tenía persianas de acero por todos lados. Bajamos de la limusina y yo me preguntaba por qué estábamos ahí, ya que parecía una fábrica abandonada. Luego se nos acercó un corpulento guarda de seguridad, que llevaba un bate de béisbol. Me dijo: "No hay problema con ustedes, muchachos. Sé quiénes son". A continuación señaló a Miles y nos preguntó: "¿Por qué tienen que traerlo aquí?". Miles pasó caminando a su lado en dirección al lúgubre edificio y yo lo seguí.

Fue directamente hacia el piano, que estaba desvencijado y desafinado. Me indicó: "Ven aquí; quiero mostrarle algo".

Le respondí "bueno" y me dirigí hacia él. Miles observaba el teclado y estiraba esos largos dedos que tenía. Hombre, podrías hacer una película completa basada solo en sus manos. Estaba haciendo lo mismo que Wayne hace en el piano: observa, espera, luego se lanza. Es gracioso, mi esposa come de esa manera: Cindy lo hace con la comida; Wayne y Miles, con los acordes. Esa noche, cuando Miles tocó sus acordes, todo el club desapareció: de repente yo me encontraba en España, en un castillo en una vieja película de aventuras. Miles me preguntó: "¿Lo oyes?".

Le respondí: "Por supuesto, es increíble. Gracias". Estaba listo para mostrarme algo más, pero un tipo se levantó, puso una moneda de veinticinco centavos en la rocola y empezó a sonar la canción "Muscles", de Diana Ross, lo que cambió por completo la atmósfera. Miles escudriñó al tipo, que sabía lo que había hecho porque le devolvía la mirada. Miles lo miró fijamente un rato más hasta que dijo: "Hombre, ¿tú sabes quién soy?". Le contestó: "Eres Miles Davis. ¿Y qué?". Como si nada. Era todo lo que Miles necesitaba oír. Sonrió y se dirigió a la barra. "Dame un maldito ron con Coca-Cola. Y sírvele lo que él quiera".

Miles empezó a aburrirse del lugar, así que volvimos todos a la limusina y preguntó: "Carlos, ¿tienes hambre?".

"Sí, podría comer algo".

"Conozco un lugar excelente donde hacen sopa de frijoles negros". Le indicó al conductor adónde ir y seguimos conversando.

De pronto Miles levantó la vista y vio que nos habíamos ido demasiado lejos. Todo esto a través de sus gafas de sol y de los vidrios polarizados. Abrió el compartimiento detrás del conductor y le gritó: "¡Eh! Te has pasado, es dos cuadras más atrás. ¡Retrocede!" El conductor le explicó: "No puedo retroceder, es una calle de un solo sentido". ¡*Zas!* Miles estiró el brazo por la pequeña ventana, ¡y le pegó en la nuca! "¡Te estoy diciendo que retrocedas!"

Así que volvimos por aquella estrecha calle de Nueva York para ir al restaurante, otro sitio particular. Encontramos una mesa y Miles exclamó: "Ya vengo, tengo que hacer pis". Camino al baño de hombres vio a una mujer, se detuvo, y comenzó a hablarle y a susurrarle cosas al oído. Cuando se fue, ella se dirigió hacia mí y me dijo: "Eres un buen hombre. ¿Por qué te juntas con este malhablado?".

Mientras Miles estaba en el baño llegó la sopa; un mesero grande y fornido de enormes brazos se acercó y dijo: "Eh, Santana, ¿quieres un poco de pan para la sopa?".

"No, gracias; así estoy bien. Solo la sopa". Pero cuando Miles volvió y no vio una cesta de pan, le dijo al tipo que viniera. "Eh, cabrón, ¿dónde está el pan?". El mesero lo miró y apoyó su enorme brazo sobre la mesa junto al rostro de Miles: "¿Cómo acabas de llamarme?".

Esta escena era digna de *Alien vs. Predator*. Los dedos de Miles eran extremadamente largos; por lo que ubicó su hermosa mano negra alrededor del brazo del tipo muy lentamente, lo miró y en un tono escalofriante lo amenazó: "Voy a rasguñarte". El mesero movió la cabeza y se alejó sigilosamente. Rashiki y yo nos miramos como diciendo: "Viejo, esto sí que fue de terror".

Una noche entera con Miles en Nueva York: a veces era todo un desafío estar con ese tipo. Esa noche concluyó cuando empezaba a salir el sol y Miles nos llevó con él para consumir unas líneas de cocaína. Fuimos hasta un vecindario donde yo no quería bajarme de la limusina, así que le expliqué que tenía que volver al hotel porque teníamos un vuelo temprano esa mañana. Rashiki y yo nos quedamos en la limusina. Tomé dinero de mi billetera y se lo di a Carabello mientras le decía: "Este dinero es para que tú y Bill Evans tomen un taxi". Saludé con la mano a Miles, pero él ya caminaba perdiéndose en el amanecer, haciéndose cada vez más y más pequeño.

Recuerdo que pensé que parecía un niño caminando por una juguetería al que le han dicho que eligiera lo que quisiera. Todo el mundo en Nueva York lo conocía. Tenía rienda suelta: era Miles Davis.

Volví a ver a Miles ese año en la Ciudad de Nueva York cuando tocó en la Avery Fisher Hall. Vino hacia mí y me dio un abrazo; esta fue la primera de las dos únicas veces que lo hizo. Yo apreciaba mucho esos momentos; no veía que abrazara a demasiada gente. En la Avery Fisher recibí el abrazo más extraño: colocó sus manos detrás de mi cabeza y su nariz frente a la mía, de modo que nos mirábamos directamente a los ojos; luego se levantó del suelo mientras se agarraba de mi cuello. Entonces quedó colgado de mí, me miró y me dijo: "Carlos, significa tanto que estés aquí".

La segunda vez que Miles me abrazó fue en la fiesta de su sexagésimo cumpleaños en 1986, en un yate que estaba parado en una dársena de Malibú. Me sentí tan conmovido después de eso que cuando fue a saludar a otra persona tuve que bajar del bote para tomarme un momento. Estaba contemplando las ondas del agua cuando su sobrino, Vince Wilburn, se me acercó. Le comenté: "Viejo, realmente me produce algo cuando me saluda así". Me dijo: "Lo vi. Apenas te fuiste, exclamó: 'Ese sí que es un cabrón excelente'".

Es importante ser validado por un gigante como ese; un gigante que, además, también era un diablillo divino. Recuerdo que ese día llegó una hora y media tarde a su propia fiesta. Mientras lo esperábamos yo conversaba con Tony Williams, que estaba fumando un cigarro junto al bote, y me aseguró: "No es la primera vez que hace esto".

Zebop fue el álbum que hice cuando comencé a tocar con una guitarra Paul Reed Smith, la que se convertiría en mi guitarra principal. Actualmente Paul sigue siendo mi lutier principal. Él y Randy, el "Hombre Boogie", han dado a luz creaciones que han logrado mucho por los guitarristas y han ampliado las fronteras de la excelencia, cada uno a su manera; Paul con sus guitarras y Randy, con los amplificadores Boogie.

Paul Reed Smith: me gustan su corazón y la gente que él contrata. Su taller es como el set de una película de ciencia ficción. Más de ciencia que de ficción. Desde el tallado, pasando por el ajuste de la afinación hasta el barnizado, conoce la ciencia del oficio y cómo lograr el balance para que la guitarra tenga... esta es la palabra perfecta: consistencia. Sin importar el clima, el lugar o las circunstancias, una guitarra PRS no te fallará porque sabe comportarse bien. Algo más: cada vez que Paul las envía, las guitarras ya salen afinadas del estuche. Es un toque personal. Lo raro es que cuando me enamoré por primera vez de dos de esas guitarras PRS, estas solo eran los prototipos. Yo tenía los modelos 1 y 3, pero, entretanto, Paul había seguido avanzando; había rediseñado sus guitarras y las estaba fabricando. No era solo la forma; el modelo nuevo de la que yo había estado tocando sonaba diferente para mí, un poco más nasal. Le pregunté a Paul si podía volver al estilo viejo, pero me dijo que el costo de rehacer la guitarra en ese momento era prohibitivo. Mi argumento era que sé lo que ocurre cuando alguien ve tocar a Tony Williams con una Gretsch, a Jimi Hendrix con una Stratocaster o a Wes Montgomery con una guitarra ancha. Solo pensaba que si los chicos podían verme con esa guitarra, querrían lo mismo; y sabía que existía la cantidad suficiente de ellos para hacer que esto funcionara en el aspecto comercial. Tenía un presentimiento con respecto a la promoción de productos: mi nombre podía vender cosas, más allá de álbumes y entradas de conciertos.

Allá por 1989 me robaron algunas de mis guitarras, incluidas las PRS originales. Había alguien en nuestra organización que confió en alguien en quien no debía confiar para que guardara algunos equipos que no debió haber guardado. Hicimos una gran campaña de APB para recuperarlas y por la gracia de Dios las encontramos en una casa de empeño, puesto que eran realmente únicas. El final feliz de la historia es que encontramos las guitarras y Paul decidió utilizar el molde original para fabricar algunas guitarras nuevas con el estilo viejo. Así es como hemos entablado una larga relación y PRS cuenta con mi aval.

He aprendido acerca del valor de las promociones de productos y, también, a confiar en mi intuición sobre algunas cosas. Otro ejemplo: igual que con Paul Reed Smith, siempre tendré afecto por Alexander Dumble y sus amplificadores y, claro está, por Randy, el "Hombre Boogie" y sus amplificadores Boogie. En 2013, Adam Fells, que trabaja en nuestra oficina, me envió un video que la gente de Sony Music había encontrado de Santana en Budokan en el 73. Lo vi, escuché el sonido de la guitarra, observé detenidamente el amplificador, y este me sorprendió: "Es mi viejo amigo. ¡Extraño ese sonido!" Era el amplificador Boogie original de cuero de víbora de Randy del que me había separado hacía mucho tiempo y del que no me había acordado durante años. "Adam, ¡tienen que conseguirme uno de esos Boogie de cuero de víbora!" Me respondió: "Todavía los tenemos; hace bastante que no los vemos, pero están en el depósito". Adam los encontró, Randy los reparó y trabajó en los contactos, y yo los conecté: ahí estaba esa voz. Eso es lo que estoy tocando ahora, junto con un Dumble, y estoy sacando lo mejor de ambos.

La cuestión es que después de esto Randy volvió al modelo viejo y también al diseño anterior. Fabricó más de setecientos amplificadores Boogie de cuero de víbora. Después él y yo los firmamos, y ahora todos quieren uno. En Japón se venden como pan caliente. Así que no me digan que algo tiene un costo prohibitivo.

Llegado 1981, parecía como si el espíritu de los 60 hubiera dejado los Estados Unidos para trasladarse al extranjero. Ese fue el año en que Santana tocó en el festival Live under the Sky en Japón, un evento que juntaba rock con jazz. Santana tocó, la banda V.S.O.P. de Herbie Hancock tocó y después tocamos todos juntos, además de que se sumaron Herbie y Tony Williams. El espíritu del viejo Auditorio Fillmore estaba vivo otra vez: por lo menos ahí, en ese momento.

En ese entonces, cuando todo en los Estados Unidos había crecido tanto y sonaba todo igual para mí, me sentí en total confianza con Bill Graham para expresar mi opinión y reclamarle por lo que estaba aconteciendo en la industria de la música. Si él podía estar en mi espectáculo tomando notas en una libreta y criticarme, bueno... lo mismo se aplica para ambas partes. Al menos teníamos ese tipo de relación. Entonces le pregunté: "¿Qué te sucedió, viejo?".

"¿Qué quieres decir con 'qué te sucedió'?".

"Antes ponías a Miles Davis, Buddy Rich y Charles Lloyd en el programa con artistas de rock. Solías llegar a la consciencia de cada uno y mostrarnos a todos que existía una música extraordinaria que no era la que escuchábamos en la radio. Pero no lo haces más".

Bajó la mirada. "Buen punto". Había dejado de organizar conciertos en salones de baile y salas de espectáculos, y había comenzado a empaquetar estrellas como Peter Frampton.

"Discúlpame", le dije, "¿pero por qué no hay más músicos de *jazz* en el programa?". Aún era posible revivir el espíritu del Fillmore; ese era mi mensaje para Bill. Sí, lo sé: la industria había cambiado. Sin embargo, era Bill quien había armado el negocio y había dado el ejemplo, y todavía tenía ese poder.

Me siento orgulloso de todos los álbumes que Santana grabó en los 80 y los 90. Cada uno de esos discos captó un momento de la historia; son como instantáneas del lugar donde me encontraba y de lo que escuchaba por aquel entonces. Cada uno tenía un espíritu identificable. Cada álbum de Santana me había enseñado a estar presente con apertura mental; a escuchar mucho y a estar abierto no solo a los músicos y a la música en sí misma, sino también a los productores, ya que Santana es como los Raiders o los Seahawks: un equipo. Quizá yo esté a cargo, pero Santana es una visión colectiva que comprende muchos espíritus, corazones y aspiraciones. Tendremos que llevar esa música fuera del estudio, a la calle, y tocarla noche tras noche: tal vez no toda, pero uno nunca sabe hasta que ve cómo se sienten las canciones y cómo son recibidas luego del lanzamiento del álbum.

Cuando hice mis propios álbumes, la única responsabilidad era conmigo mismo: solo era mi visión. En el 82 hice *Havana Moon* por cuenta propia, como Carlos Santana, con la producción de Jerry

Wexler. El álbum surgió de la idea de que Chuck Berry escribió la canción del título (que es parte de la arquitectura del rock and roll) inspirado en T-Bone Walker y Nat King Cole; especialmente "Calypso Blues" de Nat, donde solo estaba Nat acompañado por un conguero, cantando como si hubiese nacido en Jamaica. Mi papá tocó y cantó en *Havana Moon*, y grabamos la canción favorita de mi mamá, "Vereda tropical". También pude colaborar con el fabuloso organista y arreglista Booker T. Jones, así como con uno de mis vocalistas preferidos, Willie Nelson.

El compositor Greg Brown escribió una canción que Willie cantaría, llamada "They All Went to Mexico". Cuando escuché la parte de la letra que dice "creo que se fue a México", pensé: "¡Ah!, se parece a lo que Roy Rogers o Gene Autry solían cantar; son como las citas de Wayne Shorter de 'South of the Border' en sus solos". Después caí en la cuenta de que la mayoría de mis amigos veía algo de México que era diferente de lo que yo veía. Igualmente, yo seguía bastante cerca de todo eso. Crecí en Tijuana, por lo que muchas cosas de México no eran necesariamente novedosas para mí. Sin embargo, otros veían aspectos buenos del país, entonces yo trataba de ver eso y de verme a mí mismo, también, desde una perspectiva distinta. Además, empecé a pensar que Willie es de Texas, que alguna vez fue México, por lo tanto México también es parte de sus raíces. Luego reflexioné: "Todo se conecta, todos somos parte de ello. Hagamos esta canción".

Tengo que agradecerle a Willie Nelson por el impulso que me dio para que saliera esa melodía. Dos años más tarde, después de que Deborah y yo fuéramos bendecidos con la llegada de Salvador, fui solo a visitar México y comenzó la verdadera reconexión.

Como resultado de *Havana Moon* también descubrí a Jimmie Vaughan, cuya forma de tocar me encantó. Jimmie y su banda, The Fabulous Thunderbirds, podían tocar *shuffles* como nadie; y Jimmie había perfeccionado ese estilo a la Lightnin' Hopkins y Kenny Burrell. Establecimos un vínculo de inmediato y él me repetía: "Espera a que escuches a mi hermano".

Cuando conocí a Stevie Ray Vaughan, en 1983, él tenía un cierto aire de superioridad. Intentó desafiarme: "Aquí está mi guitarra; muéstrame algo". ¿Que te muestre algo? Lo miré directamente a los ojos y le dije que enfundara la pistola. "Yo lo quiero a tu hermano, te quiero a ti y quiero aquello que ustedes quieren. Empecemos con eso". Se detuvo de inmediato y pidió perdón: "Discúlpeme, señor". Le respondí que no hacía falta que me llamara "señor", pero que no me tratara con esa actitud.

Como me pasó con Jimmie, tuve una profunda conexión con Stevie desde el principio: ambos teníamos una profunda e increíble devoción por la música a la que llamamos blues. Cuando digo "profunda", quiero decir "desde el centro del corazón". Stevie Ray lo sabía y podías oírlo en su música, al igual que en la música de Eric Clapton, Jeff Beck, Jimmy Page y Peter Green antes que él. Ahora tenemos a músicos como Gary Clark Jr., Derek Trucks, Susan Tedeschi, Doyle Bramhall II y Warren Haynes, junto con muchos más, que mantienen esa llama encendida.

Lo que hacía tan diferente a Stevie Ray es que no tocaba únicamente la esencia del blues, como muchos hacían en ese momento. Tal vez puedes hacerlo con algunos tipos de música como el rock melódico, o el rock o el jazz suaves, pero no con el blues. Para que suene real, debes dedicarte por completo a ello. Y créeme, Stevie Ray sí que lo hizo. Viejo, cómo lo extraño.

En el otoño del 82, Deborah y yo fuimos a Hawái, y también fueron nuestros padres. Un día frente a todos mi mamá le dijo a Deborah: "Soñé que estabas embarazada". Recuerdo que mi papá la reprendió por haber dicho eso enfrente de todos y en voz alta, y por haberla hecho sentirse incómoda. Mamá le respondió: "¿Qué? ¿No puedo contarle a alguien sobre un sueño que tuve?". Las madres mexicanas les dan mucha importancia a los sueños; supongo que de ahí heredé esa costumbre.

Resulta que Deborah estaba embarazada de dos meses; ella me preguntó cómo mi madre pudo saberlo. "Estuvo embarazada once veces; ella sabe de eso". El mes de mayo siguiente, cuando me encontraba en casa luego de una extensa gira por Europa, nació Salvador. Así como así te conviertes en padre.

Creo que Salvador fue la culminación de muchos, muchos años de rezos por parte de nuestras madres. También vino por un plan divino. Deborah y yo meditábamos con frecuencia y pedíamos que seleccionara a un alma especial; luego cada uno se bañaba y después estábamos juntos. Salvador fue concebido con una intencionalidad divina. Igual que nuestros otros hijos.

Años más tarde le expliqué a Sal cómo había sido creado (un par de veces) y mientras más crecía, mejor lo comprendía. La primera vez fue cuando tenía solo cinco o seis años e iba a la escuela pública. Deborah y yo sabíamos que podíamos pagar una escuela privada, pero queríamos que viviera una experiencia con culturas y personas diversas, sin que estuviera separado por una cuestión de privilegio. Sal era muy inteligente; entendía lo que intentábamos hacer y no tenía problemas con ello. Cuando no comprendía algo, simplemente lo preguntaba.

En una ocasión llegué a casa y Deborah me dijo: "Tu hijo quiere hablar contigo", que era nuestro código para decir "Esto no va a ser fácil". Había escuchado unas palabras groseras en la escuela, una en particular, y por alguna razón se daba cuenta de que estaba mal y no quería hablar sobre eso con su mamá. Le pregunté a Salvador qué palabra era. "Sonaba como 'comer', pero en lugar de una 'eme' tenía una 'ge'".

Me enorgullecí de que Sal hubiera encontrado una manera de mencionar la palabra sin decirla. Le expliqué que era una mala palabra para algo que podía ser muy bueno y que eso era parte de que él estuviera aquí. Le dije: "Tu madre y yo rezamos por ti, encendimos una vela, meditamos, pedimos por tu alma y luego nos metimos en la cama e hicimos el amor, y así es como viniste al mundo. Tú fuiste hecho con amor. Esto es lo contrario de esa palabra". Recuerdo que Sal me miró con la cabeza inclinada. "Ah, bien. Gracias, papá".

Luego se quedó pensando un segundo. "¿Pero qué significa?".

"Tendrás que descubrirlo tú mismo cuando tengas la edad suficiente, hijo".

* * *

Sucedió tres veces y todas fueron prácticamente iguales. Deborah iba primero al hospital, y cuando yo llegaba veía a mis padres y suegros, que estaban esperando ahí. Luego venía la enfermera con el bebé envuelto en una manta y todos nos amontonábamos para verlo. Lo primero que veía eran sus ojos, que brillaban como diamantes. Todos nuestros hijos (Salvador en el 83, Stella en el 85 y Angelica en el 89) nacieron con los ojos abiertos. Eran tan puros: todos la mirábamos a Deborah y le decíamos "buen trabajo, mamá". Después, cada una de estas veces tuve que ir al coche y tomar algo de aire fresco porque la experiencia era muy intensa. Iba solo y me sentaba en silencio, y lentamente empezaba a escuchar una canción.

Cada niño trae consigo una canción. Depende de cada padre escucharla y grabarla o tomar un bolígrafo para registrarla de algún modo. "Blues for Salvador", "Bella" para Stella y "Angelica Faith": cada uno de nuestros hijos tiene una canción especial que escribí cuando nacieron o un tiempo después. Contemplas al bebé y automáticamente escuchas la melodía. Probablemente algunas de mis mejores melodías cayeron en el sofá y se perdieron ahí, me sentaba e iba creando una canción para que los bebés dejaran de llorar y pudieran dormirse.

A las tres de la mañana, cuando el bebé no para de llorar y la madre ha agotado todas sus baterías y ya está dormida, es tu turno. Así aprendí a tener en brazos a los bebés, con firmeza y seguridad, con la barriga hacia abajo; así se relajaban. Salían del "modo llanto". Teníamos un muñeco que era un payaso; lo derribabas pero siempre volvía a su posición. Una vez lo golpeé sin querer y el bebé dejó de llorar, mientras comenzaba a observar lo que ocurría. Lo convertimos en un juego y funcionaba casi siempre, al menos para interrumpir el ritmo del llanto. Hay recursos que cualquier padre puede utilizar para ser creativo con cosas simples que hay en el hogar.

Incluso antes de que naciera Sal, Deborah y yo acordamos que, después de que ella diera a luz, yo no saldría de gira durante más de cuatro semanas, o cinco como máximo. Pasado ese tiempo, debía volver a casa, sin excepciones. Y mientras estuviera allí, sería tiempo para la familia. Tal vez podía hacer alguna grabación, pero solo en San Francisco y eso hicimos. De esta forma, no me perdía los cumpleaños ni las graduaciones.

Tenemos muchos videos familiares en los que aparezco; estuve presente y estoy muy orgulloso de eso.

Sal solo tenía algunos meses de vida cuando lo llevamos a Japón en el verano del 83 y la pasó muy bien durante su primera visita a ese país. Era un bebé grande, una bolita de grasa. Parecía un luchador de sumo. El Sr. Udo fue de mucha ayuda. Pero, para Deborah y para mí, fue una llamada de atención debido a los cambios de horario y las necesidades del niño, y además nos enfermamos durante algunos días. Después nos dimos cuenta de todos los gérmenes que podíamos contraer cuando viajábamos en avión. Cosas de padres novatos. Decidimos que no volveríamos a hacerlo nunca más. Pero, cuando nacieron nuestros próximos dos hijos, los seguimos llevando con nosotros siempre que podíamos hasta que comenzaron la escuela. Quería que vieran a su papá trabajar, que supieran lo que él hacía cuando no podía estar en casa con ellos; quería que vieran el mundo.

Estaba asombrado, pero no sorprendido. Tan pronto como llegaron los niños, también llegó la familia. Mi mamá venía de visita, y mis hermanos y hermanas también ayudaban. Deborah también tenía el apoyo de su madre, padre y hermana, a quien los niños adoraban. Solían gritar "Tía Kitsaun" cada vez que la veían. Poco después del nacimiento de Stella, decidimos mudarnos nuevamente al condado de Marin para estar más cerca de la familia y de los amigos. También teníamos que pensar en las escuelas. Todo esto me acercó más a mis padres y me hizo pensar en que mi hijo era parte de su legado.

En 1985, Salvador tenía casi tres años. Deborah y yo visitamos México de incógnito, mi cabello todavía estaba bastante corto, por lo que nadie me reconoció. Tengo que admitir que uno de los lujos más grandes de la vida es pasar desapercibido entre la multitud. La mayor parte de las personas deberían tomárselo en serio. Habíamos decidido viajar con mi madre para visitar a sus parientes en

Cihuatlán. Entonces, dado que estábamos en Jalisco, tomamos la decisión repentina de visitar mi ciudad natal, Autlán. Teníamos un chofer pero, por alguna razón, tardamos casi todo el día en llegar allí; nos quedamos unas cuatro horas en el pueblo y tardamos seis horas en volver.

Conocimos muchas personas que se acordaban de mi madre. Todavía era un niño cuando nos fuimos. Sal todavía era un bebé pero había comenzado a crecer y para aquel entonces ya tenía pies inmensos. Todavía los tiene, calza 15, más que Michael Jordan. Lo sé porque cuando Sal era un adolescente fue al campamento de verano de baloncesto de Michael. A veces me asombran los detalles que recuerdo.

El pueblo entero cargaba a Sal, pasaba de brazo en brazo como si fuera la primera vez que veían un bebé en sus vidas. Llegó el punto en que Deborah y yo nos estábamos volviendo un poco paranoicos. "Oye, ¿dónde está nuestro bebé?".

Autlán era mucho más pequeño de lo que yo recordaba, lo cual, por supuesto, es normal porque yo era mucho más pequeño la última vez que había estado allí. Se sentía lo que era: una pequeña ciudad o un gran pueblo. Comencé a besar a mi mamá en la frente, a besar sus manos. En ese momento, comencé a darme cuenta de lo que había hecho por nosotros. Le agradecía que nos hubiera sacado de ese pueblo y que nos hubiera llevado a un lugar con más oportunidades y mejores posibilidades. Esto no es una crítica ni un comentario negativo sobre Autlán. He llegado a conocer el pueblo y me enorgullece llamarlo mi hogar natal. Y esto habla de la suprema convicción de mi madre: un día lo decidió y lo hizo, nos llevó a un lugar lejano y cambió el destino de toda la familia.

CAPÍTULO 19

Angélica, Salvador y Stella, 1990.

Yo lo llamo ritmo doméstico y es algo con lo que muchos músicos tienen problemas. Pero creo que cualquier padre que deba viajar mucho por cuestiones laborales tiene que enfrentarse con ello. Siempre hablo de esto cada vez que estoy con otros músicos: "Oye, hombre, ¿cómo va el ritmo doméstico?". Me miran, algunos lo entienden, otros preguntan: "¿Ritmo doméstico? ¿A qué te refieres?".

"Tú sabes, viejo. ¿Hace cuánto que estás de gira?".

"Ah, eso".

Incluso ahora que mis hijos han crecido y que tengo a Cindy como compañera, trato de hacer mi mejor esfuerzo para equilibrar el ritmo doméstico con los otros ritmos de mi vida, como la música, los espectáculos, los viajes y las grabaciones. Si lo analizas, la parte de la música es bastante fácil: después de haberla escrito, todo lo que realmente hay que hacer es asistir y hacer lo mejor con la banda. Pero rápidamente aprendí que con la familia, cuando es el momento de volver al hogar, hay que hacer mucho más que, simplemente, asistir. Tenía que estar dispuesto a convertirme en un trapeador, o en un plumero, o en un limpiador de alfombras, o en un secador de pelo, o ponerme a preparar emparedados. Tenía que estar dispuesto a poner la misma energía, atención e intención que ponía en un magnífico solo de guitarra en mi vida con Deborah y los niños.

Recuerdo cómo mi padre lo hacía cuando regresaba a casa después de estar ausente durante meses. Todo era una locura a su alrededor con niños entrando y saliendo del lugar; y él encontraría un lugar en el piso duro y simplemente se estiraría. Era como algún tipo de yoga mexicano, estiraría sus brazos y piernas, luego sacudiría los dedos. Intenté hacerlo una vez después de una larga gira porque sentía que las paredes daban vueltas y que nunca se detendrían. Finalmente, funcionó, las paredes dejaron de moverse y yo había llegado, estaba listo para levantarme, ayudar y decir: "Está bien, ¿cómo puedo ayudar?" o "¿Qué puedo hacer?" o simplemente me adelantaría y sacaría la basura.

Creo que pocas personas, no solo los músicos, tienen la suficiente seguridad y paz interior como para afrontar la locura del ritmo doméstico (niños gritando, padres y familiares de visita). Los parientes tienen buenas intenciones, pero, en ocasiones, sus visitas pueden aumentar las presiones. Pero ese es el ritmo que uno debería disfrutar más, ser parte de él y dejar que suceda.

Los primeros años con los niños fueron divertidos y era una nueva experiencia para mí que la familia (mis padres, mis hermanas y hermanos, y mi familia política) viniera de visita. Nunca había pensado en la familia de esa manera. Cada paso que daban los niños en sus caminos era una novedad (aprender a caminar, comer alimentos de adultos, hablar) y era emocionante ver cómo se desarrollaban sus personalidades.

Los llevábamos de gira cuando podíamos. Recuerdo una ocasión en la que Sal ya estaba en segundo grado, Stella recién había comenzado la escuela y Jelli era muy pequeño; fuimos todos juntos a Europa. Fuimos a Suiza, donde Claude Nobs fue un excelente anfitrión; luego a Londres, donde los niños amaban recorrer la ciudad en los inmensos taxis; después a Roma. Luego está la otra cara de ir de gira: la tristeza que generaba en los niños cuando se enteraban de que no podían acompañar a su papá. Yo me preparaba para salir y esperaba que me pasara a buscar el coche. Cada vez que pasaba esto, los niños buscaban sus crayones y papel, comenzaban a dibujar y se concentraban mucho, de forma tal que no tuvieran que quedarse con un sentimiento de separación. Nunca voy a olvidar el sonido de sus garabateos, con tanta fuerza y concentración. Esa era su forma de decir: "Nos duele verte partir; entonces, no vamos a esperar contigo ni mirarte. Adiós".

Maldita sea. Por supuesto, todo esto me hacía acordar a mi niñez; mi papá se iba de gira y nunca estaba en casa y recuerdo cómo esta situación me hacía sentir. "¿Dónde está? ¿Cuándo lo volveré a ver? ¿Hice algo malo para que se fuera?". Sé que los niños tienen la costumbre de echarse la culpa cuando los padres no pueden estar presentes. No quería que mis hijos pasaran por eso. Entonces, les hablaba y les explicaba lo que tenía que hacer su papá. Ninguna gira duraba más de cuatro semanas; incluso, en el medio de una gira, subiría a un avión y regresaría a casa para cumpleaños, graduaciones y ocasiones especiales. Decidí hacer todo lo que estuviera en mi poder para verlos tanto y como fuera posible. Cuando el coche llegaba para llevarme al aeropuerto, me acercaba a cada uno de ellos y les recordaba cuánto los quería.

Atravesamos ese momento muchas veces. A mediados de los 80, salíamos mucho de gira junto a otras bandas importantes. Fuimos teloneros de The Rolling Stones; siempre agradecí esas oportunidades. Bill Graham organizó muchas de esas giras y fueron todas experiencias excepcionales y memorables, incluida la de 1984, cuando Santana fue la banda telonera de Bob Dylan. Me encantaba esa banda de Santana de mediados de los 80. Era una banda divertida y poderosa, y cuando tocaba era como: "Ah, increíble". Aprendí muchísimo de todos ellos.

Alphonso Johnson era el bajista, que se integró en el 83 y tenía la experiencia y las cualidades que necesitaba Santana en ese momento. Había tocado con Billy Cobham y Phil Collins; era un perfecto caballero y único en su clase. Lo escuché por primera vez cuando fui a ver a Weather Report en el 75, en el Berkeley Community Theatre. La banda era fluida y poderosa, pero el bajista realmente me enloquecía. ¿Qué es lo que tienen los bajistas de Filadelfia? Stanley Clarke, Victor Bailey, Jimmy Garrison, Reggie Workman y Jaco Pastorius, todos nacieron allí.

Alphonso es inteligente y afectuoso, y eso se reflejaba en su música. Estuvo con nosotros durante varios años; tuvo muchos momentos excelentes con Santana, pero si debo nombrar una de sus grandes actuaciones, diría "Once It's Gotcha" de *Freedom*.

También estaba David Sancious en la banda. Lo admiro locamente. Él es igual que Alphonso, un caballero con gran espíritu y sin problemas. Además de ser un extraordinario tecladista, es un excelente guitarrista. No tenía ningún problema en enchufar una Marshall y tocar desde el corazón. Su apariencia me recuerda a Coltrane. Podría interpretar a Trane en una película, tenía ese tipo de sonoridad silenciosa.

Teníamos dos Chester Thompsons. Uno era el asombroso Chester C. Thompson, un baterista que había tocado en Weather Report con Alphonso y más tarde en Genesis. El otro Chester Thompson tocaba el órgano, el piano y los sintetizadores. Así como Ndugu había sido de vital importancia para la banda a fines de los 70, este tipo fue quien ayudó a decidir hacia dónde se dirigiría Santana después de mediados de los 80 y durante los próximos veinticinco años. Si quieren saber quién es, escuchen su solo de órgano en "Victory Is Won", la canción que escribí para el arzobispo Desmond Tutu. Chester y yo tocamos la canción por primera vez para el mismísimo Tutu cuando vino a mi casa en el año 2001.

Conocí a Chester, todos lo llaman CT, aproximadamente en 1977 o 1978, cuando hacía muchas sesiones en San Francisco, probando diferentes cosas, no necesariamente para álbumes. Recuerdo que fue muy fácil conectarme y tocar con él; pero como él era parte de Tower of Power en ese momento, no volví a pensar en él. Fue aproximadamente en 1984, después de que Tom Coster abandonara Santana, que volví a pensar en CT. Decidí que no tenía nada que perder; entonces, le pregunté si le gustaría unirse a Santana y aceptó.

CT llegó a Santana con un poco de todo lo que amo: un poco de McCoy Tyner, algo de Herbie Hancock, mucha iglesia y mucho más soul. De inmediato, supe que sería perfecto porque eso es lo que pide la música: si vas a cocinar bullabesa, tienes que saber qué ingredientes colocar en la cacerola. Con CT, todo se resumía en camaradería. Después de un concierto, podíamos quedarnos hablando hasta las seis de la mañana y hablar sobre la música que amamos. Creo que a excepción de Gregg Rolie nunca antes había tenido una relación tan estrecha con un tecladista de Santana.

Necesitaba que alguien en la banda tuviera ideas diferentes a las mías. Hacía bastante que quería que alguien me refutara las cosas, no quería estar continuamente incentivando a otros. Después de tan solo algunos espectáculos, pude darme cuenta de que CT no tendría problema en rechazar las ideas con las que no estaba de acuerdo, y de hecho, rechazó bastantes. También supe que cada vez que hiciera un solo, dejaría al público boquiabierto. Lo pueden escuchar en melodías como "Wings of Grace" y "Hong Kong Blues". Sobre el escenario, adquiría una apariencia particular, como si estuviera poseído y yo decía: "Hombre, quiero *eso* en mi banda". Luego, simplemente asumía el control, y, aunque nuestros álbumes conservaron el formato de las canciones, sobre el escenario, le gustaba estirarse y yo también lo hacía. Incluso con esa intensidad, hacía que salir de gira fuera muy simple porque es muy estable, nunca lo vi hacer un berrinche, algo desesperado o frenético. CT era tranquilo y conmovedor; y estaba muy agradecido.

También nos resultaba fácil escribir juntos. Creamos canciones como "Goodness and Mercy" y "Wings of Grace" en un abrir y cerrar de ojos. "Brotherhood", del álbum *Beyond Appearances* del 85, fue escrita por CT, Sancious y yo. Por alguna razón, Miles realmente se enfocó en esa, con sus letras modernas y su mensaje de predicador. "¿De veras, Miles?". Acercó su rostro al mío y dijo: "Sí, y ni siquiera eres negro".

En el 87, grabamos el álbum *Freedom*. Este título está muy vinculado a cosas que sucedían en ese momento, como Buddy Miles saliendo de prisión y rearmando su vida en Bay Area. Puso su cuerpo y alma cuando cantó muchas de las pistas, como "Mandela", escrita por Armando. Por supuesto, en ese momento, la atención de todo el mundo estaba enfocada en Sudáfrica y todos se preguntaban: "¿Qué podemos hacer para acelerar el cambio en el sistema del apartheid y liberar a Nelson Mandela?".

Por momentos, está época se parecía a los 60, sentíamos que la música podía ayudar a evolucionar las cosas. Fue así, que los espectáculos de Santana se volvieron a enfocar en el aspecto social y yo le recordaba al público que eran gigantes que podían hacer milagros y crear bendiciones. Llevábamos playeras con las imágenes de nuestros héroes y declarábamos que nadie sería completamente libre hasta que todos lo fuéramos, como decía Martin Luther King. Le pedí al equipo de sonido que recopile canciones especiales, canciones con mensajes, para pasar en el sistema de PA antes y después de nuestros espectáculos, y así profundizar el mensaje en el público.

Freedom también es especial porque Graham Lear había vuelto, también Tom Coster, aunque durante poco tiempo, entonces estaban TC y CT juntos. Para la gira de *Freedom* en el 87, redujimos el personal de la banda a Alphonso, CT, Graham, Armando y Alex, con Orestes Vilató y Raul Rekow en percusión. Viajamos a muchos lugares de Europa en los que ya habíamos estado y a algunos en los que no, como Berlín Oriental, con Buddy Miles como invitado especial, y a Moscú, donde realizamos un concierto estadounidense-soviético histórico con Doobie Brothers, Bonnie Raitt y James Taylor. Recuerdo que fue Steve Wozniak quién lo pagó y, como se realizó el 4 de julio, se denominó el *Interdependence Concert—Give Peace a Chance* (Concierto de interdependencia: Démosle una oportunidad a la paz).

También recuerdo que Deborah conocía a alguien que vivía en Moscú con quien había asistido a la escuela y que había sido un revolucionario en los 60. Quería tomar un taxi sola en el medio de la noche para visitar a su amigo, entonces, lo hizo. Porque así era ella: muy valiente. Existe un video en el que aparezco hablando con algunos rusos a través de una valla, algunos de los cuales eran lo suficientemente jóvenes como para haber crecido con "Black Magic Woman" y *Abraxas*. Me comentaron que nuestra música había tenido un gran efecto en la conciencia de las personas, que ayudó a las personas en tiempos difíciles.

En Moscú, el espectáculo comenzó con una banda de marcha rusa que tocó "When the Saints Go Marching In", después tocaron otras bandas rusas. Las siguieron Bonnie Raitt, James Taylor y The Doobie Brothers. Y así la intensidad del programa iba en aumento. Para cuando fue nuestro turno, el público volaba y nosotros nos subimos a esa energía, hombre. Ofrecimos un espectáculo fuera de serie. De hecho, cuando comenzamos a retirarnos del escenario, después de haber tocado la última canción, comenzamos a escuchar que el público gritaba: "¡Santana! ¡¡Santana!! ¡¡¡Santana!!!" Recuerdo que Bonnie no dejaba de mirarme, no decía nada, solo meneaba la cabeza.

Uno de los mejores cumplidos que jamás recibí fue de Bonnie, después de algún otro concierto en el que estábamos los dos.

"Oye, Carlos".

"Hola, Bon".

"Tengo un nuevo nombre para ti: Intrépido. No temes tocar con Buddy Guy, Ry Cooder o Ray Charles, ni con nadie".

Le respondí: "Gracias, Bon".

¿Por qué debería temer? Esto no son los juegos olímpicos, no es boxeo. Eso es lo que todavía pienso: tocar música debería ser una situación en la que todos ganan.

En Berlín Oriental, me di cuenta de que los rusos nunca antes habían visto una banda con nuestro tipo de energía. La música realmente rompe barreras. En ese momento, su país realmente se había comenzado a abrir; creo que tenían que actualizarse más rápido de lo que pretendían hacerlo.

En esa gira, Santana tocó por primera vez en Jerusalén, la ciudad en la que Jesús predicó y se metió en problemas. Recuerdo todas las historias de la Biblia que había escuchado en Autlán sobre esa ciudad y realmente había algo especial sobre ella. Recuerdo despertar por la mañana y ver al sol salir, como hace miles de años que sucede, y es tan hermoso. Luego se ve el crepúsculo y no puedes evitar preguntarte porque las personas luchan tanto allí. Salí a pasear y me di cuenta de que por un lado, Jerusalén es un lugar muy, muy sagrado e histórico pero, por otro lado, es como muchas otras ciudades del mundo, con vendedores, mercados y personas empujándose, tratando de, simplemente, sobrevivir. Partes de esa ciudad son tan prístinas y espirituales como el asiento trasero de un taxi neoyorkino. Pensaba que, cuando se trata del reino invisible, realmente no importa dónde estés; es lo que llevas en tu corazón lo que puede convertir un lugar en divino y sagrado.

¿Todas esas fechas en la Unión Soviética e Israel? Ese fue Bill Graham; el organizó todo. Organizaba muchas giras internacionales. El año anterior, había organizado la gira de Amnesty International (Amnistía Internacional) que supuestamente, tendría la misma esencia de los espectáculos que se llevaban a cabo un tiempo atrás en el Fillmore: rock, jazz, ritmos africanos y latinos. Todos los gustos, multidimensional. Con nombres conocidos, como Peter Gabriel y Sting. Toqué en uno de esos conciertos, en Meadowlands, Nueva Jersey, pero no con mi banda. Estuvo bien, fue la única vez que toqué con Miles.

Siendo quien era y quien todavía soy, entablé una conversación con Bill antes de la gira sobre las personas que incluía. "¿Por qué no intentas incluir a Miles Davis en el Amnesty International?".

Mi pregunta pareció sorprenderle.

"Haz lo mismo que hiciste Woodstock: diles que si quieren tu ayuda deberán incluir a Miles en ella".

Se produjo un largo silencio.

Más tarde, me encontraba de gira en Australia, cuando el

teléfono sonó en mi habitación de hotel, eran las cuatro de la mañana, hora de Nueva York. "Hola, Bill. ¿Cómo estás?".

"Miles va a tocar".

"Maldita sea, Bill. Lo lograste".

"Pero te necesito aquí y no puedo pagar para que toques con toda la banda porque ya usé todos mis contactos con Miles. ¿Puedes venir solo?".

Esa era mi recompensa por presionar para que incluyera a Miles. Por supuesto que iría. Volé de Australia a Honolulu y luego de Honolulu a San Francisco. Recogí a Deborah, volé a Nueva Jersey y fui a Meadowlands. Cuando llegué, Bill dijo: "Tocarás con Rubén Blades y Fela Kuti, y con The Neville Brothers". Hasta ahí, todo era normal, pero el continuó: "Y Miles".

Espera. "Bill, ¿tocaré con Miles?".

"Sí, y Rubén en media hora. Miles quiere verte en su remolque". Esto era épico. ¿Miles habría pedido que yo toque con él? ¿Por qué no lo había mencionado antes?

Tenía un grave caso de *jet lag*. Tenía los globos oculares rojos y mi cerebro simplemente no funcionaba. Cuando entré al remolque, Miles estaba en un estado en el que jamás lo había visto. Me miraba un poco de reojo. Miró mis zapatos y mi camisa, tomó mis pantalones y dijo: "Incluso tratas de vestirte como yo". Sorprendido, le contesté: "¿Qué?". Y comenzó a agredirme, diciéndome que yo solo lo estaba siguiendo, imitando. Puedo entender que, tal vez, él pensaba que yo había organizado ese concierto solo para poder tocar con él. Antes de que llegara demasiado lejos, le dije: "Oye, viejo. No necesito tocar contigo. Le pedí a Bill Graham que te trajera aquí porque pensé que todo esto no estaría completo sin ti. No sé qué te habrá dicho él, pero no fue parte de mi condición". Y me fui.

Guau... Bueno, así se sentía estar en la lista negra de Miles. Pensé que me iba a dar el beneficio de la duda en ese caso. Yo estaba de su lado. Él debería saberlo.

Tan solo algunos años antes, me había llamado por teléfono. "¿Qué haces?", preguntó.

"Escucho un CD, Miles, *Thriller*".

"¿Qué es eso?". Le expliqué sobre el nuevo formato, los *compact discs* (discos compactos), y del nuevo álbum de Michael Jackson que todos amaban y que Quincy había producido. "No puedo dejar de escuchar una canción llamada 'Human Nature'". Poco después, Miles la hizo en *You're under Arrest* y la tocaba en sus conciertos todas las noches.

Tenía que prepararme para tocar, incluso si Miles estaba enojado y fuera incómodo. Esperaba junto al escenario y justo antes de que llegara mi turno, se me ocurrió verificar la afinación de la guitarra. El técnico la había afinado, pero había quedado allí, sola, sin ninguna supervisión y había con muchas personas en el escenario. Quién sabe lo que podría haber pasado, pero estaba completamente desafinada. En el video de esa función, se me puede ver justo en aquel momento, antes de subir al escenario con el público tras de mí. Miro en dirección contraria a ellos, hacia la cámara, porque todavía tengo la guitarra elevada contra mi rostro para poder trabajar con las cuerdas. Justo en el momento en que logré afinarla, fue mi turno de tocar. Me di vuelta y estaba en puntas de pie, la energía era muy intensa. Luego comencé a tocar y debo admitir, que lo hice estupendamente bien. Más tarde, Deborah se acercó y me dijo: "Eso es lo que quiero escuchar. ¿Por qué no lo haces todo el tiempo?". Solía decir eso de vez en cuando.

Tocamos "Burn". Yo pensé que había tocado bien, teniendo en cuenta que estaba muy afectado por el *jet lag*, realmente agotado. Cuando salimos del escenario, Miles era un tipo completamente distinto. "Oye. ¿Qué te pareció?".

"Estuvo genial, Miles; fue realmente un honor tocar contigo".

Hombre, pensé que Miles me iba a atacar nuevamente. Esa había sido la primera vez que me hablaba de esa manera, y me di cuenta de que los nervios lo habían traicionado y que por eso había sido tan grosero conmigo. Simplemente se había puesto nervioso por tener que tocar en un festival tan importante.

"Ah, sí. Fue extraño para mí, no podía escuchar nada".

Dije: "Bueno, sabes, cuando eso me pasa a mí, me muevo como un boxeador hasta encontrar el mejor lugar entre el bajista y el baterista, y hago mi propia mezcla".

* * *

La abuela Jo, Deborah y Emelda, casada con el primo de Deborah, Junior, comenzaron a llevar a los niños cuando eran pequeños a una iglesia en Oakland. Cuando uno va a una iglesia afroamericana pura como esa, va de determinada manera y se sienta de determinada manera. Se aprende un código de conducta. Sal tiene esa iglesia dentro de él, al igual que sus hermanas; pero, como dirían los ingleses, "Sal es *correcto*". Recuerdo que los tres niños se comportaban así cuando salíamos; incluso agradecían en los restaurantes. Cuando uno es padre, empieza a observar cómo se comportan las otras familias en público. En ocasiones, veía niños descontrolados, al extremo, como la niña de *El exorcista*, y me hacía feliz que mis niños no me hicieran pasar vergüenza al comportarse de esa manera cuando salíamos de la casa.

Creo que Deborah es una excelente madre y yo, un gran padre. Considero que gran parte de nuestro éxito se debió a que nos comunicábamos honesta y claramente con los tres niños para que entendieran qué se esperaba de ellos. En todo lo que hacíamos con ellos, conservábamos un sistema coherente de ética, límites morales e integridad. Nunca golpeamos a nuestros niños, pero utilizamos palabras y miradas que transmitían el mensaje de que debían permanecer callados y debían ser respetuosos. Cuando crecieron, les decía que si no estaban completamente de acuerdo con algo, podían levantar la mano e iríamos a caminar y discutirlo. "Tienes la posibilidad de caminar y hablar del tema", les decíamos.

Por supuesto, a medida que crecían, más ponían a prueba los límites. Recuerdo que tuve que decirle a uno de ellos: "Sabes, he pasado muchísimo tiempo meditando y leyendo libros espirituales para aprender a ser pacífico y compasivo, pero voy a tirar todo eso por la ventana la próxima vez que le faltes el respeto a tu madre enfrente de mí".

Deborah tenía un palo al que llamaba *pow-pow*, que conservaba sobre el refrigerador. Estaba allí y los niños sabían que, si en algún momento se excedían, ella no dudaría en usarlo. Realmente no recuerdo si alguna vez lo usó, pero sí lo sacó unas cuantas veces. Deborah y yo éramos un buen equipo, porque los niños acudirían a mí y me dirían: "Mamá dijo que esto está bien".

Como todos, los padres también comenten errores. En nuestro caso, fuimos aprendiendo y mejorando; y ellos aprendieron que la clásica estrategia de poner a un padre en contra del otro no funcionaría con nosotros. "¿En serio? Busquemos a mamá y pidámosle que me lo diga ella misma". Nos ponían a prueba, nosotros fijábamos los límites y, si bien éramos flexibles en muchos aspectos, algunas cosas no eran negociables.

Nadie dijo que ser padre sería fácil, pero puedo decirles que fue y es divertido también. Mis hijos me han enseñado mucho y una de las cosas más importantes que aprendí es cómo reír con ellos y también de mí mismo. Recuerdo que Stella quería un pequeño chihuahua. Repetía: "Por favor, por favor, por favor". Finalmente cedimos y le compramos uno. Por supuesto que no era suyo solamente, sino que era el perro de la familia, pero ¿quién lo alimentaría y entrenaría? Una noche, volví a casa de un concierto, Stella estaba en el sofá mirando televisión con una amiga. Jelli también estaba allí. Me tranquilicé y empecé a ponerme cómodo, pero, de repente, había algo caliente y extraño entre los dedos de mis pies, y el olor era espantoso. Todos me miraban. "Stella, ¡es caca de perro!" Ella me miraba como si nada. "¡Y es *tu* perro!"

Nada. Realmente apestaba, me paré y me puse a limpiar lo que el perro había hecho, a limpiar mis dedos y a limpiar la alfombra. No lo podía creer. De repente, me di cuenta y dije: "Hombre, yo *no* debería limpiar esta caca de perro. *Soy una estrella de rock*".

Por supuesto que no lo dije completamente en serio, pero, al mismo tiempo, es justo la clase de cosas que uno escucharía de una estrella de rock; entonces, fue divertido por lo que sí quise decir y por lo que no. Se produjo un momento de silencio absoluto y de repente, Jelli comenzó a descostillarse de la risa, rodando por el sofá con lágrimas en los ojos. Luego Stella, su amiga y yo comenzamos a reír también, y pronto todos nos estábamos riendo de lo que había dicho y de cómo había sonado.

A mis hijos les deseo salud, felicidad y paz mental; como a todas las personas que amo. Pero, al mismo tiempo, esas son las tres cosas que no puedo darles. Puedo mostrarles cómo son y tal vez, enseñarles cómo alcanzarlas, pero también pienso que ellos deben obtenerlas, conservarlas y, más que nada, apreciarlas por sí mismos.

La música continuó, los niños crecieron y la disciplina espiritual también permaneció, nunca se fue. Una cosa que Deborah decidió cuando nos separamos de Sri Chinmoy fue que no nos quedaríamos atrás en nuestra carrera espiritual, éramos corredores y no bajaríamos la velocidad de la aspiración. La aspiración es la llama; el deseo de divinidad. Deborah y yo decidimos no perder nuestro amor hacia Dios ni abandonar nuestros principios y prácticas, por eso continuamos meditando por las mañanas, ingiriendo alimentos sanos y leyendo libros espirituales.

Cuando estaba de gira, en cada habitación de hotel en el que me hospedaba, encendía inciensos y velas, cerraba mis ojos y comenzaba viaje hacia mi interior. Detrás de escena, en cada camerino, antes de salir al escenario, hacía lo mismo. Si alguien de la banda quería unirse, eran bienvenidos a hacerlo. La mayor parte del tiempo, la disciplina espiritual era auto disciplina. Por más que no tuviera un gurú, seguía leyendo mucho y obtuve mucha orientación de los libros.

Había descubierto el libro The Urantia Book (traducido al español como Libro de Urantia) antes de conocer a Sri Chinmoy y lo seguía leyendo después de separarme de él. Siempre estaba en la búsqueda de libros que me brindaran una sensación tangible de ser. Seguía ascendiendo mediante la selección de libros que me ayudaran a ampliar la visión que tengo de mí mismo. A veces, por ejemplo, cuando me encontraba en el aeropuerto y me daba cuenta de que pensaba en algo, sacaba unos cuantos libros que había metido en mi equipaje y un título me llamaría la atención. "Ah, esto es exactamente lo que necesito". Subiría al avión y, en algún capítulo del medio, leería algo que era exactamente lo que necesitaba analizar y con que identificarme en ese preciso momento. "Déjame tomar este mensaje y vivir con él durante una semana".

Todavía encuentro ese tipo de libros. Esta es mi estrategia: establecer la intencionalidad como una flecha y la diana aparece. Uno atrae lo que uno es. Así es como encontré *A Course in Miracles* (traducido al español como *n curso de milagros*) y *The Book of Knowledge: The Keys of Enoch* (traducido al español como *El libro del conocimiento: Las claves de Enoc*) de J. J. y Desiree Hurtak.

Para Deborah, el camino espiritual significó volver a la iglesia. Después de un tiempo, dejó la iglesia de Oakland y descubrió Unity en Marin, una iglesia con una actitud universal y progresista. No se trataba de hacer las cosas de una sola manera, pero todavía no podía imaginarme yendo a la iglesia a menos que hubiera congas allí y, dado que no las había, no iba muy seguido. En ocasiones, iba con Deborah y los niños, pero, en general, cuando ella estaba en la iglesia, yo estaría con su padre hablando sobre cosas como la tracción espiritual.

SK decía que todos estamos aquí para excavar y hacer un poco de tracción espiritual y no para resbalarnos, deslizarnos, abandonar, provocar y dar excusas. Cuando dijo eso, contesté: "Exactamente". Amo la idea de explicar disciplina espiritual en un lenguaje más coloquial, más callejero, para que las personas no piensen: "¿De qué demonios habla?". Me gusta la idea de diseminar un virus espiritual que, en lugar de enfermar a las personas, las llene de vida. El virus puede contagiarse de una persona a otra hasta que, poco a poco, todos van notando como la violencia va disminuyendo en la comunidad.

Nuestros hijos conocieron el camino espiritual de una forma muy natural, normal y orgánica. Teníamos libros espirituales. Nosotros los leíamos y ellos comprendieron que, si querían, también podían hacerlo. Pero no hay nada que se compare con vivir un camino espiritual para que los hijos puedan ver la luz en uno. Si uno sigue un camino espiritual y lo pone en práctica todos los días, entonces ellos se sentirán motivados y querrán vivir del mismo modo. Ellos nos veían meditar e iban con Deborah a Unity en Marin. Cuando empezaron a crecer y yo les mostraba un principio o una forma de ver las cosas desde el punto de vista espiritual, ellos se resistían; pero esto era normal, así suelen actuar los niños cada vez que los padres les enseñan algo. Pero lo retenían. Tal vez una semana o un mes después, escuchaba a uno de ellos hablando por teléfono con un amigo citando exactamente lo que yo les había dicho. "No quiero realizar una inversión emocional en algo negativo". "No quiero llevar eso como una insignia de honor; ese no soy yo".

Todavía les hablo en ese nivel. Constantemente les pido a Jelli, a Stella y a Salvador que no teman mostrarse tal cual son, que las personas sepan cuáles son sus intenciones y que sean claros con lo que quieren decir. Es su verificación de la realidad espiritual diaria. Hace poco, Stella fue al estudio por primera vez para grabar música y le envíe un mensaje de texto que decía: "Pídele a Dios que ayude a tu música a llegar a todos los corazones en este glorioso planeta y a recordarles su propia divinidad". Y, hasta el día de hoy, cualquiera que haya asistido a un concierto de Salvador Santana lo escuchará decir: "Es una bendición estar aquí y poder tocar para ustedes". Adoro eso. Al final de cada gira, las bandas teloneras comienzan a expresar su gratitud al público, reconocen su presencia y les agradecen por estar allí.

En 1987, Sal tenía tan solo cuatro años de edad y yo improvisaba en el estudio con CT cuando ocurrió uno de esos momentos mágicos. Los ingenieros todavía estaban resolviendo cuestiones técnicas de calibración y queríamos grabar lo que estábamos haciendo en ese momento. "Aprieta el botón para grabar ahora mismo. Graba esto, hombre. No me importa cómo lo hagas". Entonces lo grabamos en un magnetófono de dos pistas, una pista para CT y una para mí. Justo cuando tocaba la última nota y se desvanecía, se acabó la cinta. Años más tarde, descubrí que uno de los blues de Stevie Ray Vaughan se grabó exactamente de la misma manera; sin pensarlo, en el momento, en un magnetófono de dos pistas. Y cuando tocaba el último *lick*, lo mismo ocurrió: se acabó la cinta. Lo más raro de toda esta historia es que en ambas situaciones se encontraba involucrado el mismo ingeniero, Jim Gaines.

Debo decir algo sobre Jim y sobre los demás ingenieros que acompañaron a Santana, tanto en el estudio como en las giras. Fueron una bendición. Fred Catero, Glen Kolotkin, Dave Rubinson, Jim Reitzel, todos fueron esenciales para nuestro éxito a lo largo de los años y creo que todos deben ser honrados. Antcs de trabajar con

442 · CARLOS SANTANA

nosotros, Jim Gaines trabajó con muchísimos artistas excelentes, desde Tower of Power hasta Steve Miller y Stevie Ray Vaughan. Aportó una verdadera calidad terrenal al sonido y todo lo que hizo, lo que hizo de una manera desinteresada, dejando su ego de lado. Era un placer trabajar con él. Trabajó con Santana durante la época en la que las cosas pasaban de análogo a digital, entonces nos ayudó con esa transición y era tan bueno con la computadora como lo era con las perillas. En esa época, la tecnología de grabación llegaba hasta las treinta y seis pistas antes de que aparecieran las Pro Tools, que es un sistema de audio moderno. Pero él era realmente paciente y sabía qué decir y en qué momento decirlo, de una manera muy amable, que ayudaría a que la música fluyera más.

Después de esa improvisación con CT en el 87, Jim me dio un casete con la grabación y la dejé en el coche. Al día siguiente, Deborah usó ese coche para ir de compras y, cuando regresó, me preguntó: "¿Por qué no tocas así?". Volvía a hacerme esa pregunta, la misma que me hizo después del concierto de Amnesty International; en ocasiones, ella decía eso y yo me preguntaba a qué se refería. Antes de que pudiera responderle, ella ya me había preguntado el nombre de la canción del casete.

"¿Qué canción?".

"Tú sabes, la canción que tocaste con CT. La escuché y no pude manejar. Tuve que detener el coche".

Decidí llamarla "Blues for Salvador", no solo en honor a Sal sino también como homenaje a los habitantes de San Salvador que estaban atravesando momentos muy difíciles en esa época, habían sufrido un terremoto y una guerra civil. Esa canción inspiró mi último álbum solista como Carlos Santana. Me encanta porque participa Tony Williams, Buddy Miles canta en varias partes y además por aquella banda: CT, Alphonso, Graham, Raul, Armando y el resto. Dediqué el álbum a Deborah. Además, en este disco se incluye la canción "Bella", que creé para Stella.

"Blues for Salvador" ganó un premio Grammy a la mejor interpretación instrumental de rock del año, el primer Grammy que obtuvo Santana, pero no el último.

CAPÍTULO 20

Wayne Shorter, John Lee Hooker y yo, detrás de escena en
el Fillmore, 15 de junio de 1988.

Tal vez parezca que grabaría con cualquiera, en especial, después de Supernatural, *"Carlos el colaborador". Y tal vez, tenga muchos libros espirituales
por leer, porque supuestamente debería ver lo mismo en todos, pero en la
música, no lo hago y no lo haré. Existen canciones que, aunque me las
inyectes por vía intravenosa, mi cuerpo va a rechazarlas. Es así, "Gracias
por pedirme que toque esta canción. Es decir, gracias por invitarme, pero no
logro escucharme tocando eso". He rechazado a determinados músicos porque, honestamente, no me gusta su música. Es más, hasta me sorprende
que me hayan invitado. Esto nunca fue una cuestión de dinero. Es principalmente, preguntarme si me gustará la canción dentro de diez años.*

*En los 80, grabé un álbum de McCoy Tyner, Stanley Clarke, mi viejo
amigo Gregg Rolie y Jim Capaldi de Traffic. En el 85, Clive Davis me
pidió que toque con Aretha Franklin, lo cual era perfecto porque, en ese*

momento, yo trabajaba con Narada Michael Walden y ella también. Ella es la reina del soul. No podía decirle que no. Ni a Gladys, Dionne o Patti, pero una vez sí rechacé a otra cantante de R&B porque su versión de "Oye Como Va" tenía un estilo L.A. demasiado sofisticado para mi gusto. Sé que se decepcionó, porque le había dicho que lo haría.

Sería un privilegio volver a tocar algo con Willie Nelson o Merle Haggard. Aceptaría tocar con cualquiera de la familia de músicos de Coltrane y de Miles. Le dije que no a un rapero de la costa oeste porque la canción que envió sonaba cursi y plástica, falsa. Todavía me puedo escuchar con Lou Rawls.

En la actualidad, las colaboraciones no se llevan a cabo en el estudio, son tan solo archivos enviados por correo electrónico entre ingenieros. Me he adaptado a eso. Tengo suerte de haber nacido con una imaginación muy activa. Puedo cerrar los ojos, elegir una canción de Sam Cooke y tocar sobre ella como si él estuviera al lado mío y hasta decir: "Es un honor trabajar con usted, Sr. Sam Cooke". La imaginación supera al tiempo, la distancia y la separación, y lo mismo debería suceder con cualquier colaboración. La imaginación implica decir: "Estoy aquí y tú estás aquí; hagámoslo".

Prince no le teme a nada, es un tipo que no tiene límites. Sería un honor hacer algo con él, armar algo juntos desde cero. Y sé las canciones que funcionarían. Su nivel es supremo. Es un excelente guitarrista, toca increíblemente la guitarra rítmica y ha tocado en algunas ocasiones con Santana. Lo he escuchado tocar el piano y, a veces, cuando lo hace me recuerda a Herbie. Es un genio de verdad. El único problema es que tendríamos que encontrar un equilibrio, algo del estilo de John Lee Hooker, algo africano y algo pantanoso, para que ninguno se sienta sapo de otro pozo. Me gusta lo terrenal, sucio y descalzo; y creo que es lo que él también ama de la música. Tenemos que ir a la selva, hombre.

Hoy en día, los conciertos mejor pagos de jazz son, en general, los festivales; y muchos de ellos se realizan durante el verano. El invierno anterior al verano del 88, le pregunté a Wayne Shorter si podía comenzar un rumor. "¿Un rumor sobre qué?".

"Que tú y yo estamos en una banda y que nos vamos de gira".

Sonrió y sus ojos brillaron, un gesto muy característico de él, y dijo sin pensarlo: "Sí, puedes".

Wayne y yo juntamos un grupo que pensábamos era perfecto para ambos: dos tecladistas, Patrice Rushen que trajo algo de Herbie Hancock, y CT, que aportó cosas de Joe Zawinul, de la iglesia y un poco de McCoy. Además teníamos a Alphonso, Ndugu, Chepito y Armando. Dividimos la lista de temas entre algunas canciones que generalmente tocaba Santana y los temas originales de Wayne. Le pregunté si le molestaría tocar "Sanctuary" en estilo *boogie*. Creo que varios miembros de la banda me miraron con mala cara, pero Wayne sonrió y dijo: "Sí, hagámoslo" e hizo que esa sonara nuevamente como lo hacía en sus comienzos en Newark.

Tocamos veintinueve conciertos juntos y el nombre de la gira tuvo que haber sido Hagámoslo, era divertido y diferente cada noche. Había camaradería en el grupo, y creo que Wayne podía sentirlo. Me alegra que Claude Nobs nos haya ayudado a grabar el espectáculo en Montreux. Tocamos un concierto en el Royal Festival Hall de Londres. Antes de que siguiéramos tocando, Wayne, Armando, Ndugu y yo nos encontramos detrás de escena con Greg Phillinganes y algunos tipos de la gira de Michael Jackson que estaban en Londres en esa misma época. John Lee Hooker, con su Crawling King Snake original, también estaba en Londres y pasó a saludar. Apodé a ese festival Pasando el tiempo con algunos pesos pesados. No podría haber estado más feliz esa noche.

Tocar con Wayne me enseñó la forma en la que él enfrenta una melodía. Es como un ciego que sondea una habitación por primera vez o como un bailarín probando un escenario para poder memorizarlo. A propósito, toca como si casi no supiera hacerlo, con mucha inocencia. Pero lo que toca no es ingenuo: tiene inocencia y pureza; pero no desesperación. Es como si se divirtiera mientras descubre aunque ya tenga todo lo que busca.

Tocar con Wayne me dio coraje, coraje para adentrarme más y volar más alto. Me hizo tocar con más vulnerabilidad en lugar de solo tocar los difíciles *licks* que había practicado y preparado, que puede ser como un escudo que uno talla cuidadosamente antes de salir de la habitación. Wayne me enseñó a mostrarme de una manera más abierta y más vulnerable, invitando al otro músico a presentar su sabiduría. Es una invitación a aprender juntos.

Wayne hace eso cuando hablamos: hace una pregunta, y no la hace porque no sabe la respuesta sino que porque quiere que escuches la respuesta tú mismo. Y entonces, de repente, las cosas empiezan a arreglarse solas. No tienes que hacer un esfuerzo tan grande. En ocasiones, ni si quiera tienes que esforzarte, y si te esfuerzas, terminas arruinándolo. Eso es lo que realmente aprendí de Wayne, y de Herbie también. Está bien, puedes angustiarte. Pero como Wayne le dijo a ese miembro de su banda aquella vez: "¿Qué *aprendiste?*".

En esa gira, también pasaron algunas cosas extrañas. Cada noche, parecía que Chepito atravesaba una crisis nueva. Gracias a Dios, la esposa de Wayne, Ana Maria, estaba allí para ayudarlo y lograba calmarlo. Parecía que estaba a punto de explotar todo el tiempo, decía cosas como: "Chepito está muy angustiado hoy" y "Pobre Chepito. Va a morir el próximo martes". Todo siempre iba a suceder un martes. Armando lo miraría y le diría: "¿Para qué esperar? Hazlo ahora, maldita". De repente, las lágrimas se detenían. "Está bien. ¿A qué hora es el ensayo mañana?".

Miles fue parte de la gran gira de jazz en la cual participamos. Una vez, se asomó para ver un poco de nuestro espectáculo en Rochester y, cuando se estaba yendo, Chepito casi pierde la cabeza. Fue corriendo hacia Miles. "Espera. Todavía no nos has escuchado a Wayne, a Carlos y a mí. ¿A dónde te vas?". Miles lo miró y le dijo simplemente: "Chepito, todavía eres un maldito hijo de la chingada", y se fue. "¿Escucharon lo que Miles me acaba de decir? Que soy un *maldito hijo de la chingada*". Luego comenzó a llorar nuevamente pero porque estaba feliz.

Chepito siempre me hizo acordar a Harpo Marx con voz. Payaso, buscapleitos y súper talentoso; todo en uno. Anteriormente, ese mismo año, se realizó un concierto en homenaje a Jaco Pastorius, quien fue asesinado en el 87. Había asistido a un recital nuestro en Miami la noche que murió; pero luego no pudo entrar en un club y eso ocasionó una pelea con un sacabullas. Jaco entró en un estado de coma del cual nunca salió. Detrás de escena, en el concierto homenaje en Oakland, estaban todas las personas que tenían una conexión con Jaco, Weather Report o Miles: Wayne, Joe, Herbie, Hiram Bullock, Peter Erskine, Armando, Chepito. Tengo una grabación no autorizada de Coltrane. Una vez, mientras la escuchábamos entró Marcus Miller y dijo: "Hola. ¿Cómo están? ¿Qué sucede? ¿Qué escuchan?". Esperamos un instante y dije: "Es buen material, deberías escucharlo".

"Sí, está bien. Suena excelente".

No estoy seguro de que Marcus pudiera distinguir quién era, la grabación no era de la mejor calidad, pero Chepito se dio cuenta y no pudo resistirse. Dijo: "Entonces, ¿quién eres?". Marcus lo miró y dijo: "Soy Marcus Miller, toco con Miles".

"Sí, conozco a Miles, pero nunca escuché hablar de ti. ¿Qué tocas?".

"Toco el bajo".

"Mmm... Bueno, nunca escuché hablar de ti".

Marcus había caído en la trampa y para que pudiera identificar quién era, comenzó a contarle todo sobre su carrera, pero Chepito seguía diciendo: "Nunca escuché hablar de ti, hombre. Lo siento". Por supuesto que Chepito le tomaba el pelo. Cuando lo dijo por tercera vez, Wayne, Ana Maria y Herbie no aguantaron más y estallaron en risas, y Marcus finalmente se dio cuenta: "¡Ah! Está bien, muy gracioso". Ese fue sin duda alguna uno de los mejores momentos de Chepito.

Una noche, en la gira del 88, dije: "Oye, Wayne, te vez muy feliz, hombre. ¿Qué ha pasado?".

"Miles me acaba de devolver los derechos de mi canción".

Me imagino que se refería a "Sanctuary", porque esa era una de las melodías de Wayne en *Bitches Brew* que terminó con el nombre de Miles. Estaba feliz por Wayne, pero sucedió casi veinte años después de grabar esa canción. Durante su carrera, un músico debe tener sumo cuidado con algunas cosas. En ocasiones, hay que imponerse y decir: "Mira, viejo, esta canción es mía". Y tienes que hacerlo tú mismo. Incluso si debes confrontar a alguien como Miles. Bill Graham y Armando me dieron este tipo de consejos; uno no tiene que ser grosero, vulgar o molestarse, solo hay que hacerse escuchar. Lo peor que puede pasar es recibir un "no" como respuesta.

Durante aquella gira del 88, pude ver con mis propios ojos cómo tratan a determinados músicos de jazz en comparación de cómo se manejaba una gira de Santana. Esperaba que las cosas fueran distintas en cuanto a la calidad de los hoteles y al detrás de escena; pero no voy a hablar sobre ello. Aunque sí me enojé cuando nos recogieron en lo que parecía un camión de lavandería en vez de un coche.

Me refiero a muchas cosas por las que los productores del concierto no nos pagaban ni a Wayne ni a mí, como usar nuestras imágenes en afiches y playeras, transmitir el concierto por la radio y grabarlo. No habíamos otorgado nuestro consentimiento a nada de eso; solo nos pagaban por el concierto. Incluso en esa época, era práctica habitual en la industria que, si el espectáculo se grabaría para ser transmitido por radio o televisión, debías recibir otro pago además del arancel por el concierto. Lo mismo ocurría con la mercadería y productos de promoción.

Entonces, me puse firme y me hice escuchar, y sé que para algunas personas esa era una típica actitud de diva. Recuerdo que otros músicos comenzaron a mirarme como si lo fuera. Pero simplemente no quería ser parte de una mentalidad antigua, como si fuera la época de la esclavitud que parecía ser la norma en los clubes y los festivales de jazz. "Apaga las cámaras, hombre, y no las vuelvas a encender hasta que nos soliciten consentimiento y negocien con nosotros como corresponde".

Vivir todo eso en la gira del 88 me hizo dar cuenta de que era vital que me hiciera cargo de mi propio negocio. De alguna manera, debo agradecer a Wayne por ello; porque esa gira me obligó a tomar las riendas de Santana aún más, ser un poco más líder. Me di cuenta de que algunas personas de mi entorno ni siquiera me preguntaban sobre ciertos asuntos, como si quería estar en la radio y cuál debería ser mi remuneración por ello.

"Ah, es para lanzar un CD más adelante, la idea es recaudar dinero para obras de beneficencia".

"Muy bien, ¿qué obras?".

El hecho de que estas preguntas no me llegaran comenzó a molestarme y, de repente, todo esto se convirtió en una prioridad para mí y comencé a participar más en las decisiones comerciales de la banda.

De alguna manera, estaba tomando conciencia de que la manera en que se presenta Santana es sumamente importante y requiere mucho trabajo y cuidado. Había que asegurarse de que el sentimiento, el mensaje e, incluso, la ortografía fueran correctos y precisos en las portadas de los álbumes, en los afiches, en la publicidad y en las entradas.

Muchas veces, lo que sucede es que los demás no piensan como uno, están muy ocupados o no tienen buen gusto.

Recuerdo pensar en lo abismales que eran algunas portadas de los álbumes de Miles y de Coltrane. Comencé a exigir que me muestren todo; imágenes, fotos. "Bueno, estas tres son las mejores; elegiremos alguna de estas. A estas de aquí, no quiero volver a verlas. ¿Entendido?".

El primer ejemplo de esto fue *Viva Santana!*, que salió en el 88 y fue un compilado que mostraba el camino que Santana había recorrido en veinte años. No era simplemente un álbum con "lo mejor de". Contaba la historia de Santana a través de treinta canciones e incluía un cuadernillo con nuevas imágenes originales y también usaba las imágenes de portadas de álbumes anteriores. Había muchos detalles y demandó muchísimo trabajo. Pero esta vez yo supervisé todo; realmente produje este álbum de principio a fin. También filmamos un documental en el que yo hablé sobre la banda y sobre mí, y que incluía filmaciones de espectáculos de Santana. Salió en VHS y después en DVD, y ahora creo que la mayor parte se puede encontrar en YouTube. Esa fue la primera vez que intentamos mostrar y explicar la historia completa de Santana, desde "Black Magic Woman" hasta "Blues for Salvador", en un solo paquete y con toda la nueva tecnología y en los formatos de la época.

Además queríamos hacer una gira de reencuentro por el vigésimo aniversario de la banda. Tenía sentido; *Viva Santana!* trataba y resumía nuestra historia, ¿por qué no hacerlo? Las cosas estaban bien entre Gregg, Shrieve y yo; Chepito y Armando todavía estaban en la banda; y Alphonso tocaba el bajo porque Dougie se había ido. David no estaba del todo bien; teníamos a Armando y a Chepito; entonces Carabello, que tenía su propia banda, no participó. Tocamos muchas melodías de los tres primeros álbumes mezcladas con canciones más nuevas y terminamos el espectáculo con "Soul Sacrifice".

Recuerdo que el proyecto completo (el CD, el documental y la gira) me dio más confianza a la hora de tomar las riendas y aportar opiniones sobre cuestiones que no se relacionaban directamente con la música. Además, aprendí a tener más y más confianza en mí mismo después de la gira con Wayne. De alguna manera, creo que el aniversario y la gira ayudaron a que naciera un Carlos completamente nuevo. El Carlos de antes era un tipo amable que dejaba que otras personas se encarguen de muchas cosas y no quería saber nada sobre ellas. "Yo solo tocaré la guitarra, y ustedes encárguense de eso". El nuevo Carlos no quería ser un hombre controlador pero decidió que debía participar más en ciertos asuntos. Era así de simple.

Cuando tus ojos están abiertos, la inspiración puede provenir de cualquier parte. Por ejemplo: soy un gran admirador de Anthony Quinn. Algunas personas creen que es griego, pero en realidad, es mexicano. Es mi actor preferido. *Zorba the Greek* me gustó mucho, especialmente por el consejo que le da al tipo blanco: es una parte muy importante de la película. Zorba le dice al hombre que necesita un poco de locura, porque si no, ¿de qué otra manera podría cortar la cuerda y liberarse? Anthony Quinn estaba loco, bien loco. He visto sus esculturas. Y conozco a Miles; los dos sentían una profunda admiración por el otro.

En el 75, cuando leía los libros de Sri Chinmoy u otras cosas espirituales, me interesaba más el libro de Anthony Quinn, *The Original Sin* (traducido al español como *El pecado original*), la primera autobiografía que jamás había leído. En una parte, cuenta que manejaba por las calles de Hollywood con un pequeño niño que estaba sentado en el asiento del acompañante y que lo único que hacía era tomarle el pelo y decirle que no valía nada, que era tan solo un mono mexicano que jugaba a juegos de plástico, como todas las personas de Hollywood.

Por supuesto, aquel niño era parte de él; era su culpa tratando de ponerlo en su lugar. Todos tenemos esa parte de nosotros mismos adentro. Tú eres tu peor fantasma; tú mismo eres quién peor te puede hacer sentir. Pero hay una diferencia entre ser cruelmente honesto y ser simplemente brutal. Fue verdaderamente un libro terapéutico para mí, porque se relacionaba con las mismas ideas y la filosofía que leía en otros materiales. Anthony Quinn se hacía las mismas preguntas: ¿cómo evolucionar sin cometer los mismos errores que cometen todos los que te rodean? ¿Cómo desarrollar una disciplina espiritual confiable con o sin gurú?

También escribió que no quería ir a la iglesia porque no quería disculparse por ser un ser humano. Guau, *Original Sin*. Lo entiendo. Justo lo que había estado pensando.

A fines de 1988, veía a Quinn en *Barabbas*, en la que su personaje está en prisión y es liberado porque Jesús ocupó su lugar en la cruz, y, en mi cabeza, no dejaba de escuchar: "Tienes que tocar en San Quentin". Y yo pensaba: "¿Qué?".

"Debes tocar en San Quentin; ese es el mensaje de esta película".

"¿Esta película que he visto tantas veces?".

"Toca en San Quentin".

Solía mirar la prisión desde una de mis primeras casas en el condado de Marin. En el 88, vivía a tan solo un kilómetro. Tener hijos y una familia te hace pensar en lo que tienes y en lo que no tienen otras personas, y sobre la libertad que tienes de encontrar tu propósito en la vida y alcanzarlo. En esa época, casi nadie quería tocar en prisiones. B. B. había tocado en San Quentin unos cuantos años antes y había escuchado que solo prisioneros negros habían asistido. Johnny Cash había tocado en la prisión estatal de Folsom; todos lo sabían. En aquel momento, después de la gira junto a Wayne, mi nivel de confianza estaba en alza. Entonces aproveché que los miembros de la banda del reencuentro de Santana eran lo suficientemente amables como para estar bastante locos y acompañarme.

Yo mismo organicé ese concierto; organicé una reunión con el director, Dan Vasquez, un mexicano. Dijo: "Déjame entender esto. ¿Quieres tocar en San Quentin? Tienes que acompañarme y caminar un poco por el patio, y así sabrás en lo que te estás metiendo". Le respondí que no había problema.

Entonces, así como firmé un contrato por tocar allí, también tuve que firmar un documento en el cual, mi familia y yo, renunciábamos a nuestro derecho de responsabilizar a la prisión en caso de que sucediera algún problema mientras tocaba allí, por ejemplo, si los reclusos me tomaban de rehén.

Luego salí de las oficinas y caminamos hacia las puertas de la prisión. Por supuesto, no iba solo; unos guardias venían conmigo. Entramos y recuerdo que sentí como si un hielo corriera por mi columna vertebral cuando escuché el sonido de las puertas cerrarse. Lo primero que vi fueron cuatro guardias, todos con escopeta, que llevaban a un prisionero negro a algún lugar. Arrastraba sus pies encadenados y tenía más odio en sus ojos de lo que jamás había visto en un ser humano. Luego uno de los guardias que me acompañaban me dijo: "Mira el techo". Era bastante alto, pero estaba lleno de agujeros de disparos de escopeta. "Son el producto de disparos de advertencia. En general, tenemos que disparar una sola vez hacia arriba; saben que la próxima vez les dispararemos a ellos".

Llegamos al patio, donde todos estaban inmersos en una actividad, como levantar pesas o jugar al baloncesto (blancos, negros, latinos, amerindios), y las personas comenzaron a reconocerme. "Oye, 'Tana, ¿eres tú? ¿Qué haces aquí, hombre? Oye, Carlos, ¿qué haces?". Un tipo me llamó la atención. "Carlos, solo traté de cruzar las montañas desde México y después me metieron aquí". Era simplemente un alma perdida tratando de entrar al país y terminó en San Quentin. El director dijo: "Veo que estás conectado con todos aquí, viejo".

Tocamos dos conciertos en el patio: uno para los criminales más duros y otro para los condenados a cadena perpetua. Tocamos el mismo programa que tocamos en la gira de reunión, pero incluimos algunas canciones que consideramos más óptimas para una prisión: "I Shall Be Released" de Bob Dylan, "Smooth Criminal" de Michael Jackson, "Cloud Nine" de The Temptations. Sabíamos que iba a ser un público difícil porque debíamos llegar a negros y a blancos, y porque tal vez ya nadie se veía reflejado en esta música. No puedes comprar el entusiasmo en San Quentin.

Al principio, todos nos evaluaban. Con la segunda canción, comenzaron a soltarse. Podía ver cómo cambiaba la energía en sus posturas y rostros. Para la tercera canción, sentía que pensaban: "Oye, estos tipos pueden hacerlo". Con la cuarta canción, se dejaron llevar por la música, sonrieron y, por un momento, lograron olvidarse del lugar donde estaban. Es decir, la primera vez que entré allí, podía oler el miedo y el control de las emociones, lo reprimido que estaba todo. Como si en cualquier momento fuera a explotar. Podía oler su piel, la ropa que usaban, incluso sus pensamientos.

Tengo una foto de ese espectáculo en San Quentin colgada en la pared de mi oficina. Estoy tocando, y, en un costado, se pueden ver prisioneros muy duros. Puedes enfocarte en uno de ellos y notarás que estaban escuchando la música. No dije mucho en esos conciertos; dejé que la música transmitiera el mensaje: escuchar es necesario para ayudarte a que no te conviertas en una víctima o en un prisionero de ti mismo, para ayudarte a cambiar de opinión sobre las cosas y cambiar tu destino. El mensaje es el mismo tanto dentro como fuera de la prisión.

En alguna forma rara, mi vida siempre ha sido local; todo lo que sucede se origina en donde estoy. En esa época, John Lee Hooker vivía en Bay Arca. Era el Dalai Lama del *boogie*. Era como el papa del *boogie;* en lo que a mí me concierne. Llegamos a conocernos. Cuando tocábamos, muchas ves él me decía: "Carlos, vamos a la calle" y yo le respondía: "No, John, vamos al callejón", y luego él decía: "¿Por qué detenernos allí? Vamos al pantano". Lo extraño tanto.

Un *boogie* de John Lee es como la gravedad, porque atrae a las personas con una fuerza impresionante.

Es el sonido de la profundidad en el blues, su influencia se infiltra en todo y en todos. Puedes escucharlo en "Voodoo Child (Slight Return)" de Jimi Hendrix o en los *boogies* de Canned Heat. Ese es John Lee Hooker. Cuando escuchas The Doors, escuchas una mezcla entre John Lee y John Coltrane. Eso es lo que hacen; esa es la música que aman.

Por supuesto, la primera vez que escuché a John Lee fue en Tijuana; en discos y en la radio. Como dije, había tres tipos que tenían raíces muy profundas en el blues: Lightnin' Hopkins, Jimmy Reed y John Lee Hooker. Lightnin' vivía en Texas y Jimmy Reed era probablemente el más popular en la época que escuchaba blues en México, pero para finales de los 80, ya hacía mucho que nos había dejado. Hizo que Vee-Jay Records ganara mucho dinero.

En el 89, John Lee ya era un local en Bay Area. No vivía lejos de mi casa, en San Carlos, cerca de Palo Alto. Nos encontramos varias veces y hablamos, y en determinado momento de nuestra relación, me invitó a su casa para festejar su cumpleaños. Esa fue la primera vez que realmente pasábamos el rato juntos. Le llevé una hermosa guitarra de regalo.

Cuando entré, noté que todos miraban el partido de los Dodgers por televisión, porque es el equipo preferido de John Lee. Él comía pollo frito y Junior Mints. No es en broma, Junior Mints. Tenía dos mujeres a su izquierda y dos a la derecha, y le colocaban las mentas en las manos que eran más suaves que un sofá viejo. Me adelanté y dije: "Hola, John. Feliz cumpleaños, viejo. Traje esta guitarra y escribí una canción para ti".

"Ah, ¿sí?".

"Suena como The Doors tocando blues, pero la recuperé y aquí te la devuelvo. La llamo 'The Healer'".

John Lee río entre dientes. Tenía un leve tartamudeo que era muy simpático. "D-d-déjame escucharla".

Empecé a tocar y a inventarla en el momento; sabía cómo tocaba y cantaba blues. "Blues a healer all over the world...". Tomó la canción y cuando la grabó, le agregó su propio toque. Dije: "Bueno, hay que llevar esto al estudio, pero quiero que vengas a la una o a las dos de la tarde para que no pases allí todo el día, viejo. Quiero que vengas y dejes el alma. Voy a trabajar con el ingeniero, dejar los micrófonos preparados, hacer que la banda toque en el tempo correcto. Solo tienes que presentarte".

"Bueno, C-C-Carlos".

Cuando John Lee llegó, estábamos preparados. La banda estaba lista (Chepito, Ndugu, CT y Armando) aunque sin bajo porque Alphonso no pudo participar en esa ocasión. John Lee y Armando se miraban como dos perros que se miden; eran los mayores y realmente se notaba que Armando necesitaba saber quién era este tipo mayor que él. Lo miró lentamente, por completo, de pies a cabeza. Lo medía. John Lee lo sabía, pero lo ignoró, se sentó y comenzó a afinar la guitarra, riéndose por dentro.

Armando tiró la primera bomba. "Oye, hombre, ¿alguna vez escuchaste hablar del Rhumboogie?". Se refería a uno de los clubes más antiguos del circuito de música afroamericana de Chicago, lo había inaugurado el boxeador Joe Louis, mucho antes de que yo naciera. John Lee contestó: "Sí, ho-o-mbre. Escuché hablar del Rhumboogie". Armando tenía la mano sobre la cintura como si dijera: "Te agarré". Dijo: "Bueno, yo toqué allí con Slim Gaillard".

"¿Sí? Yo toqué allí como telonero de D-D-Duke Ellington".

Me di cuenta de lo que pasaba entre ellos e interrumpí: "Armando, este es el Sr. John Lee Hooker. Sr. Hooker, el Sr. Armando Peraza".

Tocamos "The Healer" de un tirón, y el ingeniero preguntó: "¿Quieren volver a intentarlo?".

John Lee meneó la cabeza. "¿Para qué?".

Lo pensé y respondí: "¿Le molestaría volver a la cabina y cuando yo haga la señal, sería tan amable de darnos su firma, esos *mmm, mmm*?". John Lee se río entre dientes nuevamente. "Sí, puedo hacer eso". Hice la señal. Ese fue el único sonido que agregó ese día: "Mmm, mmm, mmm".

Gracias a "The Healer", John Lee volvió a los escenarios. Grabó un álbum que fue de los más vendidos y también un video de música; todo lo que se merecía. Empezamos a tocar y pasar más tiempo juntos. Lo veía en los conciertos también. Tuvo un tecladista durante muchos años, Deacon Jones, quien solía subir al escenario y decir: "Oigan. Ustedes, los de adelante, es posible que deban retroceder un poco porque esto se puede poner candente. John Lee está a punto de salir". Tengo muchísimas historias como esa y otras sobre cuando John Lee me llamaba, en ocasiones durante el día, pero, como Miles, generalmente lo hacía por las noches.

Recuerdo cuando John Lee tocó como telonero de Santana en Concord, California; habíamos terminado la prueba de sonido y me estaba esperando al costado del escenario. Mientras nos íbamos, comenzó a hablar. El sonidista vino corriendo. "Sr. Hooker, necesitamos que usted también haga una prueba de sonido".

"No necesito ninguna prueba de sonido".

"Pero tenemos que saber cómo suena".

John Lee no se detuvo. "Ya sé cómo sueno". Fin de la discusión.

Una vez hubo un festival de blues al aire libre en San Francisco, y fui para apoyar a mis héroes: Buddy Guy, Otis Rush y otros. Alguien del equipo vino corriendo hacia mí y me dijo: "John Lee está en el escenario y te llamó para que vayas a tocar con él". Ya habían preparado mi amplificador, así que fui, y allí estaba él, solo, luciendo estupendamente, como siempre, con su traje y sombrero. Tenía la guitarra sobre la rodilla. Apenas me vio, dijo: "Damas y caballeros, les presento a mi buen amigo: Carlos Santana. Ven, hombre".

Era un día hermoso, y desde el escenario podía ver el cielo, los pájaros, el puente Golden Gate, y a todos esos amantes del blues en el público. Me aferré a esa imagen, cerré los ojos y me uní a él en el escenario: solo él y yo. Era como tocar con un predicador un domingo a la mañana; esperé mi momento para entrar, pero mientras él cantaba pude sentir su voz pidiéndome que empezara a tocar. Abrí los ojos, y estábamos juntos en un mismo ritmo, acompañándonos. Escuché su voz en mi interior una vez más, diciéndome que siguiera tocando, así que cerré los ojos y seguí. Cuando terminé, hubo un enorme aplauso; la gente estaba aluci nada. Miré alrededor, ¡pero John Lee no estaba!

Toqué un poco más, le agradecí a la gente y fui al detrás de escena, donde John estaba hablando con una jovencita. Me miró con esa sonrisa que tenía. "Oye, amigo, e-e-estuviste muy bien".

"Sí, pero ¿por qué me dejaste solo, hombre?".

"B-b-bueno, yo ya no tenía nada que hacer".

Siempre supe dónde estaba mi corazón en la música, pero realmente me gustaban algunas bandas y guitarristas nuevos que estaban surgiendo en el momento. Vernon Reid me recordaba un poco a Sonny Sharrock y Jimi. Su banda, Living Colour, era de la Ciudad de Nueva York y fue una de las primeras bandas de rock con todos músicos afroamericanos. Vernon es un músico funky bien sólido; es divertido tocar con él en vivo. Es un fenómeno y tiene un corazón hermoso. Él y David Sancious tienen una expresión serena en su rostro y mucha sabiduría, y a los dos también les gusta mucho Sonny Sharrock.

Vernon tocó en *Spirits Dancing in the Flesh,* el álbum de Santana lanzado en 1990. Pienso en ese álbum y escucho el equilibro de Curtis Mayfield y John Coltrane y Jimi Hendrix haciendo canciones de gospel, cantando alabanzas a Dios y tocando rock. Oración y pasión. Alice Coltrane nos dio permiso para usar la voz de John en una canción. Fue una grabación muy linda, pero yo todavía necesitaba sentir un poco de emoción nueva, sin procesar; prefería escuchar algunos errores, si entiendes a qué me refiero.

Cantar a Dios y a Jesús no tiene por qué sonar a un lamento. La canción debe provenir de tu corazón y de lo más profundo de tu interior, no solo de tu boca. Un álbum sobre Dios tiene que ser honesto y puro. Es preferible que alguien cante un poco fuera de tono pero con total sentimiento, a que se esfuerce demasiado en sonar bien y que suene fingido.

Yo quería trabajar con Tramaine Hawkins, porque con la música espiritual uno tiene que ser muy selectivo: a veces la gente puede volverse un poco artificial cuando alaba a Jesús. No voy a mencionar ningún nombre porque no quiero herir sentimientos, pero hay una diferencia entre el quejido y el soul. Cuando escucho a Mavis Staples, Gladys Knight, Nina Simone y Etta James, escucho una enorme diferencia entre ellas y otras cantantes del otro lado de la ciudad, donde las chicas cantan en forma muy quejumbrosa, tanto las afroamericanas como las blancas. Y puede que la afinación sea perfecta, pero el sentimiento no es real.

Tramaine surgió de San Francisco y estuvo con los Edwin Hawkins Singers durante un tiempo; ella era ideal para *Spirits*. Cuando estaba haciendo ese álbum, también conocí a Benny Rietveld, que estaba con Miles en ese momento. Alphonso se había ido, así que Benny terminó tocando el bajo en el álbum y ha estado conmigo desde el 91. Ahora es el director musical de la banda. He llegado a conocerlo bien y le tengo un gran afecto a Benny.

Yo había empezado a pensar en el álbum en el año 90, y Wayne me comentó que el escritor de canciones Paolo Rustichelli, que tocaba sintetizadores y estaba grabando con Miles y Herbie, había escrito una canción para mí. Así fue como terminé tocando en el álbum *Mystic Man* de Rustichelli, ¡con Miles en algunas de las pistas! Paolo me dio para grabar la canción "Full Moon", en la que yo estaba trabajando cuando me enteré de que vendría Benny. Mientras tanto, Benny se enteró de que estábamos haciendo audiciones de bajistas. Nos encontramos y él me preguntó: "Oye, ¿puedo hacer una prueba?". Lo miré serio. "Todavía estás con Miles, ¿no? Puedes tocar con nosotros, pero tienes que decirle a él". Yo no quería que hubiera ningún tipo de tensión.

Por supuesto, te imaginas lo que pasó: Benny no le dijo nada, pero Miles se enteró de que había grabado en mi nuevo álbum, *y también* se enteró de que Benny había hablado conmigo para tener una audición. Yo estaba en el Paramount, en Oakland, donde acababa de entregarle a Miles un ramo de flores y un regalo por ganar el premio Grammy a la trayectoria. Después del espectáculo, estaba preparándome para irme, estaba en el estacionamiento con mi amigo Tony Kilbert cuando John Bingham, que tocaba percusión en la banda de Miles, vino a decirme que Miles quería verme en el detrás de escena. "Claro, enseguida voy". Así que volví y entré en su camerino. "Hola, Miles".

"Cierra la puerta".

Ay, no.

"Gracias por las flores y gracias por el regalo".

"De nada, Miles".

"¿Qué le pasa a Benny?".

"No sé qué le pasa. Está en tu banda". Benny tenía que hablar por sí mismo. Miles me la dejó pasar. Lo próximo que me enteré fue que Benny le había contado, y se unió a nuestra banda y tocó en el álbum *Spirits Dancing in the Flesh*.

Spirits salió en 1990, pero para ese entonces, Columbia y CBS se habían convertido en Sony Music, y no sabían qué hacer con ese álbum ni con los anteriores, muchos de los cuales ya no estaban disponibles. Recuerdo que, antes de que saliera *Supernatural*, yo deseaba que la compañía discográfica volviese a lanzar algunos de esos álbumes, porque estaban realmente buenos: *Freedom, Blues for Salvador, Spirits Dancing in the Flesh*. Tenía eso en mente unos años después, cuando tuve oportunidad de armar *Multi-Dimensional Warrior*, la compilación de la música de Santana de finales de los 70 y los 80.

Spirits fue el final de la relación de Santana con Columbia, CBS y Sony Music. Pusieron a cargo a un tipo llamado Donnie Ienner, y yo no podía trabajar con él. Él quería trabajar conmigo, pero yo estaba más a cargo de la parte comercial de Santana que antes, y sentía lo mismo que creo que sintió Miles cuando decidió dejar Columbia en 1986. Miles no podía trabajar con el directivo de un área de la compañía discográfica, y si te sientes así, ¿para qué quedarte? Recuerdo mi última conversación con Donnie; escuché lo que tenía que decir y le respondí diciendo algo acerca de que el manejo de la situación era como "artistas contra estafadores", y después de eso las cosas no mejoraron mucho. Yo sentía que Santana tenía que estar en otro lugar, y primero pensamos en ir a Warner Bros., luego terminamos firmando en Polydor, con Davitt Sigerson.

El año 1991 no fue fácil; lo sentí como si se me hubieran salido las ruedas de entrenamiento de la espiritualidad. Mis pilares ya no existían. Mis ángeles se habían ido. Fue muy difícil. Me hizo crecer de otra forma, como si Dios me estuviera diciendo: "Ahora debes arreglártelas por tu cuenta".

Todo sucedió en apenas un mes. Santana estaba tocando en Syracuse el día que murió Miles en California, el 28 de septiembre. Wayne me llamó y me lo contó esa noche. Dijo que había visto a Miles tocando ese verano en el Hollywood Bowl. "Tocó 'Feliz cumpleaños' para mí, y en medio de la canción me miró y vi una fatiga en su rostro que no había visto nunca antes. Fatiga de muchos, muchos años".

Yo ya había visto a Miles enfermo, pero no esperaba que se muriese. Subí al ascensor con Benny y le dije: "Benny, acaba de fallecer Miles".

"¡No!"

Los dos miramos al piso, y no recuerdo mucho más. Cuando se va alguien como Miles o Armando, queda un vacío, y puedes sentir cómo baja el nivel de energía. Esa es la mejor forma que tengo de explicarlo.

La mañana siguiente me levanté a las cinco para tomar un avión para ir a la graduación de primer grado de Stella. Todavía estaba atontado. Horas antes esa noche tocamos en el festival One World, One Heart de Ben & Jerry, en el Golden Gate Park. Estaban también los Caribbean Allstars, y tocamos "In a Silent Way" como tributo a Miles.

No había visto mucho a Miles durante el año anterior. Le había enviado flores en el hospital cuando me enteré de que estaba enfermo, y me llamó para agradecerme. "Esto significa tanto para mí, Carlos", me dijo. "¿Qué estás haciendo ahora?". Le respondí lo que siempre respondo: "Estoy aprendiendo y divirtiéndome, Miles".

"Siempre vas a estar haciendo eso; es tu forma de ver la vida".

Eso fue lo último que me dijo Miles, y ojalá más gente conociera ese lado de él. Su autobiografía había salido el año anterior, y cuando la leí pensé que las personas que la escribieron con él podrían haberlo ayudado más; podrían haberle hecho más honor. Sentí que estaban promocionando demasiado al Príncipe de la Oscuridad. No había necesidad de escribir todo lo que él alguna vez dijo. Hubiese preferido leer cosas más atrayentes sobre él y otros músicos. Me gusta el romance; yo soy un romántico de cabo a rabo.

Miles tenía una memoria de elefante. Esa vez en el 81 cuando vino al Savoy y estuvimos juntos charlando toda la noche, le había dicho cuando estábamos en el detrás de escena que el mundo siempre le estaría muy agradecido, incluso si no volvía a tocar una sola nota. "Solo queremos que estés bien y seas feliz", le dije. "¿Qué es eso?", respondió él, como si fuese algo extraño para desearle a alguien. Inmediatamente le dije: "Miles, tú no eres una de esas personas que no son felices a menos que se sientan miserables, ¿no?". Él se detuvo y me miró. Un año después, toqué en un gran evento de rock y tenis en Forest Hills, Queens, donde estaban también John McEnroe, Vitas Gerulaitis, Todd Rundgren, Joe Cocker, el bajista Jamaaladeen Tacuma y el baterista de jazz Max Roach. Terminamos de tocar y estaba preparándome para irme, cuando escuché que alguien me llamaba: "¡Carlos! ¡Oye, Carlos!"

Era Max Roach. "Necesito hablar contigo, Carlos". Se lo veía serio. Me dijo: "Miles vino a verme. ¿Qué fue lo que le dijiste?".

Guau, tuve que rebobinar mucho la cinta para recordar nuestra última conversación; había sido esa larga noche que comenzó en el detrás de escena en el Savoy. Pensé en ello y me vinieron a la mente dos cosas. Primero estaba la anécdota que Miles contaba en su libro, de principios de los años 50, cuando Max puso algo de dinero en el bolsillo de su saco cuando él había estado drogado en la calle. Miles dijo que esa vergüenza fue lo que lo hizo salir de la heroína.

La segunda cosa que recordé fue en la mirada que me dio cuando le pregunté si solo era feliz cuando era miserable. Esa noche yo le había hecho ver a Miles en qué estaba fallando, y le conté a Max la historia. Me escuchó y me dijo: "Quiero que sepas que está funcionando; está empezando a comportarse de otra manera".

¿Quién era Miles Davis? ¿Qué lo hacía hacer lo que hacía? Él perseguía la excelencia de un modo feroz y despiadado, sin importar qué estuviera haciendo o con quién: negro, blanco o de cualquier otro color. Como me dijo Tony Williams: "Antes de que existieran los Panteras Negras o el *black power* o cualquier otra revolución, Miles no se dejaba intimidar por nadie, ni blanco ni negro". Tenía la pasión y la audacia. Pero si al final era feliz o no, es otra historia.

Si miras las publicidades, las películas y las revistas, verás que todas te dicen que cuando tienes éxito, entonces eres feliz. Y, para ser feliz, debes usar esto, comer aquello, obtener esto, obtener aquello. La verdad es que es exactamente al revés. Creo que lo que más se nota cuando alguien tiene éxito, es si esa persona es realmente, verdaderamente feliz.

Unas semanas después del funeral de Miles, yo estaba en casa, sonó el teléfono por la mañana y atendió Deborah. "¡No! ¡No, no, no!", comenzó a exclamar enseguida. "¡Bill se ha ido!" Yo le pregunté: "¿Adónde se fue?". Entonces me di cuenta, y eso fue todo. Quedé como atontado durante al menos dos meses. Dos de mis mejores amigos se habían ido. De pronto Miles no estaba allí para llamar tarde por la noche y decirme cuándo esconderme. Bill no estaba allí con una libreta. Ahora yo tendría que hacerlo todo internamente.

La última vez que vi a Bill fue el mes anterior en el Teatro Griego, en Berkeley. Habíamos hecho tantos espectáculos juntos para ese entonces… fue una noche increíble. Recuerdo estar en el detrás de escena después del concierto, sosteniendo a Jelli, que solo tenía dos años. Ella me miraba con una expresión de alegría en su rostro, sin decir nada. Durante el recital, la energía nunca había decaído. Tenía la sensación de que cada canción había tenido la duración exacta y la secuencia había sido perfecta. El público era una mezcla de blancos, afroamericanos, mexicanos y filipinos: una multitud de tantos colores como el arco iris. Estuvieron de pie desde el comienzo del espectáculo. Como Jelli, yo no sabía qué decir. Había gente todo a nuestro alrededor y todos estaban felices. Una vibra perfecta.

Bill vino con su libreta y me miró. Esperé. Lentamente arrancó una página y la dio vuelta hacia mí. Estaba en blanco. "Vamos, hombre. ¿En serio? ¡Guau! Gracias, Bill".

"Gracias a *ti*". Y se fue.

CAPÍTULO 21

Mi papá, José Santana, y yo en la Plaza de Toros Monumental
de Tijuana, 21 de marzo de 1992.

*Cuando fui papá, todo el tiempo les decía a mis hijos que los quería. Y,
naturalmente, pensaba en la música, en mis obsesiones y en mis hijos. Por
supuesto que sabía que no me sentiría desilusionado si Salvador, Stella o
Jelli elegían la música como carrera; tendríamos más de qué hablar. Pero
podían elegir cualquier cosa que desearan y yo seguiría estando orgulloso
de sus elecciones de vida. Lo único que sí me desilusionaría, sería que deja-
sen que otras cosas se interpongan en el camino de lo que querían hacer.
Nuestra familia es una familia donde no hay excusas. Nuestros hijos son
responsables de la calidad de sus propios pensamientos, de modo que puedan elegir convertirlos en acciones y hechos, y crear su propia vida.*

Pero requiere fortaleza saber cuándo soltar a tus hijos; de veras, de veras dejarlos ir y confiarlos a quien los creó en primer lugar. Una vez, a mediados de los 90, cuando Sal era adolescente, sentí la necesidad de hablar con él. Yo había estado de gira durante cinco semanas y recién regresaba a casa. Entiendo que para los chicos de entre doce y veintidós años, los padres son la gente con menos onda del mundo. En ese momento, precisamente, Sal necesitaba representar eso. Yo pensaba: "Los niños lo superarán, como yo lo hice, y entonces se darán cuenta de que sus padres son excepcionales". Pero en ese momento, sentía una separación entre padre e hijo.

"¿Salvador?".

"¿Qué pasa?". Esa era su respuesta a todo entonces: "¿Qué pasa?".

"Hijo, últimamente he notado que tu tarea es contradecirme en todo lo que digo. Parece que fuera tu trabajo las veinticuatro horas, todos los días, ¿sabes?". Él seguía mirándome. "Pero mira afuera: es un día increíble; el cielo está azul y el tiempo cálido. No podemos discutir sobre eso, ¿verdad? ¿Te gustaría tomarte el día conmigo e ir a sentarnos en la cima del Monte Tamalpais, y observar a los halcones y a las águilas, y quedarnos en silencio?".

Me sorprendió un poco, porque solo lo pensó unos segundos. "Suena bien". Subimos ahí y nos tomamos nuestro tiempo; nos recostamos y nos quedamos viendo flotar a las aves en las corrientes ascendentes, y yo no dije una palabra. A los quince minutos, él se abrió y empezó a contarme cosas sobre él y su novia y la escuela, y cómo lo trataba la gente por ser un Santana, y el hecho de que la gente siempre le pedía dinero. Era un desafío estar sentado allí y escuchar, solo escuchar. Yo tenía respuestas e ideas para compartir con él. Pero traté de mirarlo y verlo como lo veían sus amigos y sus maestros y me di cuenta de que él ya estaba empezando a darse cuenta de las cosas por su cuenta. Siempre fue muy educado y respetuoso; aún lo es.

Te daré un ejemplo. En el 2005, estábamos de gira juntos (Santana y la Salvador Santana Band) y estábamos en San Antonio. Alguien llamó a la puerta de mi camerino. "¿Quién es?".

"Soy yo, papá. Salvador".

"Hijo, no necesitas llamar a la puerta. ¡Pasa!"

"Papá, necesito pedirte algo". Yo bajé mi guitarra. "¿Puedo llevarme una botella de agua de tu refrigerador? En nuestra habitación ya no tenemos más". Quiero decir, realmente hace eso. Me hace estallar el corazón de amor.

"Sal, puedes tomar lo que quieras, incluido mi corazón. Lo que tú quieras".

"Eh, de acuerdo, papá. Gracias. Que tengas un excelente recital".

Todavía lo hago sentir un poco avergonzado, lo sé. Pero yo no voy a cambiar, y él tampoco. "¿Cómo estás, Salvador?".

"Gracias por preguntar, papá. Estoy bien".

¿Sabes? Cuando crezca, quiero ser como él.

En 1997, Prince me llamó para decirme que iba a tocar en San José y me preguntó si quería ir al recital, hacer alguna improvisación y juntarnos un rato. ¿Que si quería? Me encanta Prince. Cuando llegué allí, me dijo: "Ven aquí, quiero mostrarte algo". Está bien, ¿qué cosa? ¿Quizá una guitarra nueva? Me llevó a una habitación en el detrás de escena y abrió la puerta, y allí estaba toda su banda, viendo un video. Prince sonreía. "Ellos están de testigos: siempre, antes de salir al escenario, toco *Sacred Fire*. Les digo que esto es lo que quiero que hagan". Miré a la banda y pensé: "Grandioso; aquí hay toda otra banda a la que le estoy diciendo qué hacer".

Fue un honor que Prince me mostrara eso, especialmente porque *Sacred Fire: Live in Mexico* era tan personal y especial para mí como *Havana Moon*. Era un video en vivo, y también había un álbum en vivo (*Sacred Fire: Live in South America*) que salieron juntos, la primera vez que hice esa especie de paquete coordinado: una gira, un álbum y un video.

Sacred Fire salió en el 93, y la gira venía de *Milagro*, mi primer álbum para Polydor del año anterior. Sin duda, en *Sacred Fire* hay un cierto nivel de confianza espiritual en mí mismo. Tocar en México representa para mí, lo que para Bob Dylan tocar en Jerusalén. Esta es tu gente. Mejor que pongas lo mejor de ti. De hecho, me enorgullece decir que Santana nunca ha cometido demasiados errores en Ciudad de México, Nueva York, Tokio, Sídney, París, Roma, Londres, Moscú o cualquiera de las grandes ciudades. Sí metimos la pata en otros lugares porque somos humanos y falibles, pero no porque lo planeáramos o nos faltara voluntad. Cada vez que hay un concierto grande, respiro profundo y digo: "Que todos los ángeles vengan y me ayuden con esto".

Milagro era una carta de despedida escrita especialmente para Bill y Miles. Comenzaba con la voz de Bill presentándonos como lo hacía siempre: "Desde mi corazón, ¡Santana!" Luego seguía "Milagro", porque eso es lo que fueron estos dos hombres, y lo que cada uno de nosotros es. La canción usaba una línea de "Work", de Bob Marley. La siguiente melodía era "Somewhere in Heaven", que comenzaba con Martin Luther King Jr. hablando sobre la tierra prometida. Yo no sabía exactamente dónde estaban mis ángeles, pero sabía que Bill y Miles seguirían llamando y conectándose, dándome consejos y bendiciones espirituales. Le pedí a mi viejo amigo Larry Graham que cantara en el álbum, y apareció en "Right On". Puse "Saja" como introducción; esa vino de un álbum muy extraño llamado *Aquarius* y fue escrita por el saxofonista Joe Roccisano. Cuando escuché esa canción, sonaba realmente como algo que haría Santana si hubiésemos trabajado con Cal Tjader. Agregué ese sentir de "Shadow of Your Smile", que luego se desliza a una *guajira* muy sentida.

Todavía me gustan las palabras de Marvin Gaye, como "For those of us who tend the sick and heed the people's cries / Let me say to you: Right on!" (Para aquellos de nosotros que cuidamos a los enfermos y atendemos al grito de la gente / Déjame decirte: ¡Bravo!). Tienen un mensaje importante. Creo que transmiten el mismo mensaje que la música de Santana; es lo que sentí que todavía necesitaba escucharse en los 90. Todavía necesita escucharse hoy.

Recuerdo que, después de su primera grabación de sonido, Larry me preguntó: "¿Qué te parece?".

Yo le dije: "Larry, estás dando la vuelta a la manzana... ¡tienes que meterte debajo de las sábanas!"

Él se rio. "¡De acuerdo! Entiendo". La siguiente grabación fue espectacular. Todos conocen a Larry como bajista, pero también es un increíble cantante; en esa misma sesión, hizo un increíble precalentamiento vocal. Fue al piano y tocó todo el teclado, desde la nota más grave hasta la más aguda, acompañando cada sonido con su voz.

En ese álbum, la conformación de Santana también fue estupenda: tenía a CT, Raul, Benny y Alex, y agregamos a Karl Perazzo, que había tocado congas y timbales con Sheila E. y Cal Tjader; a Tony Lindsay, que había estado cantando por Bay Area y tenía una voz clara y perfecta para R&B; y a Walfredo Reyes Jr., que es de Cuba y, antes de venir con nosotros, tocaba la batería con David Lindley y Jackson Browne. También tenía una sección de vientos que incluía a Bill Ortiz en trompeta. Bill, Tony, Benny y Karl aún están con Santana en la actualidad. Ese dúo de Raul y Karl fue especialmente bonito y flexible, porque ellos respetan la clave. La honran: saben exactamente dónde está, como lo sabía Armando, pero no están obsesionados con ella.

La gira de *Milagro* iba a ir a México, y mi hermano Jorge ya había venido y había tocado en varias etapas, así que la idea de familia estaba en el aire. El plan era filmar y grabar los recitales que hiciéramos en México: mi padre vendría para abrir el espectáculo en Tijuana; también tocarían César Rosas de Los Lobos y Larry Graham. Recuerdo que tomamos un vuelo a San Diego desde donde sea que estábamos, y las condiciones meteorológicas eran realmente preocupantes. Se puso tan mal la cosa que pensamos que el avión se iba a caer. El avión comenzó a sacudirse mucho, de repente cayó un tramo, y los vasos de café que las azafatas llevaban por el pasillo salieron disparados al techo. Una azafata corrió a su asiento y la vi persignarse. El avión cayó de nuevo, y una niñita sentada cerca de mí empezó a gritar y a reír. "¡Wiii! ¡De nuevo! ¡De nuevo!" Todos comenzaron a reírse, y eso hizo que nos relajáramos. Luego la sacudida se detuvo.

En Tijuana, el promotor local llamó al concierto un *regreso a casa*. Pusieron el nombre en afiches y obtuvieron permiso para usar la Plaza de Toros Monumental de la ciudad. Creo que podría decirse que ese fue un momento decisivo para mí, cuando acepté plenamente y me sentí a gusto con mi identidad mexicana. Fue mucho más fácil ir a Autlán porque allí muy pocos se acordaban de mí. Pero en Tijuana, todavía había muchos que me conocían, y toda la ciudad sabía sobre mis comienzos allí, en la Avenida Revolución, si bien no tuve tiempo de visitar los viejos bares o clubes, y El Convoy ya no estaba. Fuimos por la ruta, y en algunos aspectos parecía que no había cambiado mucho. Había diferentes nombres, diferentes clubes, nuevos lugares para bailar y no tanta música en vivo, pero estar en Tijuana definitivamente era como regresar a casa.

Hicimos dos noches en la plaza de toros, y el concierto siguió y siguió. Comenzó con mi padre cantando y tocando con una banda de mariachis locales; luego tocó Pato Banton, dado que el reggae realmente se estaba volviendo popular en México entonces; luego siguió Larry Graham; y finalmente tocó Santana, con mi hermano Jorge e incluso Javier Bátiz haciéndonos el regalo de subir e improvisar con nosotros. Fue la filmación y la música de otras ciudades en esa gira lo que luego se convirtió en el DVD *Sacred Fire*. También decidimos filmar algunas cosas en blanco y negro en Tijuana, y las usamos en el video de "Right On", que fue el single principal de *Milagro* (ahí me ves tocando en la plaza de toros de Tijuana). ¿Esas filmaciones de gente cruzando la frontera a la noche? Eso no fue actuado; fue real.

Años después encontré una cinta de ese concierto. Finalmente me senté y la escuché, de principio a fin. Ese concierto fue importante para mí porque fue la primera vez que escuché a mi papá validar mi música. Al final de su función con los mariachis, habló conmigo en el detrás de escena. Estaba hablando mucho más de lo que hablaba normalmente. "Sabes, Carlos, escuché tu música muchas veces en la radio, y te he visto tocar, y hay algo muy distintivo en lo que haces. Cuando escucho 'Batuka' o 'Ain't got nobody that I can depend on', *eso* es Santana".

Nunca había escuchado a mi papá decir algo así. Yo ni siquiera sabía que él conocía los nombres de algunas canciones de Santana, y mucho menos las letras. Sabía las melodías. Nos habíamos hecho tan famosos tan rápido que nunca llegué a ver cómo habían cambiado los sentimientos de papá acerca de mi música. De todos modos, él nunca hablaba mucho. Me honraba permitiéndome convertirme en lo que él había sido. Es como que yo me convertí en él, pero a mayor escala, y eso fue suficiente para que él dejara de decirme qué hacer y qué no hacer.

Tuve oportunidad de decirle a mi papá lo que me había guardado durante muchos años. En el 93, toda la familia se reunió durante dos semanas en Hawái; éramos todos mis hermanos y hermanas con sus hijos, más los padres de mi ex esposa y mis padres. Le dije: "Oye, papá, alejémonos un poco de todo este barullo; dejemos que los niños se diviertan un poco".

Empezamos a caminar y le dije: "¿Sabes? Hay algo que quiero decirte hace mucho".

"¿Qué?".

"Necesito decirte cuán orgulloso estoy de ti por haberte ocupado de todos nosotros con ese violín. Sé que tenías que viajar sin saber cuánto dinero ibas a conseguir. Nunca nos faltó una comida. Quería agradecértelo". Él simplemente me miró. Y me sentí bien. Fue como esa mirada entre cualquier padre e hijo que dice: "Estamos interconectados". Pude ver la validación no solo para él mismo, sino también para su padre y para mi hijo.

No sabía que él solo iba a vivir unos cinco años más. Todavía se me hace un nudo en la garganta cuando escucho la cinta de esa plaza de toros en Tijuana.

Tocar en Tijuana fue muy difícil debido al gobierno y la política local, y toda la corrupción que tuvimos que enfrentar, pero los muchachos de la empresa de Bill Graham (Bill Graham Presents, BGP) lo hicieron posible, y les estoy agradecido.

Pero digamos que no soy un gran admirador de lo que le ocurrió a BGP después que Bill murió. Creo que algunas de las personas que se hicieron cargo eran las que le hubieran dicho a Bill lo que él quería escuchar, y que no compartían su visión ni sus prioridades ni su compromiso con la música y con la comunidad de músicos. Yo solía decirle a Bill que nunca escucharía que yo estaba hablando de él a sus espaldas porque no me importaba decirle lo que tuviera que decirle a la cara. No iba a chuparle las medias, como algunas de las personas que trabajaban para él; pero algunas de estas personas decían cosas horribles sobre él. No creo que Bill se ocupase de ese aspecto de su negocio antes de morir, porque no había motivos para hacerlo (por supuesto, él no había planeado morir tan pronto). Actualmente, algunos de los aspectos comerciales de Santana todavía están en manos de BGP; ellos son propietarios del sitio de objetos de interés Wolfgang Vault, por ejemplo, y allí puedes encontrar afiches y playeras de Santana. Hemos aprendido a hacer negocios juntos, pero todavía siento que se traicionó una parte de lo que Bill había creado.

Bill solía describirse a sí mismo como un "dejado sentimental". Yo no soy así. Aprendí que incluso si tienes un apego sentimental a ciertas personas, en este negocio a veces es mejor no tener demasiados lazos emocionales. Así, si necesitas despedir a alguien que no está colaborando o que no puede seguirte el ritmo cuando avanzas, puedes hacerlo. Sé que hay muchas personas que he llevado y mantenido conmigo cuando debí haberlas dejado ir porque no aportaban ninguna vitalidad ni agregaban nada a la energía o a la visión de la organización. Nunca es fácil, pero en 1995, cuando finalmente inicié mi propia empresa representante, tuve que empezar a ver las cosas de ese modo.

Habíamos empezado a ocuparnos de toda la administración de Santana en el 88, y durante un tiempo Bill Graham había sido como un supervisor, con Ray Etzler como representante. Todavía compartíamos espacio en la oficina con BGP. Después Bill se murió, Ray se fue y Barry Siegel, que era nuestro contador, asumió como representante comercial y trabajaba con Deborah. Ella y yo (y luego mi cuñada, Kitsaun) nos convertimos en nuestra propia empresa representante y aprendimos una lección colectiva sobre las cuestiones prácticas del negocio, como hablar con abogados y contadores, y firmar nuestros propios cheques. Deborah iba y venía de la oficina, cuestionando si las cosas podían hacerse mejor o con menos dinero. Sus años manejando el restaurante con Kitsaun ayudaron.

Kitsaun King ya era una parte muy importante de nuestra familia. Cuando iniciamos Santana Management ella trabajaba para United Airlines. Durante los 90 finalmente pasó a formar parte de nuestra familia musical a tiempo completo. Ella podía ponerse firme (en el transcurso de los años tuvimos algunas discusiones por ciertas cuestiones de la banda) pero sus instintos por lo general eran correctos, y nunca dudé de su lealtad o de su absoluta determinación para hacer lo que era mejor para Santana. Le ofrezco mis condolencias a cualquiera que haya cometido la insensatez de hablar mal de mí o de Santana en su presencia. La tía Kitsaun no toleraba eso.

En el 95 encontramos un espacio para la oficina y depósito en San Rafael. Antes de eso estábamos desparramados por todos lados, rentando espacios para guardar cosas y salas de ensayo cuando las necesitábamos. Así que se nos ocurrió la idea de juntar todo bajo un solo techo. Deborah fue la que tuvo la visión e intención de hacer esto, y pronto habíamos establecido nuestra propia empresa. Conseguimos algunas de nuestras personas favoritas de BGP (como Rita Gentry y Marcia Sult Godinez, ambas muy capaces y fáciles de congeniar) porque queríamos algunas caras familiares. Seré el primero en decir que trabajar para mí no es fácil. De hecho, no necesito que nadie trabaje para mí: yo hago mi propio trabajo, gracias. Pero si dices que trabajamos juntos por un objetivo común, y que tu función es esta y mi función es aquella, entonces sí, deberías trabajar para mí.

Lo gracioso es que, si bien nos estábamos ocupando mejor de nuestro negocio, creo que durante esos primeros años de tener nuestra propia empresa representante, Santana pasó menos tiempo en el estudio que en toda nuestra historia. Pasamos casi siete años sin ninguna grabación nueva de Santana desde el 93 (cuando grabamos los conciertos en México y en América del Sur para el proyecto *Sacred Fire*) hasta el 99, cuando empecé a trabajar en las canciones de *Supernatural*. No es que hubiese un problema creativo o musical. Nunca dudo de mí mismo en ese sentido; no sufro del bloqueo de los escritores. Sé que la música vendrá a través de mí. Simplemente sentí que no había ninguna necesidad. No sentía deseos de grabar. Y no dejamos de tocar en vivo; nuestra agenda de giras estaba ocupada.

Prefiero no hacer nada antes que hacer un álbum solo para mantener feliz a una compañía musical. Además, Davitt Sigerson se había ido de Polydor, así que nos pasaron a Island Records, donde el encargado era Chris Blackwell. Parte del nuevo contrato fue que obtuve mi propia compañía discográfica, que llamé Guts and Grace. De allí salieron cuatro álbumes; dos de ellos por Paolo Rustichelli: uno llamado *Santana Brothers* (éramos Jorge y yo, y nuestro sobrino Carlos Hernández, que toca guitarra y es un excelente compositor) y el otro llamado *Sacred Sources: Live Forever*. Ese álbum compilaba grabaciones en vivo de Jimi Hendrix, Marvin Gaye, Bob Marley, Stevie Ray Vaughan y Coltrane: todos portadores de mensajes. Fue un desafío lograr que todas las partes aceptaran (todos los herederos y sus abogados), pero valió la pena para poder lanzar mucha de la música poco conocida de mi colección, que quizá si no nunca hubiera salido.

Guts and Grace ya no existe, pero lo bueno que salió de allí es que aprendí que cualquiera puede tener una compañía discográfica, pero si no logras que la música esté en las tiendas o en Internet y sea accesible al público, es como tener un coche sin llantas o gasolina. Necesitas tener mucha energía que te sustente en la empresa de la que eres parte. Hoy, por supuesto, con los sitios en línea y los MP3 todo es muy diferente, pero en ese entonces no sabíamos que todo el sistema de tiendas musicales y formatos físicos iba a cambiar.

Yo me sentía mal porque no tenía suficiente energía para presionar a Island para que se ocupara de mis lanzamientos. Parecía que Chris Blackwell no se estaba aplicando mucho a la tarea en ese entonces. A mis ojos, Island había hecho algunas cosas excelentes al promocionar a Bob Marley y la música reggae y toda esa música africana en Mango Records, pero hacia finales de los 90 creo que Chris estaría de acuerdo en que nadie en Island estaba realmente presente.

*   *   *

Administrar tu propia carrera no es fácil al comienzo; había muchas cosas que desconocíamos. Nos reunimos con abogados y contadores y otra gente de negocios para averiguar cómo podíamos obtener más dinero de antiguas grabaciones, y de las imágenes y portadas del grupo, y del nombre Santana. Empezamos a estudiar cómo manejaban otras bandas sus negocios; Dave Matthews, Grateful Dead y Metallica nos ayudaron y nos mostraron lo que hacían. Empezamos a preguntar lo mismo que preguntaban otras bandas: ¿cómo podemos usar nuestro dinero para ayudar a la gente directamente en vez de pagar impuestos que solo terminan apoyando al Pentágono? Aprendimos que todo en la vida es un proceso de aprendizaje.

En 1998, a través de Santana Management, creamos la Fundación Milagro (*Milagro Foundation*) para ayudar a los niños y adolescentes en crisis. Esa todavía es la misión de la fundación. Al principio, Deborah y Kitsaun ayudaban a administrarla. Luego encontramos a Shelley Brown, que había sido directora de la escuela primaria de Salvador, en San Rafael. Su experiencia en el manejo de una escuela pública, haciendo que las cosas funcionaran para una multitud de niños diferentes y, básicamente, manteniéndolos a todos unidos (afroamericanos, blancos, asiáticos y latinos), nos hizo pensar en ella como la persona adecuada. Ella ha sido increíble. Ahora están a cargo Shelley, Ruthie Moutafian, mi hermana María, y todo un equipo completo. Desde que comenzó la fundación, hemos donado casi seis millones de dólares para apoyar a los jóvenes en todas partes del mundo.

¿Por qué el nombre Milagro? Porque creo que la vida se trata de hacer que sucedan milagros; que no importa cuánto dinero demos, el regalo más valioso que podemos ofrecer a los jóvenes es ayudarlos a salirse de los límites de las creencias, alentándolos a creer que sus sueños no son imposibles y que pueden permitir que la voz de la divinidad dirija su vida. Si podemos enseñarle a la gente a lanzar canastas de tres puntos en baloncesto y cómo tener una dieta saludable, también podemos enseñarles a los niños en crisis a ser felices por solo quince minutos al día (luego, por una hora, y luego, por el día entero), y eso es un milagro. Si podemos hacer que las personas dejen de criticarse unas a otras (y a sí mismas) y vean el lado brillante de la vida, eso es un milagro. El objetivo de la fundación es elevar la consciencia y despertar la divinidad a una edad temprana, vulnerable.

Realmente es el mismo mensaje que le digo a todos los públicos: puedes hacer de cada día el mejor día de tu vida, empezando por hoy. Creo que ese es el mayor milagro que puedes darte a ti mismo, y no depende de nadie más que de ti. Puedes hacer que suceda, empezando ahora mismo.

Milagro empezó cerca de casa, dando dinero a una organización que ayuda a los fugitivos que vienen a través de Larkin Street en San Francisco, donde está la estación de autobuses. Esta organización llega a los niños antes de que lo hagan las drogas y los proxenetas, dándoles un lugar para dormir, bañarse y reponerse, para que puedan decidir cuáles serán sus próximos pasos. También apoyamos a un centro comunitario en Marin City, donde el personal les enseña a los niños a cultivar plantas, y comenzamos a patrocinar a jóvenes músicos.

Otra cosa que hace la fundación es fomentar programas que alejen a los niños de los vecindarios pobres de las ciudades, aunque sea solo por un día, y los acerquen a la naturaleza, a ver los árboles y respirar aire puro. Hemos ayudado a gente joven a salir de Oakland para ir al parque de secuoyas, donde los árboles son como enormes catedrales que te ocultan del resto del mundo y parece que hubieran estado ahí tanto tiempo que no puedes calcular su antigüedad. ¿Puedes imaginar cómo se ve eso para un niño que nunca ha visto más que calles, edificios y cemento? No solo estamos elevando la consciencia; esto es más bien como reorganizarla.

Milagro ahora también está en México. En ciudades fronterizas como Tijuana y Juárez, hay muchos niños que están en crisis, sobreviviendo en las calles y viviendo en túneles por la noche. Están hambrientos, así que inhalan mucho pegamento para no pensar en el hambre. Estamos tratando de conectarnos con ellos para salvarlos de ese tipo de existencia. En Autlán ahora hay una clínica de salud y un centro comunitario llamado Santuario de Luz, que Milagro ayudó a fundar en 2005 con el Dr. Martín Sandoval Gómez, y realmente ha tenido un impacto increíble en la ciudad. La clínica proporciona un servicio de ambulancia e instalaciones modernas que nunca antes había habido en Autlán. Yo fui allá en el 2006 y me recibieron con honores. La gente venía de diversas ciudades alrededor de Jalisco para verme y contarme cómo lo que estábamos haciendo con el Dr. Martín había afectado sus vidas. Escuchar eso fue mejor que recibir cualquier cantidad de premios Grammy.

Creo que es importante comprender que la Fundación Milagro comenzó antes de que lanzáramos *Supernatural*; no fue algo que surgió de preguntarnos: "¿qué podemos hacer con todo este dinero?". Surgió de preguntarnos: "¿cómo podemos compartir lo que tenemos?". Realmente se remonta a mucho tiempo antes, a mi mamá y su poderosa energía de compartir. Ella nos decía a mis hermanos y a mí: "Todo sabe mejor cuando lo compartes". Y luego ponía helado o tacos o frijoles frente a nosotros. Milagro es sobre proporcionar alimento para el alma y el espíritu, que, al igual que el alimento físico, sabe mejor cuando lo compartes con quienes lo necesitan.

¿Recuerdas esa pareja de Saint Louis, David y Thelma Steward, que me dijo algo que me impresionó? "Es una bendición ser una bendición". Es así. Es una bendición estar bendecido con los recursos y los contactos para ayudar a muchas personas y hacer que funcione. Yo pasé a formar parte de una comunidad de dadores, y no puedo dejarme engañar por mi ego diciendo: "Mira qué especial que soy y lo que estoy haciendo". Tengo que estar abierto a conocer y apoyar a otras personas que están haciendo el mismo trabajo.

Andre Agassi y Steffi Graf crearon una escuela en Las Vegas en medio del gueto, la cual tiene una tasa de graduación de casi el 100 por ciento. Algunos propietarios de casinos dan dinero a la escuela, y hay un concierto a beneficio cada año que la apoya; yo he tocado en el concierto, al igual que Tony Bennett y Elton John. Debería haber escuelas como esa en cada ciudad: si las hubiera, podrías ver los beneficios que trae para la gente de los alrededores en apenas unos años. Hay un dicho que me gusta decir una y otra vez: "La consciencia puede ser rentable".

Me hace feliz saber que hay una confederación de esperanza: Bill Gates, Paul Allen, Matt Damon, Sean Penn, Danny Glover, Bono, Elton John, Angelina Jolie, Morgan Freeman, Ashley Judd, George Clooney, Bruce Springsteen, el Dalái Lama, el arzobispo Desmond Tutu y muchos otros. Están todos en la misma sintonía, haciendo aquello en lo que realmente creen. Ojalá tuviéramos la oportunidad de juntar todo e implementar programas, escuelas e instalaciones que puedan ayudar a inculcar la mecánica de la igualdad, la equidad y la justicia.

También me hace feliz que a veces suene mi teléfono y sea Harry Belafonte. No creo que nadie hoy tenga la misma claridad espiritual y brújula moral que él; decididamente, nadie la ha tenido tanto tiempo como él. Él ya estaba trabajando contra el apartheid antes de que Nelson Mandela fuera a prisión, y luego luchó por la liberación de Mandela hasta que finalmente sucedió. Él es un pilar de nuestra comunidad, alguien en quien la gente puede confiar, psicológica y moralmente, que estará presente en un 100 por ciento, y que no será nada menos que su luz.

La primera vez que hablamos lo llamé Sr. Belafonte, y él me dijo que no lo viese como a alguien superior. "Tú eres uno de nosotros; estamos a la misma altura". Le dije que pensaba que yo todavía estaba tratando de llegar allí, pero podría haberme derretido ahí mismo cuando me dijo eso. Hablamos mucho, y creo que parte del motivo por el que nos hicimos amigos tan rápido es porque ambos somos defensores de la libertad y nos mantenemos firmes en nuestras palabras y creencias. Quienes producen el evento Kennedy Center Honors estaban pensando en pedirle a Harry que me presentara a mí en la ceremonia del 2013, y yo hablé con él al respecto. Harry me dijo: "Primero quiero que veas un discurso en YouTube". Era el que dio él en la cena de la NAACP (Asociación Nacional para el Progreso de las Personas de Color) para honrar a Jamie Foxx y otros, donde hablaba sobre el control de armas y el racismo: "El río de sangre que riega las calles de nuestra nación proviene mayormente de los cuerpos de nuestros niños negros".

Lo que decía Harry era verdad, y me sentí honrado de que haya aceptado presentarme. Mi amigo Hal Miller me dio un consejo: me dijo que yo iba a ir a Washington para ser honrado por la nación y que este no era el momento ni el lugar para entrar en guerra. "Disfruta y saborea la experiencia", me recomendó. Y sugirió que también le pidiera a Harry que bajara un poco el tono. Le dije a Harry: "Saquemos la parte de la guerra". Él aceptó: "De acuerdo… pero no toda".

Puedes ver la presentación de Harry en el Kennedy Center Honors en línea, incluido lo que dijo sobre mí y sobre el control de la inmigración mexicana. Decidió ir por las risas, pero aun así transmitió su mensaje. Me encanta su espíritu y lo que hizo esa noche. Estoy muy orgulloso de llamarlo mi amigo, y hemos hecho mucho trabajo juntos, especialmente en apoyo a Sudáfrica.

Creo que el compartir y el brindar apoyo siempre tienen que ver con la igualdad y la justicia. Son bendiciones, y no algo para vender o para mantener alejado de la gente. Si eso es ser político, está bien. El Sr. Belafonte, mejor dicho, Harry, no puede ser el único que expresa su opinión.

Una vez yo estaba trabajando con el actor Morgan Freeman contra una ley anti-inmigración en Atlanta, y explicó que la mayoría de la gente no comprende que cuando los políticos aprueban una ley como esa, están impidiendo que las personas hagan su aporte a la comunidad y la conviertan en un lugar mejor para todos. Él tenía razón; para que la sociedad crezca, debe cambiar. El crecimiento implica un cambio, y debe ser así para todo el mundo.

Cuando fui a la Casa Blanca para el evento Kennedy Center Honors, estaba hablando sobre esto con Shirley MacLaine, y de repente me frenó: "¿Qué acabas de decir?". Le respondí: "El patriotismo es prehistórico". Ella asintió con la cabeza. "¿Esa expresión la inventaste tú?"

Creo que lo que estaba diciendo resonó en Shirley porque ella es una persona de pensamiento progresista. Quiero decir, necesitamos actualizar el software en nuestro cerebro y empezar a mirar nuestro planeta desde la vista aérea. Incluso si jamás viajas fuera de tu ciudad natal o tu vecindario, sigues viviendo aquí en un mundo donde todo está conectado. Esa interconexión está allí para que la conozcas, la descubras y la escuches: es el Tono Universal, la vibración del sonido que nos recuerda que la distancia y la separación son una ilusión.

Hasta el día de hoy detesto a cualquiera que trate de adoctrinar a otros para que odien a los que son diferentes y a los que tratan de salir adelante y elevarse. Lo detesto tanto como detestaba cuando algunos mexicanos trataban de hacerme odiar a los gringos. Eso es lo que trataban de inculcarme en Tijuana, pero tampoco me creí esas mentiras. Todos somos personas. Las demás cuestiones (como banderas, fronteras, tercer mundo, primer mundo) son pura ilusión. Me gusta la idea de una familia mundial bajo una sola bandera: un sol y las siluetas de una mujer, un hombre, una niña y un niño. Todas esas divisiones ilusorias nos mantienen atascados en el mismo lugar donde estábamos hace cien mil años: neandertales peleando por algún maldito cerro.

Cualquier padre puede verse a sí mismo en su pequeño hijo o hija. Creo que cada uno de mis hijos heredó una parte de mí, y luego eso se amplificó. También creo que cada uno de ellos —Salvador, Stella y Jelli—tiene una convicción suprema, como su abuela Josefina. Sal es un abanderado del respeto y del compromiso espiritual. Jelli es política, la que lucha por los derechos. Ella sabe de historia y trabaja en la oficina de Santana con los archivos. Stella siempre tiene algo importante para decir; le gusta ser el foco de atención.

Solíamos decirle a Stella "CNN" porque siempre era la primera en saltar para contarme todo cuando yo llegaba a casa. Me parece verla todavía chupándose el pulgar, rascándose la ceja y diciendo: "¿Y sabes qué pasó entonces?". Yo le decía: "No, pero estoy seguro de que me lo vas a contar". Y entonces escuchábamos el relato con todos los detalles. Stella era la que, si le parecía oler que alguien estaba fumando marihuana, amenazaba: "¡Le voy a decir a mamá!"

Stella es mi Josefina, la que te pone a prueba, más que Jelli y mucho más que Salvador. También es como yo en sus sentimientos acerca de la escuela y la iglesia. Una vez recibí una llamada telefónica de una maestra de la escuela secundaria católica a la que iba Stella en ese momento. "Disculpe, Sr. Santana, pero tenemos un problema con Stella. Como sabe, somos una escuela católica y una de las materias es el estudio de la Biblia. Hoy estábamos leyendo sobre cómo Eva fue hecha de la costilla de Adán, y Stella comenzó a discutir en voz alta sobre el pasaje, diciendo cosas como: 'Chicos, ¿ustedes no creerán toda esta historia, no?'".

Esa es mi hija.

Luego los administradores me pidieron que fuera a la escuela a la mañana siguiente, y si bien generalmente me levanto tarde, me presenté allí a las 7:30. No hablamos mucho sobre Stella, pero me mostraron todas las instalaciones durante cuarenta minutos y luego ya me imaginé lo que vendría.

Me mostraron un espacio donde esperaban construir un gimnasio nuevo y me preguntaron si podría hacer algunos conciertos allí para recaudar dinero. ¿O si podía donar el dinero?

Yo estaba volviendo a casa en el coche y estaba en medio del puente Golden Gate cuando recibí una llamada de Stella. "Papá, ¿qué les dijiste?". Ella se refería a su discusión sobre la Biblia; no sabía sobre la charla por la recaudación de fondos. Le dije que había dado la misma respuesta a los dos asuntos: no, no iba a reprimirla a ella por cuestionar esas creencias, y cuando me pidieron una donación les dije: "Gracias por tomarse el tiempo para mostrarme la escuela. Tengo dos preguntas: ¿ustedes cobran una matrícula a todos los alumnos aquí, verdad? Y además, vi una foto enorme del papa cuando entré a la escuela. La Iglesia Católica tiene miles de millones, ¿no pueden pedirle a él?". El director indicó que por tal o cual motivo se habían divorciado oficialmente del Vaticano. Yo le contesté: "¿Y no recibieron ninguna pensión alimenticia?".

El modo en que resumiría a Stella es que nació para ser el centro de atención, por cómo se ve y se comporta, pero al mismo tiempo, quiere ser invisible. A veces le tomo el pelo y le pregunto cómo hace para andar de incógnito. Ella alza su mano y la ubica frente a mi cara: "Háblale a la mano". Con mis hijos siempre estoy aprendiendo nuevas formas de comunicarme.

Jelli es la hippie de la familia, la que quiere ayudar a salvar al mundo. El otro día me llamó y estaba tan emocionada: "¡Estoy con Angela Davis!" Estaba en una conferencia y acababan de conocerse. Más tarde Jelli me dijo que Angela le había dicho algo que realmente le quedó dando vueltas... que cuando era joven tenía más coraje. Yo le dije: "Hmm. ¿Qué piensas de eso, Jelli?".

Jelli tiene los pies en la tierra y es muy sensata. Tiene un pensamiento profundo y facilidad de palabras. Le encanta Dolores Huerta. El año pasado la arrestaron por meterse en una propiedad privada, en una protesta en honor a Trayvon Martin. La esposaron y tuvimos que pagar una fianza para sacarla. No sé si lo hará otra vez porque fue una experiencia bastante intensa, y nadie quiere tener eso en sus antecedentes. Pero Jelli es como es.

Cuando se graduó de la secundaria, todos los alumnos tenían que hablar y citar a alguien, y ella se levantó y dijo: "Yo soy el que tiene que morir cuando me llegue el momento, así que déjenme vivir mi vida como yo quiero". Recuerdo que pensé: "¡Diablos!" Estaba citando a Jimi Hendrix. Jelli va a ser una mujer fuerte. Recuerdo que, cuando nació, la miré a los ojos y pensé: "Esta va a ser realmente intensa; tiene un ímpetu diferente. Tiene la capacidad de crear un impacto mundial con lo que sea que decida ser y hacer". Hasta ahora no me ha fallado.

Mis hijos, cuando entran a una habitación, la iluminan con su luz. Cuando hablo con ellos, individual o colectivamente, veo que aspiran (como todos nosotros) a hacer de este mundo un mejor lugar para vivir. Y los amo por eso.

A finales de los 90, mi papá comenzó a tocar música cada vez con menos frecuencia. Aún le gustaba caminar y nunca había aprendido a conducir un coche. También le gustaba escuchar su música en casetes. Creo que uno de los mejores regalos que le hice fue un Walkman; caminaba de aquí para allá escuchando su música y luego transcribía las canciones en papel. Yo lo visitaba y nos sentábamos juntos en el sofá. Él me tomaba la mano, y sus manos eran como las de John Lee Hooker: increíblemente suaves. Solía tocarme los dedos sin decir nada. Así es como nos comunicábamos al final. José murió el 1.º de noviembre de 1997.

Cuando llegó el final, yo estaba junto a su cama, observando y esperando, mientras todo comenzaba a apagarse. El espíritu se mantenía fuerte mientras que el cuerpo se volvía más y más débil. Pasé por eso con mi papá, luego con mi mamá en el 2009, y este año (2014), con Armando. Todos comenzaron a verse como bebés recién nacidos: arrugados y casi sin cabello. Estaban llenos de una luz que se iba haciendo más y más brillante. No sentí miedo y no lloré; había llegado el momento, para cada uno de ellos. Me senté con ellos, sostuve sus manos y les dije que estaba bien que partieran si deseaban hacerlo. Que aquí todo estaría bien.

He visto llorar a mucha gente. Las únicas veces que lloré fue en los funerales de Bill Graham y Tony Williams, quizá porque sus muertes fueron muy inesperadas. No recuerdo haber llorado por mi mamá o por mi papá; creo que porque pude decirles todo lo que quería decirles. Cuando sea mi hora de partir, ruego tener la fortaleza de aceptar que todas las cosas que tuve (mi cuerpo, mis habilidades, mi cerebro y mi imaginación) eran un préstamo de Dios. Cuando él me pida que se las devuelva, le diré: "Gracias, hombre, por permitirme disfrutar de todo esto, porque realmente lo hice".

La última vez que vi a mi papá de cerca y claramente fue en un sueño que tuve, aproximadamente un año y medio después de que muriera. Él estaba en una montaña, con su chaqueta azul favorita. Yo estaba en un coche con mi hermano Jorge. "¡Ahí está papá! ¡Detén el coche!" Corrí hasta él, y él miraba hacia otro lado, a un río que destellaba como si en vez de agua llevase diamantes.

"¡Papá!" Realmente lo agarré porque, si no lo hacía, pensé que podría despertarme y perderlo. Él se dio vuelta y pude oler su perfume. Sentí su piel junto a la mía. Antes de despertarme, me miró y me dijo: "Él me está llamando. Ahora necesito ir con él. Debo decirte que no comprendí muchas cosas que hiciste o dijiste, pero quiero que sepas que ahora entiendo por qué eres como eres".

CAPÍTULO 22

No soy muy fanático de las entregas de premios, sea que las esté observando o participando de ellas; todos los artistas van en busca del big bang, de ese gran momento donde el teatro explota de aplausos. Demasiadas veces puedes sentir esa desesperación: "Este es el momento, viejo. ¡Tengo que llegar a la cima!" Es el mismo tipo de desesperación que sienten los muchachos que tienen que cantar el himno nacional, que es muy difícil de cantar, porque es una canción muy extraña. En algún momento en los 90 estaba viendo un partido de la NBA, y recuerdo un tipo que estaba vestido con un traje rojo y era una estrella del deporte (para nada

*conocido por cantar) que se levantó y dijo: "¿Están preparados?", como
advirtiendo que iba a hacer algo fenomenal. A mí me pareció una actitud
bastante engreída y pensé: "Ahora mejor que cantes como Caruso, amigo".*

*Supe que estaba en problemas desde la primera nota, porque empezó
muy alto; iba a necesitar un elevador expreso para llegar a la parte de
"rockets' red glare"… Creo que, si vas a ir por el momento, debería ser el
mismo momento que intentas lograr cada noche; el éxito es producto de
mucha práctica y de la confianza suprema en saber quién eres.*

*He mejorado mi presentación en las entregas de premios y espectá-
culos de televisión, y en saber qué decir cuando me piden que diga algunas palabras. Me gusta más cuando tocamos con la banda; me
enorgullece que Santana saque lo mejor de sí en una sola toma, no
importa cuándo se encienda la luz roja. Siempre sabemos lo que estamos haciendo y cómo vamos a sonar.*

*También me gustan los momentos en que no es Santana; es Carlos
con alguien más, como la vez que toqué "Black Magic Woman" con
Peter Green, cuando Fleetwood Mac ingresó en el Salón de la Fama del
Rock and Roll, en 1998. Me sentía orgulloso de que Santana hubiera
ingresado el año anterior, pero también fue cuando les di un buen tirón
de orejas porque todavía no habían incluido a Ritchie Valens. Quiero
decir, ¿qué es el rock and roll sin "La Bamba"? Rock and roll no significa blanco y popular; significa relevante para siempre. Finalmente, en
el 2000, Ritchie ingresó al Salón de la Fama.*

*Te contaré sobre uno de mis momentos favoritos de todos los tiem-
pos. En el 2004 me honraron con un premio Grammy Latino a la Persona del Año, en Los Ángeles. Era la escena típica: gente famosa en
trajes y vestidos largos bajando de limusinas; muchos discursos y ovacio-
nes. Quincy Jones y Salma Hayek me entregaron el premio y, antes de
que yo empezara a hablar, alguien gritó: "¡Ese es mi hermano!" Era
Jorge. La forma en que lo dijo, a viva voz y directo de su corazón, fue tan
adorable que casi pierdo la compostura.*

*Por favor, no me pidas que camine por la alfombra roja. Lo hice por
Deborah cuando salió su libro, y lo haría en cualquier momento por
Cindy. Pero la mayoría de las veces, cuando voy a este tipo de espectáculos
de premios, entro por la cocina y saludo a los cocineros, mozos y*

lavaplatos. Todavía recuerdo la sensación en los dedos del agua caliente y grasienta, y cómo se me arrugaban las manos.

Y no me pidas que cante *el himno nacional. Recibo invitaciones todo el tiempo para tocarlo en la guitarra; lo único que puedo hacer es tratar de tocarlo tan bien como lo hacía Jimi. ¿Y ese tipo que lo cantó en el partido de la NBA? Clive me lo presentó una vez en una fiesta por* Supernatural; *estaba de pie allí con el saxofonista Kenny G. No me reí ni sonreí, pero estaba como loco diciéndole a mi cerebro que no pensara en lo que sentía sobre el jazz suave y sobre esa interpretación en el partido de baloncesto. Mi voz interna decía: "No lo menciones, hombre, no lo hagas".*

En 1997 empecé a tener la sensación de que estaba concibiendo algo nuevo; tenía un nuevo álbum en mi interior, e iba a ser algo especial. En ese entonces pensaba llamarlo *Serpents and Doves*, e iba a consistir en singles: el tipo de canciones que te atrapan inmediatamente, algo poderoso, con un mensaje que puede elevar y enseñar. Era hora de hacer algo de música nueva para el nuevo milenio.

Ese año me pidieron que hablara en un documental sobre Clive Davis y su filantropía. No hablado con Clive ni lo había visto en más de veinte años, pero sabía que desde que la CBS lo dejó ir en el 73, él había iniciado su propia compañía discográfica llamada Arista, y había tenido éxitos con gente como Barry Manilow, Whitney Houston y Aretha Franklin. También escuché sobre su trabajo filantrópico por lo que estábamos haciendo en la Fundación Milagro; estábamos todos en el mismo mundo.

Dije que estaría feliz de decir algunas palabras sobre Clive. "Voy a decir la verdad: este hombre es realmente importante para el mundo de la música y también para el bienestar de las personas". Los productores enviaron un equipo con una cámara, y cuando Clive vio la entrevista que me habían hecho, me llamó. "¡Eh, Clive! ¿Cómo estás, viejo?".

"Carlos, gracias por lo que dijiste. ¿En qué andas, qué estás haciendo ahora?".

Era una buena pregunta. No había sacado un nuevo álbum de

Santana en más de cuatro años. "Estoy tratando de terminar mi contrato con Island Records. Les debo dos álbumes más".

"Bueno, apenas termines con ellos, llámame".

En ese momento, Island solo era una parte de la gran ensalada de PolyGram, y parecía que Chris Blackwell estaba por irse, así que yo me iba a quedar atascado ahí en el limbo, solo. Chris se enteró de que yo no estaba contento con la situación, así que vino a ver el recital de Santana en Londres, y sabía que el grupo estaba pateando traseros más que nunca. Luego voló a Sausalito a reunirse conmigo. Nos encontramos en un restaurante llamado Horizons. Él iba a intentar convencerme de que me quedara. Recuerdo que tuvo que atender una llamada telefónica y, cuando volvió, se estaba quejando de que tenía problemas con la nueva configuración telefónica en la compañía discográfica. "No son capaces de gastar dinero para asegurarse de que yo pueda tener una buena comunicación telefónica con mi gente".

Y yo pensé: "¡Diablos! ¿Qué clase de mensaje es ese? ¿Y ahora va a tratar de convencerme de que me quede?". No quería hacerle perder más tiempo ni perder el mío, así que comencé a decirle lo que tenía para decirle.

"Chris, yo te respeto, así que quiero ser muy sincero contigo. Admiro profundamente todo lo que has hecho con Bob Marley, Steve Winwood, Baaba Maal y tantos otros músicos de África, Haití y de todo el mundo. Para mí eres un aliado y un artista. Pero sé que el nuevo álbum que se está gestando en mi interior es realmente bueno; puedo sentirlo en mis entrañas. Realmente es importante para mí que no se lo dé a una compañía discográfica que lo va a dejar durmiendo en algún depósito y donde terminará siendo una deducción de impuestos que nadie va a escuchar.

"De un artista a otro, te lo pido, déjame ir".

Chris me miró y luego miró al techo por un momento. Pudo ver que yo no iba a cambiar de idea. Finalmente me dijo: "Carlos, dile a tu abogado que llame a mi abogado. Quedas libre". Fue así de simple. Podría haberme pedido que pagara por los álbumes que todavía le debía o podría haberme cobrado esa suma cuando saliera *Supernatural*, pero no lo hizo. Me liberó de toda atadura, y lo hizo con mucha integridad. Por ese gesto le estaré eternamente agradecido. Se podría decir que la primera persona responsable de la creación de *Supernatural* fue Chris Blackwell.

La otra persona que hizo posible el nacimiento de ese álbum al reunirme con Clive, fue Deborah. Una vez que quedé libre de Island, ella fue la que dijo: "Bien, ahora tienes que volver con Clive. Podría ser una buena oportunidad para que te enganches de nuevo con él y quizá para volver a la radio".

¿A la radio? Recuerdo que me pregunté si eso todavía existiría como posibilidad, y si tendría alguna importancia. Hacía tanto tiempo que Santana no sonaba en ninguna radio. Una parte de mí pensaba: "No tengo los medios para entender la radio ahora". No es que antes los hubiera tenido, tampoco.

Al principio me resistía a llamar a Clive porque nuestra última interacción había sido en 1973, y Clive no había estado muy feliz con la dirección de Santana en ese entonces. Sabía que trabajar con él ahora significaría más que simplemente conversar sobre una canción o dos y luego decir: "Hasta pronto; te enviaré el álbum cuando lo tengamos listo". Pero Deborah me dijo que escuchara lo que Clive tenía que decir. Ella fue clave para nuestro reencuentro. Me ayudó a salirme de mi propio camino cuando un ángel estaba tratando de ayudarme.

Lo llamé a Clive y lo invité a que viniera a escuchar a Santana en el Radio City Music Hall. En un momento, hice un alto en la función para hacerle un reconocimiento desde el escenario. "Damas y caballeros, esta noche tenemos presente a alguien que, como Bill Graham, es un arquitecto de esta música. Sin él, hubiera sido realmente difícil que ustedes conocieran a Janis Joplin, Sly Stone, Simon and Garfunkel, y muchas otras bandas, incluida la nuestra. Se trata del Sr. Clive Davis". Me sentí muy bien al hacerlo: era la primera vez que tenía la oportunidad de reconocerlo públicamente de esa manera. El público lo ovacionó de pie.

Caminamos después del concierto. En realidad, solo nos hacíamos dos preguntas: ¿queríamos trabajar juntos? Y de ser así, ¿cómo lo haríamos? Clive dijo algo que me gustó; él era muy directo y usó

488 · CARLOS SANTANA

una palabra muy espiritual. "¿Tienes la voluntad? ¿Tienes la voluntad de disciplinarte a ti mismo y de subirte al *ring* conmigo para que trabajemos juntos cuando empiece a llamar a todos en mi Rolodex? ¿Confiarás en mí?".

Explicó que no quería solamente hacer otro álbum de Santana; quería éxitos. Todo aquel que haya trabajado con él sabe que Clive Davis solo tiene una cosa en mente: tiene que ser número uno en la radio todo el tiempo. El mensaje era que él estaría involucrado de arriba abajo, eligiendo las canciones, sugiriendo cosas en el estudio y decidiendo sobre la estrategia publicitaria.

Clive me dijo algo más. Incluso antes de que nos hayamos reunido, él había hablado con un grupo de músicos con quienes estaba trabajando y les preguntó: "¿Les interesaría trabajar con Carlos Santana? ¿Quieren grabar con él?". Me sorprendió porque yo pensaba que recurriría a artistas del rock clásico, a gente de mi generación. En el 95 habíamos llevado a cabo una gira con Jeff Beck que estuvo fantástica, y Santana, la formación original, había sido reclutada para el Salón de la Fama del Rock en el 97. Yo pensaba en la vieja escuela, pero Clive dijo: "Sí, Lauryn Hill de The Fugees, Rob Thomas de Matchbox Twenty, Dave Matthews, Eagle-Eye Cherry; todos esos increíbles artistas y músicos quieren trabajar contigo". Yo conocía los nombres y algo de su música, y me gustó la idea.

"¿Quieren tocar conmigo, ayudar a Santana a volver a la radio? Perfecto, entonces; hagámoslo". Firmamos con Arista.

Después Clive me contó que lo que más lo convenció para hacer el proyecto fue que cuando comenzó a realizar los llamados telefónicos para ver a quiénes les interesaría, todos dijeron que sí. "No estoy min-tiendo: todos. Yo sabía que haría algo contigo, ya que no importaba a quién preguntara: la respuesta era 'sí' ".

Yo estaba entusiasmado porque ya había comenzado a grabar. Había algunas canciones de *Supernatural* que yo había querido grabar aun antes de que comenzáramos a hablar. Puedes adivinar cuáles. Tienen el estilo tradicional de Santana y son el tipo de canciones que mi padre hubiera escogido: "(Da Le) Yaleo" y "Africa Bamba". A medida que pasaba el tiempo, Clive se involucraba cada vez más en las sesiones debido a las colaboraciones y por ser quien es, y su manera de trabajar: ponía manos a la obra con una dedicación máxima a los detalles, tales como la forma de la canción y la combinación entre músicos y productores. Yo había trabajado en colaboraciones anteriormente, pero este álbum de Santana tendría diferentes grupos y productores en cada pista, según el estilo y la dirección de cada canción. Eso era algo nuevo para nosotros.

En esa época me sentía bendecido con una banda maravillosa; CT estaba conmigo, al igual que Benny y Rodney Holmes, que es un magnífico baterista con una energía absolutamente increíble, un genio musical. Fue un honor crear *Supernatural* con él y otros de los miembros de Santana, al igual que con los numerosos músicos que nos acompañaron en cada pista.

Por un momento debo detenerme y concentrarme en Rodney y otros bateristas. Rodney es uno de esos músicos completos: es inteligente, y puede escuchar y reaccionar, además de que posee la combinación correcta de *chops*, que son técnicas de percusión, y musicalidad. Lo vi tocar por primera vez en un club de la ciudad de Nueva York. Noté que el pianista Cecil Taylor estaba allí y se volvió loco simplemente al observarlo. Wayne Shorter lo llamaba Rodney Podney y lo incorporó a su banda en 1996.

Soy quisquilloso con los bateristas. No pido disculpas por eso, ya que desde hace mucho tiempo sé que para que Santana sea Santana necesitamos un baterista con un gran ritmo agradable y un dinamismo valiente y, además, que tenga la habilidad de escuchar y aprender, de meterse en la música y de hacerla chispear. Justo antes de tenerlo a Rodney tuvimos a Horacio "El Negro" Hernández, que trajo consigo un fuerte estilo cubano, y unos años después de Rodney, Dennis Chambers vino a la banda. Dennis quizá sea el mejor baterista de *groove* metal del planeta en este momento, con un control muy importante. Es una institución en sí mismo; con la sola mención de su nombre, la mayoría de los bateristas se arrodillan para rendirle homenaje. Dennis fue el baterista que estuvo con Santana durante más tiempo. Creo que al principio intimidaba a algunos de la banda debido a su reputación, pero a medida que lo conocían se daban cuenta de que le encanta hacer chistes y es muy fácil estar con él. Lo curioso es que conocí a Dennis cuando él estaba tocando con John McLaughlin en los 90. Justo frente a John, él preguntó: "Entonces, ¿cuándo vas a llamarme?".

Esa fue una de las rúbricas más importantes de Santana a lo largo de los años: un baterista flexible con un control importante y un dinamismo potente, y dos percusionistas que pueden tocar lo que sea y lograr que todo sea posible. Mantuvimos ese sonido para *Supernatural*.

Clive solía llamarme. "Tengo una canción para ti. Voy para allá". O decía: "Wyclef Jean tiene algo que quiere que tú escuches". Wyclef vino y cantó la canción allí mismo, en el estudio. Se me acercó y colocó su rostro cerca del mío. Era como si estuviese leyendo una partitura en mis ojos; a continuación él estaba mostrándonos la letra de "Maria Maria" como si supiera que toda mi familia veía *West Side Story* y lo que esa película significaba para los mexicanos como nosotros.

Clive tenía la capacidad de adentrarse verdaderamente en los detalles. Cierta vez en el estudio, estábamos grabando una melodía y él se dirigió a uno de los cantantes. "Hazme sentirla. Hazme sentirla *ahora*, ¿me oyes?". Las venas se le explotaban. Yo pensaba: "Oh, rayos". No conocía este costado de Clive, ¡nunca lo había visto en 1973! Pero él tenía razón, es lo mismo que yo les digo a los cantantes: no vendas algo, ofrece tu corazón. Me impresionaba que Clive pudiera escuchar la diferencia. El cantante me miraba como diciendo "¿qué está pasando?". Mientras, yo pensaba: "Deberías haberlo traído desde el primer momento, viejo".

Las sesiones eran divertidas porque todas eran diferentes. Venía gente nueva a la banda, como el "Gentleman" Jeff Cressman en el trombón, y así conocía a más músicos que de costumbre. Hubo dos a los que llegué a conocer muy bien y con los que aún tengo una relación muy estrecha: Rob Thomas y Dave Matthews. Ambos están muy presentes con su música y su espíritu, y se dedican tanto a los ámbitos espirituales como a los reinos externos. Quieren hacer que este mundo sea hermoso, y pienso que Clive sabía esto cuando los juntó.

Las últimas dos canciones que hicimos para el álbum fueron "The Calling", una sesión de *blues* con Eric Clapton, y "El Farol", que tiene una melodía que Sal me ayudó a escribir y es un verdadero testimonio del amor que mi madre y mi padre se tenían.

Cuando comenzamos la grabación, yo ya tenía un nombre para este álbum: *Mumbo Jumbo*. Me gustaba porque realmente existió un Mumbo Jumbo, que fue un rey africano. Incluso teníamos listo el diseño de la portada: una pintura llamada *Mumbo Jumbo* del artista Michael Rios, que diseñó muchas de las playeras que me gusta usar.

Sin embargo, cuando estábamos por llegar a la última canción, Clive me dijo: "Sabes, Carlos, voy a tener que disentir respetuosamente de ti. Mucha gente piensa que 'mumbo jumbo' es algo negativo, algo así como palabras mágicas que en realidad no son mágicas, y eso no es lo que queremos. Además, creo que la prensa haría de las suyas con ese nombre y no precisamente de forma halagadora". Respondí: "Pero Mumbo Jumbo efectivamente existió, tú lo sabes; fue un personaje histórico que curaba a la gente". Clive replicó: "Sí, está bien, pero… como sea, tenemos que dirigirnos a la prensa lo antes posible".

Luego se nos ocurrió *Supernatural*, que tiene dos significados: "místico" y "sobrenatural". Efectivamente a mí me agradaba lo relativo al reino invisible y a la autenticidad. Además evocaba a Peter Green y su tema instrumental "The Supernatural", una canción que todavía adoro. Así que está bien, Clive, llamémoslo *Supernatural*.

Cuando el álbum estuvo listo, Clive organizó una reunión para preparar a las tropas y quería que yo estuviera allí. Se llevó a cabo en su oficina con todos los soldados y guerreros que iban a impulsar el álbum: agentes de promoción, representantes de comercialización, publicistas. Clive reprodujo el álbum completo, y me dieron una ovación de pie. Dije que estaba muy agradecido a Clive y a cada uno de ellos porque sabía que esa era la primera vez que trabajábamos juntos. Luego hablé de la música. Comenté que trataba de asegurarme de que cada nota que tocaba fuera tan genuina, fresca y peligrosa como un primer beso en el asiento trasero de un coche; tan fresca como el ahora eterno.

De repente Clive exclamó: "Eh, Carlos, lamento mucho interrumpirte, pero acabas de decir algo que para mí expresa exactamente lo que siento con respecto a este álbum. Todos saben que tú tienes una larga trayectoria, pero eso no es lo más especial de esta música. Es totalmente nueva y diferente, como tú describías, y eso es lo que el público necesita saber. Tenemos que trabajar en ella como si fuera la primera vez que hacemos música". Yo estaba pensando lo mismo que Bill Graham señaló: "¿No es lo mismo que acabo de decir?".

Clive y yo estuvimos completamente en la misma frecuencia con *Supernatural* durante todo el proceso. Él se aseguró de que el mundo supiera que *Supernatural* pronto saldría a la luz, en junio de 1999, con anuncios publicitarios en revistas y carteleras en Manhattan y Las Vegas. Estábamos de gira ese verano con Dave Matthews y recuerdo que Dave siempre hablaba de todo el apoyo que recibíamos de Arista, y él mismo nos respaldó mucho.

Dave creía profundamente en la música. Una noche subió al escenario en Filadelfia y nos presentó, tocamos juntos "Love of My Life" y al público le encantó. La habíamos compuesto juntos. Él vino con las palabras y yo tenía la parte inicial de una melodía de Brahms que había escuchado en la radio. Después de que fui a Tower Records y la canté frente al vendedor del departamento de música clásica, él la reconoció de inmediato. Tenía el CD, y Dave y yo desarrollamos la canción sobre la base de este.

Me encantaba la manera en que Dave compartía su público conmigo, hablándole sobre la música que habíamos hecho y abriendo su corazón con respecto a cómo se sentía. Eso era lo que yo intentaba hacer con mi propio público: colocar estrías en sus cerebros y abrir algunos oídos. Esa fue la primera vez que sentí efectivamente que esta nueva música sería algo importante: cuando le encantó al público. Pocos días después de ese espectáculo de Filadelfia, nos encontrábamos tocando en el escenario del Meadowlands en Nueva Jersey, cuando Dave miró al cielo y vio un avión que llevaba un enorme cartel publicitario que decía "Este es el verano de Santana". Él dijo: "Clive los quiere mucho, viejo. Lo han logrado".

Clive lo había predicho incluso antes de que saliera el álbum: "Carlos, esto no será solo uno o dos millones de copias vendidas. Esto va a ser muy, muy grande". Después apareció la música, y "Smooth" comenzó lentamente, pero muy pronto despegó como un cohete. *Supernatural* empezó vendiendo cientos de miles de copias en una semana, y Clive solía llamarme adondequiera que yo estuviese para informarme sobre las cifras actualizadas de las ventas. En una ocasión me encontraba en un taxi, mientras él me decía por teléfono: "Carlos, están tocando tu música *por todos lados*".

No podía escucharlo bien. "Lo sé, Clive; está sonando en la radio del taxi justamente ahora".

Todo se convirtió en una locura, simplemente una locura. Después salió "Maria Maria" y llevó las ventas a otro nivel, aún más alto, y nunca más bajaron.

La formación de Santana en las primeras giras de *Supernatural* estaba en un momento único: teníamos a CT, Benny, Rodney y Karl, además de la sección de cuernos con Bill Ortiz, y Jeff Cressman en trompeta y trombón. Gracias a ellos pudimos hacer algunas melodías de uno de mis álbumes favoritos de Miles: la banda sonora que compuso para la película *Elevator to the Gallows* en 1958. También teníamos a René Martinez, un guitarrista clásico y de flamenco que en realidad era nuestro técnico de guitarras, pero tocaba con tanta dignidad y elegancia que le ofrecimos un espacio de presentación justo antes de que hiciéramos "Maria Maria" y causó sensación.

El año 2000, nuestro camino se cruzó con el de Sting en algunos festivales que se llevaron a cabo en Alemania. Según el programa, él debía tocar después de nosotros, pero la primera vez que nos escuchó, era obvio que había quedado impresionado. Sting me dijo esto una noche en mi camerino mientras yo tomaba una cerveza con mi amigo Hal Miller, que puede ser un tipo muy gracioso a veces. "Carlos, ¿quién diablos es ese baterista?".

"Es Rodney Holmes y es de Nueva York. Tocó con Wayne Shorter y con los Brecker Brothers".

"¡Es fantástico!", dijo Sting. "¿Y quién diablos es ese guitarrista?".

"Ah, ese es René Martinez, mi técnico de guitarras".

Sting se quedó sin palabras durante un segundo. "Espera, ¿es tu técnico? Increíble".

Con la precisión de un reloj, Hal intervino y exclamó: "Sí. Espera a escuchar tocar al técnico de baterías; su nombre es Elvin".

Sting se echó a reír y luego todos hicimos lo mismo. Esa era una formación absolutamente increíble y estoy orgulloso de que muchos de ellos aún sigan tocando con Santana.

Es bastante difícil describir qué se siente cuando algo alcanza semejante éxito, en todo el mundo, y estás en el medio de ello. Es como un corcho que flota en una inmensa ola en el océano, ¿cuánto controlo yo y cuánto me controla a mí? Todos los días es necesario revisar los juegos del ego y encontrar el equilibrio nuevamente.

En febrero de 2000, Clive me comunicó que *Supernatural* había sido nominado para diez premios Grammy. Deborah empezó a llamarme con un nuevo nombre aun antes de que asistiéramos al espectáculo. "Bueno, señor Grammy, ¿cuántos cree que ganará?". Los niños preguntaban: "Sí, papá, ¿cuántos?". Yo sentía que sería afortunado y estaría feliz con solo uno. Por ese motivo, cuando gané el primero durante el evento que tuvo lugar por la tarde, agradecí a todos los que pude: a Clive, a Deborah, a mi madre, a mi padre y a mis hijos. Al ganar el siguiente, agradecí a mis hermanos, a los músicos y a los compositores. Cuando llegó el momento del evento de la noche, que se emitía por televisión, me sentía como esos perros que juegan a llevar y traer un frisbee, y ocurrió algo gracioso: los ganadores de otras categorías, como música clásica y *country*, comenzaron a agradecerme por no haber hecho un álbum en sus géneros.

Tengo un recuerdo borroso de todo el evento, en realidad. Las dos cosas de las cuales me sentí más orgulloso fue cuando toqué "Smooth" sobre el escenario, en la que Rob Thomas cantó y Rodney Holmes entregó su alma. Toqué la primera nota y todos los presentes se levantaron de un salto. El segundo de mis momentos favoritos tuvo lugar cuando Lauryn Hill y mi viejo amigo Bob Dylan presentaron el premio al Álbum del Año; ese fue el octavo y último Grammy que *Supernatural* obtuvo. Abrieron el sobre y lo único que hizo Bob fue señalarme, sin pronunciar palabra. Me levanté para recibirlo y de repente tenía claro lo que debía decir.

"La música es el vehículo por el cual se transmite la magia de la sanación; la música de *Supernatural* fue destinada y designada para aportar unidad y armonía". Agradecí a los dos pilares personales que vinieron primero a mi mente: John Coltrane y John Lee Hooker.

Tengo que agradecer a tantas personas, y entre ellas a una personas a quien debo agradecer enormemente: Deborah, por ayudarme a ver el enojo que aún tenía en mi interior cuando en el año 2000 hice público, por primera vez, que había sido víctima de abusos sexuales. Odio esa palabra: *víctima*. No soy la clase de persona que entraría a una habitación y diría: "Hola, soy el tipo que fue abusado". *Sobreviviente* me gusta mucho más.

Solía encabronarme lo que me había ocurrido en Tijuana y, asimismo, que no contara con un sistema de apoyo para protegerme. Al mismo tiempo, ¿por qué no dije algo del abuso yo mismo? Entonces era enojo y sentimientos de culpa y reproches que daban vueltas uno tras otro, y yo los sentía como si fuesen grilletes y cadenas. Incluso cuando aún no sabía cómo llamarlo, yo tenía claro que deseaba un nivel de consciencia más elevado porque podía observar que la baja consciencia arrastra siempre un grillete y una cadena.

Creo que todos los individuos tienen algo del pasado, algún dolor o sufrimiento, al que deben enfrentarse; una energía negativa que necesitan transformar y dirigir hacia un lugar y un tiempo donde no sea perjudicial para ellos ni para nadie a su alrededor. Tú tienes que curarte a ti mismo. Una cosa que he aprendido en todos mis años en este planeta es que si deseas curar algo, no puedes hacerlo en la oscuridad. Debes llevarlo hacia la luz.

Ahí fue cuando el ángel Metatron me dijo que debía hacerlo: tenía que hablar públicamente sobre mi pasado.

Metatron es el arcángel de quien hablé en todas mis entrevistas ese año, el que había prometido colocar mi música en la radio y hacerla oír por todas partes, como nunca antes. "Cumplimos con nuestra promesa", me dijo. "Te hemos dado lo que dijimos que te daríamos. Ahora te pediremos algo a ti".

Para explicarlo mejor, Metatron es un arcángel, la forma celestial del patriarca judío Enoc, que aparece en muchos libros. Me hablaron de él por primera vez en el 95, cuando encontré *The Book of Knowledge: The Keys of Enoch*, que desde el principio me sacudió la cabeza. Pero mientras más lo estudiaba, más me daba cuenta de que en muchas formas era una especie de anexo de *The Urantia Book* y continuaba lo que yo ahora llamo velocidad hacia la luminosidad: la comprensión de cómo los planos físico y espiritual, el visible y el invisible, están interconectados de muchas maneras y cómo algunos libros pueden alcanzar una simultaneidad divina.

J. J. Hurtak es el autor de *The Book of Knowledge: The Keys of Enoch*, un historiador metafísico y un arqueólogo multidimensional. Lo conocí a él y a su esposa, Desiree, allá por la época de *Supernatural*, y se convirtieron para mí en simuladores de pensamiento y aceleradores de la iluminación, como Jerry y Diane, Wayne y Herbie. J. J. creó un video de imágenes simbólicas, luz y color que se corresponde con una música de plegaria de Alice Coltrane y prácticamente danza al ritmo de ella cuando los reproduzco al mismo tiempo. Esta combinación me llevó a presentarlos entre sí a los dos y a sugerirles que trabajaran juntos. El resultado fue un álbum increíble llamado *The Sacred Language of Ascension*, que combina las melodías de Turiya y de un órgano con letras y cantos religiosos en inglés, hebreo, hindú y arameo y que, espero, sea lanzado pronto.

Volviendo a Metatron, después de *The Book of Knowledge: The Keys of Enoch*, encontré *The Revelations of the Metatron* (traducido al español como *Las revelaciones de Metatron*), en el cual Metatron se ubica en el centro de la escena, y después de estudiar ese libro descubrí que en ocasiones él me hablaba mientras meditaba. Una noche me encontraba en Londres haciendo algunas cosas promocionales para *Supernatural*, espectáculos de televisión y entrevistas, cuando Metatron habló y me dijo: "Ahora que estás en la radio, debes recordar a todos que tienen la capacidad de hacer de sus vidas una obra maestra de la alegría". Pero había otra cosa.

"Luego nos gustaría que reveles que fuiste abusado sexualmente porque hay mucha gente que también ha pasado por una situación similar y que debe vivir con ese mismo tipo de herida. Invítalos a mirarse al espejo y decir: "No soy lo que me ocurrió".

Yo me resistía. Tenía que luchar contra mí mismo porque sabía que mis padres, mis hijos y todos mis hermanos verían todas las entrevistas que daría. El álbum *Supernatural* era lo máximo ese año, así que el foco estaba puesto en mí. Era hora de salir de la oscuridad y volver al público, pero me decía a mí mismo: "No, no lo haré".

Los ángeles no desistieron: Metatron requería altruismo. Próximamente tendría una entrevista con la *Rolling Stone* y otra con Charlie Rose. No quería hacerlo en ninguna de las dos; en realidad no quería hacerlo en ningún lado. No dormí durante noches pensando en eso. Finalmente, lo hice en la *Rolling Stone:* le conté al mundo lo que me había pasado cuando estaba en Tijuana. Sin detalles escabrosos; solo el hecho explícito de que había sido abusado cuando era niño y que aún conservo pureza e inocencia.

Es mi voz interior; todos la tienen. La tenía en el Tic Tock, incluso en Tijuana. Permanecía conmigo. Si no oyes esa voz, eres como un bote sin timón. Aprendes a confiar en ella. Cuando cantaba temas religiosos o cuando todo estaba en silencio y era tarde, podía escucharla y a veces, escribía lo que me decía. También le conté a la *Rolling Stone* sobre Metatron. "Mi realidad es que Dios te habla todos los días... tienes las velas, tienes el incienso y tienes los cantos religiosos, y de pronto escuchas esta voz: *Ahora, escríbelo*".

A *Supernatural* le fue tan bien y ayudó a atraer a tantos admiradores nuevos que todos los álbumes de Santana empezaron a venderse nuevamente, incluido el primer álbum y hasta *Caravanserai*. *Abraxas* fue un éxito otra vez, en CD. Los jóvenes revisaban nuestra historia, todo nuestro catálogo. Gracias a Bill Graham y a la cláusula "todos los formatos futuros" que él había incluido, ganábamos dinero por esos álbumes con los mismos porcentajes que cuando salieron por primera vez.

Santana a veces viajaba en asientos de primera clase, otras en clase turista, y en ocasiones nos alojábamos en moteles. Después de

Supernatural, comenzamos a viajar en primera clase y a hospedar-
nos en hoteles lujosos. Empezamos a hacer negocios como socios
con otras empresas, ayudándolos en la fabricación de sus productos,
no solo ofreciéndoles avales de productos. Nuestra primera asociación fue con la Brown Shoe Company. Creamos una línea completa
de zapatos con el nombre Carlos. Ahora también tenemos sombreros y tequila por medio de estos mismos tipos de relaciones.

Nuestro contrato con Arista tenía que ser reformulado porque
el pecio pautado para *Supernatural* había sido muy bajo y querían
asegurarse de tener nuestro próximo álbum. La manera habitual
en que las grandes compañías discográficas hacían el seguimiento
de un álbum megaplatino era proporcionarles a los músicos una
gran bonificación, que en realidad era un anticipo que al final debía
devolverse. Pero si al álbum siguiente no le iba tan bien, entonces
los músicos quedaban adeudando dinero hasta que lograran otro
éxito. Eso es lo que sucedió con Prince y Warner Bros.

A Deborah se le ocurrió otra idea, y se la comentamos a nuestro
abogado: "Pidamos una bonificación no reembolsable, no un anticipo
que después debamos devolver". Sería mucho menos, pero no nos
importaba. "Veamos qué ofrecen", dijimos. Arista realizó una linda
oferta, y así es como *Shaman* vio la luz de la mano de Arista. El
dinero real es aquel que no tienes que devolver.

El álbum cambió nuestros espectáculos en vivo, también. Nuestras
listas de temas volvían a ser canciones. Nos alejamos de las sesiones
improvisadas de música, y Chester y yo no componíamos tanto como
antes. CT se quedó con nosotros hasta el 2009, pero pienso que su
deseo de marcharse comenzó con las giras de *Supernatural* y en vista
de los cambios que estábamos atravesando. Después de *Supernatural,* proseguimos con algunos álbumes que surgieron de la misma
idea, trabajando con muchos artistas que volcaron gentilmente sus
corazones en las colaboraciones: desde Michelle Branch y Macy Gray,
pasando por Los Lonely Boys, Big Boi, Mary J. Blige y muchos otros.

Todos querían a Santana en los espectáculos de televisión y en las entregas de premios e intentábamos complacer a todos, pero era una locura. Incluso tuvimos problemas para asistir a *The Tonight Show*, así que cuando finalmente pudimos ir a Los Angeles con tiempo suficiente, programamos dos grabaciones en una semana. Fue divertido, y recuerdo que Jay Leno fue muy amable: se me acercó una vez que concluimos para decirme lo agradecido que estaba de que hubiéramos estado tan dispuestos a colaborar y si había algo que pudiera hacer por mí, simplemente tenía que decírselo.

Yo sabía exactamente lo que quería. "Jay, tú sabes que soy un gran admirador de Rodney Dangerfield". Él había estado en *The Tonight Show* muchas veces, incluso en los días de Johnny Carson, por lo que le pregunté a Jay si podía conseguirme algunas grabaciones de esas apariciones para mirar mientras estuviéramos de gira.

La mañana siguiente, recibí en mi oficina un paquete que contenía algunos DVD, una grabación de tres horas de Rodney Dangerfield en *The Tonight Show*, desde los 60 hasta su aparición más reciente. Contó algunos de sus chistes más graciosos en ese espectáculo. Viejo, aún veo esos DVD. Creo que mis partes favoritas son aquellas en las que Rodney dice algo que se sale de los límites de la televisión tradicional, entonces Jay agrega: "¡Ahí va el *show*!" y Rodney le recuerda: "Está bien, son las once y media de la noche". Me encanta ese intercambio, ese ida y vuelta; Johnny o Jay reaccionan ante el otro, pero, en realidad, se están estimulando mutuamente.

En el verano del 2000 tocamos *Supernatural* en vivo en Pasadena, todas las canciones con todos los cantantes, y Arista lo grabó para hacer un video doméstico. Me preguntaron quién más me gustaría que estuviera en el espectáculo y les respondí de inmediato: Wayne Shorter. Él no había participado en el álbum y era el único que no encajaba, pero yo sabía que Arista tenía que decir que sí. Wayne y yo decidimos tocar "Love Song from *Apache*", que Coleman Hawkins grabó y que yo había tocado en el 94 en Montreux con Joe Henderson.

Wayne tocó un solo durante un ensayo que cautivó los oídos de todos los presentes; todo se desarrolló en cámara lenta y la última nota sonó como una estrella fugaz. Este puede escucharse en una de las pistas adicionales del DVD. Me sentí muy agradecido de haber podido hacer ese concierto porque todos los que tocaron en *Supernatural* vinieron y dieron lo mejor de sí mimos. Pero Wayne es ese ángel luminoso que está en la punta del árbol de Navidad. Esto es lo que dijo esa noche acerca de *Supernatural:* "Este tipo de álbum que llega a tanta gente ni siquiera se trata de música. Revela un encuentro social y conocimiento común sobre los humanos".

Y yo pensaba que eso era absolutamente correcto. Woodstock fue un encuentro y *Supernatural* también lo es. Es la esperanza que debemos tener cada vez que hacemos un álbum o un espectáculo: estoy tocando esta noche y esto no se tratará únicamente de música: será un encuentro".

Supernatural tuvo lugar porque no participé solamente a mi manera. Tuve la iniciativa de confiar en Clive, y él se comunicó por teléfono con todos y logró que sucediera. Durante años, se escuchaba hablar de Santana en todas partes: estaciones de radio, centros comerciales, películas. Lo extraño es que Arista despidió a Clive al poco tiempo que salió *Supernatural* y puso a L. A. Reid a cargo. El contrato para *Shaman* había sido todo para él.

El mayor impacto de *Supernatural* se produjo en mi cronograma. El período más largo en que estuve de gira con Santana fue desde el verano del 99 hasta el año 2000, y requirió de mucha energía. Me encontré a mí mismo haciendo entre cinco y diez veces más entrevistas de las que había hecho para un álbum en el pasado. Tocábamos, viajábamos, y yo me levantaba por la mañana para otra conferencia de prensa. Sé que esto es parte del trabajo; siempre lo fue. Solo estoy diciendo que era más intenso que nunca, y que me requería estar presente y ser elocuente en muchas estaciones de radio, así como hablar de la producción del álbum una y otra vez. La gente es curiosa; quiere tener información sobre su música favorita y uno quiere dársela, pero puede resultar perjudicial.

Lo bueno es que Santana es una banda que siempre ha sido fuerte y ha estado preparada para las giras, entonces cuando llegó el éxito de *Supernatural*, pudimos manejar todas las fechas que se nos presentaban. No es que estábamos saliendo del retiro ni nada por el estilo. Pero las giras a veces duraban más de cinco semanas, por lo tanto tuvimos que suspender la regla de la familia Santana por un tiempo. A fines del año 2000, hice la promesa de disminuir el ritmo al menos por un año; ni siquiera comenzamos a grabar nuevamente durante unos seis meses.

Mientras tanto, la gente, en especial muchas corporaciones, comenzaron a tratar de tentarnos con montos de dinero obscenos para que viajáramos y tocáramos solo en una función. "Pagaremos todos los hoteles y los boletos aéreos, y a ustedes les pagaremos dos millones y medio de dólares por cuarenta y cinco minutos".

No, no, no. Dije: "No hay Santana en este momento; ninguno". Conozco la expresión "la ocasión es como el fierro: se ha de machacar caliente", pero yo dejé enfriar el fierro. Tenía que detenerme. Había problemas por el hecho de que yo estaba tanto tiempo lejos y quería evitar que la familia se desmoronara. Esto me hizo dar cuenta de que el amor no debe estar a la venta.

Hace poco tiempo, me hicieron una entrevista para un periódico en Australia y el entrevistador me preguntó por qué yo era uno de los pocos sobrevivientes de la familia Woodstock. Respondí que yo había aprendido a escuchar mi voz interior, y esta me decía que me ayudaría a no producirme una sobredosis. Muchas personas que ya no están entre nosotros murieron a causa de una sobredosis.

Después le conté: "Cuando vas a mi casa, viejo, no está Santana ahí. Es solo Carlos".

"¿Cómo?".

"Claro, no hay fotos ni afiches ni discos de oro de Santana en la casa. Necesito separar la persona de la personalidad". Todavía tengo que recordarme a mí mismo de hacerlo. A veces es como Miles señaló en las notas de del disco de *Sketches of Spain:* "Un día me llamaré por teléfono a mí mismo y me diré que me calle".

En la época en que salió *Supernatural,* este era nuestro ritmo doméstico: vivíamos en San Rafael en una linda casa frente a una colina, con hermosas cercas y flores. Cerca de allí había un edificio con techo a dos aguas al que yo llamaba "Iglesia Eléctrica", un término que tomé de Jimi Hendrix. Ahí es donde conservaba mi vida musical, donde recibía las llamadas telefónicas sobre trabajo y pasaba tiempo por la noche cuando quería tocar música o escuchar discos, o mirar baloncesto o boxeo. Era donde guardaba todas mis guitarras, un órgano Hammond y uno Fender, baterías, congas y otros instrumentos de percusión. Tenía un lugar especial para mis discos y colecciones de audio y video. Cuando me visitaban amigos como Hal Miller y Rashiki, estos se quedaban en la Iglesia, tenía una habitación para huéspedes y una cocina, y yo llegaba alrededor de las diez y hacíamos planes para el día o simplemente iban a hacer las compras conmigo. En los 90 me encantaba ir en el coche a recoger a Sal de la escuela, aunque él ya estuviera un poco grande para eso. A unos noventa metros de donde vivíamos estaba la casa que construimos para Jo y SK, los padres de Deborah. Mi mamá y mis hermanos no vivían demasiado lejos, en Bay Area, por lo que los niños pudieron conocer bien a su familia. Toda nuestra casa estaba enfocada en Deborah y los niños, nada de Santana. Cuando Jelli y yo empezamos a pasar más tiempo juntos, nos gustaba ver *MADtv*. Yo grababa los episodios, y luego ella venía a la Iglesia Eléctrica y reía hasta rodar por el suelo. Pero si el espectáculo mostraba algo para adultos, yo le decía que se tapara las orejas. Y ella reía aún más fuerte.

Todos los niños se dedicaron a tocar música por un tiempo. Estudiaban piano con Marcia Miget, y yo solía llevarlos a sus lecciones. Marcia se llama a sí misma "rata de río de Saint Louis": sabía todo sobre la historia musical de su ciudad, incluidos Clark Terry, Miles Davis y Chuck Berry. Les enseñaba piano a Sal y a Jelli, y Stella estudiaba saxofón alto. Me alegra no haber faltado jamás a ninguno de sus "recitales de graduación". Recuerdo que Sal hizo un excelente trabajo con "Blue Monk" y Stella tocó una balada de Pharoah Sanders con un tono y un flujo hermosos. Solo Sal continuó por el camino de la música, lo que está absolutamente bien. Me gusta la idea de que los tres sepan qué se siente tener un instrumento en las manos y hacer música. Marcia fue como un miembro de la familia Santana por un tiempo. Ahora dirige su propia escuela en San Rafael, llamada Miraflores Academie.

Teníamos un enorme pastor alemán llamado Jacob; los niños lo llamaban Jacobee. A veces pasaba por debajo de la cerca y salía a correr por el vecindario, entonces Deborah me llamaba. "Oye, tu perro se escapó de nuevo y los Smiths quieren que lo agarres antes de que se coma a su gato, ¿sí?". Yo soltaba la guitarra y dejaba de ver televisión. "Espera: ¿quiénes son The Smiths?". Luego iba a buscar a Jacob.

Me encantaba observar a ese perro mientras saltaba y corría por todas partes, con la lengua colgando como si intentara recuperar el aire. Una vez llevé a Jacob y a los niños a Stinson Beach, a una media hora de distancia de nuestra casa, y el perro encontró una gaviota muerta sobre la arena. Para él fue como hallar una comida *gourmet*; se abalanzó sobre ella, la mordisqueó y comenzó a revolcarse sobre ella. Necesitaba perfumarse con ese apestoso olor.

Yo pensaba: "¡Vaya!, ¿Cuánto tienes que querer algo para arrojar todo tu cuerpo encima de eso de esa manera?". Lo deseas tanto que quieres usar su olor. Empecé a pensar cómo esto ocurre también en la música; de qué forma algunos músicos van a buscarla, se meten en una canción y estrujan su cuerpo entre las notas.

En una ocasión Jaco Pastorius y yo estábamos tocando con unos músicos de *jazz* en una sesión especial, y los demás le preguntaron qué quería tocar. Me sonrió y luego respondió: "Fannie Mae", que es una vieja canción de rocola de Buster Brown; no el niño que vivía en un zapato, sino un cantante de blues de los 50 y los 60. La melodía consta de un *blues* simple con un *shuffle*. Los otros músicos no la conocían o no querían tocarla, pero Jaco comenzó a hacerlo y se metió en ella del mismo modo en que Jacob lo hizo la gaviota en la playa. Estaba totalmente abstraído en el sentimiento y el corazón de aquella canción. Yo continuaba pensando: "Ese es el tipo de espíritu y de convicción que quiero tener en Santana".

Les dije a los niños que se metieran en el mar para que Jacob los siguiera, se metiera y se quitara ese olor horrible. La verdad, es muy lindo ver cuando alguien es auténtico.

CAPÍTULO 23

(De izq. a der.) Salvador, Angélica, Deborah,
Stella y yo, 1998.

En 1998, Santana acababa de ingresar al Salón de la Fama del Rock y
para algunos eso significaba que ya habíamos logrado nuestro mejor
trabajo; como dijo un amigo: "Han llegado a la cima, ahora deben dis-
frutarla". ¿Sabes a qué se parecía Supernatural? Era como entrar en el
Salón de la Fama del Béisbol, retirarse, luego volver al ruedo y llevar
nuevamente a tu equipo a la Serie Mundial. ¿Retiro? No todavía.

He hablado mucho acerca de aquellos momentos en que el teléfono sonaba y oía a Miles o a Bill Graham o a John Lee al otro lado de la línea y sentía que eso era una validación. Después de Supernatural, si tenía una idea para un concierto especial o benéfico o simplemente deseaba elogiar a alguien, sentía que podía tomar el teléfono y llamar a cualquiera. Y la gente me devolvía la llamada. Podía ser alguien de HBO, de MTV o de la Rolling Stone. O podía ser alguien de Hollywood.

O Plácido Domingo: le pedimos que cantara en Shaman, y lo hizo en una sola toma. Terminó la melodía como un torero que acababa de lidiar con el diablo y resultó victorioso. Me gustaría poder hacer un álbum completo solo con él. Ese tipo es bestialmente extraordinario.

De hecho, quería hacer muchas cosas y ahora las he logrado; como los álbumes Guitar Heaven y Corazón. Quiero hacer un álbum llamado Sangre, en honor a mi papá, y grabarlo con mis hijos, con Cindy y con mi cuñada Tracy, que es una excelente cantante y compositora, y yo la llamo Sil. Además, estamos trabajando en Santana IV, que finalmente reunirá a los músicos que están disponibles de la formación original: Shrieve, Carabello, Rolie y Schon, y algunos de la banda Santana actual. Cuando hablamos sobre esto hay un tono diferente en nuestras voces, como si todos anhelaran volver una vez más. En realidad ya hemos ensayado algunas veces, y la química estuvo allí de inmediato: lo sagrado y una química natural. Quizá podamos hacer una gira con esta banda y con Journey; cada una tocaría por separado y después nos uniríamos al final. Debo aplaudir a Neal por haber iniciado y trabajado diligentemente en pos de esta idea, y por hacerme pensar: "Está bien, tal vez podamos juntarnos todos nuevamente, subirnos a nuestros caballos y cabalgar; no hacia el atardecer, sino hacia un nuevo amanecer.

Ahora puedo respirar hondo y decir que es un buen momento para estar vivo porque hay muy pocos obstáculos, y ya no existe una lucha por poner de manifiesto una música que reúna a mucha gente. Uno de los mejores halagos que recibí fue de parte del bajista Dave Holland. En una ocasión nos encontramos detrás de escena en el Hollywood Bowl con Wayne, Herbie, el gran percusionista hindú Zakir Hussain, Cindy y otros. Dave dijo que necesitaba decirme algo, como si lo hubiera estado conteniendo por un tiempo. Dijo: "Cada vez que he escuchado tu *música o te he visto en alguna configuración, siempre logras compartir aspectos comunes con toda la gente: jóvenes y viejos, negros, blancos y marrones". Tengo mucho respeto por Dave y por lo que ha hecho con Miles y por sí solo después. Me estaba dando una lección de humildad. "Gracias, hombre. Esto significa mucho".*

Me encanta crear música que conecte la mayor cantidad de gente posible, no solo entre sí, sino también con su propia divinidad. Mi concepto es utilizar lo que tengo para intentar abrir los corazones y las mentes, y ayudar a las personas a cristalizar su propia existencia, alcanzar una consciencia más profunda y encontrar el objetivo real en su vida. Así es. Es el alfa y la omega.

C uando finalmente volvimos al estudio en 2001, la presión consistía en continuar después de *Supernatural* con algo que fuera igual de grande. Comenzamos a trabajar en *Shaman*, y teníamos una melodía que yo sabía iba a ser tan grande como todo lo que había tenido lugar antes. "The Game of Love" no solo era una excelente canción; habíamos invitado a Tina Turner para que la cantara y el resultado fue increíble. Lamentablemente no pudimos lanzarla en el momento, entonces Michelle Branch realizó un fantástico trabajo con la canción, lo que le aportó un estilo diferente y se convirtió en un éxito. De todos modos, estoy feliz de que hayamos podido incluir la versión de Tina en *The Ultimate Santana Collection* en 2007, de modo que el público pueda saber por qué me siento así con respecto a la canción.

Mientras hacíamos ese álbum yo estaba en el estudio todos los días, y esto ponía a prueba mi cerebro porque debía concentrarme mucho en cada canción para lograr la mezcla correcta y juntar todas las partes. Volvía a casa tarde e iba directo a la Iglesia Eléctrica. Seguía recibiendo llamadas durante la noche de John Lee Hooker. Una vez lo sorprendí y lo llamé por su cumpleaños, y me dijo: "Amigo, ¡oír tu voz es como comer un gran trozo de p-p-pastel de chocolate!" Le respondí: "Viejo, es *tu* cumpleaños y siento como si tú me dieras el presente a *mí*".

Una noche, estaba tan cansado, que en lugar de ir a la Iglesia para relajarme, fui directamente a la cama. Me levanté a la mañana siguiente y sonó el teléfono: alguien me llamaba para comunicarme que John Lee había fallecido la noche anterior. La noticia me paralizó. Necesitaba estar solo y dejar que los sentimientos me atravesaran, tomar una guitarra. Me dirigí a la Iglesia y vi la contestadora automática. Tenía un mensaje: era de John Lee, de la noche anterior. "C-C-Carlos. Solo quería oír tu voz y decirte que yo *amar* a Dios y yo *amar* a la gente". Colgó el teléfono, y eso fue todo.

Mi filosofía es que ser consciente implica saber que eres un creador. Sí, está el creador supremo, pero él te dio libre albedrío para que tú puedas ser el creador de la película que es tu vida. Sé ese creador: trabaja con lo que te ha sido concedido.

Alrededor de 2003 volví a Autlán, pero esta vez con toda mi familia: todos mis hermanos y mi mamá en una silla de ruedas. Ella estaba en la gloria, porque todos los que la recordaban formaron una fila junto a ella para estrecharle la mano. "¡Oh, Josefina! Te extrañamos; te hemos echado mucho de menos".

El motivo de la visita era que el municipio había colocado una estatua en mi honor: era el Carlos de *Supernatural*, no el Carlos joven y hippie. Recuerdo que pensé que era demasiado grande: mis manos eran enormes y la guitarra no era de ningún modelo que yo conociera. Tal vez era única en su tipo.

Esta fue una oportunidad para agradecer y celebrarme a mí mismo, así como para compartir quién soy con otros, pero también fue una oportunidad para no cometer una sobredosis de mí mismo. Aún siento que estoy aprendiendo a recibir, sonreír y ser amable.

Entonces cuando me preguntaron qué pensaba de la estatua, hice un chiste acerca de que las palomas la usarían para practicar tiro al blanco, y los presentes se echaron a reír.

En ese viaje me sentí abrumado por los recuerdos de mi papá, cuando vivíamos en Autlán y yo era muy pequeño; de cuando andábamos en bicicleta y del olor de su jabón español. Recordaba cómo me sentía al saber que él tenía otro trato para conmigo. Pero esta vez yo estaba orgulloso de eso y ya no me sentía incómodo al respecto.

En un momento me di cuenta, repentinamente, de que mi papá faltaba en nuestro grupo y comencé a sollozar. Nunca pensé que eso sucedería. Era como si algo se hubiese acumulado desde que él falleció y llegó un punto en que debía explotar, entonces me excusé. Fui al baño y tenía los ojos totalmente enrojecidos. Recuerdo que me estaba enjuagando el rostro, cuando entró mi hermano Tony y me preguntó: "¿Estás bien?".

"Sí, viejo. Estaré bien".

"¿Qué pasa?".

"No puedo dejar de pensar en que papá ya no está aquí. Lamento no haber organizado antes un evento como este".

"No, Carlos, está aquí, él está aquí". Los funcionarios del municipio acababan de colocar una gran imagen de José y aparecieron algunos mariachis que comenzaron a tocar música, y ahí estaba él.

El municipio de Autlán se encargó de todo: la estatua, la música de mariachis, todo. Yo no participé. Al poco tiempo, robaron la guitarra de la estatua que estaba adherida, no construida en el mismo bloque; pero como era tan grande supongo que el ladrón pensó: "¿Cómo puedo esconder esto?". Más tarde, la encontraron en una zanja y volvieron a colocarla donde correspondía para que yo no estuviera tocando solo una guitarra de aire.

En 2005 Santana tocó en la Ciudad de México para más de cien mil personas en la plaza al aire libre más grande del país: el Zócalo. Quería ofrecerle a la multitud lo más posible de la vieja Santana, como hice con *Supernatural*. Para mí era como si Santana y México nunca hubieran tenido la oportunidad de conocerse bien, entonces quería mostrarles la historia completa de la banda. Empezamos sonando como Sun Ra; Sun Ra y Jimi Hendrix. La gente se miraba entre sí: "¿Dónde está 'Maria Maria'?". Fue una linda interrupción de las rígidas listas de temas de *Supernatural*. Fue casi como un viaje colectivo de LSD en el que se veía a los músicos expandirse, divertirse y tocar como niños otra vez. Después tocamos canciones de *Supernatural*, y para ese entonces el público ya había enloquecido. Descubrí que en México, cuando te reclaman, *realmente* te reclaman.

Por estos días mis listas de temas siguen siendo iguales, abiertas y flexibles, respetando a las distintas Santanas, desde *Abraxas* a *Supernatural* y, ahora, le damos la bienvenida a *Corazón*.

En 2003, The Milagro Foundation tenía cinco años y Deborah y yo constantemente buscábamos formas de utilizar la energía y de dar esperanza y apoyo espiritual a la gente. El máximo apoyo que alguien puede brindar es recordar a las personas que son importantes y que tienen valor; que son un rayo de luz más allá de lo que hayan hecho o no. La filantropía real no se trata de hacer dinero: se trata de mover luz, y no importa cuántos ceros tengas a la derecha en tu cuenta bancaria, siempre y cuando tengas un 1 a la izquierda.

Ese año Deborah organizó una fiesta en nuestra casa para el arzobispo Desmond Tutu y Artists for a New South Africa con el objetivo de luchar contra la crisis de sida que había en Sudáfrica. Había escuchado por primera vez al arzobispo Tutu en *Larry King Live* allá por 1983, y sus palabras en ese entonces fueron verdaderamente sorprendentes. Él habló del *apartheid* y de la manera en que el brutal gobierno sudafricano oprimía a los sudafricanos negros. Sin embargo, lo que en realidad ocurría era que los sudafricanos negros buscaban a los opresores y les decían: "Únanse a nosotros en nuestra victoria; celebren con nosotros. Ya hemos ganado". Entonces uno pensaba... "Espera un minuto: ¿qué acaba de decir?". Escuché una canción ahí mismo.

Veinte años más tarde el *apartheid* ya no existía y el Congreso Nacional Africano, que ya no era una organización terrorista, dirigía el país. Ese verano destinamos todas las ganancias de la gira completa de Santana a ANSA para apoyar a las organizaciones que luchaban contra el sida. El alcalde Brown vino a nuestro hogar junto a otras personas importantes, y Santana tocó, y luego Sal tocó. El arzobispo dio un corto discurso, y todos donaron dinero para ayudar a cubrir los costos de su viaje. Quizá fue el mejor ejemplo de cómo podía reunir todo lo que tenía; mi música y mis espectáculos, mi familia, mis amigos y mis contactos, para contribuir a lograr algo que debía hacerse.

La esposa de Bill Cosby, Camille, era la conexión con ANSA; Deborah y Camille son amigas desde hace mucho tiempo. Además, Camille había producido un documental sobre la crisis del sida. Cuando vi la película, exclamé: "¡Vaya! Esta situación es de lo más real y desesperante". Era un ciclo de negligencia que recién estaba comenzando, y podía detenerse con la medicina y la compasión correctas en los lugares correctos. El documental de Camille me convenció de que el problema persistiría durante un largo tiempo si no se hacía algo de inmediato.

En agosto pudimos juntar y proveer a la organización más de dos millones de dólares. Además, nos mantuvimos en contacto con ANSA y el arzobispo Tutu. Tres años más tarde, en septiembre de 2006, Deborah y yo organizamos un evento especial en Beverly Hills para celebrar el cumpleaños número setenta y cinco del arzobispo, y hablar acerca de las vidas que fueron salvadas y lo que se había hecho para detener la epidemia. Un mes después fuimos a visitar Sudáfrica junto con un grupo de amigos, incluido Samuel L. Jackson, para ver qué se había logrado.

Puedo mencionar mi encuentro con Nelson Mandela y otras experiencias que siempre atesoraré. Sin embargo, lo que nunca olvidaré son dos cosas: la primera fue cuando observé a unas cincuenta personas llevar a cabo una danza tradicional en una zona rural muy, muy distante, donde no había electricidad ni agua corriente. Mientras bailaban, uno de ellos se apartó del grupo. Pasó una pierna por encima de su cabeza y luego la bajó estrepitosamente al suelo, a la vez que los demás aplaudían, cantaban y marcaban el 1. Recuerdo que Sal comentó: "No es un patrón *flam*" (es decir, dos golpes casi simultáneos que suenan como una nota única), y estaba en lo cierto. "Sé cómo lo hacen, y por qué es tan firme y sincronizado".

Samuel Jackson preguntó: "¿Cómo, Sal?".

"Gracias a dos cosas: está en su historia, en su ADN. No es un ritmo actual. Y no tienen televisión ni nada por el estilo, así que no tienen distracciones".

Lo otro que recuerdo de ese viaje es que visité una clínica y vi los rostros reales del sida: las personas que habían estado al borde de la muerte, pero que estaban recuperándose. Pero no se trataba solo de la enfermedad; además se veía una pobreza extrema, desesperanza y tristeza. Eso es lo que sentí en el fondo. Recuerdo que mientras Deborah, Jelli, Sal y yo estábamos ayudando a distribuir cajas de provisiones para las familias de pacientes con sida, una mujer mayor permanecía sentada allí desde hacía un largo rato, sola, perdida en sus pensamientos y con una mirada vacía y lejana. Cuando nos acercamos a ella, miró a Deborah, y luego a mí y a Salvador, mientras lentamente comenzó a hacerse más presente. Después se dio cuenta de que la caja de harina, azúcar y comidas enlatadas que teníamos en las manos era para ella, entonces repentinamente comenzó a llorar.

Es un recuerdo que nunca podré quitarme de la cabeza. Solo pensar en él ahora me provoca escalofríos. Algunos podemos no percatarnos de lo afortunados que somos en este mundo hasta que nos topamos con alguien que ha atravesado la desolación y ha conocido el infierno. No se puede evitar pensar en lo que tenemos en este país. Yo creo que demasiada gente piensa que la oportunidad es algo que uno recibe y luego debe conservarla para sí mismo. ¿Cómo la recibiste en primer lugar? Debiste tomarla de alguien que no deseaba compartirla, ¿entonces ahora todo el mundo tiene que hacer lo mismo?

Los Estados Unidos toman lo que quieren y explican que eso es lo correcto y lo que se debe hacer, sin analizar las consecuencias. Pero todas esas justificaciones vienen del miedo y del prejuicio. Podemos pensar que tenemos a Dios de nuestro lado, pero si empiezas con temor, esto solo puede conducirte a justificaciones y a la pérdida de oportunidades. No hay consciencia en eso, nada divino. Pensemos en todos los desastres que han ocurrido recientemente, como el 9/11, el huracán Katrina y el huracán Sandy. Aun en esos acontecimientos hemos tenido problemas para aunar fuerzas y ayudarnos los unos a los otros. De parte del gobierno hubo más miedo, con respecto a los individuos que se llevaban demasiado y a quién debía pagar las cuentas, por ende hubo un esfuerzo por hacer lo correcto y ayudar.

Lo que necesitamos es liberarnos del miedo y del prejuicio. Esa es una bendición que todos pueden utilizar.

En 2006 sucedieron algunas cosas, una tras otra, incluso antes de que fuéramos a Sudáfrica. Deborah publicó su libro, *Space Between the Stars* (traducido al español como *El espacio entre las estrellas*), donde hablaba de su vida y de la historia de nuestra familia, y reveló muchas cosas sobre nosotros. Le brindé mi apoyo y di entrevistas junto a ella para promocionarla; fue ahí cuando caminé por la alfombra roja con ella para celebrar su honestidad al escribirlo.

Unos meses después, a mediados del verano, su madre falleció. SK ya había partido y yo sabía que Deborah necesitaría algún tiempo para recomponerse. En esa época nuestra agenda estaba completa, con una gira mundial y, un poco más tarde, el viaje de ANSA a Sudáfrica.

Había hablado con Jo un par de semanas antes; ella había llamado a casa una noche, y yo atendí. "Hola, mamá. ¿Cómo estás? Déjame pasarte con Deborah". Respondió: "Estoy bien, querido. En realidad, quiero hablar contigo. Nunca he dicho esto, pero quería decirte que desde el primer día en que Deborah te trajo a nuestra casa, me diste una gran tranquilidad porque supe que siempre cuidarías de ella y la protegerías".

Deborah y yo estábamos juntos desde hacía casi treinta y cuatro años. Pienso que los ejemplos de ambas parejas de padres jugaron un papel importante en la forma en que manejamos nuestro matrimonio. Nos ayudaron a ser sabios y a no detenernos en pequeñeces. También nos enseñaron la importancia del mantenimiento constante; el hecho de prestar atención al romanticismo interior y de honrar los sentimientos del otro, porque el amor incondicional surge primero y viene antes que nuestro aspecto individual.

Durante el 2006, Deborah estuvo tan ocupada como yo; cuidando a la familia, promocionando su libro y dirigiendo Santana Management. Según me comentó posteriormente, yo era el único que aportaba ideas y visiones de proyectos, y ella era la encargada de los aspectos básicos: "Yo soy la que trata con los agentes, los abogados y los contadores. Superviso todo: el negocio y las regalías y las casas". En aquel entonces teníamos una casa en Maui; "Simplemente es demasiado".

Esto sucedió en febrero de 2007 y lo recuerdo con total claridad. Nos encontrábamos en la casa de San Rafael; yo estaba tocando la guitarra cuando Deborah vino y empezó a contarme cómo se sentía. "Tu mundo me está aplastando". Así lo describió. "Necesito encontrarme a mí misma y hacer mis propias cosas. Necesito ocuparme de mí ahora, porque siento que estoy desapareciendo en tu mundo".

Dije: "Rayos, Deborah, ¿qué puedo hacer?" y ella me respondió: "Tú no estás haciendo nada malo. Solo es la forma en que se han dado las cosas. Necesito hacer algo por mí ahora mismo porque me estoy ahogando en todas estas obligaciones: ocuparme de los niños, el negocio, tu familia y mi familia. Necesito alejarme al menos durante seis meses. "Te pido que no me llames ni me contactes. Estaré en la oficina una vez por semana para ocuparme del negocio, pero por favor, no estés ahí cuando yo vaya".

Nunca pensé que ocurriría esto, en absoluto. Fue totalmente inesperado para mí. Habíamos decidido suspender la actividad de Santana durante la mayor parte de 2007, sin giras ni álbumes, solo unos pocos espectáculos, por lo que yo había pensado que destinaríamos este año a estar más tiempo juntos. Deborah se dio cuenta de que yo no me lo esperaba. Agregó: "Sé que esto es una sorpresa. ¿Por qué no vas una semana a Hawái y ves a tu amigo Tony Kilbert, así tú y yo podemos pensar mejor en esto?". Entonces fui a Hawái.

Solo había pasado unos pocos días allí con todos estos pensamientos en mi cabeza, atravesando estas dimensiones de dolor y de frustración, sin entender qué estaba ocurriendo realmente, cuando una noche se desató una tormenta extremadamente fuerte. Sacudió la casa y todo se movía sin clemencia. Yo estaba solo, enfrentando todos estos miedos y preguntándome si alguna de las ventanas se rompería. Cuando finalmente terminó y salió el sol al día siguiente, me sentí tan bien por estar al aire libre y vivo que el miedo de enfrentar lo que verdaderamente podía estar ocurriendo con Deborah fue eclipsado. Entonces la llamé esa mañana y le dije: "Oye, ¿qué está pasando?". Me respondió: "Te lo dije: por favor, no me llames por un tiempo". Tenía que preguntarlo, así es que lo hice. "¿Vamos a divorciarnos?". El tono de su voz cambió de inmediato. "Bueno, ¿necesitas saberlo ahora?".

Yo pensaba: "Rayos". No he oído ese tono muchas veces; sonaba como si hubiera guardado algo en su interior durante un largo tiempo. Una parte de mí quería decirle que ella siempre había recibido ayuda en la casa y con los niños, y que en la oficina, ella contaba con gente que la ayudaba. Había deseado decirle esto incluso antes de que me marchara a Hawái, pero pensé que no estaría preparada para oírlo en ese momento, entonces no lo hice. Ahora pensaba: "Espera: sabías quién era yo y lo que yo hacía antes de que nos casáramos, sabías de la música y las giras y los compromisos".

Ahí pude ver que eso no importaba. Durante unos días tuve la esperanza de que aún existiera la posibilidad de que la relación mejorara, y que Deborah cambiaría de idea con respecto al lapso de seis meses. Incluso durante los meses siguientes seguí anhelando que solo se tratara de una especie de prueba. Hice lo que ella me pidió y me mantuve alejado, pasando el tiempo con mis amigos, que hicieron lo mejor para levantarme el ánimo. "Esto se trata de Deborah, como ella te dijo", solían decir mis amigos. "Así que no te culpes, viejo". No obstante, mi mente no podía dejar de pensar y pensar, preguntarme: "¿Qué significa? ¿Qué salió mal? ¿Por qué ella no puede vivir más conmigo? ¿Por qué esto es tan insoportable? ¿Por qué, por qué, por qué?".

Cuando volví a casa, Deborah se había mudado y los niños estaban en la escuela o viviendo su vida, y eso era lo peor: la noche más oscura del alma. Todo se volvió muy intenso. Recuerdo que era un hermoso verano y solía levantarme por la mañana, el sol brillaba y sentía un delicioso perfume de flores cuando entraba en la cocina, pero no había nadie ahí con quien disfrutarlo, con quien compartirlo. Todo se estaba volviendo muy, muy intenso. Toda la casa empezó a sentirse como un ataúd, y yo era el único que estaba allí.

Tenía a mis hermanos y hermanas que constantemente me llamaban y preguntaban cómo estaba. Tenía a mis amigos, con quienes me reunía aunque sabía que yo no siempre era la mejor compañía. Tenía a viejos amigos, como Quincy Jones, que me llamaban. Tenía a un amigo que me dijo que era hora de subir a un avión con él e ir a un lugar de Brasil porque conocía a unas chicas que yo tenía que conocer. "Todo lo que necesitas es un poco de...". Le respondí: "Gracias, pero no. Gracias. Necesito eso como necesito un agujero en mi cabeza, viejo".

Recuerdo que la reacción de mi mamá fue: "¿Qué le hiciste? ¿Qué le hiciste a Deborah para que hiciera esto?". "Mamá, ¿por qué no le preguntas a ella?", repliqué. Ya tenía suficiente lidiando con mi cerebro que me torturaba, esforzándome por librarme de toda esa culpa y esa vergüenza.

Fue unos meses después, mientras Deborah y yo hablábamos por teléfono, cuando me dijo que quería hablar de lo que necesitábamos hacer ahora que nuestro matrimonio había terminado. Esa fue la primera vez que utilizó esas palabras. Dije: "¿Entonces vas a apretar el gatillo?". No dijo que sí ni que no, solo agregó: "Necesitaremos hacer esto y atravesar este proceso y...". Me acuerdo de que le pregunté: "¿Dónde quedó nuestro amor; aún sientes algo por mí?". Me respondió: "Bueno, no necesito decirte eso". Solo respondí: "Está bien".

Ciertamente nunca recibí con claridad un "ya no siento nada" o "no te amo más"; y lo que lo hizo aún más difícil fue que nunca peleamos ni discutimos ni dejamos fluir nuestras emociones.

Pero ahí fue cuando finalmente me dije a mí mismo que había terminado, punto final; cuando está roto, está roto. Estábamos hablando de que necesitábamos arreglar todo por nuestra cuenta para no tener que hacer todo el trámite con abogados; en ese momento yo oía una voz interior que me decía: "Simplemente afloja la tensión. No pelees, no te resistas, no discutas y no regatees. Esto no se trata de dinero para ti y nunca lo ha sido. Dale lo que quiere".

Los niños se enteraron del divorcio antes que nadie. Sabían que Deborah se mudaría e iría a su propio lugar y todos tenían su propia manera de afrontarlo. Desde el principio les dije que los

llamaría y les enviaría mensajes de texto con la misma frecuencia
que antes, más allá de cómo se sintieran y, les aclaré que siempre
estaría con ellos y dispuesto a responder todas sus preguntas con la
mayor honestidad posible. Incluso cuando las cosas empeoraban y
yo me sentía deprimido o enojado, mi plan solo consistía en creer
que cualquiera puede hacer de cada día el mejor de su vida, aunque
sea en otra configuración. Efectivamente, siempre creí que esa era
la mejor manera de mostrar todo aspecto de la vida a nuestros hijos;
por medio del ejemplo, en lugar de hablar.

De algún modo era bueno que no estuvieran presentes y siguie-
ran con sus cosas. Salvador venía con frecuencia a ver cómo me
encontraba, y él era como la "Suiza" de la situación: muy neutral, sin
tomar partido por nadie, solo quería estar allí tanto para su madre
como para su padre. No es que las chicas no estuvieran de la misma
manera, solo que Sal era mayor y tenía más capacidad para demos-
trar sabiduría, compasión e imparcialidad. Eso verdaderamente
repercutió en mí y me ayudó mucho. Él había entablado una relación más estrecha con Keith Jarrett en ese momento, entonces solía
venir y tocar el piano, y simplemente dejarme embelesado. Keith era
uno de mis pianistas favoritos de todos los tiempos y podía ser el
distribuidor espiritual de melodías sumamente románticas, puras y
hermosas. Hay algo muy terapéutico y sanador en ello.

Recuerdo una vez que conducía por Napa solo, cerca de esta
época, cuando empezó a sonar la versión de Keith de "It's All in the
Game". De pronto comencé a sollozar y tuve que detener el coche.
Lo que estuviera por hacer ya no era importante, entonces di la
vuelta y volví a casa para estar solo, buscar alguna guía interior y
curarme un poco más.

El divorcio es algo muy personal y yo carecía de experiencia para
lidiar con algo así en público. Hablar de lo que me había ocurrido
años atrás era una cosa, pero hablar de los temas personales que
estaban ocurriendo en ese momento, cosas que pueden tratarse en
TMZ con tanta facilidad, era otra. Nadie quiere alimentar esa

máquina. Tenía la sensación de que en cierto modo Deborah y yo nos habíamos ganado el respeto de los periódicos y los programas de televisión para mantenerlos alejados durante este período; no sentían la necesidad de hablar de nuestros temas. También creo que conscientemente ambos realizamos el compromiso de tomar el camino más correcto por el bien de nuestros hijos y familias. Cuando finalmente fue anunciado que nos separábamos por motivos irreconciliables, respiré hondo y por un largo tiempo. Considero una bendición que no se hiciera un gran despliegue de esto en los medios. A fines de 2007 el tiempo transcurría muy, muy lentamente. Todavía me estaba recuperando, viejo; todo era dolor. Estaba realizando un trabajo mucho más interno, haciendo lo que a Wayne Shorter le gusta llamar la "jardinería interior": quitar la maleza. Leía mucho para mantener mi cerebro alejado de la tortura, de la culpa, de la vergüenza y de toda la cuestión del ego, y estaba hallando sabiduría en muchos libros diferentes. En una revista, *Sedona Journal of Emergence*, encontré una línea de un poema persa: "El sol nunca le dirá a la Tierra 'Tú me debes algo'". ¿Puedes imaginar una benevolencia o una luz que sea más suprema?

Una noche cerca del Día de Acción de Gracias, encendí una vela y comencé a buscar ayuda; esa voz interior volvió y me dijo: "Estoy junto a ti: ¿eso no es suficiente? Debes dejar ir a Deborah y a tus hijos. Ellos están bien, están conmigo y están bien. Cuídate a ti".

Eso fue alrededor de la época en que me contacté con la autora Marianne Williamson. Ella y yo hablamos por primera vez justo antes de que Deborah se fuera, y al final de ese verano, después de que nos separamos, algo me decía que la buscara y viera si Marianne podía ayudarme. Era como si estuviese haciendo buceo en un lago de dolor y realmente necesitara que alguien me volviera a enseñar a respirar. Ella me escuchó y percibió algo en mi voz, así que de inmediato me recomendó a Jerry Jampolsky y Diane Cirincione, que están casados y viven en Sausalito. Jerry y Diane son terapeutas que usan el libro *A Course in Miracles* en su trabajo. También dirigen una red de centros de asesoramiento que ayudan a las personas, brindándoles lecciones de espiritualidad y transformación.

Fui a visitar a Jerry y Diane a su casa y verdaderamente me salvaron la vida. Recuerdo que la primera vez que nos sentamos juntos, Jerry me pidió que me definiera a mí mismo, sin mis hermanos, mi familia y mis amigos. Le dije que me veía a mí mismo como el perrito que se aleja del resto de la camada porque se distrae jugando con algo, como una pantufla, y luego pasa de jugar con ella a romperla con los dientes: *grrrr*.

Jerry dijo que eso era bastante interesante. Después me preguntó: "¿Pero por qué no te ves a ti mismo primero como un hijo de Dios?". Fue una revelación para mí la manera en que me abrió los ojos sobre cuánto me había alejado del camino de la divinidad, especialmente después de la ruptura con Deborah. También me abrió los ojos respecto de lo mucho que había luchado y batallado contra todo, tanto en mi interior como en la situación. Me dije a mí mismo que había pasado un largo tiempo desde que había visto las cosas desde esa perspectiva. Tal vez otras personas me hayan dicho algo similar, pero cuando Jerry me lo dijo, las cosas realmente cambiaron para mí y comencé a curarme con una honestidad y una energía que no había tenido antes. Volví al camino en el que había estado anteriormente, afianzando mi entereza.

Comenzamos a hablar casi todos los días, leyendo *A Course in Miracles* a través del teléfono, que se convirtió en una fuente de inspiración y guía, con la orientación de Jerry y Diane. Aún lo hacemos; creo que estamos en la cuarta o quinta lectura del libro. Ellos me llaman todos los días entre las siete y media y las ocho de la mañana, ya sea que esté en casa o de gira, lo que es increíble para mí, porque a veces mi mañana puede ser la mitad de la noche en Sausalito. Leemos juntos la lección del día, lecciones que aplico a todo lo que ocurre en mi vida. Fueron Jerry y Diane quienes me ayudaron finalmente a superar mi enojo por los abusos que sufrí cuando estaba en Tijuana y a perdonar al hombre que me lo hizo. Me dijeron que lo imaginara frente a mí y que lo convirtiera en un niño de seis años con un resplandor de luz divina detrás. Lo miré, lo perdoné y lo envié hacia la luz, y así nos liberé a ambos del pasado. Por último, pude respirar; sentí como si ese capítulo de mi vida hubiera concluido.

Jerry y Diane me ayudaron a recomponerme después de que Deborah se fue. Encontrarme con ellos me dio otra oportunidad para ver que mi vida siempre se ha basado en reconocer a los ángeles que aparecen cuando más los necesito. Pude volver al punto en que podía levantarme y estar feliz conmigo mismo. Estoy seguro de que una de las razones por las que Deborah y yo nos separamos fue porque debía ser cansador para ella comenzar el día con alguien que no podía aceptarse a sí mismo y creaba distancia entre él y el resto del mundo. ¿Quién puede saberlo con seguridad?

Ese primer año y medio fue doloroso, pero la vida continuó. Al principio resultó especialmente difícil porque Santana estaba tomando un descanso de las giras. Realicé algunas sesiones. Smokey Robinson me llamó y me pidió que tocara en una canción llamada "Please Don't Take Your Love", de la que hice dos versiones y él seleccionó lo mejor de cada una. En 2008, Santana volvió a las giras y eso me ayudó a dejar de pensar en el pasado, a estar en el presente y a volver a mi marcha usual.

Siete años después me encuentro en un punto donde todo lo que quedó de mi vida con Deborah, sus padres y mi excuñada, Kitsaun, es belleza y bendiciones. Ahora estoy en un lugar donde puedo desearle sinceramente lo mejor a Deborah y agradecerle por todo. Puedo honrarla a ella y a todo lo que tuvimos y al mismo tiempo estrechar lo que vino después: la manera en que crecí, cambié y después recibí a Cindy, mi amor y mi esposa. Nunca en mi vida he sido tan feliz como en este momento.

El recuerdo de todo lo que ocurrió en 2006 y 2007 (ANSA y el arzobispo Tutu y Deborah) me volvió a la mente en 2014, cuando fui a Sudáfrica a tocar por primera vez. Había visitado el país, pero nunca había tocado allí, y fue increíble. Creo que para cualquier músico la primera vez que toca en Sudáfrica debe ser increíble, especialmente para aquellos que atravesaron los días del *apartheid* y de los boicots y que descubrieron a todos los magníficos artistas que surgieron de allí, incluidos Hugh Masekela y Ladysmith Black Mambazo.

Llamé al arzobispo Tutu y le pregunté si podíamos reunirnos; bueno, en realidad mi asistente Chad lo hizo. Estábamos tocando en Ciudad del Cabo, donde vive el arzobispo y está construyendo un centro para su fundación espiritual; es una de las ciudades más hermosas que he conocido. Nos invitó a su casa y después de conversar durante un rato le recordé algo que él había dicho recientemente: que si el cielo discrimina a los homosexuales, entonces él no quería ir ahí. También mencioné que dos meses después de que dijera eso el papa hizo el mismo comentario, lo que demuestra que el arzobispo realmente sabe cómo utilizar las palabras de modo tal que las personas se despierten y reciban el mensaje.

Adhiero a su mensaje con el conocimiento de que está dirigido a todos y que igualmente habla de aspectos que es necesario corregir; él no bajó los brazos una vez que el *apartheid* hubiera terminado. Es similar a lo que dijo Martin Luther King Jr. con respecto a que ningún hombre es libre hasta que todos somos libres.

La noche anterior a que visitara al arzobispo, Stella me había enviado un mensaje de texto con una foto de mi exesposa, Deborah, en la que se encontraba con el dalái lama y me encantó saber que ambos todavía nos encontrábamos en el mismo camino, aunque no estuviéramos allí juntos. Pensaba: "¿Cuántas posibilidades hay de que esto ocurra al mismo tiempo, que Deborah y yo nos encontremos cada uno con dos de los líderes espirituales más inspiradores del mundo?". Luego, de repente, tuve una visión.

Empecé a pensar quién podría canalizar toda esta energía. ¿Qué sucedería si pudiéramos reunir al arzobispo Tutu, al Dalái Lama, al papa y a los principales líderes del mundo judío y el musulmán en un avión? Podrían viajar a lugares como Ucrania, Siria y Venezuela, y a sitios que la CNN ni siquiera menciona, llevando luz a la oscuridad y desarticulando el odio que está comenzando allí antes de que esto se acreciente y produzca guerras. Iría junto con

Santana y tocaríamos, y ayudaría a reclutar otros grupos que encabezan titulares, además, con el fin de salir en las noticias de todo el mundo y detener la matanza antes de que pueda ocurrir.

Le comenté esta idea al arzobispo y le pregunté si podía imaginarse haciendo esto y ayudándonos a llegar a otros líderes, como el papa. Abrió grandes los ojos, luego se mostró humilde y preguntó: "¿Pero por qué me escucharían a mí?". Ahí fue cuando mi amigo Hal Miller, que estaba con nosotros, intervino y dijo lo que él necesitaba oír: "Porque cuando usted habla, el mundo escucha".

El arzobispo sonrió y cuando nos fuimos me pidió que siguiéramos en contacto con respecto a la idea. Lo sé: es un sueño, ingenioso y audaz. Pero ese es el tipo de audacia con la que quiero vivir. Tengo fe en los principios de John Lennon y de John Coltrane, de Jesús y de Martin Luther King Jr. Tengo fe en aquellos que creen con todo su ser que nunca es demasiado tarde para reparar este planeta.

CAPÍTULO 24

Recordando el pasado: Cindy y yo en nuestra boda en Maui,
19 de diciembre de 2010.

*Fui a Suecia recientemente. Era mi cumpleaños, estaba afeitándome y
en mis ojos reflejados en el espejo pude ver a mis padres. "Hola, mamá",
les dije. "Hola, papá". Ambos ya se han ido, pero aún están conmigo y
juntos uno con el otro. Todavía encuentro mucha fuerza en la lealtad
que se tuvieron entre sí. Recuerdo cómo se miraban desde distintos puntos del salón en la fiesta de su quincuagésimo aniversario: era como si
los demás no estuviésemos allí. Ese cariño aún estaba presente, incluso
después de que todo lo que pasó entre ellos. Puedes preguntarle a cualquiera de nosotros, sus hijos; a mis hermanos o hermanas. No creo que*

alguno de nosotros tenga el recuerdo de mis padres besándose o abra-
zándose. Pero mi mamá quedó embarazada once veces.

Una vez los interrumpí. Yo tenía diecisiete y vivíamos en el distrito
The Mission. Había llegado de la escuela y tenía prisa por ir a mi tra-
bajo en el Tic Tock. Abrí la puerta y estaban en la cama. Me miraron
como diciendo: "Ahora no". Cerré rápidamente la puerta y de repente
todo ocurrió en cámara lenta. ¡Por supuesto! Lo hacían, tenía que
haber intimidad. Salí sintiendo como si tuviera una manta cálida sobre
el cuerpo. No hay nada que te haga sentir más seguro que ver a tus
padres enamorados uno del otro. Entonces todo el mundo es un lugar
feliz. Esa es la base que me gustaría que cada niño tuviera y el tipo de
amor que espero tener en mi vida: una relación que dure y se sienta
como el primer día, aunque sea el último.

Alrededor de dos años después de mi divorcio, finalmente respiré
hondo y me dije a mí mismo: "Está bien, afrontemos el nuevo día. No
tengo dudas de que Dios enviará a alguien a mi camino, porque tengo
que tener una reina". Tengo todos estos logros y una casa grande y viajo
y me alojo en hoteles fantásticos; aún recibo muchas bendiciones y
honores. Disfruto de la abundancia y de una increíble belleza. Pero
está incompleta a menos que tenga una reina con quien compartirla.

En 2009 yo me encontraba en Las Vegas, era un domingo por la
noche. Recibí una llamada en la que me avisaban que mi mamá
se había caído y estaba en coma en el hospital. Contraté un vuelo
privado y toda la familia se reunió al lado de su cama. Todo el mundo
se turnaba para sentarse a su lado, susurrarle cosas al oído y decirle
lo que necesitábamos decirle. "Mamá, soy Carlos de nuevo. Estoy sos-
teniéndote la mano y quiero que sepas que recuerdo todo lo que me
dijiste. Me acuerdo de que me dijiste que todo lo que tengo le perte-
nece a Dios: mi guitarra, mi música, mi sonido, mi cuerpo, mi respiración. Todo es prestado y cuando él me pida que se lo devuelva, debo
abrir la mano y dárselo. ¿Recuerdas que dijiste eso, mamá?".

Mi mamá había hablado conmigo acerca de la muerte unos
meses antes. Me preguntó: "¿Tienes miedo a la muerte?". Le

respondí: "No, en absoluto". Se quedó pensando en eso y aseguró: "Yo tampoco". Pero algunas personas mueren antes de su hora porque ya están petrificadas por ella. Le dan a la muerte demasiado poder".

Les pedí a todos que se tomaran de las manos, incluida mamá, y formaran un gran círculo. Luego le dije: "Mamá, todos estamos aquí y te damos permiso para marcharte, si lo deseas". Unos minutos después, se fue.

Conozco a mucha gente y tengo una gran cantidad de amigos y parientes, pero tengo muy pocos amigos *amigos:* personas con quienes comparto un nivel de intimidad profundo y sincero. Esto no es una queja. Esos pocos amigos son lo que llamo mi sistema de apoyo espiritual; a veces me conocen a mí y a mi corazón mejor de lo que yo me conozco a mí mismo. La palabra clave es *confianza.* Confío en ellos para ver cosas que quizá yo no vea, y he aprendido a prestar atención y a escuchar lo que me dicen.

Después del divorcio, me apoyé realmente en mis mejores amigos y ellos no me defraudaron. Para mí es importante reconocer su presencia en mi vida y el hecho de que me hayan presentado todo tipo de divertidas posibilidades con dignidad, benevolencia y modernidad, dependiendo de su naturaleza, ya que son todos muy diferentes.

Gary Rashid, Rashiki, como decidió llamarlo Armando, es a quien conozco desde hace más tiempo. Empezó a trabajar con Bill Graham en el 73, lo que significa que estuvo cerca de Santana mucho tiempo. En esa época él estaba comenzando a realmente escuchar la música y a descubrir su propio camino. Para el 79, era uno de mis mejores amigos y estábamos conociendo más profundamente a Little Walter, Slim Harpo y John Coltrane, descubriendo cosas en la música que le mostraba que yo jamás había detectado. Me encantaba ver cómo él se desarrollaba hasta el punto en que comenzaba a enseñarme a mí. Al día de hoy, cuando me encuentro en Bay Area, una de las cosas que más disfruto hacer es subirme al coche con Gary y dar un paseo de una hora bordeando la costa y escuchando a Miles.

Hay algo más acerca de Gary que yo recibo con los brazos abiertos: se caracteriza por su pureza e inocencia: es infantil, pero no inmaduro y nunca es insensible o demasiado dogmático. Sé que en ocasiones yo puedo ser como un león y rugir. Él, a su vez, puede ser como una paloma y yo necesito eso cerca de mí. Además es un jugador de tenis implacable, pero lo suficientemente amable como para permitirme ganar algunas veces.

Tony Kilbert, Brother TK, como yo lo llamo, es mi ancla en Hawái. Podemos pasar el rato juntos en la playa, mientras él bucea durante horas y horas. Esa es su meditación. Es un tipo alto y guapo, que era uno de los *disc jockeys* con esas voces perfectas de la radio de Bay Area cuando nos conocimos, en los 70. Recuerdo la dedicación que empleaba en sus preguntas cuando me entrevistaba. Pienso que a todos los periodistas se les debería exigir que escuchen la entrevista que le hizo a Bob Marley cerca de esa época, por el respeto y la consciencia con que TK la llevó a cabo. Se puede sentir cómo Bob abre su corazón frente a él.

TK tenía una buena vida y residía en San Rafael, pero luego casi todos sus familiares (su madre y sus tías) fallecieron en un lapso de cinco años, por lo que decidió abandonar su carrera ahí y mudarse a Maui. Aún trabaja con la música y enseña. Además, se dedica a luchar por causas que defienden la integridad natural de las islas y los derechos de los lugareños. Admiro la forma en que sigue su voz interior. Nos gustan los mismos músicos, la misma música y los mismos principios de vida.

Hal Miller es mi amigo que vive en Albany. Era cantante y baterista de doo wop y es originario de la Ciudad de Nueva York. Veía y escuchaba tocar a Coltrane y a Miles por la ciudad. Me encanta cuando habla de las épocas en que creció viendo a estas leyendas y a otras más. Conocí a Hal en la década de 1980 y actualmente es uno de los coleccionistas de videos de jazz más importantes del mundo. Tiene un sentido del humor tan cáustico que si enciendes un fósforo en su presencia, todo se quemará. En realidad creo que la palabra es *irreverente*: nada es demasiado sagrado o santo para él. En una ocasión Dennis Chambers se emocionó demasiado con la música que estábamos tocando y se retiró del equipo de batería por un minuto; fue la primera vez que lo vi hacer eso. Después estábamos hablando y Hal me dijo: "Ah, no es la primera vez que veo llorar a Dennis. La última vez fue cuando volvió a su hogar después de una gira; entró y exclamó: 'Querida, llegué' y de repente me vio en su sala de estar, sentado en su silla favorita ¡y usando su bata!" Viejo, quedamos todos en el suelo después de eso, incluido Dennis. Hal siempre hace bromas ingeniosas con las que entretiene a la gente.

Ese es uno de los motivos por los cuales me gusta que Hal salga de gira con Santana. A veces participa con las congas, pero además conoce nuestra historia y a todos los músicos personalmente. Puede escuchar la banda con precisión y elegancia año tras año. Amo sus oídos y la forma en la que encuentra las palabras para describir lo que está funcionando en nuestra música y lo que podría mejorarse. Aunque tiene algo: Hal no se involucra con nada demasiado espiritual o metafísico. Si la conversación se torna demasiado cósmica, dirá que necesita abandonar la habitación, y está bien. Yo conozco su espíritu, y con eso me basta.

Uno de mis mejores amigos a quien no puedo dejar de mencionar es Chad Wilson, mi primer encargado de seguridad, que llegó a Santana alrededor de la época de *Supernatural,* cuando todo explotó y se volvió enorme. Es de Ohio y me acuerdo de la primera vez que fuimos a París. Teníamos un día libre, así que salimos a caminar y él parecía Dorothy fuera de Kansas, simplemente paralizado cuando vio el Arco del Triunfo por primera vez. Luego se recuperó rápidamente, como si necesitara estar alerta, y yo lo miraba a los ojos y me reía. "Adelante, amigo. Cómete el lugar con los ojos; yo cuidaré de ambos".

Es extraordinario observar a Chad. Al principio él era admirador de Metallica (yo también lo soy) pero ahora escucha *Kind of Blue* y le gusta muchísimo. Al igual que Rashiki, ha recorrido un largo camino. Por un tiempo, le tocó ser como el saco de boxeo de la banda, pero aprendió muchas cosas de eso. Al estar con nosotros, se ha dado cuenta de que existen muchas dimensiones para expandirse y él se ha permitido crecer sin temor.

Ahora Chad se ocupa de mucho más que la seguridad. Es mi asistente personal, mi compañero y parte de la familia, ya que es el padrino de Jelli. Lo más curioso es que me llevó casi seis meses decir su nombre correctamente; mi mamá nunca lo logró, así que lo llamaba Ramón. Cuando él venía conmigo a visitarla, ella le decía: "Oye, Ramón, ¿quieres unos chiles rellenos?". . Y eso fue todo: ahí se enamoró de la comida mexicana y desde entonces le ha quedado Ramón.

Dicen que si vas a nadar al mar y una gran ola te arrastra y te pierdes por completo, lo que debes hacer es encontrar la luz y nadar hacia ella. Cuando tuve mis altibajos después del divorcio, la fuerza y la gentileza que Chad, Rashiki, TK y Hal me demostraron evitó que eligiera el camino incorrecto y me perdiera en mí mismo. Aprendí a reconocer lo afortunado que soy de tener estos amigos, así como su constancia y fuerza de carácter a mi alrededor. De ellos aprendí a tomar consejos aun cuando no haya querido escucharlos.

Si me hubieran preguntado sobre Las Vegas incluso unos años antes de que comenzara a tocar ahí regularmente, en 2009, lo único que sabría de ese lugar era que allí vivían los miembros del Rat Pack y que era un sitio de gente convencional que frecuentaba salones públicos. Después surgieron artistas como Donnie Osmond, Wayne Newton y Tom Jones. Nunca hubiera relacionado Las Vegas con la música de John Lee Hooker. La primera vez que tocamos allí fue en 1969, con Grateful Dead, y esto nos daba temor porque podías sentir lo que la gente que vivía ahí pensaba acerca de los tipos de pelo largo; en aquel entonces no permitían que los hippies estuvieran cerca de los casinos. Era un lugar para pasar una noche y luego largarse de ahí.

Pero las cosas han cambiado en Las Vegas y la mayoría de las personas que la visita crecieron con Santana, es su música. Esa es la cuestión: yo no me había dado cuenta de que la gente que iba a escucharnos tocar en Las Vegas no necesariamente vivía allí. Iban de todas partes del mundo. Además, ahora cuando tocamos allí no es como antes, cuando no eras más que música de fondo mientras la gente hablaba y bebía. Ahora somos la atracción principal y ¿qué mejor lugar para proporcionar una dosis de un virus espiritual que el público pueda llevarse a su hogar, junto con las playeras, las gorras y cualquier artículo que haya ganado en los casinos? Verdaderamente no encuentro más barreras con lo que hacemos sobre en el escenario con el público de Las Vegas que en cualquier otro lugar.

La relación de Santana con Las Vegas se inició en 2009 en el Hard Rock Hotel y en 2011 la House of Blues nos propuso un contrato para que hagamos nuestro espectáculo allí. La House of Blues nos honra al presentarnos de una manera que no es superficial ni sintética; las instalaciones y los técnicos son profesionales y nos brindan el tipo de apoyo publicitario que reciben las principales actuaciones en Las Vegas. Con el Hard Rock Hotel pasaba lo mismo. El público puede acercarse bastante y me gusta eso. En algunos aspectos es mejor que los estadios y auditorios porque puedo oír si quieren más intensidad o alguna canción en particular; puedo saber cómo se están sintiendo.

Cuando nos trasladamos a la House of Blues, nos dimos cuenta de que la ciudad podía funcionar no solo como sede de la banda, sino que también podía ser un buen sitio para que yo viviera allí. Había varias razones; podíamos ahorrar dinero al no tener que salir de gira todo el tiempo y no incurrir en gastos de viajes. El casino Mandalay Bay, que está asociado a la House of Blues, nos brinda las habitaciones de hotel, las comidas y los pasajes aéreos para nuestros traslados. Además, como residente de Nevada, pagaría muchos menos impuestos que en California. Una vez más, el tema no era solo cómo ahorrar dinero, sino, como sucede con la Fundación Milagro, controlar adónde es dirigido para que no engrose simplemente las arcas del gobierno y sea invertido en personas de carne y hueso e instituciones reales que puedan servir a la humanidad en general.

La persona que descubrió esto y logró que sucediera es Michael Vrionis, que ahora es mi representante. Después del divorcio, cuando era necesario que alguien ocupara el puesto de director ejecutivo del negocio de Santana, Michael pudo intervenir sin sentirse abrumado por el trabajo. Yo sabía que su plan era bueno porque nuestros abogados y contadores me llamaron de inmediato para decirme que había tenido un golpe de suerte y que esa idea nos permitiría ahorrar mucho dinero. Michael es un veterano del mundo de los negocios y habla ese idioma muy bien. Además, está casado con mi hermana María, y juntos conforman un equipo extraordinario que mantiene los estándares de Santana muy altos. En 2011 reformamos la administración del grupo, la emplazamos en Las Vegas y la llamamos Universal Tone. A fin de cuentas no se trata solo de algo monetario. Michael ha sido muy bueno a la hora de conservar las relaciones: está en contacto permanentemente y mantiene los vínculos activos con los principales representantes de HBO y Sony Music, incluso con Clive Davis. En 2012 nos ayudó a comenzar Starfaith, nuestra nueva compañía discográfica, que produjo el álbum de Santana *Shape Shifter*.

Hoy Santana se encuentra bendecida con músicos que aportan convicción y coherencia. Benny Rietveld sigue siendo nuestro director musical y bajista, y sus solos destacados, como su soplido en "Imagine" de John Lennon, constituyen una parte importante de nuestros espectáculos. Karl Perazzo es quien ha estado con Santana durante más tiempo, y su potencia y gracia son nuestra conexión con el increíble ambiente latino de San Francisco: tocó con Sheila E. y hasta con Prince durante un cierto período. Me encanta darme vuelta y ubicarme frente a él cuando intercambiamos *riffs* en la guitarra y los timbales. Bill Ortiz y Jeff Cressman componen la sección de vientos de Santana y también surgieron de la increíble tradición de jazz de Bay Area. Bill ha grabado un álbum excelente en el que toca la trompeta sobre pistas de hip-hop, y los expresivos solos de Jeff con un sabor caribeño me recuerdan a grandes trombonistas de ska, como Don Drummond. Andy Vargas y Tony Lindsay son las voces de Santana, y entre ambos cubren la gama completa de matices: desde el gospel y los sonidos más turbios (*gutbucket*) hasta los claros y suaves; y ayudan a retener la energía, puesto que siempre están ubicados al frente y en el borde del escenario.

Ahora también tenemos a Tommy Anthony, que vino con nosotros de la banda de Gloria Estefan y tiene tres talentos claros: es un cantante de voz clara y aguda; un guitarrista rítmico con un vocabulario de acordes de rock sorprendente; y es uno de los mejores solistas de guitarra de Miami. Además tenemos a David K. Mathews en teclados, que estuvo con Etta James y Tower of Power antes de venir con nosotros. Se ha convertido en alguien indispensable para la banda, porque conoce de todo, desde Otis Spann y McCoy Tyner hasta Randy Weston y Eddie Palmieri. También tiene tatuadas a las leyendas del piano Fats Waller y James Booker.

Los dos miembros más recientes son Paoli Mejias Ramos, en las congas, y José Pepe Jiménez, en batería. Ambos tienen orígenes portorriqueños y han traído su propia autenticidad y compromiso, lo que brinda una nueva sensación a la música, pero nos mantiene en una situación de banda: no soy únicamente yo ubicado al frente con tipos que tocan distintas partes y visten la chaqueta de Santana. Prefiero oírnos correr riesgos, probar nuevas canciones y tener una mala actuación, antes que hacer una actuación adecuada que únicamente haga sonar todos los viejos éxitos.

Antes de cada concierto de Santana aún medito entre quince y veinte minutos, y todos en la banda están invitados a acompañarme; no es un requisito, pero casi todos vienen y se unen al círculo al menos una vez cada tanto. Siempre les digo: "Nada es obligatorio, únicamente que estén el cien por ciento presentes y que toquen lo mejor posible sobre el escenario". Después de meditar, organizo una reunión previa al espectáculo para hablar sobre este y repasar las nuevas melodías, transiciones o partes de una canción que mantienen el espectáculo renovado y en movimiento. A veces intentamos algo que se nos ocurre por algo que alguien dijo o algo que escuché en mi iPod. Recientemente estuvimos en Mónaco y yo decidí que debíamos probar una canción de O'Jays que conozco, "I Love Music", que habla de unirse y ayudarse los unos a los otros, y tiene una fabulosa energía de *gospel*. Un mensaje perfecto para una cena lujosa con espectáculo en esa parte del mundo, ¿no? Quizá deberíamos haber hecho "Rich Get Richer". De todos modos, la trabajamos en la prueba de sonido y detrás de escena antes del espectáculo. Solo la hicimos una vez, pero valió la pena.

* * *

En Las Vegas hay mucho dinero, *mucho*. Sé que esto no es una novedad para nadie. Para mí, hay un sentimiento de posibilidad en esa atmósfera de desierto: la cristalización de un objetivo que podría alcanzar a habitantes de todas partes del mundo, que es algo que no se siente en otros lugares. Es como la diferencia entre millones y miles de millones. No es difícil encontrarse allí con gente como el director del Mandalay Bay u otros artistas que difunden ideas sobre cómo invertir parte de ese dinero y realmente lograr una diferencia. Está empezando a ocurrir; simplemente mira la fundación de Andre Agassi y Steffi Graff, y lo que hacen allí con los niños y las escuelas de Las Vegas.

Una noche no muy lejana, mi abogado, John Branca, Michael, Cindy y yo cenamos con algunos de los principales ejecutivos del casino y sus esposas, y preguntaban cómo hacíamos para mantener a Santana siempre renovada y con tanta energía después de todo este tiempo. Les conté, pero luego dije: "Bueno, me alegra responder estas preguntas, pero necesito que sepan dos cosas directamente de mi corazón. La primera es que la consciencia puede ser muy rentable. La segunda es la siguiente: aquí en Las Vegas tienen los medios, el dinero y el talento para asociarse y crear un espectáculo de televisión de entrevistas y música todas las noches que supere todo lo que viene de Nueva York o Los Ángeles. Solo hay que encontrar al presentador adecuado, alguien que sea gracioso pero no predecible y que pueda transmitir el mensaje correcto sobre de qué manera todos podemos ayudar al planeta".

Me miraron como preguntándose qué tan en serio lo decía y comprendieron que lo decía muy en serio. Después de un momento dije: "No hay nada que no sea posible cuando tienes una determinación suprema y una visión decidida".

Extraño algunas cosas de la costa oeste, pero tan solo se encuentra a un vuelo de noventa minutos de distancia, y he aprendido a amar Las Vegas y a compartirla con Cindy, la nueva reina de mi corazón; contemplando el amanecer y el atardecer juntos, pasando hermosos momentos en el desierto, meditando, haciendo ejercicios, tocando la guitarra, escuchando mi música favorita o comiendo con ella en un fantástico restaurante del cual ya conozco muy bien al chef y al personal. Después está otra de mis cosas favoritas: levantarme al día siguiente con Cindy, que es tan suave: no solo su piel, sino su mente y su corazón; y luego comenzar todo de nuevo.

En febrero de 2010, Salvador lanzó un nuevo disco y organizó una fiesta en Los Angeles. Deborah estaba allí, y cuando llegué vino a saludarme y me dio un abrazo de cortesía. Yo sabía que todos nuestros hijos nos estaban mirando. Al día siguiente volé de regreso a Las Vegas y recibí una tarjeta de ella en la que me decía que había sido lindo verme. La llamé y le agradecí la tarjeta. Aún estábamos tratando de resolver cómo nos comportábamos el uno con el otro, pero nuestra prioridad era hacer lo que fuera mejor para nuestros hijos: ser sinceros, positivos y respetuosos.

En ese momento ocurrieron dos cosas: logré liberarme de manera consciente de mi sentimiento de culpa sobre Deborah, tanto emocional como psicológicamente, y dejé de fumar, pero esta vez totalmente y no de forma parcial. Continué con el trabajo interno, pero era diferente, como si una enorme puerta se abriera hacia una habitación que había estado cerrada por un largo tiempo. Cuando entré en la habitación, pude oír una voz que decía: "Respira profundamente, limpia el lugar, cepíllate los dientes, abre la puerta, abre tu corazón y vuelve a ser vulnerable". Respiré hondo, el aire era refrescante y lo sentí diferente en mis pulmones. Luego escuché: "Ahora invita a tu reina".

La primera vez que Cindy Blackman y yo nos vimos en realidad no ocurrió nada. Me gustaría decir que sí, pero ambos estábamos en distintos lugares en nuestras vidas, y parte de la alegría de vivir consiste en no tener todo a tu alcance al mismo tiempo. Solo cuando miras en retrospectiva ves cómo la historia cobra sentido. Corría el año 2002, ella tocaba la batería con Lenny Kravitz y todos nos encontrábamos en un festival de rock en Alemania. Dennis Chambers hacía tiempo que me decía: "Amigo, espera hasta que veas tocar a esta chica. Es fantástica". Así que me quedé a ver el espectáculo de Lenny, y quizá fueron las dos canciones que escuché, pero no escuché lo que él me había dicho. Pensaba: "Bueno, hum… ¿Cuándo empezará a tocar?". Básicamente, lo que ella estaba haciendo era mantener un ritmo estable, como si estuviera sosteniendo una bandeja para alguien; la música no quería dejarla ir. Pero la siguiente noche fue una revelación. Cindy hizo algunos solos fantásticos y tocó unos alocados pasajes de relleno. Ahí fue cuando supe que ella realmente podía tocar.

Mientras más escuchaba, más cambiaba mi percepción acerca de Lenny y su música. Debo agradecerle a él desde el centro de mi corazón porque hizo posible que yo supiera que Cindy existía. Unos años después, Tracy, la hermana de Cindy, que es cantante y guitarrista, me vio comiendo en un restaurante de Bay Area llamado Comforts. De repente había una mujer de hermoso cabello rojo y pecas parada junto a mí, que con total confianza me dijo: "Tú eres Carlos Santana". Le dije "hola" y pensé que quería que le firmara algo o tomarse una foto. Pero en cambio, tenía un mensaje para darme: "Debes conocer a mi hermana, ella toca la batería". Por supuesto que reconocí el nombre cuando me lo dijo. Le respondí: "De acuerdo, te lo agradezco mucho".

Todavía no significaba nada para mí, Cupido aún no había arrojado ninguna flecha. Luego, en mayo, tocamos en un espectáculo privado para una compañía de electrónica alemana en Orlando y Dennis no podía ir porque había sido contratado por otra persona. Oí una voz que me dijo: "Llama a Cindy".

"¿Cindy?".

"¿Te acuerdas de Cindy Blackman, que tocaba con Lenny?". Entonces le pedí a mi gerente de producción que la contactara; y ya la habíamos confirmado cuando Rashiki y yo finalmente tuvimos tiempo para descargar sus álbumes y escucharlos mientras dábamos vueltas en el coche. Exclamé: "¡Ay, no! ¡No es la misma persona que escuché aquella vez en Alemania!"

Cindy estaba tocando música en un nivel diferente del que yo me esperaba, improvisando y estableciendo ritmos muy evolucionados, y tocaba con artistas como Patrice Rushen y Buster Williams.

Podía adivinar que tenía bastante de Tony Williams y algo de Elvin Jones en su colección de música; después supe que había aprendido mucho por haber pasado tiempo con Art Blakey. Me dejó un correo de voz en el teléfono para que habláramos sobre la música del espectáculo. La llamé y conversamos sobre la lista de temas; después yo seguí con mi historia sobre la marca del *wah*, que le cuento a cada persona nueva que ingresa en la banda.

Esto se remonta a algo que vi en África cuando tocamos en 1971: un círculo de seis o siete mujeres que empezaron a cantar juntas "ey ya na na na…" cada vez más y más rápido; sus voces cantaban partes diferentes hasta que unieron todo en el mismo instante con un gigantesco *"¡¡wah!!"* Fue increíble toda esa energía a la vez. Después de eso empecé a distinguir el *wah* en la música de Buddy Rich, James Brown, Duke Ellington y Tito Puente, y cómo cada uno tiene su propia forma de marcar el *wah*, o el 1. Pero la banda no puede marcar el *wah* demasiado fuerte o pasarse de la raya; debe llegar a él en la medida suficiente y en el momento preciso para suministrarle una consciencia colectiva.

Estábamos preparándonos para hacer la prueba de sonido en Florida un día antes del espectáculo de Orlando, cuando vi a Cindy que caminaba lentamente desde la sala hasta el escenario, sonrió y me saludó con la mano. Había venido a ver la banda antes de tocar con nosotros y llevaba algo consigo. Estaba vestida de modo muy sencillo, como si fuera a una clase de yoga; simple, pero moderna y sin maquillaje, lo que para mí puede ser diez veces más magnético que el *glamour*. Escuchó la banda, mientras yo la miraba con el rabillo del ojo. Tenía un espíritu que yo podía sentir. Yo sabía que ella estaba muy entusiasmada por estar allí y tocar con nosotros, y eso es exactamente lo que espero que le ocurra a cada músico.

Nos encontramos detrás de escena después de la prueba de sonido y me mostró un libro: el catálogo de una exhibición de Miles Davis en Montreal. Entonces busqué mi iPod en el bolso de mano que siempre llevo conmigo y se lo di; estaba lleno de todos los fragmentos de música de Miles que había recopilado durante años, muchos de los cuales son muy difíciles de encontrar. Volvió a su habitación del hotel, escuchó el iPod y encontró "Capri", de Paolo Rustichelli, una bella melodía en la que toca Miles. Es una melodía tan hermosa que, si pienso en eso, estoy casi seguro de que en ese momento a ella le dieron ganas de casarse conmigo. Estoy bromeando, pero realmente con música como esa no creo que ella tuviera otra opción.

Hicimos el espectáculo juntos en Orlando y salió fantástico; ella estuvo genial. Sabía todas las partes y su percusión me recordaba a un colibrí o a una abeja enojada. Cindy tiene muy buen ritmo, pero no se dedica solamente a marcar el compás, no se conforma solamente con tocar de forma correcta. Después el resto es personal, pero mencionaré esto: nos encontramos y hablamos durante horas, y de repente yo estaba mostrándole lo que hacíamos con Santana, la Fundación Milagro y un sitio web llamado Architects of a New Dawn, que tiene algunos de mis videos favoritos. Ahora me doy cuenta de que yo estaba intentando mostrarle quién soy verdaderamente, como persona, más allá del Santana guitarrista.

Al día siguiente Cindy me dijo que tenía que irse a un concierto con un guitarrista y cantante de rock amerindio: "Me voy a Santa Fe para tocar con Micki Free y su banda". No intenté ocultar mi desilusión. "¿En serio? ¿Por qué tienes que irte?". No podía creer que me estuviera oyendo a mí mismo decirle eso a otro músico. "¿Por qué no te quedas?".

"No, de veras; tengo que hacer este concierto".

Así que Cindy se marchó; tomé del brazo a Chad y le dije: "Tenemos que ir a Disney World".

¿"A Disney World? ¿Para qué?". No tenía tiempo para explicarle todo, pero de algún modo Cindy y yo habíamos terminado hablando sobre Mickey y Minnie Mouse la noche anterior, entonces le dije: "Tengo que encontrar unas orejas con brillo de Minnie Mouse para enviárselas a Cindy". Caminamos durante casi dos horas y entramos a todas las tiendas del lugar, y había muchas. Los vendedores nos decían "por allá" y "ahí", pero la mayoría no entendían de qué les estábamos hablando. Chad estaba listo para encargarlas a medida.

536 · CARLOS SANTANA

Justo cuando estábamos por rendirnos encontré a dos vendedoras que me preguntaron: "Ah, ¿te refieres a las que son para niñas pequeñas? Esas son las únicas que tienen brillo. Aquí están".

Me relajé, pedí que las empaquetaran especialmente y las traje a casa: en cierta forma tenía el presentimiento de que una vez que se las diera a Cindy, algo realmente importante ocurriría. Y así fue.

Si bien soy residente de Nevada, también tengo una casa en lo alto de las colinas en Tiburon, con una increíble vista de North Bay y del puente Golden Gate. Invité a Cindy a que me visitara allí cuando ambos hubiéramos concluido las giras en junio, y ella aceptó. Recuerdo que la observé caminar mientras entraba en mi casa, con el andar elegante de una pantera, mirando todo a su alrededor. La casa tiene grandes ventanas y el día no podía ser más hermoso, con el sol resplandeciente por todas partes, mientras el cielo y la bahía lucían un increíble tono azul. Vino y me dio lo que yo llamo un "abrazo de cocina", no por el sitio donde tuvo lugar, sino porque fue largo, afectuoso y lleno de una promesa de devoción familiar. Quedó sellado en ese preciso instante; y luego le coloqué las orejas de Minnie Mouse en la cabeza. Viejo, sentí que tenía diecisiete años y estaba en la preparatoria otra vez, sintiendo en un momento toda la pasión y la emoción que piensas que alguna vez experimentarás en tu vida. Bueno, mejor dicho, catorce años y en la secundaria.

Nos sentamos y recuerdo que le tomé las manos, la miré a los ojos y después oí mi propia voz que le decía muy suavemente: "Cindy, ¿quieres ser mi esposa?". Parecía una niñita. Los ojos le brillaron y los abrió bien grandes mientras respondía "sí".

Por supuesto, yo tenía que pedirle permiso a su padre, Daddy Dude, que así es como lo llamo. Debido a que le pregunté a Cindy si quería venir con Santana ese verano y unirse a nosotros cada noche, esperamos unas semanas hasta que la gira nos llevó a Chicago, donde vivía él. Fuimos a un restaurante de comida sureña estadounidense y aguardé su respuesta. Me miró, luego miró a Cindy durante un largo rato y me dijo: "Creo que nunca la he visto más feliz, Carlos".

La noche siguiente ya no aguantármelo ni un segundo más. El padre de Cindy y su pareja fueron al concierto, junto con las esposas de Buddy Guy y de Otis Rush. Se sentía como una gran familia. Después de que Cindy tocó un solo de batería en "Corazón Espinado", me dirigí hasta el micrófono y aproveché la oportunidad frente al público del First Midwest Bank Amphitheater en Tinley Park, Illinois, para pedirle una vez más que fuera mi esposa. Su respuesta fue la misma que la primera vez.

Cindy viajó con Santana hasta fines de 2010 y participó casi todas las noches; de hecho, eso sigue ocurriendo. Ella sale de gira con nosotros o toca cuando estamos en la House of Blues en Las Vegas y continúa haciendo su propia música, incluida su banda tributo a Tony Williams Lifetime, con Vernon Reid, el organista John Medeski y el bajista Jack Bruce. En casa la veo tocar la batería, tocarla de verdad, y veo su rostro y me digo a mí mismo: "Ella nació para hacer esto, conmigo o sin mí", y no hay ningún problema. Me da pena cualquiera que trate de interponerse entre alguien como ella y lo que ella ama, diciendo: "Soy yo o la música". ¿Discúlpame? Bueno, ya sabes lo que opino de eso.

Me encanta la confianza en las mujeres, y realmente la necesito en mi mujer. Cindy tiene una confianza callada que le surge de no tener que probarle nada a nadie. Es una bendición para mí estar con una persona que se siente tan cómoda en su propia piel.

Además de ser mi pareja y amiga, ella es paciente, compasiva y atenta: siempre me pregunta si me estoy hidratando, lo que es muy importante en un lugar como Las Vegas. Si trae una botella de agua para un paseo en coche, siempre trae una segunda para mí. La llevé a su primer juego de baloncesto profesional, y ahora es admiradora de los Golden State Warriors y me ha despertado el interés en algunos equipos de Chicago. Ahora tengo una compañera con quien hacer frente a admiradores del baloncesto como Hal Miller y Chad Wilson, que siempre me atacan en grupo y apuestan en mi contra. Yo les digo lo que pienso acerca de los Heat o los Spurs y ellos exclaman: "¡Ay, ahora es 'Cindy y yo'!"

Sí, así es. Cindy es uno más de los muchachos; es decir, ella viene de pasar tiempo con Art Blakey & the Jazz Messengers y Tony Williams, oyendo todas las conversaciones de hombres, riendo y observando que nadie se salga de las casillas. Como cualquier pareja, aún estamos aprendiendo a comunicarnos. Lo hacemos por teléfono y por mensajes de texto y, cuando vuelvo a casa, en palabras y en contacto físico.

Hay un dicho que reza: no atraes necesariamente lo que deseas o necesitas, atraes lo que eres. No me sorprendí al saber que Cindy estudiaba la cábala y es profundamente espiritual. Cuando hablé por primera vez con ella de temas como los ángeles y el reino invisible, fue como si estuviéramos retomando una conversación que habíamos iniciado hacía un largo tiempo. Cuando les comenté a Jerry y a Diane, dijeron: "Sabes, Cindy es una creación de tu espíritu. Tú la creaste y ella te creó a ti. Ambos rezaron por el otro y ambos realizaron el trabajo interno. Cindy también está aquí para ayudarte a limpiar tu clóset interno". Pregunté: "¿Clóset interno?". Jerry me explicó que necesitaba abrir todos los cajones y dejar salir todas mis compulsiones, turbaciones y fantasías, así como olvidar la culpa, la vergüenza, los prejuicios y los miedos.

Ahora Cindy y yo tenemos la misma aspiración; compartimos el deseo de divinidad. Cindy y yo leemos juntos todos los días para recargar nuestra creencia y afianzar nuestra esperanza, confianza y fe, de modo que cuando necesitemos fuerza tengamos la necesaria para librar de obstáculos nuestros caminos y apartar nuestros egos. Juntos escribimos poemas y mensajes espirituales que publicamos en Facebook y compartimos con todo el mundo. Escribimos juntos el siguiente poema, "Yo soy el Tono Universal", el 8 de julio de 2011:

Yo soy el tono universal
del que surgen la inspiración, la visión, la motivación y la aspiración.
Tú eres el ritmo que está en contacto con el pulso de todos los corazones.
Somos las vasijas que encauzan la luz y el amor de Dios.
Todas y cada una de las cosas del reino de Dios son precursoras de su
    esencia
Dulce armonía, unidad sólida, gracia gentil, divinidad y belleza
Es lo que somos y quiénes somos cuando estamos conscientes de
    estar en el centro de nuestro corazón

Y cuando estamos en un flujo de armonía perfecta con nuestro
Creador y el universo
Permanecemos abiertos a recibir su luz y encauzarla hacia TODO lo
que existe.
Sonríe y deja que la luz brille y eleve, transforme, ilumine todo y a
todos
Con la alegría, la paz, la luz y el amor de tu espíritu.
Sé feliz y llénate de amor en tu suprema divinidad.

Cuatro años después me siento agradecido; muy, muy agradecido. Aún me cuesta creer que entre todas las personas de este mundo Dios me eligiera una compañera tan compatible con mi energía y mis principios y la pusiera frente a mí. Como dice Wayne, para ser feliz hay que tener coraje, y en este preciso momento creo que soy la persona más feliz de este planeta. Mi tesoro más preciado actualmente es una nueva guitarra que mi esposa le encargó a Paul Reed Smith y me obsequió cuando nos casamos, el 19 de diciembre de 2010, en Hawái. Escritas en la parte posterior entre las perillas de afinación, pueden leerse las siguientes palabras: "La primera vez, todo. Eternamente tuya, Cindy".

En nuestra boda estuvieron todas las personas importantes para nosotros: nuestras familias y nuestros mejores amigos, mis hijos, y Jerry y Diane, que hablaron y pidieron unos minutos de silencio para que todos nos contemplemos sin distracción alguna de palabras o de pensamientos. Herbie y Wayne estaban ahí, también, y nos honraron con su presencia y su música, ya que tocaron "Afro Blue" y "Stella by Starlight". Antes de la ceremonia le pregunté a Sal si le parecía bien lo que estaba haciendo y lo que me respondió todavía me lleva a preguntarme cómo logró un nivel tan elevado de consciencia espiritual. Nos pidió a Cindy y a mí, como parte de la ceremonia, que llenáramos un tazón de madera con agua de lluvia y nos laváramos las manos mutuamente para simbolizar el perdón por todas las cosas de nuestro pasado, para así comenzar renovados y purificados. Lo hicimos, a continuación Cindy leyó sus votos en su iPhone y yo los leí en mi iPad, y luego bailamos al son de la grabación de Ronald Isley de "The Look of Love", de Burt Bacharach.

La segunda vez que caminé por la alfombra roja lo hice con Cindy, en diciembre de 2013, para la proyección del especial de HBO de nuestro concierto en Guadalajara. Esa fue su primera vez, y estaba deslumbrante, yo no podía dejar de mirarla—. De todas maneras yo miro a Cindy constantemente: tiene una nariz tan hermosa, sus labios y su cabello son increíbles y, para mí, su corazón integra todo a la perfección. Cuando llegó el momento de detenernos frente a los fotógrafos esa noche, ella se olvidó de mirar a las cámaras, como se supone que debe hacerse, y en cambio me miraba a *mí*. Recuerdo que nos reímos de eso, luego Cindy se puso seria y destacó: "¿Pero puedes ver la forma en que te estoy mirando?". Viejo, podía sentir que me estaban brotando lágrimas de alegría, así que tenía que decir lo que estaba pensando rápidamente en ese instante, las únicas palabras que me venían a la mente en ese momento.

"Oh, sí. *Sí*".

EPÍLOGO

Hoy y mañana

El arzobispo Desmond Tutu y yo, 24 de febrero de 2014.

Cuando tocamos en vivo en el Festival de Jazz de Montreux en 1988 con Wayne Shorter, Wayne contó en una entrevista: "Busco libros que nunca terminan". Me encanta esa idea. Este libro es así: aún faltan muchas cosas por ocurrir y, sin embargo, vive en el instante sagrado, en un santuario donde no hay que preocuparse por el futuro ni quedarse estancado en el pasado. Nadie está loco si está el cien por ciento presente en el ahora, ¿sabes?

En mi vida, el ahora que aún se está escribiendo siempre ha incluido tres partes: mi música, el reino espiritual y el ritmo doméstico.

Lo dije anteriormente y lo repito: en mi familia, incluso después del divorcio, solo quedan bendiciones y belleza. Le agradezco a Deborah por nuestros años juntos y nuestros tres hermosos hijos. Estoy muy orgulloso de ellos; nunca se han metido en problemas y cada uno tiene una sensibilidad natural para mantenerse en el ritmo con elegancia e integridad. Puedo ver a miembros de mi familia reflejados en cada uno de ellos y puedo observar que todos provienen de un largo río de música: mi padre era músico, su padre era músico municipal y también lo fue su padre antes que él. Por el lado de su madre, SK era el rey original del R&B, y tocaba *blues* y baladas antes de que B. B., Albert o Freddie lo hicieran. A través de Sal, Stella y Jelli, el río sigue corriendo.

Mientras trabajaba en este libro pensé mucho en mis hijos. "¿Qué pensarán cuando lo lean?". Sé que van a decir que fui honesto, puro y compasivo, y con eso me basta.

He aprendido de mis hijos cómo ser padre: cuándo hablar y cuándo no hablar. De Santana, en el ámbito musical, he aprendido a ser el líder de una banda. Incluso antes de Santana, yo pensaba que a veces alguien tiene que dar un paso al frente y decir algo y, si nadie lo hace, entonces me toca ser el chef de la cocina. Aprendí que un líder no duda en expresar su opinión y decir: "Las papas todavía están crudas y demasiado duras. Dejemos que se cocinen un poco más".

Santana surgió porque yo escuchaba a un nuevo músico como Michael Shrieve, Chepito o Neal Schon y pensaba: "Podría funcionar con la banda que tenemos ahora", y esto sigue siendo así. Siempre hay lugar para el crecimiento y el cambio. Santana en 2014 no es lo que era en el 68, el 73 o el 89. Tampoco pretendemos que sea lo mismo. Creo que ese es el distintivo de Santana: lo único que se ha mantenido igual en nuestra música es la coherencia de una presentación cada vez más elevada.

Pienso que ese es el motivo por el cual la música de Santana se mantiene fuerte y vital. También creo que nuestra música les recuerda a las personas que no tienen que esperar a que llegue el cielo; este ya está aquí. Tiene el poder de inspirar, de transportar y de cambiar a la gente, incluso en un nivel físico. Recibo cartas, correos electrónicos y publicaciones en línea de admiradores que cuentan que un concierto los ayudó a curarse de formas que necesitaban, pero que nunca habían esperado. Tan solo durante el año pasado he oído de personas de Dayton y Spokane que han manifestado que nuestra música llegó a sus almas y transformó sus cuerpos. Todo ha sido puesto en marcha y conectado por el sonido, por ende cuando hablo sobre mi vida musical y el reino espiritual, deben comprender que estos no pueden separarse. El sonido asalta tus sentidos y bombardea tus moléculas, y tu cuerpo sabe que más allá de lo que la mente piense, la conexión siempre está allí.

Más que un recorrido por la senda de los recuerdos, este libro pretende sacar a la luz todas las historias de mi vida para que las personas puedan ver que siempre hay espacio para el crecimiento y la iluminación espiritual. Con "iluminación espiritual" me refiero a tomarse todo con calma, a disfrutar de la vida. Aun cuando mi vida estaba totalmente equilibrada; cuando el aspecto familiar, musical y espiritual se habían manifestado en los más altos niveles (incluso en Woodstock y en los premios Grammy) me costaba mucho aceptarme a mí mismo y verme como los demás me veían. Pero ahora puedo hacerlo, y me relajo y me tomo las cosas con calma. A veces estoy cepillándome los dientes o peinándome el cabello y de repente grito: "¡Rayos!" Cindy viene y me pregunta: "¿Qué sucede; estás bien?". Sigo mirándome al espejo y le contesto: "Este sí que es un mexicano muy guapo. No es de extrañar que me hayas perseguido por todos lados". Ella me mira y se limita a mover la cabeza.

En este momento tengo sesenta y siete años de juventud y me siento estupendo, con toneladas de energía. Un día mío habitual comienza temprano y termina tarde por la noche. Creo que todos estos años de dieta vegetariana estricta, aunque ahora coma carne, a la larga han ayudado a mi cuerpo. Sigo siendo quisquilloso con las comidas: trato de no comer en exceso y de consumir ensaladas cuando puedo. Disfruto de una cerveza o un vaso de vino, pero no soy de beber mucho. Además hago ejercicio todos los días. Me alegra decir que mis ojos y oídos no necesitan ayuda alguna, y todo lo otro que debe funcionar, como músico y como hombre, está funcionando bien, por suerte.

Wayne y yo hemos hablado sobre qué ocurriría si alguna vez llegamos a un momento en que algunas cosas ya no nos funcionen, cuando nuestros dedos ya no quieran trabajar más, y dijo que eso no le preocupaba. "Las personas creativas siempre encuentran una forma de crear". Esta frase me reconforta mucho y todos los días le agradezco a Dios que mis dedos puedan sostener una guitarra, tocar los acordes y encontrar las notas que pueden transformar e inspirar. Si alguna vez llega un momento en que mis dedos ya no puedan hacerlo, estaré agradecido por el tiempo en que sí pudieron.

Si mis habilidades me abandonan, creo que fundaré una pequeña iglesia en Hawái. La llamaré Iglesia de la Sagrada Elección porque eso es lo que todos tenemos: una elección. Será diferente de las demás iglesias, ya que el único requerimiento será que cada persona se comprometa internamente a lograr un cambio tangible en su interior, a asumir una responsabilidad y a dejar de ser una víctima amargada. Tienes que ser como un perro que se sacude el agua, quitarte todo aquello que no deberías cargar.

Me imagino la iglesia con bancos y abierta al mundo exterior; y con una música vibrante y vital, cuya parte principal será el ritmo. Puede ser música local, pero deberá tener congas para derribar el falso concepto de que los tambores y la percusión son los instrumentos del demonio. Yo hablaré y habrá cantos religiosos, y aunque todavía pueda tocar un poco la guitarra, la reservaré a un lado para eventos especiales. Cuando llegue el momento, esa parte de mi vida se dedicará a presentar lo que el Espíritu Santo quiere que presente.

Estoy en este hermoso planeta desde el 20 de julio de 1947 y nunca jamás le recé o le pedí nada a Satán, a Lucifer, a los demonios ni a ninguna otra fuerza oscura. Creo en los ángeles, los arcángeles, los sintonizadores de pensamiento, los seres sensitivos, los espíritus benévolos y los familiares que han fallecido y aún están aquí para guiarme y protegerme. Sigo leyendo y meditando, y hago lo que puedo para fortalecer los músculos de mi pensamiento, como desarrollo el resto de mis músculos en el gimnasio. Algunas personas piensan que una vez que comienzas a descubrir las cosas divinas y recorres el camino de la iluminación espiritual tienes que perder el apetito por el mundo, y eso no es cierto. Esa no es la manera en que he vivido mi vida y esto no cambiará.

Creo que existe un ser supremo, un creador supremo, y ya sea Jesús, Buda, Krishna o Alá. Es como dijo John Coltrane: "Todos los caminos conducen a Dios". La divinidad tiene muchos nombres, pero un solo destino. Dios es pura armonía; no solo un acorde o una nota. Decir que uno de ellos es el único y que todo aquel que adore a otro está equivocado e irá al infierno es un pensamiento momificado y petrificado.

Yo no quiero ir al cielo si este es selectivo. Y hay otra cosa por la cual rezo: solo quiero ir al cielo si allá arriba hay congas.

Mi libro comenzó con un desfile y termina en una isla.

Pienso mucho en las islas. A veces los entrevistadores quieren saber qué música u otras cosas me llevaría a un lugar desierto. Generalmente les respondo *Sketches of Spain*, de Miles Davis, mi guitarra y una copia del libro *A Course in Miracles*. A fines de 2013 estaba casi listo para mudarme a una isla: fuimos desde el Kennedy Center Honors directamente a México para filmar el especial de HBO y terminamos *Corazón* alrededor de esa época.

Ese es un sueño que aún tengo: vender todo y mudarme a algún lugar como Hawái, pero como era hace cien años. Todavía hay lugares de ese tipo en todo el mundo, adonde puedes escaparte, esconderte y coexistir con la naturaleza; donde el cielo es tu techo, el océano es tu tina de baño y la temperatura siempre es la ideal. Si tienes hambre, simplemente tomas una papaya, un coco o un mango de un árbol.

Solía decirme a mí mismo: "¡Guau!, qué existencia increíble que debe ser". Ahora escucho una voz que me dice: "No te engañes a ti mismo, viejo. En dos horas estarías muerto de aburrimiento".

La parte de mi vida que es agotadora es la dicotomía entre tener tanta energía y sentir que realmente necesito descubrir cómo relajarme, y disminuir las giras y la planificación para ponerme a tono conmigo mismo y obtener una mejor visión del futuro. Estar con Cindy me ha ayudado en eso; he realizado conscientemente un compromiso para dejar de ir de gira y dejar de hacer cosas relacionadas con Santana de tanto en tanto, para salirme de la locura. Ahora, como siempre, para mí todo se trata del instante sagrado, del estado de gracia al que siempre intento llegar y mantenerme, y de estar preparado en todas partes y de todas las formas para recibir el Tono Universal.

Reconocimientos

Hubo una serie de personas que fueron sumamente importantes gracias a la ayuda que me brindaron para presentar este libro. Ashley Kahn aportó sus habilidades de escritura y su consciencia para captar mi voz, y tomar momentos y recuerdos para construir con ellos un edificio que yo sintiera como un hogar y que es una invitación abierta para todos los que quieran aprender, descubrir y experimentar una alegría eterna. Hal Miller se sentó y viajó conmigo, grabando mis historias y preservando los detalles, los nombres y las fechas; e hizo un resumen de todo eso para asegurarse de mostrar un panorama completo y, además, mantuvo un equilibrio entre las distintas partes de mi vida: la familiar, la musical y la psicología callejera moderna comprobada. Agradezco al equipo que hizo posible todo esto: a mi agente literaria, Jillian Manus; a mi representante de relaciones públicas, Michael Jensen; y a Michael Pietsch y John Parsley de Little, Brown. Todos creyeron en este libro desde el principio. Llevo siempre en mi corazón a mis dos viejos amigos de la preparatoria, Michael Carabello y Linda Houston, por compartir lo que recordaban sobre nosotros durante mis primeros tiempos en los Estados Unidos. Estaré eternamente agradecido a mi hermana María y a su esposo, Michael Vrionis, por cuidarme durante este proceso y a mi esposa, Cindy, por leer cada palabra y estar en el centro de mis sistemas de apoyo interno y externo.

En Santana, actualmente soy el maquinista de un tren rápido, y soy responsable de muchas cosas que ocurren a medida que avanzamos: conciertos y grabaciones y productos; y ahora, este libro. Aun cuando mi Brigada A de profesionales de la música y la producción no esté directamente involucrada en las palabras de estas páginas, su espíritu está aquí. Quiero recordarles que si la gente no nota nada de lo que ellos hacen o su combinación de experiencia, audacia y enfoque absoluto es porque están realizando un trabajo perfecto. Debo agradecerle a este equipo por su dedicación divina y nombrar a cada uno de sus integrantes.

Skip Rickert, nuestro coordinador de gira, trabajó anteriormente con Stevie Ray Vaughan durante toda su carrera y también con artistas importantes como Barbra Streisand, Guns N' Roses, ZZ Top y Backstreet Boys. Es quien se asegura de que no surjan problemas cuando estamos de gira y fue quien expandió nuestras posibilidades al presentarnos en nuevos sitios en África, India y Europa. El asistente del coordinador de gira, Libby "Mr. Thousand Rainbows" Fabro, trabaja con una elegancia y un propósito discretos y eficientes, y siempre trata de hacer que la vida durante las giras sea tan cómoda y previsible como sea posible. Nuestro coordinador de producción, Michael "Hoss" Keifer, se ocupa de todo lo que necesitamos en el escenario, sin importar el país o la situación en la que nos encontremos, y supervisa a los técnicos para asegurarse de que el sonido, las luces y el video alcancen el alto nivel de presentación que tiene la música. El equipo de Santana es la envidia de muchas otras bandas que salen gira (lo sé porque, con los años, lo escuché una y otra vez), y, en gran parte, esto se debe a Hoss. Chris "Stubby" McNair puede hacer casi cualquier cosa que se le pueda pedir a un técnico de escenario y tenerlo listo de inmediato. Es el Sr. Súper Confiable, el muchacho responsable de mantener nuestros equipos y cerciorarse de que estén seguros durante todo el año. Mi técnico de guitarra, Ed Adair, comenzó a trabajar con Santana durante la década de 1980. Gracias a ellos dos, puedo estar seguro de que todos los instrumentos estarán listos a la hora de tocar. Sin importar dónde sea el concierto, sé que Ed estará siempre a mi lado asegurándose que todo esté listo y afinado. Gracias a nuestros ingenieros de sonido (Rob Mailman en el sitio y Brian Montgomery en el escenario), sé que el sonido de Santana va a llegar al público de la mejor manera posible. Cumplen una función muy importante ya que deben asegurarse de que Santana tenga una consistencia sumamente notable y poderosa todas las noches. Bob Higgins es el director que está a cargo de los videos que se proyectan durante los conciertos. Es un experto en coordinar los efectos visuales con el centro espiritual y el ritmo de cada canción. También me gustaría agradecer muy especialmente, a Sean Guthrie, nuestro encargado de seguridad, que realiza su trabajo con sensibilidad, humor y encanto sureño.

Hace décadas que la gente de Universal Tone Management acompaña a Santana, y se trata de personas leales e inestimables. Debo agradecer a Adam Fells, que ha estado con nosotros desde antes de *Supernatural*. Comenzó a trabajar con nosotros mientras estábamos de gira, y ahora participa en todo lo que hacemos. Es la persona que, día a día, se asegura de que las cosas realmente se hagan y además conoce la historia de Santana prácticamente mejor que nadie. Rita Gentry, nuestra conexión con Bill Graham y nuestro increíble recurso que hace todo realidad, sabe cómo ocuparse de cualquier desafío o de cualquier persona. Micki Alboff ha sido nuestra directora de oficina durante más de doce años. Tiene el increíble talento de saber qué está pasando con todo lo que estamos haciendo en cualquier momento. Mi hija Jelli administra los archivos de Santana y está realizando un valioso trabajo para preservar la historia de la banda. Hay muchas otras personas que trabajan en la oficina, y sin ellas no puedo ni concebir como Santana o yo podríamos hacer lo que hacemos: todos los conciertos, las grabaciones, los negocios y los viajes. Incluso este libro.

Por último, estoy eternamente agradecido de los admiradores de Santana. Muchos de ellos ya son como parte de la familia. Es por ellos que, después de todos estos años de gira, aún me entusiasma y me siento ansioso de ir a una prueba de sonido, ensayar nuevas canciones y mostrarles que Santana sigue teniendo el mismo encanto. A muchos los conozco por nombre: Kristin, Phillipine,

Lisa y Natalie, las cuatro chicas que conocí en Viena en 1989 y que crecieron con la música de Santana, que venían a escucharnos fielmente todos los años y que ahora son mujeres adultas que tienen sus propias familias. Y Sara, la mujer de Montreux que siempre se ponía de pie y bailaba de una manera hermosa, siempre y cuando tocáramos una guajira, por lo que nos aseguramos de tocar una cada vez que estamos allí.

Le dediqué este libro a mi mamá, pero no podría haberlo hecho ni tendría historias para contar sin los admiradores que han apoyado a Santana desde nuestros comienzos en San Francisco y que ahora están en todas partes del mundo. Su amor supremo y apoyo constante son el motivo por el cual seguimos haciendo lo que hacemos. Este libro es un intento de agradecimiento a todos ellos.

Ashley Kahn desearía volver a manifestar personalmente su gratitud a John Parsley, Michael Jensen, Jillian Manus, y Michael y Maria Vrionis, y además agradecer a su agente literario, Dave Dunton de Harvey Klinger, Inc., como también a Adam Fells, Chad Wilson, Cynthia Colonna, Abigail Royle, Johnny O'Brien, Sonny Schneidau, Laurent Masson y especialmente a Hal Miller, su compañero de discusiones en este recorrido literario y espiritual. Se reserva un profundo reconocimiento al mismo Carlos, a quien le agradece la oportunidad de haber podido escuchar, aprender y saber qué se siente no tener miedo de soñar con lo infinito.

Créditos fotográficos

Introducción: © Archivos de Santana
Capítulo 1: © Archivos de Santana
Capítulo 2: © Archivos de Santana
Capítulo 3: © Archivos de Santana
Capítulo 4: © Harry Crosby/Universidad de California, San Diego
Capítulo 5: © Archivos de Santana
Capítulo 6: © Archivos de Santana
Capítulo 7: © Jim Marshall Photography LLC
Capítulo 8: © Archivos de Michael Ochs/Getty Images
Capítulo 9: © Bill Eppridge/Time Life Pictures/Getty Images
Capítulo 10: © Sony Music Entertainment
Capítulo 11: © The Estate of David Gahr/Getty Images
Capítulo 12: © Archivos de Michael Ochs/Getty Images
Capítulo 13: © Sony Music Entertainment
Capítulo 14: © Archivos de Michael Ochs/Getty Images
Capítulo 15: © Archivos de Michael Ochs/Getty Images
Capítulo 16: © Jim Marshall Photography LLC
Capítulo 17: © Sony Music Entertainment
Capítulo 18: © Ebet Roberts
Capítulo 19: © Archivos de Santana
Capítulo 20: © Ken Friedman

Capítulo 21: © Peter A. Distefano
Capítulo 22: © Sony Music Entertainment
Capítulo 23: © Linda J. Russell
Capítulo 24: © Jimmy Bruch
Epílogo: © Benny Gool

Índice

Abdul-Jabbar, Kareem, 332
Abraxas, 220, 248–49, 251, 254–57, 277, 281, 326, 385, 402, 433, 497, 509
Adams, Greg, 366
Adderley, Cannonball, 153
Aerosmith, 233, 402
Africa/Brass, 260
Afrika Bambaataa, 402
"Afro Blue", 195, 265, 291, 539
Agassi, Andre, 476, 531
Aguabella, Francisco, 323, 325
Aldrin, Buzz, 113
Alias, Don, 318, 337
Allen, Paul, 477
Allman, Duane, 196, 279
"All Your Love (I Miss Loving)", 197, 239, 250
Alpert, Herb, 75
"Amazing Grace", 175
Amigos, 403–404, 406
Ammons, Gene, 280, 289
"Angelica Faith", 424
"Angel of Air/Angel of Water", 385
"Angel of Sunlight", 386
Anka, Paul, 69, 90
Anthony, Tommy, 407, 529
"Apache", 80
Aquarius, 467
Areas, José "Chepito", 184, 201, 216, 353
    álbumes con, 240, 272, 274, 303, 305, 316, 345, 385
    integrante, 190, 204–5, 207–8, 356
    relación con, 265–66, 284, 296–97, 369
    de gira con, 283, 358, 361, 422–24, 426
    Woodstock y, 210, 215, 219, 222
Are You Experienced, 174

Armstrong, Louis, 332
Arnaz, Desi, 194
Arroyo, Martina, 222
Astaire, Fred, 25, 310
"As the Years Go Passing By", 162, 170, 190
"Astral Traveling", 321
Autry, Gene, 25, 421
"Ave Maria", 8, 94, 120
Ayler, Albert, 199, 370

"Babalu", 194
Bacharach, Burt, 540
Baez, Joan, 233
Bailey, Victor, 430
Baker, Ginger, 171
"Ballad of a Thin Man", 150
"Ball and Chain", 159
"Bamba, La", 70, 74, 85, 484
Banton, Pato, 469
Barbieri, Gato, 119
Barkan, Todd, 372
Barragán, Josefina. *Ver* Santana, Josefina B. (madre), 3, 5
Barret, Carlton y "Family Man", 401
Barretto, Ray, 195–96, 201–2, 251, 299
Bartz, Gary, 265, 270, 396
Basie, Count, 108, 383
Bátiz, Javier, 76, 117, 469
"Batuka", 288, 469
"Batukada", 288
Beach Boys, 104, 113, 127, 191
Bean, Richard, 134
Beatles, 127, 133, 136, 139, 156, 158–59, 164, 174–76, 187, 191, 196, 277, 301, 308, 310, 344, 349, 370, 377
    popularidad de, 127–28, 130, 150

Beatles *(seguido)*
espiritualidad de, 286, 327, 332
Szabó y, 132, 155
Beck, Jeff, 134, 187, 189, 393, 422, 488
Belafonte, Harry, 477–78
"Bella", 424, 442
Bennett, Tony, 476
Bennett, Wayne, 81
Benson, George, 161, 308, 404
Bernstein, Leonard, 130, 288
Berry, Chuck, 409, 421, 502
"Bésame mucho", 63, 74
Big Boi, 498
Big Brother, 145, 178, 203, 211
"Billie Jean", 404
Bingham, John, 459
Birch, Gaylord, 404, 406
Bishop, Elvin, 116, 279, 329
Bitches Brew, 254, 260, 265, 272–73,
299, 318, 447
"Black Magic Woman", 109, 197, 250,
269, 277, 327, 334, 346, 366, 399,
405, 433, 450, 484
Blackman, Cindy. *Ver* Santana, Cindy
Blackman (esposa), 532–33
Blackwell, Chris, 364, 473, 486–87
Blades, Rubén, 435
Blakey, Art, 9, 534, 537
Bland, Bobby "Blue", 81, 126
Blige, Mary J., 498
Bloomfield, Michael, 116, 137, 141, 154–55,
203, 211
"Blue Monk", 139, 502
Bluesbreakers, 170
Blues Breakers with Eric Clapton, The,
153
Blues for Salvador, 459
"Blues for Salvador", 90, 424, 442,
450
Bobo, Willie, 138–39, 187, 196, 198–200,
209–10, 258, 289–90, 294
Bogart, Humphrey, 18
Bono, 477
*Book of Knowledge: The Keys of Enoch,
The*, 440, 496
Borboletta, 387–88
Bowie, David, 90, 387
Branca, John, 531
Branch, Michelle, 498, 506
"Breezin'", 308
Brooks, Mel, 383
"Brotherhood", 432
Broussard, Jules, 364, 386
Brown, Buster, 503

Brown, David, 173, 184, 201, 259, 299,
319, 387
despido, 288–89, 309
integrante, 177, 190, 205–8, 367
de gira con, 196–97, 245, 426
Woodstock y, 210, 215
Brown, Greg, 421
Brown, James, 80, 84, 127, 145, 198, 209,
264, 292, 402, 530, 534
Brown, Jerry, 113–14
Brown, Milton, 289
Brown, Pat, 14
Brown, Shelley, 474
Bruce, Jack, 171, 212, 272, 537
Burdett, Al, 137
"Burn", 436
Burrell, Kenny, 108, 126, 179, 196,
393–94, 421
Butler, Billy, 81
Butterfield, Paul, 159, 187
Butterfield Blues Band, 116, 137, 149, 153,
159, 170, 203, 240, 279
Byrd, Donald, 263
Byrds, 164

Cables, George, 306
Caliman, Hadley, 316, 321
"Calling, The", 490
"Calypso Blues", 421
Canned Heat, 225–26, 454
Cantinflas (Mario Morena), 381–82
Capaldi, Jim, 443
"Capri", 535
Carabello, Michael, 106, 135, 137–39,
143, 145, 151, 163, 167, 170, 179–80,
184–85, 187, 193, 195–96, 198, 201,
214–17, 220, 232, 245, 249–50,
252, 254–56, 268–69, 271, 273,
280, 284, 288, 291, 295, 306–9,
316, 319, 324–25, 412–14, 416, 450,
505, 547
álbumes con, 236, 238, 240–42, 272,
478
despido, 175, 290, 292–93, 309
conciertos con, 133, 136, 145, 161, 183
integrante, 177, 190, 207–8
Miles Davis y, 254, 391–93, 395
relación con, 129–30, 138, 144, 155,
158, 170–71, 185, 202–4, 232,
259, 265, 268–69, 292, 300,
303, 391
de gira con, 276, 280, 426
Woodstock y, 210, 219
Caramba!, 307

Caravanserai, 306, 310, 312–13, 319, 321–23, 325–28, 333–36, 340–41, 348, 363–64, 387, 497
Caribbean Allstars, 460
Carillo, Lco, 71
Carlos Santana & Buddy Miles! Live!, 328
Carson, Johnny, 277, 499
Carter, Ron, 408
Cash, Johnny, 211, 452
Cassidy, Hopalong, 25
Castro, Fidel, 310
Catch a Fire, 401
Catero, Fred, 248, 441
Cesena, Josefina "Chepa", 16
Chakiris, George, 131
Chambers, Dennis, 489, 526, 532
Chambers Brothers, 144, 264
Champs, 75
Chancler, Ndugu, 265, 387
"Change Is Gonna Come, A", 352
Charles, Ray, 69, 76, 78, 93, 96, 126, 154, 197, 251, 263, 277, 290, 327, 433
Chávez, César, 114, 188
Cheech y Chong, 381
Chico, El, 138–39
"Chim Chim Cheree", 170
Chinmoy, Sri, 64, 273, 335, 337, 340, 348, 350–51, 353–54, 359, 362, 367, 374, 386, 439, 451
    partida, 376–77, 388, 416
    música inspirada por, 345–46, 386
    guía espiritual, 323, 331–33, 335–39, 341, 348, 355, 359–60, 379, 388–89
Christian, Charlie, 2 241–42, 331
Christian, Yvonne, 105
Cirincione, Diane, 351, 517
Clapton, Eric, 90, 134, 165, 171, 181, 189, 212–13, 238, 269, 279, 393–94, 411, 422, 490
    sesiones improvisadas con, 86, 372–73, 464
Clarke, Stanley, 387, 430, 443
Clash, 402
Cleaver, Eldridge, 303
Cliff, Jimmy, 401
Clooney, George, 477
"Cloud Nine", 453
Cobham, Billy, 325, 337, 365, 430
Cochran, Todd, 375
Cole, Natalie, 180
Cole, Nat King, 74, 120, 421
Coleman, Ornette, 297
Collins, Albert, 109, 181
Colombo, Chris, 126

Coltrane, 260
Coltrane, Alice, 8, 263, 301, 318–19, 367, 370, 373, 385–86, 457, 496
Coltrane, John, 8–9, 11, 68, 73–74, 84, 164–65, 175, 184, 186–87, 190, 220, 242, 244–45, 250, 259–60, 263, 266, 273, 299, 302–3, 318–19, 334–35, 337, 340, 344, 349, 352, 364, 366–67, 369–70, 372–73, 375, 392, 403, 430, 444, 447, 454, 457, 495, 521, 524–25, 545
    comparaciones con, 229, 408, 430
    Love Supreme de, 9, 327, 334
    música de, 71–72, 156, 166, 177–78, 180, 232, 237, 245–46, 252, 284, 287, 302–3, 318, 320, 334, 345, 350–51, 354, 433, 447
    camino espiritual de, 332, 349–50, 355–56, 515
Coltrane, Kathleen, 373
Coltrane, Ravi, 373
"Comin' Home Baby", 162
Commodores, 401
"Concierto de Aranjuez", 321
"Confidential Friend", 106
Conklin, Lee, 221
Contours, 135
Cooder, Ry, 210, 433
Cooke, Sam, 352, 444
Copeland, Miles, 205
Corazón, 509, 545
"Corazón Espinado", 537
Corea, Chick, 265, 333, 396
Coryell, Larry, 334, 337, 397
Cosby, Bill, 157, 180, 290, 382, 510
Cosby, Camille, 510
Cosey, Pete, 249, 280
Coster, Tom, 307, 320, 341, 353, 364, 367, 386, 431–32
    y Szabó, 291, 304
Cotton, James, 190, 218
Country Joe and the Fish, 229
Course in Miracles, A, 351, 440, 517–18, 545
Crazy World of Arthur Brown, 179
Cream, 149, 171–72, 187, 212, 252, 269, 272
"Creator Has a Master Plan, The", 366
Creedence Clearwater Revival, 189
Cressman, Jeff, 490, 493, 529
Crockett, Davy, 24
Crossings, 321, 375
"Crying Beasts", 249
Cuba, Joe, 195
Cuscuna, Michael, 244

Dalai Lama, 453, 477, 520
Damon, Matt, 477
"Dance Sister Dance", 320, 403–4
"Dance to the Music", 198, 288
Dangerfield, Brent, 217, 221
Dangerfield, Rodney, 382, 499
Davis, Angela, 481
Davis, Clive, 16, 64, 210–11, 221, 225,
    240, 255, 258, 267, 325, 358, 363,
    402, 443, 485, 487–88, 529
  despido, 311–12, 345, 364, 381
  filantropía, 459
  álbumes de Santana y, 227, 241–42,
    309–12, 460–67, 473
Davis, Miles, 8, 11, 23, 40, 55, 64, 68, 115,
    148, 164–65, 190, 195, 198, 211, 240,
    244, 256, 262–63, 268, 318, 323,
    326, 411, 415, 417, 420, 434, 462,
    502, 534, 545
  Bill Graham y, 141, 193, 398
  reservas en clubes, 184, 227, 381
  amigos de, 204, 231, 427
  Milagro tributo a, 442
  músicos que tocaron con, 257–58, 318,
    365–67, 375, 383, 386, 388, 412–14,
    423–24, 434–35, 479
  música de, 23, 66, 156, 169, 180,
    183, 187, 229, 232, 236–37, 245–46,
    284, 286–87, 299, 302, 305, 311,
    323–24, 348, 379, 466–67, 506,
    516
  relación con, 39, 53, 62, 242,
    244, 248–57, 262, 265, 278,
    295–96, 374–76, 387, 391–96,
    409, 478
  palabras de, 110, 198, 474
Davis, Sammy, Jr., 159, 166
Deep Purple, 261
DeJohnette, Jack, 159, 193, 264–65, 273,
    318, 385, 387–88, 396
De La Rosa, Steve, 132, 183
Delorme, Michel, 244, 373
Derek and the Dominos, 279
"Desolation Row", 392
Diddley, Bo, 127, 196
"Directly from My Heart to You", 394
Doggett, Bill, 81
Domingo, Plácido, 505
Doors, 159, 164–65, 187, 190, 252, 344,
    400, 454
"Do You Love Me", 135
Drummond, Don, 529
Dumble, Alexander, 419
Dunn, Joyce, 135

Dylan, Bob, 156, 158, 179, 190, 205, 211,
    227, 383, 391–92, 430, 453, 466,
    494
Dynamics, 134

Eagle-Eye Cherry, 488
"East-West", 154
East-West, 153
Eastwood, Clint, 113
Eddy, Duane, 75, 80
"Eight Miles High", 164
Elders, Joycelyn, 132
Elevator to the Gallows, 260, 493
Ellington, Duke, 69, 78, 263, 455, 534
Elton John, 476–77
Emperors, 289
Errico, Greg, 133, 288, 316
Escovedo, Coke, 288, 299, 316
Escovedo, Neal, 316
Escovedo, Pete, 273
Escovedo, Sheila, 273
Estrada, Ron, 155
Etzler, Ray, 384, 471
"Europa", 142, 207, 320, 403–4
Evans, Bill, 261, 273, 414, 416
Evans, Gil, 23, 340, 394
"Everybody's Everything", 287, 289
"Every Step of the Way", 321
"Everything's Coming Our Way", 289
"Evil Ways", 200, 210, 220–21, 236, 240,
    278, 334
"Exodus", 400

Fabulous Thunderbirds, 116, 421
"Faith Interlude", 317
"Fannie Mae", 503
Farlow, Tal, 242
"Farol, El", 64, 490
"Farolito", 7, 64
Farrell, Joe, 273, 306, 364
Farrés, Osvaldo, 74
"Fascination", 63
Feliciano, José, 254
Fells, Adam, 419, 549–50
Festival, 215, 403–4
Festival Pop de Monterey, 174, 184, 211
First Light, 190
"First Light", 321
Fischer, Clare, 410
Flack, Roberta, 290, 323
"Flame-Sky", 364–65
Fleetwood Mac, 116, 149, 197, 279, 406,
    484
"Follow Your Heart", 273

"Fool on the Hill, The", 277
Ford, Dee Dee, 135
Ford, Glenn, 167
For Those Who Chant, 307
Four Tops, 298
Foxx, Jamie, 477
Frank, Sid, 246
Franklin, Aretha, 15, 175, 290–91, 341, 443, 485
Fraser, Tom, 161
Freak Out!, 394
Freddie and the Stone Souls, 133
"Free Angela", 375
Freedom, 430, 432, 459
Freeman, Morgan, 477–78
Freeway Jam, 215
"Fried Neckbones and Some Home Fries", 139, 196, 209, 219, 231
"Fuente del Ritmo, La", 320
Fujioka, Yasuhiro "Fuji", 244
"Full Moon", 458

Gabriel, Peter, 434
Gaines, Jim, 441–42
"Game of Love, The", 506
Garcia, Jerry, 146, 154, 160, 229
Gardner, Don, 135
Garland, Red, 409
Garrison, Jimmy, 184, 334, 430
Gasca, Luis, 287, 307, 316
Gates, Bill, 477
Gaye, Marvin, 9, 115, 125, 175, 245, 271, 298, 315, 352, 388, 400, 404, 467, 473
Gentry, Rita, 472, 549
"Georgia on My Mind", 86, 90–91
Getz, Stan, 125
Gianquinto, Alberto, 218–19, 248, 254, 289, 303
Gillespie, Dizzy, 196, 242, 266, 332
Gilmore, John, 370
Gimme Shelter, 239, 277
Gleason, Ralph J., 193, 243, 260, 286, 328
Glover, Danny, 477
"God Bless the Child", 100
Godinez, Marcia Sult, 472
"Going Home", 366–67
"Goin' Out of My Head", 139, 166
Gómez, Martín Sandoval, 476
Goodman, Benny, 331
"Good Morning Little Schoolgirl", 137, 160
"Goodness and Mercy", 431

Gordon, Dexter, 119
Graf, Steffi, 476, 531
Graham, Bill, 16, 146, 148, 152, 160, 170–71, 179–80, 186, 199, 203, 209, 214, 223, 231, 233, 240, 246, 256–57, 261, 266, 271, 300, 311, 326–27, 341, 358, 376, 383, 390, 403, 405, 413, 420, 429, 434–35, 448, 470–1, 482, 487, 492, 497, 505, 524, 549
    muerte de, 364, 438, 445, 456
    reservas en el Fillmore, 141–42, 144–45, 151–52, 161–63, 170, 192–93, 213, 227
    guía, 177, 198–99, 214, 242, 285, 340–41, 369, 398–99, 424, 465, 478
    Milagro tributo a, 442
    músicos que trabajaron con, 193–94, 252–53, 256, 264, 496
    representante de Santana, 243–44, 263–64, 309, 311, 382, 445–46, 471
    giras organizadas por, 212, 324, 377, 392, 407, 412–13
    Woodstock y, 211–12, 215, 219, 221
Graham, Larry, 198, 264, 467–69
Grant, Cary, 25, 176
Grateful Dead, 137, 145, 156, 174–75, 178, 204, 210, 218, 221, 243, 267, 303, 378, 474, 527
Grávátt, Eric, 341
Gray, Macy, 498
Green, Al, 400
Green, Freddie, 108
Green, Grant, 108, 179, 393
Green, Peter, 116, 134, 165, 197, 250–51, 422, 484, 491
Griffith, Emile, 52
"Guajira", 287, 289, 467, 550
Guaraldi, Vince, 126, 137, 219
Guitar Forms, 394
Guitar Heaven, 505
Guy, Buddy, 8, 55, 88, 137, 169, 181, 213, 238, 262, 272, 395, 433, 456, 537
"Gypsy Queen", 139, 197, 250, 366

Haas, Wendy, 321
Hakim, Omar, 205
Hamilton, Chico, 138, 153, 187, 189, 195, 197, 209, 259, 299, 308
Hammer, Jan, 337, 403
Hancock, Herbie, 10, 222, 262, 269, 321, 370, 380, 408, 419, 431, 445
    Miles Davis y, 375, 386, 391–92, 434

Hancock *(seguido)*
  música de, 248, 254, 305, 351, 382,
    387–88, 398, 422
  relación con, 360, 387, 424, 510
Handy, John, 148, 193–94, 219, 301
"Hannibal", 242
Harder They Come, The, 401
Hard Road, A, 165
Haro, Danny, 106, 119, 123, 143, 176
  distanciamiento de, 154–55, 168–69
  familia de, 102, 118
Harper, Rod, 184
Harris, Eddie, 164, 220, 290, 293, 387
Harrison, George, 177, 196, 393
Havana Moon, 420–21, 466
Havens, Richie, 233
Hawkins, Coleman, 80, 119, 499
Hawkins, Tramaine, 458
Hayek, Salma, 484
Haynes, Roy, 318
"Healer, The", 454–56
Heider, Wally, 248, 279
Helms, Chet, 149, 152, 154
"Help, I'm a Rock", 394
Henderson, Joe, 80, 307, 499
Henderson, Michael, 264–65, 395
Hendrix, Jimi, 8, 137, 159, 165, 171, 174,
    179, 187–91, 205, 213, 215, 219, 227,
    234–35, 249, 251, 264, 272–73, 275,
    316, 401, 410, 418, 454, 457, 473, 481,
    502, 508
  muerte de, 262, 289
  guitarra eléctrica y, 110, 179, 201, 229,
    397
  Festival Pop de Monterey y, 165, 178,
    192
  música de, 150, 157, 169, 180, 203, 236,
    238, 250, 254, 286, 299, 430, 433,
    447, 481
  Woodstock y, 215, 219, 222–23
  palabras de, 156, 388, 455, 475
Henry, Sonny, 210
Herb Alpert and the Tijuana Brass, 75
Hernández, Carlos, 473
Hernández, Horacio "El Negro", 489
Hesse, Hermann, 254
Hidalgo, Padre Miguel, 24
Hill, Lauryn, 488, 494
Holiday, Billie, 1, 100, 331
Holland, Dave, 264–65, 385, 396, 505
Holmes, Rodney, 489, 493–94
"Honky Tonk", 81
Hoodoo Man Blues, 137

Hooker, John Lee, 8, 88, 107–8, 121, 129,
    139, 190, 226, 249, 260, 394, 443–
    45, 453–55, 482, 495, 506, 527
  relación con, 8, 420, 422, 430–33,
    468, 478–80
Hope, Bob, 383
"Hope You're Feeling Better", 252, 255,
  269
Hopkins, Lightnin', 8, 107, 109, 121, 141,
    421, 454
"Hound Dog", 159
Houston, Linda, 105, 547
Houston, Whitney, 485
Hubbard, Freddie, 190, 321, 375
Huerta, Dolores, 14, 481
"Human Nature", 436
Humble Pie, 240
Hurtak, Desiree, 440
Hurtak, J. J., 417, 496
Hussain, Zakir, 505

"I Am the Walrus", 176
Ienner, Donnie, 459
"I Feel Fine", 196
Ike Turner and the Ikettes, 108
  Ver también Turner, Ike, 108
Illuminations, 385–87
"I Love Music", 530
"I Loves You, Porgy", 91
"Imagine", 352, 529
"I'm Blue", 108
Impressions, 125
In a Silent Way, 260, 272–73, 335,
  396
"In a Silent Way", 260, 272–73,
  460
"Incident at Neshabur", 220, 248
Indios Tabajaras, Los, 79
"I Need Your Lovin' ", 135
Inner Mounting Flame, The, 303, 335
Inner Secrets, 403, 406–7
Intergalactic Wayne Shorter, 245
"In the Midnight Hour", 191, 293, 318
"Iron Lion Zion", 80
"I Say a Little Prayer", 341
"I Shall Be Released", 453
Isley, Ronald, 540
It's a Beautiful Day, 257
"It's All in the Game", 516

Jack Johnson, 271, 335
Jackson, Al, Jr., 318
Jackson, Mahalia, 9, 113, 302

Jackson, Michael, 51, 115, 315, 404, 436, 445, 453
Jackson, Paul, 404
Jackson, Samuel L., 510
Jagger, Mick, 271, 277
James, Elmore, 108, 116
James, Etta, 94, 108, 127, 458, 530
Jampolsky, Jerry, 351, 517
Jan and Dean, 104
Jarrett, Keith, 159, 265, 268, 270, 333, 341, 396, 516
Jean, Wyclef, 130, 490
Jefferson, Thomas, 233
Jefferson Airplane, 145, 159–60, 219, 239
Jesucristo, 296, 358
Jiménez, José Pepe, 530
Jimi Hendrix Experience, 191
"Jingo", 139, 148, 154, 170, 184–85, 195–96, 220–21, 230–31, 236, 262
Jobim, Antônio Carlos, 318
Joel, Billy, 222
Joey Dee & the Starliters, 82
Johnny Rotten, 402
Johnson, Alphonso, 430
Johnson, Jimmy, 409
Johnson, Magic, 113
Johnson, Robert, 153, 393
Jolie, Angelina, 477
Jones, Booker T., 421
Jones, Darryl, 205
Jones, Deacon, 456
Jones, Elvin, 318, 334, 388, 394, 409, 534
Jones, Hank, 180
Jones, Jim, 356
Jones, Quincy, 327, 484, 515
Joplin, Janis, 146, 203, 487
Jordan, Michael, 426
Journey, 299, 319, 505
Juárez, Benito, 24
Judd, Ashley, 477
"Jungle Strut", 280, 289

Kahn, Steve, 311
Kanté, Mory, 286
"Karate", 289
Karma, 366
Kaukonen, Jorma, 160
Kelly, Wynton, 409
Kennedy, Robert, 188
Kermode, Richard, 333, 341, 353, 364, 367
Khan, Ali Akbar, 117, 153
Kilbert, Tony, 74, 459, 513, 525
Kind of Blue, 259–60, 526

King, Albert, 8, 88, 901, 109, 162, 181, 190, 292, 391, 393, 404
King, B. B., 8, 10, 29, 69, 76, 78, 85, 88, 90, 108, 116, 121, 126, 136, 139, 169, 179–82, 196, 203, 213, 220, 224, 288, 332, 391, 394
música de, 67, 76, 85, 103–4, 111, 130–31, 186, 202, 229, 273, 373
sitios, 121, 170–71, 173, 428
King, Ben E., 386
King, Deborah. Ver Santana, Deborah (esposa), 50–51, 55, 64, 131, 307, 329–41, 343, 349, 353, 355–63, 367, 371, 379, 385, 390, 397–98, 408, 410, 412, 421–26, 428, 433, 435–40, 442, 462, 471–72, 474, 484, 487, 494–95, 498, 502–4, 509–11, 512–20, 532, 542
King, Freddie, 81, 88, 94, 127, 129, 153, 238, 333–34, 391
King, Kitsaun (cuñada), 472
King, Martin Luther, Jr., 185, 188, 302–303, 432, 467, 520–21
King, Saunders (suegro), 78, 242, 331–32
King Curtis, 253–54
Kings, 81
Kinks, 134
Kirk, Rahsaan Roland, 225, 270, 294, 394
Kirwan, Danny, 279
Klarwein, Mati, 254
Knight, Gladys, 458
Knudsen, Paul, 16, 140–42
Kolotkin, Glen, 319–20, 441
Kooper, Al, 155, 21–12, 249
Kramer, Eddie, 275, 289
Kravitz, Lenny, 532
Krieger, Robby, 164
Krishnamurti, 301, 349
Kuti, Fela, 298, 435

Ladysmith Black Mambazo, 520
Lancaster, Burt, 80
Lang, Michael, 223
Lara, Agustín, 7, 64, 72
Lear, Graham, 406, 432
Led Zeppelin, 187, 224, 251, 314, 400
Lee, Stan, 301
Lennon, John, 175, 352, 521, 529
Leno, Jay, 247, 499
"Let's Dance", 90
"Let the Good Times Roll", 91, 108

"Let Us Go into the House of the Lord", 337, 365, 372
Lewis, Jerry, 382
Lewis, John, 409
Lewis, Mingo, 309
Liberace, 113, 166
Liebre Chica (Little Jackrabbit), 85
"Life Divine, The", 337
Ligertwood, Alex, 407
"Light My Fire", 164, 400
"Light of Life", 366
Lindsay, Tony, 407, 468, 529
"Listen Here", 220, 293
"Little Latin Lupe Lu", 135
Little Richard, 69, 75–76
Little Walter, 134, 153, 196, 524
Live Adventures of Mike Bloomfield and Al Kooper, The, 212
Live at the Fillmore 1968, 208
Live at the Regal, 16, 136
Living Colour, 402, 457
Livingston, Doc, 173, 184, 187, 217–18
Lloyd, Charles, 148, 159, 164, 196, 301, 344, 370, 420
Loading Zone, 170, 264, 288, 329
Lobo aullador, 196, 315
Lohmann, Jan, 244
Lonely Boys, Los, 498
"Look of Love, The", 539
Lopez, George, 382
Lotus, 384–85, 392, 405
Louis, Joe, 455
Love Devotion Surrender, 337, 367
"Love Is Strange", 80
"Love of My Life", 492
"Love on a Two-Way Street", 321
"Love Song from *Apache*", 499
Love Supreme, A, 187, 259–60, 302–303, 322, 337, 369, 566
"Love Supreme, A", 352, 373, 401
Lucas, Reggie, 280

Mabry, Betty, 216, 264
MacLaine, Shirley, 222, 478
Magic Sam, 196, 238
Maharaj Ji, 301
Maharishi Mahesh Yogi, 301
Mahavishnu Orchestra, 273, 302
Malo, 134, 287, 329, 333, 359
Malone, Marcus, 173, 185
Mamas and the Papas, 139, 308
"Mandela", 432
Mandela, Nelson, 336, 432, 477, 510

Manilow, Barry, 485
Manitas de Plata, 394
Mann, Herbie, 162, 261
"Manteca", 196
Marcum, Stan, 155, 176, 257, 278, 306
despido, 290, 292–93, 309
relación con, 16, 148–52, 158–59, 167–70, 174, 184, 303
Mares, Tony, 101
"Maria Maria", 130, 250, 346, 490, 493
Marley, Bob, 9, 11, 80, 85, 175, 213, 245, 352, 400–2, 467, 473, 486, 525
Marsalis, Branford, 205, 396
Marsalis, Wynton, 370
Marshall, Eddie, 307
Martin, Dean, 382
Martin, Trayvon, 481
Martinez, Jimmy, 138
Martinez, René, 493
Martini, Jerry, 329
"Mary Ann", 154
Masekela, Hugh, 520
"Mask, The", 265
Mathis, Johnny, 126, 211
Mathews, David K., 530
Mayall, John, 134, 153, 165, 187
Mayfield, Curtis, 289, 298, 457
McCann, Les, 164, 290
McCartney, Paul, 277
McClure, Ron, 159
McDuff, Jack, 161, 187, 196
McGriff, Jimmy, 161
McLaughlin, Eve, 385
McLaughlin, John, 51, 262, 271–72, 302, 323, 335, 337, 349, 354–55, 364, 370–71, 373, 385, 396–97, 403, 490
y Miles Davis, 257–58, 332, 375
Medeiros, Lynn, 329
Medeski, John, 537
"Meditation", 337
Meditations, 369
Mehta, Zubin, 288
"Mercy, Mercy, Mercy", 323
Metallica, 474, 526
Metaphysical Meditations, 322
Metatrón, 495–97
Mickey & Sylvia, 80
Miget, Marcia, 502
Milagro, 407, 466–69
"Milagro", 467
Milagro Foundation, 474, 485, 509, 528, 535

Miles, Buddy, 316–18, 328–29, 335, 432, 442
Miller, Hal, 72, 74, 244, 478, 493, 502, 521, 525, 537, 547, 550
Miller, Steve, 179, 262, 267, 442
Mimram, Colette, 216
"Minor Swing", 190
"Misty", 90, 126
Mitchell, Mitch, 219, 318
Moby Grape, 145, 214
Mocker Manor, 156–57
Monk, Thelonious, 68, 86, 139
Montgomery, Wes, 8, 108, 120, 126, 139, 165, 166, 179, 196, 242, 259, 308, 393, 418
  influencia de, 8, 104, 158
Festival de Jazz de Montreux, 261, 299, 541
Moon, Keith, 170
Moonflower, 403, 405–6
Moreira, Airto, 265, 387
Moreno, Mario, 381
Morgan, Lee, 126, 190, 272, 307
Morrison, Jim, 224, 304
Moss, Tyrone, 289
Moutafian, Ruthie, 474
Muddy Waters, 69, 108, 121, 153, 391, 393
Muktananda, Swami, 301
Multi-Dimensional Warrior, 459
Mumbo Jumbo, 491
Musselwhite, Charlie, 192
Mysterious Traveller, 408
Mystic Man, 458

Naftalin, Mark, 160
"Naima", 337, 369, 373
"Nature Boy", 321
Nelson, Willie, 421, 444
Neville Brothers, 435
Newton, Huey P., 218, 303
"Night Train", 80
Nobs, Claude, 80, 261, 286, 341, 376, 429, 445
"No One to Depend On", 288
"No Woman, No Cry", 400

Obama, Barack, 98, 222
Ochoa, Mario, 287
O'Jays, 530
Olatunji, Babatunde, 139, 194, 262
"Once It's Gotcha", 430
"One Love", 175, 352, 401
Oneness, 407–8, 410

"One Way Out", 196
Original Sin, The (libro), 451
Orlando, Tony, 400
Orozco, Carlos Barragán, 18
Ortega, Gaspar "El Indio", 52
Ortiz, Bill, 468, 493, 529
"Out of This World", 260
"Oye Como Va", 64, 142, 251–52, 254, 280, 287, 334, 346, 399, 405, 444

Page, Jimmy, 134, 238, 273, 393, 411, 422
Palmieri, Eddie, 194, 530
Panteras Negras, 188, 303–4, 462
Pantoja, Victor, 138, 299, 316
"Para Los Rumberos", 287
Parker, Bobby, 196, 262
Parker, Charlie, 74, 109, 242, 260, 266, 270, 272, 323, 331, 392
Pastorius, Jaco, 400, 430, 447, 503
Patillo, Leon, 387, 403
"Peace on Earth", 373
Penn, Sean, 477
"Peppermint Twist", 82
Peraza, Armando, 270, 322, 353, 364, 377, 455
  álbumes con, 306, 320, 345–46, 365, 367, 409–10, 419
  integrante, 306–8, 335, 356
  de gira con, 316, 357–58, 422–24, 426
Perazzo, Karl, 468, 529
Perry, Lee, 401
"Persuasion", 231
Pickett, Wilson, 290, 292, 294, 298, 316, 394
"Piel Canela", 26
"Please Don't Take Your Love", 519
Police, 402
Pozo, Chano, 196
"Practice What You Preach", 90
Prado, Pérez, 45, 71
Presley, Elvis, 69, 90, 107, 195
Prestia, Rocco, 264
Preston, Billy, 392
Prince, 412, 444, 466, 498, 529
Procol Harum, 179, 204
"Promise of a Fisherman", 387
Pryor, Richard, 382, 395
Puente, Tito, 10, 125, 128, 148, 194, 201–203, 251, 275, 277, 287, 299, 534
Purim, Flora, 366, 387

Quicksilver, 145–46
Quinn, Anthony, 450–51
"Quizás, Quizás, Quizás", 74

Rae, Johnny, 218
Rainey, Chuck, 184, 264
Raitt, Bonnie, 432–33
Ramos, Paoli Mejias, 530
Rashid, Gary "Rashiki", 74, 265, 318,
    366, 524
Rashied Ali, 318
Rauch, Dougie, 264, 298, 306–7, 320,
    330, 353
Ray, Daniel "Big Black", 195
Reagan, Ronald, 114
Redding, Otis, 188, 318
Reed, Jimmy, 8, 69, 77, 107, 129, 139, 454
Reid, Vernon, 457, 537
Reinhardt, Django, 190
Reitzel, Jim, 441
Rekow, Raul, 432
Representantes de Santana, 156
Reyes, Rico, 255, 287, 289, 299, 321
Reyes, Walfredo, Jr., 468
Rich, Buddy, 172, 202, 270, 291, 311, 323,
    420, 534
"Rich Get Richer", 530
Rietveld, Benny, 458, 529
Righteous Brothers, 135
"Right On", 467, 469
"Right On Be Free", 298
Rios, Michael, 491
"Riviera Paradise", 393
Roach, Max, 461
Robinson, Smokey, 591
Roccisano, Joe, 467
Rockefeller, Nelson, 227–28
Rodrigues, Doug, 321
Rodriguez, Sergio "Gus", 106, 119, 143
    distanciamiento de, 154–55, 168–69
Rogers, Roy, 25, 35, 421
Rolie, Gregg, 161, 173, 201, 431, 443
    álbumes con, 236, 238, 240, 303, 420,
        478
    contribuciones de, 182, 186–87, 264,
        272, 347
    integrante, 164, 190, 206–8
    relación con, 170–71, 185, 203–5, 232,
        284, 292–93, 296, 339, 409
    Woodstock y, 216, 219
Rolland, Gilbert, 35
Rolling Stones, 133, 136, 156, 174, 239,
    277, 314, 381, 391–92, 429

"Room Full of Mirrors", 275
Rosas, César, 468
Ross, Gene, 76, 91, 92, 117
Royals, 84, 106
Rubinson, David, 214, 403–4, 408, 413, 441
Run-DMC, 402
Rush, Otis, 8, 88, 107, 109, 153, 179,
        196–97, 236–37, 250, 333, 393,
        395, 456, 537
    influencia de, 8, 103, 105, 224–26
Rushen, Patrice, 445, 533
Rustichelli, Paolo, 458, 473, 535
Rutley, Tom, 305, 320

Saaveda, Don Lauro, 91
Sacred Fire, 466, 469, 472
Sacred Language of Ascension, The, 496
Sacred Sources: Live Forever, 473
"Saeta", 23
"Saja", 467
Salvador Santana Band, 465
"Samba Pa Ti", 252–54, 277, 307
Sam the Sham and the Pharaohs, 136, 161
Sanchez, Mimi, 307, 412
Sancious, David, 205, 407, 430, 432, 457
"Sanctuary", 445, 447
Sanders, Pharoah, 73, 119, 318, 321, 366,
        370, 502
Sangre, 505
San Pacu, 255
Santamaría, Mongo, 125, 165, 194–95,
        202, 214, 249, 291, 323
Santana (álbum), 208–9, 213, 227, 230
Santana (grupo), 86, 169, 189, 192
    premios, 62, 419, 458, 462, 467–68, 477
    disolución, 284–85, 290, 292–93,
        296–97, 309
    identidad, 164–65, 176–77, 298–300,
        302
    miembros de, 164, 190, 205, 207–8,
        249–50, 255, 264–65, 289–90,
        293, 303–4, 306, 312, 316, 345, 347,
        356, 367, 369, 381–83, 385–86,
        407–10, 422, 426, 434–35, 442–43,
        463, 466–67, 478, 501
"Santana" (canción), 404–405
Santana, Angelica "Jelli" (hija), 402,
        405–7, 415–18, 429, 438–39, 441,
        453–55, 462–63, 464, 475–77, 479,
        481, 527, 542, 549
Santana, Antonio (abuelo), 27
Santana, Carlos, 6, 11–12, 17–18, 52, 57,
        61, 64, 67, 69, 77–78, 106, 112, 117,

123, 128, 141, 160, 180, 182, 204, 207, 239, 254, 263, 293–94, 308, 318, 324, 326, 328, 340, 342, 386, 390, 392, 394–95, 398, 405, 407, 414, 415, 417, 420, 433, 442, 443, 446, 450, 452, 454–56, 460–61, 469, 484–86, 488, 491–93, 498, 501, 507–8, 523, 533, 550

ángeles de, 15–16, 101–2, 124, 154, 168, 211, 308–9, 441–42, 491

premios de, 108–9, 210, 451–52, 458, 516

ritmo doméstico de, 4, 405–6, 439–41, 474–76, 512–13

héroes de, 8, 50, 116, 131, 248, 257, 432, 468

trayectoria musical de, 4, 66–73, 84–86, 114–15, 190–91, 201–2, 245–46, 270–72, 512–15

dimensión espiritual de, 4, 11, 91–92, 106–7, 280–82, 285–87, 305–6, 321–23, 330–37, 348–50, 355–56, 359–60, 388–89, 416–18, 509–10, 512, 515–16

Tono Universal de, 9–11, 326–27, 329, 351, 453

Santana, Cindy Blackman (esposa), 532–33

Santana, Deborah (esposa), 50–51, 55, 64, 131, 307, 329–41, 343, 349, 353, 355–63, 367, 371, 379, 385, 390, 397–98, 408, 410, 412, 421–26, 428, 433, 435–40, 442, 462, 471–72, 474, 484, 487, 494–95, 498, 502–4, 509–20, 532, 542

libro escrito por, 458, 484

contribuciones de, 369, 413–14, 419, 446–47, 460–61, 471

divorcio de, 484–89, 491, 503

vida doméstica con, 391, 400–404, 406, 414–15, 475–76

agradecimiento a, 467–68, 491, 513

matrimonio con, 341–44

encuentro, 312–18

filantropía, 448, 481–83

restaurante de, 337, 359–60

familia Santana y, 53, 62, 326, 404

camino espiritual de, 320, 322–23, 335, 337–40, 348, 359, 377, 388, 416–18, 492

de gira con, 319–20, 324, 410

Santana, Irma (hermana), 15, 17, 48–9, 51, 59, 63, 101, 103–4, 123–24, 167, 195, 207, 243

Santana, Jorge (hermano), 15, 20, 49, 73, 98, 102, 104, 123, 126, 128, 134, 195, 287, 333, 381, 468–69, 473, 482, 484

Santana, José (padre), 3, 5–7, 30, 33, 36–37, 41–43, 61, 65, 81, 91, 126, 201, 216, 254, 274, 464, 466, 482, 508, 530

Autlán y, 17, 19–21, 28, 30–34, 36, 480–81

muerte de, 35, 62, 455–56

carrera musical de, 7–8, 17, 25–26, 34–35, 62–63, 69–70, 118, 216, 234, 399, 513

relación con, 55, 62, 163, 340, 407, 444–45

San Francisco y, 73, 94, 97–98, 115–16, 169, 230

apoyo de, 75, 81, 158, 443–44

Tijuana y, 41–43, 46, 48, 57–61, 63, 65, 67, 106, 112–13

Santana, Josefina B. (madre), 3, 5, 7, 16, 29, 31–32, 479, 507

Autlán y, 16–25, 27–34, 36–37, 480

Cihuatlán y, 5–7, 29–30, 404

muerte de, 456, 495–96

Deborah y, 343, 401, 487

nietos de, 403, 453, 475

enseñanzas de, 45, 47–48, 50–52, 55, 60, 107, 163, 174, 373, 450

promesa a, 42–43, 90, 230

relación con, 55–57, 62, 65, 73, 75, 105–6, 159, 166, 169, 195–97, 317, 340, 344, 361

San Francisco y, 95–99, 108, 115, 118, 150, 230

Tijuana y, 40–43, 45–46, 49, 52–55, 59, 61, 64–67, 69–70, 94, 112–13

Santana, Laura (hermana), 15, 17, 31, 38, 48–49, 51, 59, 103, 122, 136, 158, 362

Santana, Leticia (hermana), 49, 103–4

Santana, María (hermana), 6, 8, 15, 28, 36, 49, 55, 94, 103–4, 130, 158, 195, 206, 208, 243, 250, 346, 381, 446, 474, 490, 493, 529, 547

Santana, Salvador (hijo), 6, 57–58, 73, 421, 423–25, 427, 441, 464–66, 474, 479, 504, 511, 516, 532

nacimiento de, 6, 55–56, 400–401

infancia de, 401–4, 406–7, 414, 475–76

música de, 464, 482, 503, 513

relación con, 439–41, 488, 513

camino espiritual de, 417–18, 510–11

Santana, Stella (hija), 424–25, 427, 429, 438, 441–42, 460, 464, 479, 480, 502, 504, 520, 539, 542
Santana, Tony (hermano), 15, 17, 20, 28, 33, 38, 42, 44, 48–50, 54, 59–61, 74, 81, 101, 103, 106, 111, 114, 117–18, 121–24, 130, 136, 158, 202, 206, 217, 273, 381
  Autlán y, 17, 20, 27, 32, 36
  San Francisco y, 97–99, 102, 116–18, 124, 150, 195
  Tijuana y, 40–41, 43, 46–49, 52, 57–59, 79, 107, 112–13
Santana Blues Band, 89, 143, 170, 172, 174, 186, 190, 193
Santana Brothers, 473
Santana III, 286–89, 299, 312–13, 319
Santana IV, 505
Santana-Shorter Band, 404
Santo & Johnny, 79
Saphore, Steven, 255
Satchidananda, Swami, 301, 330, 340, 358, 367
Schon, Neal, 255, 279, 542
Schwarzenegger, Arnold, 114
Scofield, John, 280
Seale, Bobby, 303
Seeff, Norman, 406
Serpents and Doves, 485
Sete, Bola, 8, 126, 148, 194, 213, 219, 393
"Shades of Time", 220
Shadows, 80
Shaman, 498, 500, 505–6
Shankar, Ravi, 117, 153, 164, 188
Shape Shifter, 529
Sharrock, Sonny, 242, 261, 273, 404, 457
Sheila E., 288, 468, 529
"She's Not There", 405–6
Shorter, Ana Maria, 446–47
Shorter, Wayne, 10, 80, 176, 191, 245, 259, 262, 266, 272, 299, 306, 315, 342, 370, 395, 408, 421, 443, 444, 489, 493, 499, 517, 541
  Miles Davis y, 251, 375, 394, 436
  música de, 231, 245, 248, 258, 351, 399
  tocar y salir de gira con, 78, 290, 386, 421–26, 472–73, 512
  Weather Report y, 342
  palabras de, 166, 181, 489, 510, 514
Shrieve, Michael, 68, 201, 219, 232, 235, 250, 255, 260, 268, 291, 299–301, 303, 305–6, 308, 313, 318–19, 321–22, 325–26, 333–35, 337, 340, 353, 358,

364, 366–67, 374–75, 383, 387–89, 450, 505, 542
  álbumes con, 236–37, 303, 305, 309, 316, 345, 347–48, 367, 478
  guía, 246, 284–85, 287, 290, 302, 369
  integrante, 190, 207–8, 335, 356
  relación con, 66, 254, 292–93, 296–97, 323, 340, 355, 368–69
  de gira con, 276, 320, 426
  Woodstock y, 210, 219, 222
Shut Up 'n Play Yer Guitar, 395
"Sidewinder, The", 126, 162
Siegel, Barry, 471
Sigerson, Davitt, 460, 473
Silver, Horace, 220
"Silver Dreams Golden Smiles", 410
Simon and Garfunkel, 211, 487
Simone, Nina, 458
Simpson, O. J., 187, 362
Sinatra, Frank, 74, 176, 370, 385
"Singing Winds", 249–50
"S.K. Blues", 331
Sketches of Spain, 23, 260, 268, 397, 414, 501, 545
Sly & the Family Stone, 146, 187, 198, 329
  Ver también Stone, Sly
Sly & the Stoners, 145
Smith, Jimmy, 126, 161, 163, 187
Smith, Linda, 207
Smith, Paul Reed, 79, 417–19, 539
Smith, Randy, 249
"Smoke on the Water", 261
"Smooth", 130, 250, 492, 494
"Smooth Criminal", 453
Snoop Dogg, 409
"Solamente una Vez", 26
"Something's Got a Hold on Me", 91, 108
"Somewhere in Heaven", 407, 467
"Song of the Wind", 319
"Sonny Boy Williamson", 212
"Soul Sacrifice", 185, 197, 220, 222–23, 231, 450
"Soul Serenade", 253–54
"Soul to Soul", 298
"Soy el Tono universal", 538
Space Between the Stars, 512
Spann, Otis, 409, 530
Spencer, Jeremy, 279
Spirits Dancing in the Flesh, 457, 459
Springsteen, Bruce, 407, 477
Staples, Mavis, 290, 458
Staple Singers, 204, 221, 290
Starr, Ringo, 156

"Stella by Starlight", 539
Steppenwolf, 179, 204
Stern, Mike, 280
Steward, David y Thelma, 476
Sting, 205, 402, 434, 493–94
Stone, Freddie, 133
Stone, Sly, 126, 198, 487
"Stone Flower", 320–21, 334
Strangers, 73, 83
Streisand, Barbra, 205, 211, 548
Strummer, Joe, 402
Sumlin, Hubert, 88
"Summertime", 86, 91, 126
Sunlight, 409
Sunnyland Slim, 409
Sun Ra, 508
Supernatural, 4, 64, 80, 90, 130, 165, 175,
    279, 381, 411, 443, 459, 472, 476,
    485–501, 504–9, 526
"Supernatural, The", 165, 491, 549
"Supernatural Thing", 386
Super Nova, 272
"Suzie Q", 189
Swing of Delight, The, 407–8
"Sympathy for the Devil", 392
Szabó, Gábor, 8, 126, 138–39, 141, 148,
    153, 164, 167, 189, 194, 197, 213, 218,
    251, 259, 264, 307, 321, 337
    música de, 121, 132–33, 135, 145, 155–56,
    158, 179, 184, 186–87, 201, 237, 245,
    305, 347
    relación con, 259, 291–92, 320

Taj Mahal, 210, 214, 257
Tan, Amy, 113
Tanglewood (festival), 259, 262–63,
    265–66, 268, 298
Temptations, 198, 264, 453
"Tequila", 75, 196
"They All Went to Mexico", 421
Thiele, Bob, 366
"Think", 84
"Third Stone from the Sun", 189
Thomas, Leon, 324, 353, 366, 375, 387
Thomas, Rob, 130, 488, 490, 494
Thompson, Chester, 430–32, 441–42,
    445, 455, 468, 489, 493, 498, 498
Thompson, Chester C., 430
Thornton, Big Mama, 159
Thriller, 435
Tillery, Linda, 288
Time Has Come, The, 144
"Time Has Come Today", 144

"Time of the Season", 405
Tjader, Cal, 125–26, 165, 218, 288, 324,
    467–68
TJs, Los, 76–77, 81–84
Tony Williams Lifetime, 261, 272, 400,
    537
"Toussaint L'Ouverture", 288
Tower of Power, 255, 258, 264, 287, 329,
    431, 442, 530
Townshend, Pete, 170
"Treat", 220
Turner, Ike, 108, 290, 293
Turner, Tina, 290, 295, 506
Turtles, 136
Tutu, arzobispo Desmond, 72, 430, 477,
    509–10, 519–20, 541
Tyner, McCoy, 431, 443, 530

Ultimate Santana, 506
Urantia Book, The, 301, 439, 496

Valdez, Patato, 323
Valens, Ritchie, 70, 85, 484
Vanilla Fudge, 179
Vargas, Andy, 134, 407, 529
Vargas, Pedro, 26, 41, 70
"Variations on the Carlos Santana Secret
    Chord Progression", 394
Vasquez, Dan, 452
Vaughan, Jimmie, 421
Vaughan, Stevie Ray, 8, 90, 117, 393, 421,
    441–42, 473, 548
Ventures, 79
"Vereda tropical", 29, 421
"Victory Is Won", 430
Vilató, Orestes, 432
Vitous, Miroslav, 341
Viva Santana!, 449–50
Voices of East Harlem, 262–63, 290,
    298
Volunteered Slavery, 271, 294
"Voodoo Child (Slight Return)", 454
Vrionis, Michael, 528, 547, 550
V.S.O.P., 419

"Waiting", 219, 230
Walden, Narada Michael, 444
Walker, Greg, 403, 407
Walker, T-Bone, 81, 88, 331, 393, 421
Warwick, Dionne, 115
"Watch Your Step", 196
"Watermelon Man", 125, 325
"Watusi, El", 195

"Waves Within", 321
Wayne, John, 252, 311
Weasels Ripped My Flesh, 394
Weather Report, 205, 299, 318, 323, 326, 341–43, 403, 408, 430, 447
Webster, Ben, 119
Welch, Raquel, 277
Welcome, 363–64, 366, 384, 387
"Welcome", 364, 373
Wells, Junior, 137
West Side Story, 130–31, 490
Wexler, Jerry, 421
"What's Going On", 175, 298, 352
What's Going On, 9, 322
"When I Look into Your Eyes", 366
White, Lenny, 318, 407
Whitfield, Norman, 198
Who, the, 136, 149, 155, 170, 188, 235, 314, 402
Wilburn, Vince, 417
William Penn and His Pals, 161
Williams, Buster, 533
Williams, Richard, 340
Williams, Tony, 50, 202, 217, 261, 271–72, 318, 324, 364, 387, 400, 408, 417–19, 442, 462, 482, 534, 537
   y Miles Davis, 49, 257, 318, 386, 396, 437
Williamson, Marianne, 517
"Will o' the Wisp", 414
Wilson, Chad, 526, 537, 550
Wilson, Devon, 216, 234
Winter, Johnny, 257
Winwood, Steve, 234, 486
"Within You Without You", 177

"Woke Up This Morning", 196
Womack, Bobby, 308, 333
Wonder, Stevie, 127, 270–71, 370, 388
Wong, Linda, 68, 96
Woodstock, 122, 175, 188, 203, 222–24, 227–29, 231–36, 239, 241, 258, 263, 275, 277–79, 282, 326, 390, 434, 500–501, 543
"Wooly Bully", 136
"Work", 467
Workman, Reggie, 430
"Work Song", 153, 170
Wozniak, Steve, 432
Wray, Link, 80

"X factor" (banda), 193

Yasgur, Max, 234
Yogananda, Paramahansa, 244, 301, 322, 330
Young, Larry, 51, 272–73, 337, 365, 367
Young, Lester, 119
Young, Neil, 262, 267, 383
Youngbloods, 210
Young Rascals, 179, 254
"Yours Is the Light", 366

Zamudio, Domingo, 136
Zapata, Emiliano, 24, 140
Zappa, Frank, 179, 394
Zawinul, Joe, 60, 299, 342, 445
Zebop, 417
Zeffirelli, Franco, 296
Zombies, 405

Acerca de los autores

CARLOS SANTANA nació en Autlán de Navarro, México, en 1947. Es guitarrista, compositor y miembro fundador de Santana. Grabó y participó en más de noventa álbumes. Vive en Las Vegas con su esposa, la baterista Cindy Blackman.

ASHLEY KAHN nació en el Bronx, Nueva York, en 1960. Es autor, periodista, educador y coordinador de producción, y ha estado involucrado en el negocio de la música desde la década de 1980. Entre sus libros, se puede mencionar *A Love Supreme: The Story of John Coltrane's Signature Album*. Vive en Fort Lee, Nueva Jersey.

HAL MILLER nació en el Bronx, Nueva York, en 1941. Es baterista de jazz, escritor y orador frecuente en escuelas de música, y es uno de los principales coleccionistas de videos de jazz del mundo. Hace casi treinta años que es amigo íntimo de Carlos Santana. Vive en Albany, Nueva York.